CW00348727

Language to La

A practical and theoretical gu
Italian/English translators

Christopher Taylor

CAMBRIDGE
UNIVERSITY PRESS

CAMBRIDGE UNIVERSITY PRESS
Cambridge, New York, Melbourne, Madrid, Cape Town,
Singapore, São Paulo, Delhi, Tokyo, Mexico City

Cambridge University Press
The Edinburgh Building, Cambridge CB2 8RU, UK

Published in the United States of America by Cambridge University Press, New York

www.cambridge.org
Information on this title: www.cambridge.org/9780521597234

© Cambridge University Press 1998

First published 1998
7th printing 2009

A catalogue record for this publication is available from the British Library

ISBN 978-0-521-59723-4 Paperback

Thanks

This book is the fruit of many happy years teaching at the University of Trieste's Advanced School of Modern Languages for Translators and Interpreters. Thanks are therefore due to all the friends and colleagues whose precious advice and encouragement have made it possible – John, Clyde, Laura, David and all the others too numerous to mention. Special thanks go to Carol Taylor Torsello for her invaluable help in checking over the various manuscript stages and keeping me on the right path. Any remaining flaws are entirely my responsibility. For their patience and understanding, heartfelt thanks to Daniela, Riccardo and Stephanie.

Contents

Part One

Theoretical Background

Introduction

The purpose of 'Language to Language' is to provide students, teachers and all interested parties with an account of what is involved in the translation of many different kinds of English and Italian texts. The book consists of two distinct yet connected parts. Part One explores some of the more theoretical issues affecting translation studies, while Part Two takes a practical look at what is involved in translating a specific text. The material in Part One thus provides the background for the task of Part Two, which is to analyse the <u>process</u> of translation. This involves trying to discover what goes through translators' minds as they attempt to transfer the meaning of a source text A to the language of a target text B.

The layout of the material, as explained above, enables readers to use the book in a variety of ways, depending on their specific requirements at any particular time. Teachers can use the material for lessons on theory or practice. The theoretical considerations contained in Part One can provide material for class lectures, points of reference for practical exercises, and topics for home reading assignments. Whether translating from Italian to English or from English to Italian, the actual translations in Part Two, with their detailed explanations, can be used for the analysis and interpretation of texts in class, or for home study prior to their discussion with students. During such discussion, students should be encouraged to be critical of the translations provided, if they feel any parts can be improved. The practice texts provide vehicles for homework. Students can use the book for private study of the theoretical aspects and for home practice. The annotated texts can be translated and then compared with the versions provided, while most of the examples are followed by further practice texts.

'Language to Language', although dealing with eminently academic subject matter, seeks to maintain a lively, modern style, and to be user-friendly. As such it should be of interest to anyone involved in any way in the fascinating world of language and translation. In order to facilitate readers' access to the material contained in Part One of the book, each chapter is preceded by an overview of the content, and an extensive glossary of key words and expressions is provided at the end of the book. These words and expressions are printed in bold type when they first appear in the text.

This Introduction explains the basic rationale behind 'Language to Language' and provides an initial series of examples by way of illustration of the issues involved. The process of translation is rarely straightforward, and until translators have explored every angle of a **source text** in order to make the correct **target text** choice at all levels, a translation remains a kind of 'virtual' text, in the sense of being in a state of only partial completion, always requiring at least some finishing touch. During this phase of being neither source nor target text, it is constantly open to re-interpretation, re-thinking and reformulation. The inherent difficulty of the translation task lies in the fact that the translator has to work simultaneously at several levels of meaning: the literal sense of the words on the page, the **semantic connotations** that may lie behind the literal sense, the **pragmatic** force that the original writer may have intended, and the **stylistic** conventions relating to the **register** or **genre** of the text. This book follows the journey through the virtual translation, and examines precisely how the translator deals with all these layers of meaning.

Part One

Part One of the book consists of three chapters of a partially theoretical nature. Each chapter contains a large number of translation examples in line with the notion that theory must be tied to practice to be of any real benefit. The three chapters cover the relevance to translation of: 1. theoretical and applied linguistics, 2. the study of meaning in context, and 3. the concept of genre, all of which interconnect, but which are treated separately to match the 'layers of meaning' approach outlined above and adopted in Part Two. Basically, in working towards the target version of a text, the translator mentally manipulates the competing claims of its linguistic, semantic, pragmatic, cultural and stylistic components, the number and complexity of which will vary greatly from text to text. Any text for translation may contain elements pertaining to any or all of the 'layers'. The various parts of a single text may require the application of different parameters. The aim of Part One, therefore, is to sensitise students of translation, and anyone interested in this fascinating field of human activity, to the varied nature of text by presenting an analysis of its various components and discussing some of the modes of thinking that surround text and translation studies.

Some texts, or parts of texts, will require mere **contrastive lexicogrammatical** skills, others will require detailed and accurate knowledge of specific **terminology**. Others still will require attention to how the **discourse** is structured, to **phonological** features, or the **semantics** of word play. Yet others will require a wide knowledge of the world, or a heightened sensitivity to the pragmatic content of a text not written merely to inform. Before entering into more detail on these points, some of the translation strategies required to deal with such textual features will be illustrated by an initial series of examples:

1   Use of contrastive lexicogrammatical skills:

E' arrivato il direttore
The manager has arrived

English usually lacks the option of **fronting** the verb in **declaratives**; the auxiliary verb in the present perfect tense is always *have* in English, the **transparent translation** of *direttore/director* has usually to be rejected in favour of an alternative such as *manager*.

2   Use of specific technical terminology:

Primarily degenerative dementia is a disorder whose essential feature is the presence of dementia of insidious onset and gradually progressive course.

Demenza degenerativa primaria è un disturbo la cui caratteristica essenziale è la presenza di una demenza ad insorgenza subdola e a decorso gradualmente progressivo.

(de Vanna, Marinucci, Melato, Taylor, Valenti 1989:144)

This kind of terminology has exact equivalents which can be found in sources such as specialised technical dictionaries, glossaries, and databanks, as in the source quoted here.

3   Attention to discourse structure:

Guardavano fuori dalla porta, si guardavano l'un l'altro, sbadigliavano, sospiravano.

(C. Cassola, 'Il taglio del bosco')

They would look out of the door, they would look at each other, they would yawn, they would sigh.

(in Dodds 1994:199)

In this case the **syntactic equivalence** apparent in the position of the verb and the repetition of the tense must be maintained.

4   Recognition of phonological features:

... ma neanche con lei dicevo una parola, anche con lei chinavo il capo.
(E. Vittorini, 'Conversazione in Sicilia')

... not even with her did I say a word, even with her my head hung heavily.
(in Dodds 1994:234)

In this extract the **alliteration** of the *k* **plosives** in the original is matched by the *h* **fricatives** in the translation.

5   Word play:

TOAD   ... I could eat a horse.
ALBERT (*a horse*) Oh, could you? Well, I wouldn't say no to some toad-in-the-hole.
(from A. Bennett, 'The Wind in the Willows' 1991)

ROSPO ... Potrei mangiarmi un cavallo.
ALBERT Ah sì? Beh, io non rifiuterei di certo qualche coda di rospo.
(trans. C. Zamponi, 1995)

Here, the animal/culinary reference in Albert's reply, which is where the play on words lies, cannot be translated literally. However, as the 'meaning' lies in the word play rather than the object itself, a change in image that still incorporates the *toad* reference and 'plays' in the same way, provides an example of successfully inventive translation.

6   Knowledge of the world:

Pandora's father has come out of the closet and admitted he is a Bennite.
(S. Townsend, 1982, 'The Secret Diary of Adrian Mole')

Il padre di Pandora si è tolto la maschera a ha ammesso di simpatizzare addirittura per Tony Benn e la sinistra laborista.
(trans. C. Brera 1984)

In order to understand the reference to a *Bennite*, a knowledge of contemporary political affairs, backed by historical and cultural awareness, is required.

7   Sensitivity to pragmatic content:

What say we adjourn to yonder hostelry, see what mine host can do in the way of fodder?

Che ne dici di andare in quella locanda, e vedere che vettovaglie può offrirci il mio oste?

In the above extract from 'The Wind in the Willows', there is a deliberate attempt to create an old-fashioned flavour for humorous reasons with the use of archaic vocabulary.

In order to give readers the opportunity to explore further any of the points raised, each chapter is followed by suggestions for further reading. There is now a copious literature available on all aspects of translation studies, containing many interesting ideas on the subject. It is the absorption of these ideas from reading and discussion that prove useful to translators in their work, rather than any direct reference facility. Unfortunately, it is not as easy for a translator to refer to a book on translation theory to resolve a particular problem as it is for a physics student to look up the correct procedure for an experiment, nor would any explanation be as precise as in a strictly scientific discipline. However, this should not in any way discourage students from reading on and around the subject. The format of this book, with its many examples, is designed to generate ideas that may subsequently find their way onto the written translated page.

Part Two

The fact that texts may be amalgams of a number of different linguistic, pragmatic or stylistic components, all leads to the conclusion that a text needs to be analysed thoroughly before it is translated. This means more (and less) than simply reading through the text before beginning work. It means more in the sense that many of the elements that affect a text's translation may not be immediately apparent and therefore it is necessary to 'read between the lines'. It means less in the sense that a quick skim may be sufficient for a first reading and certain translation solutions may indeed be immediately evident. Translators will then proceed to 'read' the text many times as they revise and modify the work, until the **holistic** picture forms and what was earlier termed the 'virtual' translation becomes a finished translation product.

Depending on the complexity of the text, the translator will be called upon to work at the various levels referred to earlier, either simultaneously or in stages. The first level is that of the lexicogrammatical 'skeleton' of the text, namely correct syntactic structures with appropriate vocabulary. It is essential that this is sound, even in the most liberal translation, as this is the framework that must carry any further level of meaning, that is any possible pragmatic or stylistic load.

Consider the following translation from Tim Park's novel 'Tongues of Flame' (1985:19):

> Then that next Thursday he was expelled from school. He was caught smoking cannabis with two friends in the cricket nets so they scarcely had any choice really, and it was very embarrassing for Father because this was a church school and he was the chaplain. They had a furious row about it in the study and Adrian said he was quite happy to be expelled because now he could apply to a sixth-form college to do his A-levels in music and art.

> Poi il giovedì seguente fu espulso dalla scuola. Era stato sorpreso a fumare la marijuana con due amici nel campo di cricket, perciò il preside non poteva agire diversamente, e per mio padre era doppiamente imbarazzante perché era una scuola religiosa e il cappellano era proprio lui. Litigarono come due belve nello studio e Adrian disse che gli faceva molto comodo quell'espulsione, perché adesso poteva andare altrove per studiare musica e arte.

(trans. R. Baldassare 1995:32)

A number of questions evidently arose in the translator's mind: whether to change the tense of *He was caught*; how to substitute *cricket nets*, incomprehensible to an Italian readership, and deciding on an inaccurate but suitably general *campo di cricket*; deciding to insert a definite subject *il preside* where the original author adopts the lazy (but deliberate) *they* with its connotations of despised authority, in fact embodied by *il preside*; consciously shifting the **information focus** to the father in the syntactic change *e il cappellano era proprio lui*; the decision to use the *belve* simile; reaching the conclusion that the subjects Adrian wished to choose (*musica e arte*) were more important to the theme of the novel than the **culture-bound** institution in which he would study them and therefore opting not to even attempt to translate either *sixth-form college* or *A-levels*.

It is possible that all the above translation choices were made spontaneously and instantaneously, though it is reasonable to assume that some of them may have been the result of rethinking due to changes elsewhere in the immediate **co-text** or to subsequent changes of outlook as the result of new insights from the wider text. In any case, the translator has made decisions as to lexicogrammatical, semantic, pragmatic, cultural and stylistic aspects of the passage, which for the sake of convenience can be seen as separate layers of meaning blended together to form a target text.

It is just this idea of layering that provides the basis for the translation methodology adopted in Part Two of this book. The basic premise is that in order to organise the various layers into a coherent whole, those layers must first be identified and understood through a pre-translation analysis. Experienced translators are often able to work through the layers simultaneously to a certain extent; they are able to recognise and understand pragmatic, stylistic and cultural elements at more or less the same time as they process the purely linguistic signs. However, the printed page inevitably restricts representation to a more mechanical step-by-step approach, and this is more useful for students, who need to dissect the texts and deal with the layers in a more methodical way. So, while an attempt has been made to keep the artificial division in perspective, Part Two takes the reader through the preparatory, pre-translation phase of a number of different texts and then, in the case of Italian/English, introduces the device of the 'rolling translation'. Here the translation of the source text is seen to unfold in interim versions as the results of a lexicogrammatical analysis are superimposed on an initial 'literal' translation, a mere abstraction, showing how a text would be translated if no strategy at all were employed. This purely lexicogrammatical analysis is then subjected to further modification following semantico-pragmatic, stylistic and cultural analyses until a complete picture emerges. J.R. Firth, when he spoke of translation method, did so in terms of a translation typology which distinguishes between similar 'levels' (1968:149):

1 Interlinear word-for-word – literal transposition
2 Bit-for-bit – a more flexible method involving the freer translation of larger chunks of a text where literal translation would result in incomprehensibility or at least poor grammar
3 Free – a much freer approach based on the semantic message of the discourse

Following the processing of the various levels, the finished version is then often compared to an 'official' translation of the text. In the case of the English/Italian translation examples, the 'rolling' is not made explicit, though the process described is the same; again, 'official' translations are provided to assist the analysis. Further texts are provided for translation practice, including continuations of those passages taken from longer works.

Chapter One

Linguistics and Translation

Although translation as a discipline falls within the wider area of applied linguistics, the influence of linguistic theory on translation studies has perhaps been less evident than that of other sectors such as semantics, stylistics and cultural studies (see Chapters Two and Three). However, translation is undeniably a linguistic phenomenon, at least in part, and translators can certainly benefit from a consideration of some of the more important developments that have taken place over the last hundred years or so with regard to the lexicogrammar. Chapter One therefore looks at a number of theoretical concepts concerning both grammatical and lexical aspects of language.

OVERVIEW OF CHAPTER

1 Language structure (and the organisation of information)

Structuralism

The way words are put together in logical and grammatical sequences, and the way particular words are chosen by speakers/writers as they communicate, is studied in terms of syntagmatic structure and paradigmatic system. The way to identify meaningful stretches of text, so useful in translation, is analysed through an examination of various forms of constituent analysis. These ideas are associated with a number of different linguists, starting from de Saussure at the beginning of the century, and including the later group of American linguists (particularly Bloomfield) who were actually known as Structuralists.

The Prague School

The way texts are organised and how they present information is explained in terms of functional sentence perspective and communicative dynamism, ideas developed by the Prague School of linguists.

A functional approach (Halliday)

The organisation of information in a text is seen from a slightly different perspective through M.A.K. Halliday's treatment of theme and rheme and information structure.

2 Lexis and terminology

The meaning attached to items of general lexis is discussed in terms of componential analysis, and the way words 'go together' is analysed through an explanation of what is meant by the concept of collocation. Proper names receive separate treatment.

Terminology is discussed as a distinct discipline, particularly in its application to languages for special purposes. Comments on lexicography and the use of dictionaries and corpora complete this section.

3 Translation strategies

Finally, Chapter One explores a series of translation strategies in order to illustrate the linguistic reasoning behind translation.

The usefulness of Chapter One can be seen in terms of providing a first layer in the preparation of a full translation, where the surface features of a text are transferred from one idiom to another and are made to blend together in a syntactically satisfactory, cohesive and communicative whole.

1.1   Language structure (and the organisation of information)

The Swiss linguist Ferdinand de Saussure (1857-1913), one of the most important early exponents of modern linguistics, made a major contribution to the study of language structure. He first described the horizontal nature of structure in terms of the joining of words or longer units (**syntagms**) to form grammatically acceptable and meaningful clauses and sentences. For example, the clause *He leaves tomorrow* consists of three words arranged in what we consider to be a logical, and grammatical, order. In this case, what is known as the **syntagmatic sequence** consists of pronoun + verb + temporal adverb.

He then compared this structure with the vertical nature of **system**, that is the choosing of competing **linguistic options** available to speakers within a syntagmatic sequence. For example, in this same clause *He leaves tomorrow*, the pronoun *He* could be replaced by *She, You,* etc., the verb form *leaves* could be replaced by *goes, sails to Rio,* and the adverbial *tomorrow* could be replaced by *next week,* or by a more complicated phrase such as *as soon as the weather improves.*

He	leave(s)	tomorrow
She		
You		

He	leave(s)	tomorrow
	goes	
	sails to Rio	

He	leaves	tomorrow
		next week
		as soon as the weather improves

This relationship between the 'competing linguistic options' is referred to as **paradigmatic**. Once words or word groups have been (subconsciously) 'chosen' from the paradigmatic axis by the speaker/writer, then they must be combined **syntagmatically** in a logical order to create meaning.

1.1.1 Structuralism

Structuralists, a name given in particular to a group of American linguists who analysed the constituent parts of sentence structure, further developed these essential **parsing** techniques. Leonard Bloomfield (1887-1949), for example, introduced the notion of *Immediate Constituent Analysis*. The methodology involved in this kind of analysis enabled grammarians to split sentences, clauses and clause constituents (noun phrases, verb phrases, adverb phrases, etc.) into their component parts:

The meeting broke up at midnight and the delegates went home (*sentence*)

The meeting broke up at midnight (*clause*)
and (*conjunction*)
the delegates went home (*clause*)

The meeting (*noun phrase*)
broke up (*verb phrase*)
at midnight (*temporal adverb phrase*)
and (*conjunction*)
the delegates (*noun phrase*)
went home (*verb phrase*)

The meeting (*determiner + noun*)
broke up (*verb + particle*)
at midnight (*preposition + noun*)
etc.

Even single words could be split into meaningful **morphemes**:

quick − ly
(*adjective + adverbial suffix*)

Translators, it must be said, rarely need to parse so deeply; it is sufficient for them to be able to recognise 'autonomous units' at clause, phrase or word level. The term 'autonomous unit' is to be understood here as a stretch of language that can be translated as a single unit in the target text. In the clause *The meeting broke up at midnight* the three units *The meeting/broke up/at midnight* stand up on their own and can be translated successfully: *La riunione/si è sciolta/a mezzanotte*. The division into *The/meeting broke/up at midnight* does not provide such easily manageable units. This is a very simple example, but it is possible that much longer stretches of text can be considered as autonomous units. The curious expression *It's raining cats and dogs* must be translated as a single unit: *Piove a catinelle* or *Piove a dirotto*. In the case of consecutive interpreting, where the interpreter listens to a speech, takes notes, and then delivers the message in the target language, an amusing anecdote or a joke (easily remembered in the short term) can be treated as extended autonomous units of language. A joke will be translated as a unit rather than as a succession of words and phrases. To return to written translation, by parsing and isolating units of language, the translator can create at least an initial sketch of the units of meaning in a text. Of course, these units may then need to be re-arranged or modified in some way in the target version.

Take the following complex sentence:

Nasce da questa esigenza la figura dell'integratore d'impresa, di chi, cioè sappia costruire sistemi integrati su misura.
(Advertisement for Bull Information Systems) (from Taylor 1990:72)

The translator should first identify those items that stand as autonomous units. In this sentence the noun phrases *the idea of the company integrator, someone, custom-made integration systems*, the verb phrases *arose, (is) able to construct*, the adverb phrase *from this need* and the conjunction *that is* function as such, that is they 'stand on their own'. The translator can thus translate them as units and then fit the pieces together according to the syntactic rules of the target language:

(The idea of the company integrator), (that is) (someone)
(able to construct) (custom-made integration systems), (arose)
(from this need).

1.1.2 Universal structure

The idea that there are universal structural elements common to all languages has been an ongoing theme in linguistic theory. The American linguist Noam Chomsky, in the development of his theory of universal **'deep' grammar** (see 'Syntactic Structures' 1957), suggested that the underlying structures of language may be stable over time, and that the 'core' language that is innate in all human beings does not change. Only the **'surface' grammar** changes, that which manifests itself in the many different languages spoken in the world. Although Chomsky did not relate his theory to the question of translation, the translation scholar Eugene Nida's concept of 'kernel sentences' (1964:66) owes something to deep structure theory. By introducing the idea of kernel sentences, Nida attempted to isolate 'core' elements in all languages. Kernels, according to Nida, are the minimal structures in a language (e.g. subject + verb; article + noun) from which the rest can be derived, either by addition, omission or some form of permutation. There are more parallels between languages at this level, and therefore if source texts can be reduced to their kernel form, they will be easier to translate; subsequently they can be retransformed into more complex and acceptable target text constructions. A biblical example of Nida and Taber's (1974:52) comes from Ephesians 1:7.

in whom we have redemption through his blood, the forgiveness of sins, according to the riches of his grace

The basic kernels are identified as *God redeems us, Christ dies (sheds his blood), God forgives, We sin* and *God shows grace richly*. This provides for the creation of a congruent version:

> God redeemed us through Christ's shedding of his blood, and God forgave our sins. All this indicates how richly God showed his grace.

This can then be elaborated appropriately in the target language.

1.1.3 The Prague School

At more or less the same time as Bloomfield and the early American structuralists were developing their ideas, the Prague School was emerging in Europe. One of the most important legacies of this school's studies, particularly associated with the names of Mathesius, and later Firbas, is that concerning **functional sentence perspective** (**FSP**) and the concept of **communicative dynamism** (**CD**). The FSP theory sees clauses divided into a **theme** and a **rheme**. The theme contains information that is to some extent dependent on the immediate context or co-text of the communicative act; it is somehow 'known' or it has already been mentioned in the text: it is **given information**. It generally appears at or near the beginning of a clause and 'prepares the ground' for what follows. Consider, for example, this line from the preface to Bernard Shaw's 'Pygmalion':

> The English have no respect for their language ...

The theme in this clause is *The English*, retrievable from both the situation (the English are being talked about) and the text (the English have been previously mentioned). It sets the scene for the rheme, which in this case is what is said about the English.

The rheme contains 'context-independent' information, that is **new information** which generally comes at the end of a clause and which is particularly useful in the development of the discourse. If all information in clauses were given, it would be of little interest to anyone; it is the new element that keeps us interested, that tells us something we do not already know. On the other hand, if all the information were new, without any 'anchor' in shared knowledge, we would not be able to absorb the load. The relative weighting of the new information determines the level of communicative dynamism. Theme is therefore seen as consisting of those elements within a clause that form the basis of the information content (*The English* in the example above), even if they are not necessarily the first items. This part of the clause has a <u>low</u> communicative dynamism. The rheme (in this case *have no respect for their language*) completes the information and fulfils the communicative purpose. It is often new information and has a <u>high</u> communicative dynamism. Consider the sequence:

> Interest rates fell by 2%. This drop caused panic on the Stock Market as brokers rushed to inform clients.

The theme in the first clause *Interest rates* is followed by the rheme *fell by 2%*. This rheme is re-worked as the theme of the next clause (*This drop*), and is already known (given information), to be followed by the more interesting new information *caused panic on the Stock Market*; it is this latter information that provides a high degree of communicative dynamism. Similarly, in the next clause *brokers* refers to the people who constitute the Stock Market and is thus at least partially given, while the communicative dynamism is enhanced by the new information *rushed to inform clients*.

In terms of Italian/English translation, an example of how communicative dynamism may be differently constructed is illustrated by the following sequence:

> Jack ha pagato il conto, e siccome era molto caro, ha contribuito anche Mary.

In the first two clauses a linear progression is followed where a part of the rheme of the first clause *il conto* is picked up as the theme of the second clause *(esso) era* and is given information. The fact that *il conto* was *caro* is new information and the sentence achieves dynamism as it proceeds. New information keeps interest aroused as to how the discourse will continue. In the third clause, the Italian construction puts what might be construed as the newest element (*Mary*) in final position. A more spontaneous (**unmarked**) English translation, with the more colloquial verb *chipped in* justified by the informal nature of the discourse, might be:

> Jack paid the bill and since it was expensive, Mary chipped in too.

This creates the same communicative dynamism in the first two clauses, whereas in the third, although there is a phonological stress on *Mary*, she is shifted to initial position, more usually associated with theme. The communicative dynamism seems to move the whole sentence forward in slightly different ways in the two cases, but both the noun *Mary* and the verb *ha contribuito/chipped in* are items of new information and simply illustrate how the dictates of comparative syntax affect the presentation of information. *Mary* in the Italian clause is in fact an example of subject in final position as opposed to a grammatically acceptable, though stylistically less common, position before the verb, as in English. Student translators must be constantly aware of this kind of postverbal subject option, which is so frequent in Italian and so rare in English. As Baker (1992:166) says:

... generally speaking, in languages with relatively free word order (e.g. Italian) there will be less tension between the requirements of syntax and those of communicative function. Conversely, in languages with relatively fixed word order (e.g. English) there will be greater instances of tension between syntax and communicative function.

1.1.4 Theme in Halliday

M.A.K. Halliday, in his 1985 (reprinted 1994) work 'An Introduction to Functional Grammar', developed his own concept of theme and rheme as elements of information structure. The Prague School linguists tended to equate theme with given and rheme with new, and could account for rheme preceding theme on some occasions (see example of *Mary* above). But for Halliday theme is invariably found in initial position, and may consist of either given or new information, as may the rheme. However, the unmarked clause (i.e., the normal structure, the default position) in the Hallidayan scheme also sees the conflation of the traditional grammatical subject and theme in a declarative clause (i.e., not in an interrogative or an **imperative** clause where the verb form, coming first, is theme). Consider the famous line from chapter ten of George Orwell's 'Animal Farm' (1945):

All animals are equal but some animals are more equal than others.

In both declarative clauses the theme (in initial position) is the subject. It is common, also in the Hallidayan approach, for the subject/theme to be given information, either previously mentioned in the co-text or implicitly known to be shared knowledge. In the second clause of the example above, *(some) animals* is at least partially given in the previous clause. The information focus, where the important new information is stored (in this case *more equal than others*), generally falls at the end of an English clause, and in the spoken language is stressed phonologically, and this is the unmarked option.

However, as clauses in any stretch of discourse are analysed in terms of theme/rheme, given/new, and information focus, it becomes clear that many of them are **marked** in some way. Perhaps an adverbial expression is found in theme position:

On the first day of Christmas my true love gave to me a partridge in a pear tree or some new information is presented first in a clause, as theme. Note in the following example how the theme of the second clause *Bearing gifts* (which precedes the subject *we*) is new:

> We three kings of orient are
> <u>Bearing gifts</u> we traverse afar

Such examples require special attention on the part of the translator precisely because there may be valid syntactic, semantic or stylistic reasons for their 'markedness'. Such considerations can assist in the organisation of the translation of a sentence such as the following, where the Italian sentence actually thematises the verb:

> Si avvia al termine la pausa estiva che, come ogni anno, ha determinato la sospensione dell'attività parlamentare.
>
> The summer break which, as every year, has brought about an adjournment of parliamentary activity, is drawing to a close.

(Taylor 1990:78)

A mere copying of the Italian construction could distort the logic or at least sound clumsy, given that the unmarked English language option is always to equate the theme with the subject.

An analysis of the theme structure of both unmarked and marked English clauses shows how information is presented in typical English constructions (themes underlined):

1   the passive voice:

<u>Only the best tennis</u> is played at Wimbledon.

2   the interrogative pre-positioning of the operator:

<u>Do</u> you play tennis?

3   the **cleft sentence**:

<u>It</u> was Rush who scored the goal.

4   the **pseudo cleft sentence**:

<u>What</u> Rush <u>did was</u> galvanise the rest of the team.

5   an **embedded clause** as subject:

<u>That Rush would come back to Liverpool</u> was never in doubt.

6   the thematisation of adverbs:

<u>Against all the odds</u>, Liverpool managed to win.

The syntactic flexibility of the Italian language and its frequently different thematic organisation enable constructions such as those above to be translated in a number of ways. For example, the verb is regularly thematised (*A segnare è stato Rush*), where a parallel construction would be impossible in English. Imagine the arrival of a king being presented in the following manner:

E' arrivato il Re! E' arrivato il Re!

In English *Has arrived the King* is ungrammatical. But the very thematic organisation in Italian in this instance may push the translator to reject the congruent syntax of the following:

The King is here! The King is here!

and opt for a simple **presentative** construction with the subject shifted to the right:

Here is the King! Here is the King!

1.1.5 Cohesion

Another concept of major importance in the analysis of text organisation, and of great relevance to translation, largely attributable to Halliday and in particular to Halliday and Hasan (1975) is that of **cohesion**.

> The topic of cohesion ... has always appeared to me the most
> useful constituent of discourse analysis or text linguistics applicable
> to translation.   (Newmark 1991:69)

Cohesion is created in a number of ways within a text and indeed refers only to the links that exist <u>within</u> the discourse, within the co-text, that is, created by the words themselves. The extralinguistic semantic links that tie a text together, and which are of course crucial in the understanding of discourse, are referred to by a corresponding term, coherence, which will be examined in Chapter Two. Cohesion is achieved in various ways, both grammatically and lexically:

1   through **conjunction**:

Bond arrived <u>and</u> sat down.

2   through **reference** (generally **pro-forms** that refer back or ahead within a text):

a) Pronouns that refer back to a previously-mentioned entity are said to constitute '**anaphoric** reference':

> John came in, he did x, he did y, he did z ...

b) Where the reference is to an entity further ahead in the discourse, it is termed '**cataphoric** reference':

> This is not good news for any of you. You are all fired!

3   through substitution or **ellipsis**:

> It might rain but I hope it doesn't. (verb phrase substituted by auxiliary)

> I voted for the Greens. Why (...)?

4   through the repetition of words:

> The only thing we have to fear is fear itself.

5   through the use of **synonyms** or near-synonyms:

> Having lost one opportunity, he won't get a second chance.

6   through the use of semantically-related items:

> a) That's the top and bottom of it. (relationship of **antonymy**)

> b) The tiger is an endangered animal. (relationship of **hyponymy**, that is a superordinate term *animal* is associated with a subordinate, hyponymous term *tiger*)

> c) Clear away the tables and chairs. (items in same **semantic field**)

> d) She sewed a new button on her jacket. (part/whole relationship). Another example of a part/whole relation might be an estate agent's description of a house on a room by room basis.

The following passage from Margaret Atwood's short story 'Dancing Girls' (1977:210) illustrates the concept of cohesion:

> The first sign of the new man was the knock on the door. It was the landlady, knocking not at Ann's door, as she'd thought, but on the other door, the one east of the bathroom. Knock, knock, knock; then a pause,

soft footsteps, the sound of unlocking. Ann, who had been reading a book on canals, put it down and lit herself a cigarette. It wasn't that she tried to overhear: in this house you couldn't help it.

There are several examples of **lexical cohesion**, starting from the repetition of the key words *knock* and *door*. The semantic field is maintained throughout via lexical chains (*landlady–door–unlocking–house*, etc.) and a part/whole relationship is expressed through *house–bathroom–door*. Anaphoric reference is created by the pronouns *she, the one, who* and *it*. In fact, the pronoun *it* appears four times though with four different functions, and this is the feature that differs most markedly from Italian in this instance. Firstly, *It was the landlady* refers back anaphorically to the entire locution *knock on the door*. The second occurrence of *it* (*put it down*) refers to the concrete entity *cigarette*, while in the last sentence *It wasn't that she tried to overhear: in this house you couldn't help it* the first instance refers cataphorically to the act of trying to overhear, and the second refers back to the same. Only in the second case would Italian need to use an overt pronoun, while this dummy or empty *it* plays a vital role in English grammar. This use of *it* represents only one case of where the Italian suppression of pronouns could potentially limit comprehension in translation. Another short story by Atwood (op.cit:38) begins in the following cataphoric way:

He hadn't seen her around for a week, which was unusual: he asked her if she'd been sick.
'No', she said, 'working'. She always spoke ...

He is identified as Morrison in line seven but *she* is not revealed as Louise until a further ten pronominal references (*she, her*) have been made to her, and another nine (*he, him*) to him. The two characters are once referred to together as *they*, and *she* refers to *him* once as *you*. Italian can use gender-marking morphemes to avoid ambiguity (*Io so che tu sai che lei è bugiarda*), but there is a need in a text of this sort to adopt a more marked overt subject pronominalisation in Italian too.

1.2   **Lexis and terminology**

The analysis of **lexis** as if it were a separate field of study is a convenience rather than a reflection of linguistic reality. It is not easy to divorce grammar from lexis, which is why we speak of the **lexicogrammar** of a language: the paradigmatic selection of grammatical structures and words (i.e., between competing linguistic options) and the syntagmatic possibilities offered by the grammar rules and lexical collocations enable us to create language. However, as the title of this section suggests, a distinction will be made between lexis (words) and **terms**. The problem for translators is that 'words' are slippery; they can be ambiguous, **polysemous**, **collocation-bound**, **register**-sensitive. Terms, on the other hand, at least according to theory (see Sager 1990, Baker 1993) are unambiguous, **monosemic**, invariable, independent of context. Translators must wrestle with 'words' to fit them to the meanings they require and the contexts within which they are working, while their only problem with terms is finding the right equivalent, because in theory there can only be one equivalent – there are as many term units as there are concepts (see Sager, 1990, for a detailed account of all aspects of terminology). Naturally, the real life picture is not so 'clear cut', but the theoretical distinction is sufficiently useful to justify separate treatment. Thus **1.2.1** will deal with general lexis and the translator's necessarily flexible attitude towards dealing with 'words', and **1.2.2** will concentrate on terminology, as a discipline and as the raw material for term databases, and on the translator's use of this constantly evolving instrument. Finally, **1.2.3** will examine **lexicography** as a discipline and, consequently, the use of dictionaries, the most obvious tool of the translator's trade.

1.2.1 General lexis

Clearly, the translator's task is not simply a question of finding dictionary equivalents to a series of **lexical items** in the source text and arranging them in the target text, paying attention merely to the constraints of comparative syntax. Translators must be particularly sensitive to the meanings of the words on the page, because words are what have to be translated, though there may be a great deal more behind those words than may seem the case at first glance. The 'words' that will here be considered are those that are, in one sense, readily available to the educated translator, but in another sense, can be elusive when required to express source language concepts in target language form. Firstly, the technique of **componential analysis** will be examined as a means of creating the complete semantic picture of a lexical item. The way lexical items combine will then be considered in a discussion of collocation. Finally, the separate issue of proper names will be addressed.

Componential analysis

From Hjelmslev (1953) and Coseriu (1967) in Europe, to Katz and Fodor (1964) in America, the original ideas surrounding what was called componential analysis enjoyed considerable consensus before other approaches to lexical semantics joined the debate. The basic idea was that of breaking a word down into its components (e.g. man = + male + human + adult) in order to arrive at its total meaning. Fowler (1977:34) talks of componential analysis as a valid instrument of measurement for the semantic features of words:

> Each lexical item is regarded as a set or cluster of components called distinctive features or semantic features.

Lexical items are thus considered in terms of their semantic components; lexical translation can take its cue from this concept. Newmark (1981:27) shows how the word *bawdy* can be broken down into its sense components and thus prepared for translation (within the particular context in which its translation is required) much more convincingly than by weighing up synonyms listed in bilingual dictionaries. He breaks down this particular lexical item as follows:

BAWDY

A ESSENTIAL (FUNCTIONAL) COMPONENTS

1 Shocking (emotive)

2 Related to the sex act (factual)

3 Humorous (emotive/factual)

B SECONDARY (DESCRIPTIVE) COMPONENTS

1 Loud

2 'Vulgar' (in relation to social class)

The item, having been stripped down, so to speak, to reveal all its possible components, can be measured against the competing claims, in the target language, of near-synonyms, paraphrasal expressions, compensatory solutions or even replacement by zero, depending on the particular **context of situation**.

As an example of componential analysis at work, consider the following text, an extract from 'The Secret Diary of Adrian Mole, aged $13\frac{3}{4}$' (Townsend, 1982:110). This humorous and highly perceptive best-seller takes the form of an adolescent's diary and is thus conveniently divided into the days of the year. The following entry is for Saturday, August 15th, when the boy

Adrian is being driven to Scotland by his mother and her 'boyfriend'. The latter caresses the mother while driving along, and is observed by Adrian himself in the back seat.

> My mother and creep Lucas met me at Sheffield. My mother looked dead thin and has started dressing in clothes that are too young for her. Lucas creep was wearing jeans! His belly was hanging over his belt. I pretended to be asleep until we got to Scotland. Lucas mauled my mother about whilst he was driving.

Perhaps the most difficult vocabulary item in the text in terms of frequency and **idiomatic** use is the verb *to maul*. Good translation here calls for a certain dictionary skill, which will be covered in more detail in **1.2.3**, and the use of componential analysis. First, a good bilingual English/Italian dictionary (S.E.I./Oxford, 1984) provides the following entry:

> **to maul** *vt*, maltrattare, malmenare, bistrattare

All of these mean precisely the opposite of what Adrian intended, though it is clear that he considers Lucas a vulgar, indelicate kind of man. The Concise Oxford monolingual dictionary gives the following definition:

> *to maul* is *to handle sb/sth roughly or brutally*, even metaphorically, (e.g. *his article was mauled by the critics*)

We are left in the same position. The English-speaking reader knows that an ironic **metaphor** is being used, the kind of metaphor that works through overstatement, and which would be difficult to find even in a dictionary of current idiom. In such circumstances, translators must gain what they can from the context and take what they can from the word. Thus, knowing that Lucas would be unlikely to mistreat Adrian's mother, especially with Adrian in the car with them, the components *roughly and brutally* can be removed from the English dictionary definition, and *handle* can be used as a new base term. This provides us with

> maneggiare, manipolare, toccare con le mani

Working back through an Italian thesaurus (Quartu, 1986), amongst the many entries, the term *coccolare* is to be found, which the various contextual clues would indicate as being an appropriate term.

However, it is not only rare, obscure or polysemous words that can benefit from the rigours of componential analysis. A number of commonly used, seemingly 'innocent', lexical items are often the victims of varying degrees of mistranslation. The following is a verse from Bob Dylan's song-poem 'Chimes of Freedom' (Rizzo, 1972:96):

> striking for the gentle
> striking for the kind
> striking for the guardians
> and protectors of the mind

The first line raises just such a recurring lexical dilemma: the translation of *gentle* which, apart from all other considerations, provides a very useful example of the dangers of transparency and **false cognates**, otherwise known as 'false friends'. It is much more subtle than the classic examples of false cognates such as *actually/attualmente*, *evident/evidente*, *trivial/triviale* and therefore much more insidious, as it appears over a whole range of semantically-related areas. In the context of this Dylan song, the term is used to describe those who 'never do any harm to anyone' and to make a net distinction between such people and the perpetrators of evil. It recalls the biblical *'Blessed are the meek ...'*. A quick look at any bilingual dictionary will produce a range of options for the translation of *gentle* including *dolce, mite, moderato, lieve, fine, tenero, leggero, benevolo, garbato, cortese, eletto, distinto, nobile* and, of course, the one which should practically always be avoided, *gentile*. Cross-checking any one of these in a dictionary of synonyms will provide another set of bewildering possibilities. However, a componential analysis of the item in its protest song-cum-poetry context should help to eliminate a number of the above synonym-definitions, e.g. *lieve, fine, leggero, benevolo, garbato, cortese, eletto, distinto, nobile* and indeed *gentile*. This leaves *dolce, mite* and *moderato*, terms that are echoed in English dictionary and thesaurus definitions, showing the value of a judicious use of monolingual sources. The Cambridge International Dictionary of English, for example, tells us that *gentle* means *calm, kind* or *soft*. Roget's Thesaurus gives us *moderate* and *temperate*, but then the thesaurus entries for both *calm* and *soft*, among other options, point to *mild*. In this way the translator should be in a position to work his or her way through the various lists and by process of elimination arrive at an equivalent item such as *mite*. Ironically, the next line throws up the word *kind*, and there is a strong case for translating this, in the context, with *gentile*. Indeed, Rizzo does precisely this:

> rintoccavano per il mite
> rintoccavano per il gentile

Collocation

> You shall know a word by the company it keeps.
>
> (J.R. Firth 1968:106)

Firth was referring to the binding properties of lexical items; in simple terms, how words 'go together'. Some **collocations**, as these combinations of words are called, are more predictable than others – examples such as *leggere un libro* or *blue sky* are very predictable, very common and often mirrored in other languages: *read a book* and *cielo azzurro*; some, however, may be almost tautologous and therefore expendable in translation: *garage mechanic/meccanico, medical doctor/medico, motor car/macchina.* Fixed idioms may have obscure origins – *campa cavallo, topsy-turvy* – but are predictable in their collocational power. *Topsy* and *turvy*, for example, collocate with no other words. Other items collocate more capriciously and at times in surprising combinations: *to ride a horse, bicycle, elephant,* etc., but *to ride the storm, ride a cock horse, to ride along, to be taken for a ride, a sixpenny ride, 'Ride 'em Cowboy'* and, for example – by extension of 'the storm' collocation – *to ride a crisis, problem,* etc., then *to ride the bandwagon* extrapolated from the expression *to jump on the bandwagon* and so on, with a potentially huge number of variations recognisable as collocates. This is of interest in terms of the flexibility and inventiveness of the language within the confines of acceptable collocation formation, but at the same time poses enormous problems for translators, the most obvious of which being that the patterns of collocation in one language are often not mirrored in another, however closely related.

Sinclair (1992:83), however, claimed that

> each utterance provides a framework within which the next
> utterance is placed.

This is presumably true of any language and especially true in the case of written language which is so often partially retrospective. Thus, the **interlingual** identifying of extended collocational patterns should be very useful for translators, and this is becoming more and more feasible through the kind of corpus work Sinclair has been involved with for some years (see **1.2.3**).

In the case of predictable collocations there is widespread **equivalence**, though Crystal warns, for example, that in Japanese, the verb for 'drink' collocates with water and soup, but also with tablets and cigarettes. (1987:105)

Italians *mangiano spaghetti* but also *si mangiano le unghie*, whereas the English *bite their nails*. The case of idioms and colloquial language is more complex, as idioms often belong only to individual languages, though there is a certain amount of equivalence in set expressions, for example *time flies/ il tempo vola*, and proverbs: *Don't look a gift horse in the mouth/A caval donato non si guarda in bocca*. Alternatively, set equivalents exist, for example *Ci mancherebbe altro!/What next!*, *Tutto il mondo è paese/It's the same the world over*. In less accessible cases of colloquial and idiomatic language, the translator needs to be well aware of (and well read in) the idiosyncrasies of the two languages to be able to render, for example *Ci sono molti treni che fanno servizio tra Londra e Brighton* with *There are frequent trains running between London and Brighton* and *i ragazzi giocavano bene (professional football team)* with *the lads played well*.

Let us now examine some of the ways the item *gentle*, discussed above, may collocate: *gentle slope, a gentle rebuke, gentle reader, gentle breeze, gentle rain, gentle manner, gentle voice, gentle smile, gentle exercise, gentle movement, the gentle sex, of gentle birth*. The most frequent corresponding collocations in Italian would show a great deal of variation (*gentle slope/ leggero pendio, gentle breeze/brezza leggera, of gentle birth/di nobile origine*) and perhaps only one – *gentle reader* – could claim equivalence in *gentile*.

Having discussed the various ramifications of the concept of collocation and how crucial these are to a translator's understanding of language use, the way collocation can be played with by writers, in order to create a range of effects, will now be examined. The substitution of an unusually marked term in place of one of the items in an expected collocation is common in, for example, journalism or in playful exchange amongst imaginative interlocutors, e.g:

> Never on a Tuesday cf: Never on a Sunday
> He's a heavy non-smoker cf: He's a heavy smoker
> It's just not ice-hockey cf: It's just not cricket

The problem for the translator arises when the marked collocation makes no sense, even with a leap of imagination on the part of the reader, in the target language. In the case of a) above, the translation *Mai di martedì* (cf: *Mai di domenica*) is transparent and works – the source of the original collocation is known across the two cultures. In the case of b) it is arguable whether the mechanism needed to produce *E' un non-fumatore accanito* (cf:

E' un fumatore accanito) is as common or as psycholinguistically successful as its equivalent in English. It is unlikely that the translation-enforced 'battuta' in Italian would sound as amusing as the 'witty remark' in English, as any comparison of national humour conventions would confirm. However, translation b) would not be impenetrable and could even be justified in the right context as mirroring the thought processes of the original. In the case of c), the translator is faced with a substitution that works on so many levels that she or he cannot hope to capture it in literal (or probably any other kind of) translation.

Analysing it, we can see that the original phrase is idiomatic and culture-bound; cricket certainly was, and to a certain extent still is, regarded as the game of English gentlemen and this led to its being used idiomatically to stand as a metaphor for 'fair play'. Its replacement with a term from the same semantic field of sport can probably be understood by many British English speakers, but irony is created by the fact that the sport chosen was not in fact practised in Britain until recently. What doubles the irony is that ice-hockey is reputed to be extremely violent and the sport that most flouts the idea of fair play. In an earlier work (Aspects of Language and Translation: Contrastive Approaches for Italian/English Translators, 1990) I argued that *It's just not cricket* could be translated by *Non è fair play*, given that the latter expression exists as a **loan** in Italian, but in the case of c), a resort to congruent meaning may be in order and something along the lines of *Non è gioco sporco* might be necessary. This may win no prizes for originality but it is safe; the important thing initially is for a translator to be able to recognise this kind of false collocation when it appears.

Partington (1995) identified three kinds of transformation adopted by writer/speakers according to their **illocutionary intent**. He labelled them:

1 reformulation: *The kooky that didn't crumble (That's the way the cookie crumbles)*
2 abbreviation: *Once a Catholic (Once a Catholic, always a Catholic)*
3 expansion: *Songs from an Age of Innocence (Songs of Innocence + The Age of Innocence)*

(A. Partington 1995)

In cases such as these, if translators can see what is meant and what is being done with the language, they are at liberty to experiment in the same way. In the case of 3 above, where the William Blake poems would not be unknown to an educated Italian readership and the *Age of Innocence/Età dell'innocenza* are transparently translatable, there is no reason not to translate the unusual collocation with *Canti da un età d'innocenza*.

In the case of 1, however, the idiomatic American expression *That's the way the cookie crumbles* unfortunately finds no similarly idiomatic equivalent in Italian. The meaning is *Sono cose che succedono*, but an attempt to imitate the source language play with, for example, *La cosa che non è successa* runs the risk of not being understood for the very reason that it does not present an obviously (un)usual collocation. In the case of the following example, let us assume a relevant context (e.g. European Union milk quotas):

The milk they cry over (cf: Don't cry over spilt milk)

The translator is invited to join the game, and would indeed be ill-advised not to attempt a similar device, perhaps *Il latte su cui si piange* (cf: *Non piangere sul latte versato*). In both languages the collocational force existing between the lexical items *milk/latte* and *cry/piangere*, due solely to the existence of the proverb, is strong enough to maintain the effect.

Example 2, on the other hand, highlights another interesting discovery, again by Partington et al working with the Bank of English corpora, that many proverbial expressions are used in truncated form more often than in their canonical form. People are more likely to say '*Silver linings and all that*' than they are to recite the complete proverb '*Every cloud has a silver lining*', presumably on the assumption that the collocational force of these words is such as to preclude the necessity for total explicitness. The important message here is that while translators must be faithful to the linguistic conventions of each language, they must beware of ascribing the same conventions to the two languages with which they are dealing. Does Italian truncate proverbial expressions to the same extent, and for the same reasons? There are observable reasons to suggest that this is so in some cases ('*Campo cavallo*' '*Acqua passata*') but not in all. For example, it is very common in English to find the proverb *It was the (last) straw that broke the camel's back* shortened to *It was the last straw*. The Italian proverbial equivalent *Era la goccia che faceva traboccare il vaso* does not display this same propensity to abbreviate, though a semantically related short expression *Era il colmo* could very often fill the gap. It is to be hoped that future work on frequency counts and collocation will be able to assist the translator immensely in this kind of matching work.

Proper names

It would seem that with regard to the proper names of real people, the criteria for the translation of such names across languages are those of historical importance and rank. Great figures from the past in all fields of human endeavour find their names translated: the further back in time, the more chance of their being systematically translated, as is the case with biblical figures, Romans and Greeks. The nearer we get to the present day the less this usage persists; now the only proper names of people that are translated regularly between related European languages are those of royalty (*Principe Carlo, Princess Caroline*) and titles of address (*Signora Thatcher, President Scalfaro*). In the case of the names of places and geographical phenomena there again appears to be no norm, though the names of many countries, principal cities, major rivers, etc. are translated: *Deutschland/ Germany/Germania; Genève/Geneva/Ginevra; Rhein/Rhine/Reno.*

The names of modern world figures tend to cross borders intact, though they may suffer certain indignities in pronunciation. Modern communications and an ever-increasing knowledge of other cultures, deriving from increased contact between peoples, have meant that translating the name of the president of the United States into Italian (e.g. *Guglielmo Clinton*) has become superfluous, and indeed ridiculous.

In the case of lesser-known individuals, while their names will not be translated, it will often be necessary to leave clues as to their identity, role, position or importance. In a single report on the death of the Israeli leader Yitzhak Rabin, the Italian daily newspaper L'Unità (5/11/95), dealt with the various personalities involved in the following manner: the headline *ASSASSINATO RABIN* needed no further explanation and neither did the mentioning of the American president *La condanna di Clinton* or the leader of the Palestine Liberation Organisation *Arafat piange l'amico israeliano.* The article presumably passed through various stages of semi-translation as the news made its way through the press agencies, to be enhanced by subsequent press releases in Hebrew and English, and as the reportage moved through the lower ranks of politicians and public figures involved in the Rabin scenario, all well-known to the Israeli public, further elucidation was deemed necessary in Italian:

> … giunge l'annuncio ufficiale del direttore del gabinetto Eytan Haber …
>
> Piange Jean Friedman, uno degli organizzatori della manifestazione …

> Si dispera Shulamit Aloni, ministra delle Comunicazioni e leader del
> Meretz, la sinistra laica israeliana.

Even the name of Ezer Weizmann is preceded by the information tag *il capo dello stato*. As can be seen, the neatest and most economical way of providing any information the translator believes necessary is by adding it in the form of embedded phrases or clauses in apposition to the name itself. There are other ways, but the use of footnotes or endnotes, or even brackets, is only justified if the information considered necessary is of an encyclopaedic kind and length.

The discussion so far has centred on the names of real people, living or dead. Generally speaking such names refer to the people in question and no longer carry any significant semantic load: it is true that *Johnson* once referred to 'John's son', or that place names such as *Cedar Falls, Fontanafredda* form partial descriptions of the places in question, but such names have become **fossilised** and do not require translation.

Different considerations come into play when the focus turns to the names of fictitious characters, and particularly contemporary fictional names. Generally speaking, names of a purely onomastic nature do not translate, except occasionally: *Davide Copperfield*. However, if the name carries any other kind of meaning, this is when the translator's imaginative faculties are truly tested. Self-explanatory names such as *Bluebeard/Barbablù* and even *Cappuccetto Rosso/Little Red Riding Hood* are easily dealt with. Others require varying degrees of ingenuity. Consider some of the inventions in Aldo Busi's (1993) translation of 'Alice in Wonderland'. *Alice* is *Alice* logically enough (only the pronunciation changes between English and Italian), *the White Rabbit* is *il Coniglio Bianco* (a straight enough translation), and *Dinah* the cat remains *Dinah* (there is no hidden meaning here, though some translators might have been tempted, unnecessarily, to omit the final *h* in accordance with Italian phono-graphological norms). So far Busi has not been stretched, and even *the March Hare* (*la Lepre Marzolina*) and *the Hatter* (*il Cappellaio*) have a certain predictability and have appeared before. He then plays safe with *the Cheshire Cat/il Gatto del Cheshire* and is neat with *the Fish-Footman/il Valletto-Pesce* in spite of losing the alliteration, but the real touch of genius comes with *the Mock Turtle* whom Busi dubs *la Tartaruga d'Egitto*, from the Italian expression of doubt '*Ma che X d'Egitto!*'. In this case both the character itself and the extra connotation have been successfully portrayed. This kind of invention is also splendidly exemplified by the translation by Corbolante (1987) of the name of an 'Adrian Mole' character, a boy called *Maxwell House* (with all that that name implies for a British English reader: trendiness, pretension, amusing association with a well-known brand of coffee). In the Italian version he becomes *Teo Lipton*, thereby maintaining all the ingredients of pretension, humour, and even the association with an English drink product, but this time well-known in Italy.

Another work that illustrates the kind of difficulties involved in translating fictional names is Alan Bennett's stage version of Kenneth Grahame's 'The Wind in the Willows'. The character Mole calls one of the rabbits *Flopsy*, immediately conjuring up a series of images for the British reader. The name reflects the 'lop-sided' movement of the animals themselves and also the way the ears 'flop'. The translator of this work (Zampone 1994), provides the solution *Orecchielunghe*, remaining within the same semantic field, and maintaining the image. The buxom washer-woman *Bouncing Betty* becomes *Betty la Prosperosa* in a fairly effortless transfer of imagery, though again entailing the sacrifice of the alliteration. Betty, in her everyday work, uses a product called *Rinso*, **calqued** on the verb *to rinse*:

> She gets him his tub, washboard and a packet of Rinso soapflakes.

The translator's strategy in this case is to work back from the obvious connotation, producing a name that is consonant with the target language culture. Hence:

> Gli dà la tinozza, l'asse per lavare e un pacchetto di sapone in scaglie Sciacqua.

But a more subtle problem arose in the translation of this work regarding the names of the main characters, who are all animals personified. *Toad* is unarguably *Rospo* and *Badger* is *Tasso*. *Rat* is *Topo* but this is not so clear-cut; the Italian *topo* tends to bring to mind a smaller creature (mouse), but other considerations rule against the use of the more ugly sounding *Ratto*. Firstly, *Rat* may be a 'rat', but only in the zoological sense, as he is quite a sympathetic character in the play. Secondly, the characters often call each other by their nicknames, which are derivations of their actual names, and easily dealt with in Italian with 'vezzeggiativi': *Toady/Rospetto, Moley/ Talpetta*. *Ratto* would not fit the pattern as well as *Topo/Topino*. *Mole* created problems initially, as the translator wished to use the definite article and call the characters *Il Topo, Il Tasso*, etc., in line with Italian usage. *Talpa* is feminine and would require the misleading feminine article; hence the decision to use articleless nouns for all of them. And so it can be seen how a whole series of parameters must be considered when dealing with meaningful, fictitious names, but also how rewarding it can be to the translator, and ultimately to the reader, to effect this particular kind of componential and semantic analysis.

1.2.2 Terminology

Interest in terminology, initially as a separate field, and now as a fully-fledged discipline in its own right, has gone hand in hand with the information explosion of the post-war years. The constant development of science and technology has led to the creation of a multiplicity of subject areas, as disciplines expand, split and create their own autonomies. The expansion of interest in ever wider (and narrower) aspects of established fields of study is dependent on the constant formulation of new concepts, as new ideas take hold, new discoveries are made and new pathways are explored. Such new concepts need to be labelled, and as unequivocably as possible, within the confines of a finite language set.

Languages for special purposes

The emergence of distinct linguistic categorisations based on the idea of languages for special purposes (LSP) has introduced a degree of order into the labelling process, and will be discussed in more detail in Chapter Three. All major languages (English is the prime example as it has become the international vehicle for the transfer of scientific and technological information) accommodate a dynamic, ever-growing series of subsets of inter-linking 'technical' disciplines. Texts of special purpose languages consist of appositely labelled <u>terms</u> bound together by appropriate <u>words</u> from the general vocabulary stock.

So, as concepts are formulated, terms are created to represent those concepts in the lexicon of the language. The adoption of a particular term to represent a concept does not, however, occur haphazardly. Elements of componential analysis and the semantic environment of the subject area, allied to pre-ordained rules of term formation based on pre-existing items, provide a considerable level of consistency in the naming process. Nonetheless, in theory, one term represents one concept and should be free of any ambiguity. Sometimes the lexical item representing the term also exists in the general language, but is considered to be a separate lexical unit. A topical example would be *window* in its traditional and computer-connected senses. In other cases the technical term may be more common than its non-technical double; this is the case with a medical term such as *abortion*. The same lexical item may appear in different subject fields, but it will be fulfilling a different terminological job in each case, and will be translated correspondingly differently. The term *enlargement*, which in the general language has the basic meaning of *ampliamento*, translates as *ingrossamento* in medical terminology and *ingrandimento* in the field of photography, cf: *flap* in brain surgery, in aeronautics, in construction science, and also in the general vocabulary of the language. In fact, the number of analysable components of the item *flap* will be much more restricted where the item is used terminologically. Whereas clues are often required to comprehend a textual message in general language in the form of contextual and co-textual items, clues should be superfluous in special language texts. Dictionary definitions of 'words' are often given in the form of synonyms; special language glossaries or technical dictionaries should not need to follow this practice because terms should have no synonyms. Ideally, terms should be defined analytically, fixing their meaning in a hermetic way in relation to all other associated terms, though it must be said that very often this ideal is mere wishful thinking. Before examining the importance of these distinctions in terms of translation, it is time to provide an interim definition of terminology.

Juan Sager, who has written extensively on the subject, and whose ideas have contributed greatly to this section, formally defines terminology in the following way:

> Terminology is the study of and the field of activity concerned with the collection, description, processing and presentation of terms, i.e. lexical items belonging to specialised areas of usage of one or more languages.

He adds that:

> In its objectives it is akin to lexicography which combines the double aim of generally collecting data about the lexicon of a language with providing an information, and sometimes even an advisory, service to language users.   (1990:2)

Translators are, of course, among the principal users of this service, both from lexicographers and terminologists. As regards the presentation of terms, dictionaries in the traditional sense are losing ground to modern subject field glossaries which are able to respond to the way terms are classified and categorised, and thereby introduce some order into term accessibility. The **generic** and **partitive** relations subsisting between terms leads to subcategorising on the following model. 'Generic' refers to the class of objects or concepts, while 'partitive' refers to the various types within the general class:

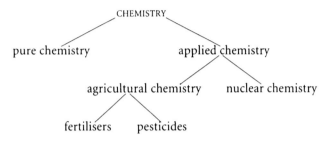

This is of great assistance in the organisation of data and, in the case of multilingual glossaries, the Elsevier collection of highly specialised technical dictionaries is a prime example of term categorisation coming some way towards helping the translator, by presenting associated and related terms together in easily-accessible form.

Terms and translators

The specialised language planning carried out by terminologists is designed to assist the users of terminology, who in the first instance are the specialists themselves. It is they who have needed, over the years, the terminological discipline provided by dictionaries, specialised glossaries, and now ever more sophisticated data banks. In the early days of international information exchange, the specialists themselves often found they had to function as rudimentary translators. They would have provided the analytical definitions mentioned earlier which today's translators can look to when checking whether a bilingual equivalence is to be trusted or not. Their knowledge of the subject compensated for many linguistic shortcomings, but as science and technology developed rapidly and efficient international communication was called for, the inevitable process of the division of labour brought professional translators (of varying competence) onto the scene. The monolingual data collections were followed by bilingual equivalents, initially of limited reliability, but gradual improvements and ever greater specialisation have now led to the availability of a vast range of valid materials. But before looking at the latest that information technology and

computational linguistics can offer, let us examine just how terms are dealt with in collected form, and how the translator should use them.

The formulation of a concept leads to the coining of a term in a particular language, let's say English. For the term to have an equivalent in another language, let's say Italian, which is to have the same terminological status, the respective conceptual fields must be the same. As Sager (1990:47) explains

> Coincidence of conceptual fields is likely to exist in the taxonomic sciences, and in other sciences in which there has been a considerable amount of knowledge transfer and linguistic borrowing so that the two conceptual fields show a great similarity.

In fact, what normally happens between two closely-related languages such as English and Italian, is that terms are either translated satisfactorily, calqued, or borrowed intact. Often a time lag operates between these three options. That is, sometimes a new term is translated immediately and the translation sticks and becomes an accepted part of that language's terminology stock. In other cases, the term is either not translated because the foreign term is preferred, or the translation does not take hold and loses ground over time to the loan or to a crude calque. Different users in the same field, e.g. banking (financial experts, bankers, clerks, customers), may show diverse preferences for a translated, calqued or borrowed term, and thus prolong the confusion as to how to translate individual items. For example, the results of a questionnaire given to various operators in the field of factoring (Guerra 1987) showed that English terms were used even where a translation existed (*acceptance/tratta accettata*) or where a neologism had been devised (*advising bank/banca corrispondente di avviso del credito*), but that in time Italian usage can prevail (*approved debt/debito approvato, aged balanced report/distinta dei debiti scaduti*). Other terms were found to be in a state of flux: for example, the term *merchant bank* is used 80% of the time and the corresponding Italian term *banca d'affari* 20% of the time. *Demurrage* enjoys 50% popularity together with *spese di controstallia*. *Depositi a vista* is used 80% of the time at the expense of the now disappearing *call deposits*. English terms are used where Italian equivalents have not yet been created and particularly where there is no legal jurisdiction. Such data indicate the importance to the translator of a sound knowledge of the readership.

Translators, usually not specialists and often with no technical background, look to the data collections (dictionaries, glossaries, data-banks, etc.) to help them find target language equivalents of terms. It is at this point that it becomes clear that the 'one concept-one term' ideal of terminology is not always applicable, or is not evident to the non-specialist. Standardisation procedures are still being refined and are still far from complete. On the other hand, technological progress shows no signs of slowing down, and consequently scientific innovation and the creation of new terminology proceeds rapidly. Thus it is now acknowledged that supplementary information regarding usage is often required in dictionary material, and it is being increasingly provided in the form of usage notes, terms found in context, encyclopedic definitions and pragmatic assistance. The data banks of the future will contain more and more of this type of information in line with developments in lexicography (see **1.2.3**).

Term formation

New terms are practically always formed on the model of existing terms, themselves often derived from Latin or Greek, by affixation, compounding or abbreviating. Parallel patterns can be seen to operate. For example, in the rapidly-expanding field of computers, lexical items are generated on established models: *software, hardware, shareware, bannerware, crippleware,* etc. Very often the same macro-processes of term formation can be seen at work across languages, where the purpose is to qualify, classify, identify, specify a use, or whatever. The *supermarket* is the *supermercato,* the *pressure screw* is the *vite a pressione, bionic* is *bionico, anti-freeze* is *anti-gelo.* The case of *pressure screw/vite a pressione* is instructive for two reasons. First, it is indicative of how terms do not necessarily consist of just one lexical word; compounds of various types become lexicalised and appear as separate, individualised terms: *closed-circuit television, thoracic outlet syndrome, titoli di credito a breve termine, cavo ad alta frequenza,* etc. They translate as such: *televisione a circuito chiuso, sindrome dell'apertura toracica superiore, short term paper, high-frequency cable.* The second point, however, as can be seen from analysing these examples internally, is that term formation processes may differ across languages at a micro-level. The *pressure screw* two-noun cluster in English translates as a noun + preposition + noun *vite a pressione* in Italian. The processes and the models they create can also, at times, lead to semantic confusion. *Diamond drilling* and *Concrete drilling* (see Sager 1990:66) would appear to be based on the same formation model but, in fact, in the first case the drilling is carried out <u>with</u> a diamond tip and in the second case the drilling is done <u>into</u> concrete – *trapanare con la punta di diamante* and *trapanare nel cemento* respectively.

More importantly, all these examples point us in the direction of that peculiarly English linguistic habit of creating potentially infinite noun strings. This process, which is common in the general language (*press conference, Speech Day Programme, Health Service Minister Pay Award Scandal*) is extremely widespread also in terminology (*microcomputer database management system software evaluation guidelines*). Note how the Italian compound *gradino di caduta* becomes *straw walker step* in this example of technical English taken from the field of mechanised agriculture. Each noun determines the one following, whereas the typical Italian prepositional phrase construction, occasionally varied by adjective use, works the other way with each term being determined by the following unit.

The noun string is often complicated by the addition of adjectives or participles qualifying or classifying nouns in the sequence: *parallel bench vice/ morsa parallela, single-side finishing method/finitura di un fianco per volta, bag-filling machine/insacchettatrice*. The translations in these cases do not reveal determining patterns and must be considered as single term units.

Lexical density (term density)

Lexical density refers to the proportion of **lexical words** (words with recognisable concrete or abstract referents, be they nouns, verbs, adjectives or adverbs, e.g. *table, elephant, intelligence, go, beautiful, quickly*) in a text compared to the number of **function words** (prepositions, conjunctions, copular verbs, etc.). Written language, for example, is lexically more dense than spoken language, as the writer has time to compose a more concentrated discourse.

One of the distinguishing features of technical, 'term-ridden' text at a macro-level is assumed to be the greater than normal level of lexical density and, more particularly, the greater level of 'term' density, that is the ratio of technical <u>terms</u> to ordinary lexical words and function words. The information load is considered to be heavier, often to the extent of being impenetrable to the non-expert. Abstracts for articles that appear in medical journals are a good example, though most scientific sectors are the same. This impenetrability is assumed to be the product of a densely-presented mass of unknown, unshared information. According to the notion of equivalent-effect, the translator should attempt to create the same effect on a target language audience as the original writer created on the source language readership. Although this whole concept has been challenged by translation scholars (see Snell-Hornby 1988) the measuring of lexical density can provide a parameter in assessing whether a translator has achieved the right register and right balance of technical expression. It is also possible, with the use of **corpus**-based devices, to see whether different parts of texts are more term-dense than others, and organise a translation accordingly.

Compare the two texts below:

Catalytic incineration

Incineration in the context of this article is the combining of oxygen with noxious material to form harmless compounds, usually carbon dioxide and water. It can be carried out by two methods: *thermal incineration* – whereby a flame is maintained – and *catalytic incineration* – whereby the combustion is carried out in the presence of a solid catalyst without a flame.

Incenerimento catalitico

L'incenerimento, nel contesto di questo articolo, è la combinazione di ossigeno con sostanze nocive per formare composti innocui, di solito biossido di carbonio e acqua. Può essere effettuato con due metodi: *incenerimento termico* – in cui si mantiene la fiamma – e *incerimento catalitico* – in cui la combustione viene effettuata in presenza di un catalizzatore solido senza fiamma.

The English original from Princeton Chemical Research Inc. (AC 1994) has a lexical density of about 50%, faithfully adhered to in the Italian translation, and a very high term density of circa 17%, also reproduced in the target text.

The next example text, on the same subject of atmospheric pollution, is taken from Complete Car (December 1994), aimed at the enthusiastic amateur. It therefore displays a more informal style, even when dealing with technical matters.

Clearing the air

It's getting tougher to justify owning a car if you care about the world we live in. The car is under attack as never before as the bad guy in the environment debate. Its critics say it kills and injures millions and chokes us with its fumes; it squanders valuable resources; it causes whole districts to be demolished to make way for its advance; and it leaves crime and destruction in its wake. Yet most of us would admit it's still an essential part of our lives: we all want to own one – and without it we would more or less grind to a halt.

Aria da pulire

Diventa sempre più difficile giustificare il possesso di un'automobile se vi preoccupate del mondo in cui viviamo. L'auto è sotto accusa come non lo è mai stata prima d'ora, come il cattivo del dibattito ambientale. Chi la critica dice che uccide e ferisce milioni di persone e ci soffoca con i suoi fumi; sperpera risorse di grande valore; è la causa della demolizione di interi distretti per lasciar posto al suo passaggio e nella sua scia lascia crimine e distruzione. Eppure molti di noi ammetterebbero che è ancora una parte essenziale della nostra vita: noi tutti ne vogliamo una, e senza ci fermeremmo quasi completamente.

In this case, the lexical density is only 40% and the term density almost zero; the translator has translated accordingly and thus made a definite effort to maintain the style of the original, even though a more far-reaching investigation into 'colloquial language density' would have suggested further thought to the translation of *tougher*, *bad guy* and *grind to a halt*. Moreover, *it causes whole districts to be demolished* is grammatically clumsy and perhaps not worthy of the **nominalisation** created for the target language version. But these considerations apart, the statistics of lexical density can be seen to confirm or otherwise the translator's adherence to style and register.

1.2.3 Lexicography and the use of dictionaries

Unlike Dr. Johnson's quirky dictionary of 1755 (the work of 'a harmless drudge'), modern monolingual and bilingual dictionaries (e.g. Collins Cobuild English Dictionary, I Dizionari Sansoni) provide ever more systematic data on all aspects of the lexical items they list. Advances in lexicography, in line with what is happening in the field of terminology, can be seen on the pages of all the latest dictionaries and glossaries the market now offers. Information on **morphology** (irregular plurals, prepositional constructions such as *pensare a*, *pensare di*, *impedire a*, *prevent from*), spelling and pronunciation is followed by a serious lexical breakdown. Words are presented in their base form, but all affixes are considered as well as other forms of that word making up a vocabulary block (e.g. *passion*, *passionate*, *impassioned*, *passion-killer*, *passion fruit*, etc.). The problem of ambiguity caused through **homonymy** (the phenomenon of identical words referring to widely different referents), polysemy (words having more than one meaning though connected in some way) and **homography** (words having the same form but different pronunciation and meaning, e.g. *permit* noun and *permit* verb) is also tackled. The difference between homonymy, polysemy and homography is a grey, contentious area but the distinction as outlined above is useful in lexicographical terms, and therefore useful to the translator. In the dictionaries, homonymous items usually form separate headwords and polysemous items are labelled in some way, e.g. (1), (2), (3), according to their different meanings. Such sources of ambiguity are more common in English, also due to the lack of morphological variation between grammatical categories (e.g. *round* can be noun, verb, adjective, adverb or preposition).

Thus in the Sansoni bilingual Third Edition (1991) the Italian item *porto* can be seen to be homonymous in its widely different meanings of *harbour*, *licence* (*porto d'armi*) and *port wine*, represented as three different (head)words. Its polysemy is evident from the various numbered entries: *1. harbour ..., 2. port (città portuale) ..., 3. aim, goal ...* etc. All the above information is arranged in an increasingly user-friendly way, and should provide translators with enough options to fit the particular context-bound solution they are seeking. Items like *la politica* and *l'economia* used to cause problems through their partial polysemy, and the dictionaries now provide examples to guide the choice between *politics/policy* and *economics/economy*.

> **politica** f. **1** (*scienza*) politics *pl* (*costr. sing o pl.*) **2** (*linea di condotta*) policy: **una — lungimirante** a far-sighted policy.
> (Sansoni 1991:1916)

> **economia** f. **1** (*scienza*) economics *pl* (*costr. sing*) **2** (*sistema economico*) economy: **— agraria** agricultural economy
> (Sansoni 1991:1578)

Morphology sometimes intervenes in cases of homonymy: the lexical item *wave*, apart from its salutational meaning, can be used both congruently and metaphorically (*the waves washed up on the shore, a wave of sympathy swept the hall*), but in translation Italian would distinguish between *onda(e)* and *ondata*. Cf: *walk* (verb & noun) – *camminare, camminata*.

Certainly, the powers of semantic association have made polysemy a very useful instrument in the hands of the language user and it is difficult for the lifeless printed page to capture all possible uses of a word, and even more difficult to provide a list of all possible translation options. Very often, translators will have to meet the bilingual dictionary halfway by taking what they can from the various entries and applying them to the context of situation. By way of example, here are some of the entries provided for the verbs *cuocere* and *cook* in the Dizionari Sansoni (Schmid 1995:36):

> cuocere = to cook
> to roast
> to boil
> to bake
> to stew
> to grill
> to burn
> to tan
> to make fall in love (cotto)
>
> to cook = cuocere
> cucinare
> falsificare
> alterare
> manipolare

A number of sample sentences are also provided, and **markers** indicating whether the word is being used technically, familiarly, ironically, etc. are also extremely useful. Thus a translator faced with the English expression *cooking the books* would find, under the headword *cook*, that it means *falsificare i registri* but would also be given the information that the expression is familiar *(fam)* and may seek a similarly colloquial equivalent.

This example is indicative of how it is very often the commonest words that appear over a whole range of expressions which at times show little semantic affinity with the root meaning of that word, and which dictionaries do not always pick up. The polysemy of the verb/noun *play* in English is well known, but the instruction on a cassette recorder *PLAY* cannot be dealt with by either *suonare* or *giocare*. However, many figurative expressions and examples of proverbial language, idioms and **tropes** are now presented, in context, even within the confines of the printed page, though this is a tall order for bilingual dictionaries. The latest monolingual editions, however, are able to fill many a gap. Idioms are generally listed now under the headword(s), even at the risk of repetition. Therefore, it is now possible to track down slippery idiomatic expressions such as '*You reckon?*', '*mark* *you!*' and '*I'll be bound*'. Indeed, the judicious use of both mono- and bilingual dictionaries is the real secret to the translator's lexicographical skills (see previous discussion of the verb *to maul*). Identifying first the right semantic area and then homing in on nuance can be very rewarding. In translating a passage containing the sentence

> Il progetto si presentava irto di difficoltà.

the translator can easily detect the semantic field, but may feel that a particular collocation is required to do justice to *irto*. The bilingual dictionary can provide a series of options (*bristly, thick, filled*), none of which are remotely suitable, but also *fraught with difficulties* as an example sentence, though the latter may be a little melodramatic in some contexts. Checking back through the monolingual dictionaries and exploring the *pieno di, afflitto di* direction in Italian and then how *difficulties* collocates in English, translators can compare competing items (*full of, assailed by, chocker-block with*) as they see them in context, possibly opting finally for:

> The project was beset by difficulties.

The Longman Activator (1993) and the bilingual Cambridge Word Routes (1995) are designed to help word seekers in this way, that is starting from the general meaning and tracking down the specific, though a traditional thesaurus and indeed a modern dictionary of the Cobuild type are useful.

The new monolingual dictionaries are also useful in providing examples of the kind of colloquial usage that until recently was lacking in any dictionary, especially those involving false or semi-false cognates. For example, the Cobuild includes the following uses of *actually, evidently* and *question*.

> **actually** You use **actually** to introduce a new topic into a conversation. *Well actually, John, I rang you for some advice.*

> **evidently** You can use **evidently** to introduce a statement or opinion and to emphasise that you feel that it is true or correct: a formal use. *Quite evidently, it has nothing to do with social background.*

> **question** A **question** is a problem, matter or point which needs to be considered. .... *It was just a question of having the time to re-adjust.*

It presents them in an informal way now adopted for 'user-friendly' reasons. In these three cases, translators also have the benefit of the sample sentences on which to base their target texts. If they are able to apply those sentences to the text they are translating, they might then opt respectively for *in effetti, chiaramente* and *si tratta di* . . . .

Corpora

Baker (1995:223) points out that

> Within translation studies . . . , Lindquist (1984) has advocated the use of corpora for training translators, and Baker (1993) has argued that theoretical research into the nature of translation will receive a powerful impetus from corpus-based studies.

So what is the current state of affairs regarding corpora and translation studies? First of all, what is meant by a corpus and what corpora are available? A corpus, for the purposes of translators, is a large body of recorded text material, written and/or spoken, stored on computer and available to the user at the push of a button, available not only in the form of a mechanised dictionary, but also manipulable in the sense that information such as a term's frequency of use or collocational range can be extracted. This latter information is so diffuse that it cannot be recorded in any meaningful way in standard dictionaries. There is now a substantial (and growing) selection of corpora available, in a growing number of languages including Italian. Some of these contain text fragments chosen randomly or within predefined genres, while others contain whole texts of varying length, complexity and content, allowing for the study of units in their entirety as well as selected pieces of text. The purpose is to provide as wide a representative sample as possible of language in use. A well-known general corpus such as the Cobuild/Bank of English collection now contains up to 500 million words of contemporary English. In addition, a growing number of subject-specific corpora are appearing, prepared by terminologists and information scientists for the use of, amongst others, translators.

This amount of material is statistically viable in the sense that it provides a sufficient range of language use to be able to locate meanings of words in context through sheer force of illustration. For example, any word (or term) can be consulted in hundreds or thousands of different contexts – the computer can display a single lexical item surrounded by long series of diverse co-texts. Through the process of **concordancing**, all the collocates of an item can be called up and their frequency patterns can be analysed within a given span of words, that is a given distance to the right or left of that item:

> ... the plan to close 60 of its 481 **branches** across the country was part of its long ...
>
> ... the Royal Ulster Constabulary **Branch**. Although the Army and MI5 still retain ...
>
> ... bronze leaves and balding **branches** and to paint the walls with abstract ...
>
> ... or in person to their local **branches**. Customers who do nothing will be ...
>
> ... death (killed by a falling **branch** in the Champs-Elysees) while in exile ...
>
> (Gavioli 1996)

A printout such as this, of indefinite length, can provide exhaustive information about the behaviour of a lexical item, in this case *branch(es)*, in relation to its co-text. Statistical probabilities can be calculated regarding a word's main collocates, e.g. *local branch*, *falling branches*, etc. Such information, and other data discovered through corpus study, may clash surprisingly with the conventional wisdom and with an individual's intuitions regarding language use. For example, Sinclair (1994:24) examined the common co-occurrence of a series of adjectives + nouns:

general trend	physical assault
general drift	physical attack
general consent	physical bodies
general perception	physical damage
general opinion	physical proximity
etc.	etc.

These examples challenge the idea that adjectives are totally autonomous in nature, and that when found in juxtapostion with a noun merely enhance or restrict the meaning of that noun. It would seem rather that the words **co-select**, or are co-selected by the speaker, in the sense that their meanings overlap, or blend together to form a single unit. For example, an *assault* is usually construed as *physical*, whether or not the adjective is used; the item *general* adds nothing to the nouns it is theoretically modifying apart from underlining a part of the meaning. In a noun group such as *dry land*, it would seem that the adjective *dry* is co-selected with the noun, rather than selected from a paradigm of possible descriptions of land.

This is where the term lexicogrammar really comes into its own as words themselves are seen to dictate their linguistic environment. Traditional grammatical borders become blurred as examples of usage force re-thinking. In the expression *in one's declining years*, is *declining* a verb or an adjective? (see Sinclair, 1991 for a full account). Sinclair also points out how the data from corpora have led to a rethinking, for example, of phrasal verb semantics; attention paid to the particle (*turn up, round up, pull up, show up*) rather than the verb (*turn up, turn out, turn off*) makes it possible to group phrasal verbs according to sense. That is, in terms of phrasal verb logic, checking one word to the left of a long list of uses of the adverbial particle or preposition *up* would produce a more meaningful series of examples than checking one word to the right of the verb/noun *turn*. The English preposition or adverb particle needs semanticising in some way in Italian: the common element in the *ups* in the examples above seems to be a point of arrival. *Show up* and *turn up* can both be glossed by *arrive, round up* implies the completion of an act of gathering together, and *pull up* means to come to a halt.

Corpora also reveal discrepancies in the use of single lexical items in the singular and plural. English terms such as *advice* or *evidence* will never be found in the plural, though the latter will be found with a final *s* on the rare occasions it is used as a verb. However, an item such as *ear/ears* may throw up some seeming anomalies, e.g:

> He has an ear for music
> They have an ear for music
> *They have ears for music
> I'm all ears
> He's got a good ear (he understands music well)
> He's got good ears (he hears well)

Furthermore, if the corpus demonstrates that an expression such as *a good ear for* only appears in the context outlined above, it can be considered a single unit that chooses its own environment. Future research will be able to ascertain how many such expressions can be isolated and how many words they consist of. The next stage will be to check whether such findings correlate across language boundaries. As this work continues, the whole face of lexicography (and grammar!) will change.

For the moment, research carried out using corpora within the field of translation has shown, apart from the above, how certain types of lexis may be more frequent in one language than in another (see Shamaa (1978) on Arabic/English, mentioned in Baker 1995). It also indicates how translated texts compare with their originals over a whole range of examples. This at least implies that predictions can be made as to translation solutions in given contexts, and also how it may be possible to identify a genre of 'translationese' (Baker 1995), and what this may mean in terms of checks and balances to the translator's work. But as Sinclair has repeatedly pointed out, what seemed impossible only a few years ago is now standard practice, and the future of corpus-based linguistics undoubtedly holds tremendously exciting prospects for a whole range of disciplines. Moreover, a sufficient number of scholars and researchers are at work in the field of translation to make sure that the discipline is in a position to gain the maximum benefit in the years to come.

1.3   Translation strategies

This chapter will move on now to discuss the various ways translators can deal with structural and lexical differences between the two languages English and Italian. It will deal almost exclusively with contemporary language and the various ideas and theories that link up modern **synchronic linguistics** with translation studies. The value of this approach is summed up by Malone, whose terminology will be adopted in this section.

> Synchronic linguistics, which views language functionally and
> structurally, is of paramount importance to the study of
> translation.   (Malone 1988:3)

Using examples from the most diverse of languages, Malone (1988:15) provides a list of nine strategies the translator can apply in translating at a structural, lexicogrammatical level:

> Equation and Substitution
> Divergence and Convergence
> Amplification and Reduction
> Diffusion and Condensation
> Reordering

The first eight are presented as pairs, as they are mirror images of one another. For example, if translation from English to Italian 'diverges', then the corresponding back translation from Italian to English will 'converge'. The basic tenets of this classification are useful in providing the translator with the justification for making adjustments of form in line with the semantic, stylistic and communicative requirements of the target text.

In simple terms, Equation suggests some form of automatic equivalence, while Substitution is necessary if that automatism is not present. In Divergence the one-to-one relationship associated with Equation is replaced by a rapport of one-to-many, Convergence representing the many-to-one formula. Amplification requires the addition of some element, Reduction the opposite. Diffusion, as opposed to the simple addition associated with Amplification, requires that a source text item be expanded without adding extra information, while Condensation calls for the corresponding contraction of a source item. Reordering is self-explanatory and refers to basic comparative syntax: it has no counterpart, being in itself reciprocal in nature. These various strategies will now be discussed in terms of Italian/ English translation.

1.3.1 Equation and Substitution

Equation

The most obvious form of Equation is that of the loan word, where equality would seem absolute. Culturally specific words are often loaned; Italians play *baseball* and the English eat *lasagna*. This can even occur where equivalent terms exist in the two languages. English supermarkets now sell *rucola*, even though a bilingual dictionary would provide the translation *rocket*; Italians enjoy *un po' di relax* as often as *un riposo*. Neologisms in technical fields (created daily) generally originate in the English language owing to the international role played by that idiom in the world of science, technology and business. They also often appear as loans (*software, screening, factoring*), as do terms coined for particular sub-cultures (*videogames, rap*, etc.). However, the 'absolute' equivalence of these terms must be questioned, given that they are used outside their home context. Although *lasagna* is now a familiar part of the British diet, the term will not conjure up the same associations as it does in an Italian context. Moreover, at a phonetic level, such terms undergo quite drastic changes in pronunciation, often due to the total lack of similar vowel or consonant sounds in the borrower language. For example, the two vowel sounds in the English word *corner* are elongated when adopted for Italian football terminology, and the two *r* consonants are rolled. Nevertheless, from the strictly linguistic point of view, such loans provide a 'soft' translation option.

A second form of Equation is provided by the calque, where the target language adapts the source language term to its own morpho-phonological framework. The Italian football terms *dribblare* and *crossare*, derived from the English verbs *to dribble* and *to cross*, are now well-entrenched in Italian. Another example is the shout of approval *Bravo!* in English, particularly in musical contexts, which is addressed to one or more people of either sex, given the lack of English gender and plural markers for adjectives. More disturbingly for Italian language purists, certain English expressions and constructions which fit uncomfortably within the Italian language are beginning to be calqued in ever more frequent situations. The influence of hastily-dubbed television series is currently being blamed for the creeping infiltration of expressions like *Buon pomeriggio*, calqued on the common English greeting *Good afternoon*. Caldiron and Hochkefler (1992:39) identified the calque *bisogna che realizziate* . . . from *You must realise* . . . .

But Equation refers also, and more widely, to the default position whereby if no other pressing reason exists, a term should be translated by its clear one-to-one equivalent: *man = uomo*. That is, if all other options have been discarded because there is no semantic, pragmatic, culturally-motivated or stylistic reason for translating *man* in any other way, e.g:

> Man = l'umanità
> Hey man! = Eh, capo!
> You've already moved your man = Hai già spostato il tuo pezzo
> (draughts match)
> It's a man's game = E' un gioco da maschi

then the Equation mechanism comes naturally into force.

In a translation such as the following:

> Lorenzo fermò la macchina e si voltò verso il giovane: 'Allora tu vieni su o vuoi restare qui?'
>
> Lorenzo stopped the car and turned towards the youth: 'Well then, are you coming up or d'you want to stay here?'
> (Moravia, trans. Davidson 1965:134)

there are no compelling reasons not to translate the first sentence in the easiest way the target language provides. It is a faithful translation in every way, not least in its effortless syntax.

The direct speech that follows is not translated word-for-word, but strays from the literal only inasmuch as the rules of English grammar dictate it. The continuous tense must replace the simple present to express the imminent future of the event in the first clause, and the addition of the auxiliary to form the interrogative is mandatory in the second. However, as the story progresses, the translator is obliged to stray ever further from the transparent option:

> . . . Come se l'avesse aspettato, ecco, tosto, sorgere dall'ombra Gigliola: . . .
> 'Ma chi parla? Però lei dovrebbe convincersene.'

...As though she had been waiting for him, there was Gigliola, emerging from the shadows...

'But who's saying anything? However, you ought to be convinced.'

(ibidem)

And this, of course, is the norm.

One of the most well-known traps associated with the word-for-word equation is that of false cognates ('false friends'), where the meanings of deceptively similar terms do not match across languages. The classic examples are well known to all language students: *actual/attuale*, *simpatico/ sympathetic*, *editor/editore*, etc. There are also partial cognates where the transparent translation is valid in some situations but not in others. For example:

direttore/director
Rivolgersi al direttore

(in a company)	Ask the Director (cf: Manager, Managing Director)
(newspaper office)	Ask the Editor
(school)	Ask the Headmaster
(orchestra)	Ask the Conductor

As can be seen, in many instances the potential *director/direttore* equation is totally misleading, and in the business context is merely an alternative (see Divergence below). Interestingly, one example of where the English term has found credence is in the context of private language schools and similar establishments in Italy where the *direttore* is referred to by students and staff alike as the *Director*, even by native-speakers. A different example is that of *città*, where the semantic field remains basically the same, but the Italian term covers a much greater variety of urban conglomeration than the English *city*, which theoretically refers to an urban area containing a cathedral, but in practice is generally used to refer to large urban areas. Smaller Italian *città* are *towns*, even large *villages*. By extension, *andare in città* is usually rendered by *going to town*.

Lexical items such as *problema*, *situazione*, *realtà* and *possibilità* would seem to have unassailable equivalents in *problem*, *situation*, *reality* and *possibility*, but this is far from always the case. These four terms have a particularly high frequency in Italian, much higher than their English 'equivalents', and appear over a wide range of contexts. Taking *realtà* as an example, this word often has too high a level of abstraction for many English contexts. Approaching its translation case by case, Browne and Natali (1989:141) offer the following array of options:

l'arte come imitazione della realtà/art as imitation of nature
la realtà è dura/life is hard (it's a hard life)
la sua malattia è una realtà/her illness is genuine
progetti che diventano realtà/plans which are realised (come to fruition)
spesso la realtà ci sfugge/often we don't see things as they really are
ha il senso della realtà/he's realistic
bisogna tenere in considerazione la realtà locale/we must keep local
    needs in mind
gli editori devono conoscere bene la realtà sociale/publishers need to
    have a thorough knowledge of the social scene
la realtà economica/the economic situation

Thus it can be seen how English often has to resort to more specific terms, to circumlocutions, to paraphrase and at times to zero translation e.g. *la realtà del mondo della moda/the world of fashion*. *Problema* is often translated by *question, issue, matter*; *situazione* by *position, circumstance, place*; *possibilità* by *chance, opportunity, occasion*. It must not, however, be forgotten that in some contexts the above four terms selected as examples act as true cognates, and in those circumstances, Equation must be the rule. Indeed, word-for-word translation is justified precisely in those cases of the matching of true cognates where meanings actually coincide.

The latter premise is never more relevant than in the case of standard translations, where there should be no deviation from the fixed Equation. *The Holy Bible* is *La Sacra Bibbia* and not *La Santa Bibbia* or *The Sacred Bible*. The *United Nations Organisation* is the *Organizzazione delle Nazioni Unite* and so on. These terms have absolute authority, though there are many others whose ubiquity suggests a certain standardisation, for example, prohibitions like *No smoking/Vietato fumare*, and universal metaphors such as the *Third World/Terzo Mondo*. Well-reputed passages of authoritative works of literature and well-known quotations from political speeches have often acquired a standard translation, though in the former case these can be superceded by later versions. Shakespeare's *To be or not to be, that is the question*, for years quoted knowingly as *Essere o non essere, questo è il problema* (see trans. Baldini, 1963 cf: Montale, 1949 *Essere ... o non essere. E' il problema*), is now being challenged by succinct existential alternatives such as *Essere o non essere, tutto qui* as featured in the dubbed version of the Zeffirelli film of 'Hamlet'.

However, returning to the most authoritative text of all, the Bible, the question of standard translation was seen to emerge in the context of the simultaneous interpretation of film. Interpreting professor David Snelling

(1995), on the occasion of a Bologna University conference on 'translation for the media', mentioned the example of a film containing a series of biblical references, including mention of the *burning bush*. In a case like this, the literal translation as *cespuglio ardente* must be discarded in favour of the standard biblical translation *rovo ardente*.

After having discussed the various ramifications of the concept of Equation, it must be reiterated that literal translation is a default mechanism and that in most translations of more than two or three words, some other strategy has to be brought into play.

Substitution

The antithesis of Equation, to return to Malone's terminology, is Substitution, in which a translation is used that may bear little or no morpho-syntactic or semantic relation to the source text. There is no 'equivalent' as such. For example, at a purely grammatical level, the Italian prepositional phrase replaces (substitutes) the English Saxon genitive:

> Gulliver's Travels/I viaggi di Gulliver

The Italian subjunctive can be replaced by an English infinitive:

> Farò in modo che si interessi ...
> I'll try to get her to ...

At a more semantic rather than morpho-syntactic level, the proverb *the straw that broke the camel's back* is replaced by *la goccia che fa traboccare il vaso*. Two examples show further strategies of Substitution at work. At the beginning of the Walt Disney Pictures version of 'Alice in Wonderland' (1951), Alice is given a song to sing, all about 'Cats and Rabbits'. Cartoon films for children represent a typical genre where even songs must be translated in foreign language versions, as the audience is demanding in terms of comprehension. However, while translational accuracy is expendable, diligent translators will provide compensatory mechanisms in their substitutions. Take the third verse of the song:

There'd be new birds	Gli uccellini
lots of nice and friendly howdy do birds	sempre allegri, affabili e carini
everyone would own a dozen blue birds	canterebber l'aria di Puccini
within that world of my own	in quel mio mondo ideal
	(see Taylor 1994:149)

Much liberty is taken in translation, though the source-language semantic field is untouched. However, the third line *everyone would own a dozen blue birds* has been clearly 'substituted' by *canterebber l'aria di Puccini*. The reasons for the change are not merely linguistic (there are questions of rhyme, of scanning and of cultural relocation), but it can be seen that from the very beginning linguistic fidelity had to be rejected in the interest of a greater good – in the final analysis, the entertainment of children.

The second example is taken from a translation of Sue Townsend's bestseller 'The Growing Pains of Adrian Mole'. One character in the book, an Alsatian dog of a not particularly benevolent nature, is named *Sabre*; the name has warlike overtones and fits its owner well. It also has, in English, the advantage of being a highly credible name for a dog; not so its direct translation equivalent – *Sciabola*. The translator quoted here (Corbolante, 1987) opted for a substitution that maintained the semantic quotient of ferocity, was linguistically suitable as a name, and had the further advantage of being an English word used currently in Italian – *Killer*.

1.3.2 Divergence and Convergence

Divergence

The strategy of Divergence is that of choosing a suitable term from a potential range of alternatives. There may be a limited number of alternatives to diverge towards (*cream = panna* or *crema*) or a bewildering selection (*girare = to turn, to switch on, to pass on, to twist, to go round, to avoid, to tour, to travel, to endorse, to invest, to shoot, to spin, to circle, to wind*, etc.). Bilingual dictionaries give an idea of the extent of the Divergence phenomenon, and it is not restricted to lexical words such as nouns, adjectives and verbs. For example, there is Divergence in the meaning and function of the Italian frequency adverb *sempre*:

> Viene sempre di venerdì/He always comes on Fridays
> Il Parma preme ma la Juventus è sempre prima in classifica/Parma are putting on the pressure but Juventus are still top of the table

and in the pronoun cum interjection cum adverb cum adjective cum noun *niente*:

> Non ho niente da dire/I have nothing to say
> venti-tre, venti-quattro – Niente! – ricominciamo/twenty-three, twenty-four – No! – let's start again
> Niente male!/Not bad!

> Ho fatto tutto questo lavoro per niente/I've done all this work for nothing
> Non per niente accettano solo ragazze/Not for nothing do they only
>   accept girls
> Niente scherzi!/No messing about!
> Non hanno un bel niente/They've got nothing at all

Furthermore, the translator is often called upon to select from grammatical paradigms, where more than one construction may be acceptable.

> Se dovesse succedere
> If it should happen/Should it happen/Were it to happen/If it were to
>   happen
>
> You had better go early
> Faresti meglio ad andare presto/Sarebbe meglio se andassi presto
>
> Non serve lamentarsi
> There is no point (in) complaining/It's no use complaining/Complaining
>   will get you nowhere

Making the right choice (or <u>a</u> right choice) in all circumstances is the translator's aim and there are generally linguistic or extralinguistic clues available. As a simple example, in the case of a letter from Mozart to his wife, the great composer talks of his mother:

> I am taking *Mamma* tomorrow. Hofer has already given her the libretto to read. In her case what will probably happen will be that she will *see* the opera, but not *hear* it.
>
> Domani ci porto *Mama*; Hofer le ha già dato da leggere il libretto. Nel caso di *Mama*, andrà probabilmente a finire che lei *vedrà* l'opera, ma non l'*ascolterà*.
>
> (for greater detail see Part Two)

In the third sentence the possessive adjective *her* can diverge in Italian to *suo/suoi/sua/sue* or *di qualcuno/a*. The singular *case* means the translator can exclude *suoi/sue*, and the masculine gender of the Equation translation *caso* excludes *sua*. Although the feminine pronoun *lei* further down the clause indicates that the *case* indeed refers to the mother, the translator decides against *Nel suo caso* in favour of *Nel caso di Mama*, possibly to avoid any danger of temporary ambiguity between the mother and Hofer. In any case the translator makes use of any co-textual linguistic clues to assist decision-making.

Convergence

Convergence is the opposite of Divergence. Malone (1988:36), in one of his rare examples from Italian, cites the personal pronouns *tu/Lei/voi/Loro* all converging into *you*, depending on the context of use. The three Italian terms *commercialista*, *ragioniere* and *contabile* would converge in a commercial context to provide the single translation equivalent *accountant* in most circumstances when translating into English, without causing any embarrassment. Care must be taken when going in the opposite direction, where professional jealousies might well require a fine distinction between the diverging *commercialista*, *ragioniere* and *contabile*.

1.3.3 Amplification and Reduction

Amplification

Amplification requires that the translator add some element to the source text for reasons of greater comprehensibility. The most obvious form of Amplification is the translator's note, be it an endnote, a footnote or a bracketed addition following the item in question. Very often the addition is not so obtrusive, however, and may be purely structural. It may be necessary in the case of a collocation gap, that is, where a single lexical item in one language needs a collocational partner in the other.

> Hanno interesse a tenere il prezzo basso/They have a vested interest in keeping the price low

Amplification is also required where the source language 'takes for granted' certain components, which may be cultural, semantic or linguistic or a mixture thereof. In Alan Sillitoe's novel 'Saturday Night and Sunday Morning', an unromantic story of life in working class Nottingham in the late 1950s, one of the characters expains that:

> County lost four none   (Sillitoe 1975:196)

For the British English reader, knowing the Nottingham context of the novel and the interests of the characters, deducing that *County* refers to Notts. County Football Club is fairly automatic. For the Italian reader, an amplification is required; without resorting to the rather clumsy device of the footnote, an addition indicating the football connection is required, for example *County Calcio*, *i ragazzi del County*, or *Il Nottingham County*.

Cortese (1996:256) provides the example of translating *after Courtrai* in a text not designed for history specialists with *dopo la battaglia di Courtrai*.

The Amplification device is also found in technical writing. For example, in the geological field of tectonics the following amplifications have been made in Italian to aid comprehension:

> breached duplex/struttura di duplicazione sconnessa
> footwall flat/superficie concordante di scollamento di letto
> pop-up/cuneo di espulsione

It should be pointed out that the Amplification device can be abused. Di Sabato (1993:29) gives a current example where *political problems* was translated into Italian as *sviluppi di Tangentopoli*, giving far too much extra information.

Reduction

Reduction, as the term suggests, consists of omitting elements in a target text because they are redundant or even misleading. The Italian *carta geografica* is merely a *map* in English, and the English *three-toed sloth* translates as *bradipo* in Italian, and these are examples of 'built-in' forms of Reduction. But translators should always be ready to make decisions on when to reduce. Author-translator Tim Parks (1994) offers the example of a car-park instruction as to what to do with one's ticket that read in Italian *Esporre in modo visibile*, translatable as simply *Display*. The EARN Association in May 1994 issued a set of instructions for gaining access to the Internet, using a sub-heading *Guide to Network Resource Tools*. The Italian translator deemed it sufficient to head the Italian version with *Guida agli strumenti della rete*.

1.3.4 Diffusion and Condensation

Diffusion

While Amplification and Reduction refer to the actual adding or subtracting of elements deemed to be respectively helpful or superfluous in some way, Diffusion and Condensation are concerned with the phenomenon of linguistically slackening or tightening source text expressions for the target text version, that is, providing more or less elaboration. The Italian exclamation *Magari!* requires diffusing into a locution of the type:

If only I could!
Would that it were!
I wish that were the case!

Italian subjunctive and conditional usage can express a wide range of meanings, often requiring Diffusion in English translation. The perfect conditional in sentences like

La banda avrebbe rapinato altre tre banche.

requires the use of a conventional passive voice expression of the type

The gang is alleged/said/reported to have robbed three other banks.

Similarly, the common use of the imperfect form of the Italian verb *dovere* in clauses such as *doveva arrivare alle tre* needs diffusing to *he was supposed to arrive at three o'clock*. There are some particularly common verbs in Italian that do not always require a direct object, where their most suitable equivalents do: *A permette di fare B/A enables <u>us</u> to do B.*

Italian plural lexemes such as *informazioni, consigli, mobili* and so on are expressed as uncountable nouns (*some information, some advice, some furniture*) in English, or may even take the form *items of information, pieces of advice, articles of furniture*. Malone gives an example from Spanish that works equally well in Italian: the lexical item *attentato* in the sense of attack must be diffused in English into an *attempt on (somebody's) life*.

Condensation

In the case of Condensation, the target text expression is more linguistically economic. English is generally reputed to be more succinct than Italian, though often this is more a question of stylistics than linguistics. Certain common adjectives and verbal expressions, however, can be condensed:

a buon prezzo, a buon mercato/cheap
far vedere/show

In the other direction, prepositional verbs and phrasal verbs are typical of this phenomenon:

to look at/guardare
to make up/inventare
to make up for/compensare

Another English linguistic phenomenon that is highly indicative of the tendency towards **concision** is the well-developed facility for creating strings of adjectives and nouns, and particularly strings of just nouns, to form lexically-dense noun phrases. It is particularly the juxtaposing of nouns in potentially infinite sequences that distinguishes such noun phrases from their Italian counterparts, which are constrained by Italian syntax into containing verbs, adjectivals and complex adverbial and/or prepositional phrases:

> Environment Department Air Pollution Report Findings Scandal

> Lo scandalo suscitato dai risultati del rapporto del Ministero dell'Ambiente sull'inquinamento dell'aria

It must be said, however, that this facility can lead to ambiguity at times, e.g. *criminal lawyer*, an ambiguity that is immediately cleared in translation: *avvocato criminale* or *avvocato penalista*. Categories such as newspaper headlines and noun groups in technical writing provide endless examples of what are known as multivariate or univariate **strings**. In the case of multivariate strings, the elements comprising a noun group each have a distinct function:

> those two beautiful film stars

The above noun group consists of a demonstrative *those*, a numeral *two*, an adjective *beautiful*, and two nouns *film* and *stars*. The adjective is an example of an **epithet** and its function is to indicate some quality of what is represented by the head noun, which in this case is *stars*. The noun *film* is an example of a **classifier** whose purpose is to indicate a subclass of the head noun object (cf: TV stars, pop stars). To return to the beginning of the group, the demonstrative *those* is a **deictic** term which serves to show that a specific subset is being referred to. Each element thus has a distinct function in relation to the entity represented by the head noun.

In the case of univariate structures, there is a recurrence of the same function. Each element to the left of the head noun has the same function of modifying the term that follows it:

> 1 Overseas immigrants entry limit controversy
> 2 Opera donation scandal
> 3 Hospital doctors strike row

Example 1 contains an adjective followed by four nouns, while 2 and 3 are examples of noun groups consisting entirely of nouns. This type of construction can be found in most genres of English, with the notable exception of casual conversation. This is in line with the notion expressed in Halliday's (1995) work on written language (and by extension scientific language in particular), namely that in the written (especially technical) mode, the kind of grammar that people learn as children and continue to use in informal conversation, based largely on the verbal expression of 'events', is superceded by a more lexically dense and less dynamic grammar that condenses information into a more nominal style. This trend is clearly exemplified by the univariate string, where nouns in particular can be juxtaposed, modifying one another in succession, thus creating highly compact and meaning-packed noun groups.

Taking some currently widely-used technical terms from the field of atmospheric pollution, the univariate string can be seen to operate:

1   simple two-word compounds (noun + adjective in Italian)

   acid rain/pioggia acida

2   three-item strings (prepositional phrase constructions in Italian)

   air quality criteria/criteri di qualità dell'aria
   flue gas treatment/trattamento dei gas di combustione

Italian occasionally provides examples of two-item noun strings; in this same field the topical concept of the *greenhouse effect* translates as *effetto serra*. Psychiatry provides further examples of noun strings in English: *adjustment disorder/disturbo dell'adattamento, attention deficit disorder/disturbo da deficit dell'attenzione.* Within the construction sector we find four-item strings such as *program evaluation review technique/calcolo del grafo organizzativo della produzione.*

Condensation can also be seen to occur when a wider view of language use is taken. In more extended stretches of discourse, text cohesion is maintained in a number of ways, though essentially via a network of cross-references which may be both grammatical and lexical. Typically anaphoric (backward searching) and cataphoric (forward searching) **pronominal** reference (see **1.1.5**), and lexical cohesion achieved through repetition or synonymy, can be identified. The repeated presence in a text of persons or things or events, or even entire scenarios, will reveal an array of reiterative devices. Consider this song by The Beatles:

   Good day sunshine
   Good day sunshine
   Good day sunshine
   I need to laugh
   and when the sun is out

I've got something I can laugh about
I feel good
in a special way
I'm in love
and it's a sunny day
Good day sunshine
Good day sunshine
Good day sunshine

(Lennon, McCartney 1968:54)

The reiterative devices consist of pure choral repetition of the title line (plus one instance of *good* and one instance of *day* in the verse) and then partial repetition through morphological variation in *sun* and *sunny*. The first main theme, the personal pronoun *I* (initially an **exophoric** reference, i.e. from outside the strict confines of the text), is repeated verbatim five times in a straightforward sequence of pronouns in anaphoric relation expressing the author's feelings, and the pronoun *something* refers back to the whole idea of the sunny day. In translation, and for the moment thinking in linguistic rather than poetic terms, there would be room for both Diffusion and Condensation techniques. The key line *Good day sunshine* is tricky: it could simply be a description of the situation (*What a nice day, the sun is shining*) or a greeting to a beautiful day. In either case, the compound noun *sunshine* (itself a compound noun string) may need to be Diffused. On the other hand, the five mandatory uses of the pronoun *I* would likely disappear in Italian in an automatic process of Condensation to zero. A published translation of the words of this song demonstrates as much:

Buon giorno luce del sole
Buon giorno luce del sole
Buon giorno luce del sole
Ho bisogno di ridere
e quando è uscito il sole
ho trovato qualcosa di cui poter ridere
Mi sento bene
in un modo tutto speciale
sono innamorato
ed è un giorno pieno di sole
Buon giorno luce del sole
Buon giorno luce del sole
Buon giorno luce del sole

(A. Aldridge 1972)

1.3.5 Reordering

Coming now to the strategy of Reordering, we enter very definitely into the field of comparative syntax. At its simplest, it requires the translator to operate basic inversion procedures with, for example, adjective-noun sequences (*white horse/cavallo bianco*), and verb-object positioning (*(io) ti amo/I love you*). It is, however, equally important for the translator to know when not to activate these mechanisms, whether for linguistic or rhetorical reasons. *Pressione alta* is the correct translation for medical *high (blood) pressure*, but not in the meteorological sense where banks of *high pressure* have to be rendered by *alta pressione*. The desperate lover, in trying to wrest the vital words *Ti amo* from his loved one, may lay emphasis to his own feelings with *ma io amo te!*

Set collocations of two or more items exist in both languages

1 vita e morte/life and death
2 sano e salvo/fit and well
3 bianco e nero/black and white
4 il diavolo e l'acqua santa/(between) the devil and the deep blue sea
5a pochi ma buoni
5b spick and span

which respectively indicate how such pairings can:
1 match perfectly;
2 match partly but belong very definitely in the same semantic field;
3 match perfectly but in inverted form;
4 maintain half the pairing;
5 have no equivalent binomial form at all.

The third type provides another obvious example of the need to activate the Reordering strategy.

At sentence level it is often necessary for whole phrases or clauses to be re-ordered. Meaning is first carried in semantic units rather than in syntagmatic patterns, and thus a certain grammatical 'skewing', or rearranging, is often required. Word order is formal, and functional, and meaning-oriented. Italian will typically front a verb phrase, for example, when an intransitive verb is used to introduce a new phenomenon into the discussion, e.g. *è successa una disgrazia*. The English version of such clauses is usually the typical subject-verb structure: *something terrible has happened*. Falinski (1990:308) provides other examples:

> Non è ancora giunto il tempo
> Passavano i plotoni
> Spuntò una donna alla svolta

Intransitive structures are not, however, the only cases where Italian adopts the post placement of the subject. In the following examples (Falinski, 1990:306) the subject is post-placed and the direct object is shifted to the left and supported by its corresponding pronoun:

> Certi lavori li faceva lui
> Anche la storia della luna e i falò la sapevo (io)

These are cases of 'dislocazione a sinistra' (Salvi & Vanelli 1992:182) where the topic is shifted because

> è il costituente attorno a cui vogliamo dire qualcosa.

The pronoun with the same grammatical function appears in such cases before the verb.

Translators should generally attempt to 'skew' such structures into more congruent English syntax, or modify them in some way. They can, for example, change tense or aspect, front verbs or objects for emphasis or for requirements of theme or information focus, add particles to verbs, or use cleft sentences. Cf:

> The time has not yet come/It is not yet time
> The platoons passed by/?Past came the platoons
> A woman appeared from round the bend/There appeared a woman from
>   round the bend
> He did some of the jobs/Some of the jobs, he did
> I also knew the story about the moon and the bonfires/The story about
>   the moon and the bonfires, I knew that as well

In the absence of semantic or stylistic reasons for doing otherwise, including thematic and information structure considerations, the general rule in cases such as those illustrated above, should be to re-order the syntactic units into the most familiar patterns of the target language. Through the play-off of different forces, meaning will, as it were, look after itself.

One result of Reordering from Italian into English is that the flow of discourse can be interrupted and elements may need to be repeated so as not to create a disjointed sequence:

> Questi risultati si raggiungono attraverso forme di comunicazione
> direttamente operative in quanto predisposte ...

> These results can be achieved through directly operative forms of communication, <u>directly operative</u> in that ...

The very frequent use of the passive voice in English creates another need for Reordering in translation. The comparatively rigid theme/rheme organisation of English requires the logical object of a clause very often to be thematised and therefore placed in subject position. Italian responds with:

1 its own identical passive form, which must not be ignored although it is less frequently employed than in English:

> E' amato da tutti
> La porta viene chiusa

2 an impersonal *si* construction:

> le tigri si trovano in India/tigers are found in India
> i risultati si possono vedere/the results can be seen
> si sentono voci/rumours are heard

3 an active form using verbs with impersonal agents whose nominal or pronominal identity never appears:

> mi hanno detto che/I have been told that
> possiamo dedurre che/it can be deduced that

The more infrequent use of the passive in Italian is also due to the fact that it is impossible to use continuous verb forms in the passive voice:

> he is being interrogated = lo si interroga/lo stanno interrogando but also viene interrogato

In place of the full passive, both English and Italian sometimes revert to a simple participle construction:

> The motive for the crime, (which was) revealed by the defendant's lawyer, ...
> Il motivo del reato, rivelato dall'avvocato dell'imputato, ...

With all these observations in mind, it would seem clear that translation is a language-based task, and that a thorough knowledge of the lexico-grammar of the two languages is indispensable for a translator. As Newmark says:

> Grammar gives you the general and main facts about a text: statements, questions, requests, purpose, reason, condition, time, place, doubt, feeling, certainty. Grammar indicates who does what

to whom, why, where, when, how … we are interested in grammar … as a transmitter of meaning

(Newmark 1988:125)

So any attempt to analyse the various elements that make up a text, including those that are the subject of the following chapters, must not lose sight of the central 'linguistic' core; in the final analysis it is the graphically-represented lexicogrammar that forms the concrete element that translators have to mould into a 'target language version'.

Chapter One: Suggested further reading

Baker, M. 1992. *In Other Words*. London and New York: Routledge.

Bassnett, S. 1980. *Translation Studies*. London: Routledge.

Chomsky, N. 1957. *Syntactic Structures*. The Hague: Mouton.

Crystal, D. 1987. *The Cambridge Encyclopedia of Language*.
    Cambridge: Cambridge University Press.

de Beaugrande, R. & Dressler, W. 1981. *Introduction to Text Linguistics*.
    Harlow: Longman.

Gerot, L. & Wignell, P. 1994. *Making Sense of Functional Grammar*.
    Cammeray NSW: Antipodean Educational Enterprises.

Halliday, M.A.K. & Hasan, R. 1975. *Cohesion in English*. London: Longman.

Halliday, M.A.K. & Hasan, R. 1989. *Language, Context, and Text: Aspects of
    Language in a Social-semiotic Perspective*. Oxford: Oxford University Press.

Malone, J.L. 1988. *The Science of Linguistics in the Art of Translation*.
    Albany: State University of New York Press.

Neubert, A. 1985. *Text and Translation*. Leipzig: Verlag Enzyklopaedie.

Newmark, P. 1988. *A Textbook of Translation*. Hemel Hempstead: Prentice Hall.

Nida, E.A. 1964. *Towards a Science of Translation*. Leiden: Brill.

Sinclair, J. 1991. *Corpus, Concordance, Collocation*.
    Oxford: Oxford University Press.

Snell-Hornby, M. 1988. *Translation Studies: An Integrated Approach*.
    Amsterdam and Philadelphia: John Benjamins.

Ulrych, M. 1992. *Translating Texts*. Rapallo: Cideb Editrice.

Widdowson, H. 1979. *Explorations in Applied Linguistics*.
    Oxford: Oxford University Press.

Chapter Two

Translating Meaning in Context

The aim of Chapter Two is to examine the relevance to translation of a number of concepts that fall within the broad domain of semantics, thereby exploring in more detail the layer of meaning in texts. From a consideration of the basic principles of semantics, the chapter moves to a detailed study of 'context'. This fundamental concept is first examined by imagining context as a kind of mental picture that people can create, composed of the various features that surround the particular situations within which they communicate. Then a more scientific description is provided, associated particularly with the works of M.A.K. Halliday and Juliane House. The chapter then concentrates on the study of 'speaker meaning' – what speakers actually mean by what they say – often regardless of the superficial, literal sense of the language elements they use. This branch of semantics, known as pragmatics, requires acute sensitivity on the part of the translator in interpreting communication strategies, and a wide understanding of the cultural worlds involved. Indeed, the final part of this chapter examines the influence of cultural factors and analyses the problem of culture-bound language.

Overview of Chapter

1 Semantics (Basic concepts)

Reference

The way language relates to the world it describes. This is considered in terms of referents and referring expressions.

Semantic units

An attempt is made to isolate translatable units (chunks) of meaning.

Equivalence

Examples are used to show how elusive the concept of equivalence can be for the translator.

2 Context

Scenarios, frames, etc.

The visualising of context as a mental picture consisting of the sets of features that make up a situation has been proposed in various forms by several scholars. This section begins by examining a number of these ideas.

The context of situation

The context of situation, with its components field, tenor and mode, is examined from the Hallidayan perspective, providing an introduction to a practical contextual model devised by Juliane House.

Denotation and connotation

The semantic distinction between denotative and connotative language is explained, and particular reference is made to the modern phenomenon of politically correct language use.

Semantic/lexical fields

The question of the association of words from a semantic point of view is examined through a broad interpretation of the idea of lexical cohesion and semantic fields in discourse.

3 Pragmatics

The cooperative principle

Grice's cooperative maxims controlling the way conversation develops and the associated implicatures are discussed as a key to understanding how successful communication works.

Knowledge of the world

For translators, a general knowledge of the world surrounding them needs to be supplemented by an understanding of the universe of discourse and the context of culture. This enables meaning to be interpreted in relation to the personal set of beliefs held by the speaker/writer and the cultural beliefs and mores of both the source and target culture.

Speech acts

With particular reference to the scholars Austin and Searle, the idea of 'speaker meaning' and the interpersonal element in communication is examined through an explanation of locutionary and illocutionary (speech) acts, perlocutionary effect and felicity conditions.

4 Culture

The final section of Chapter Two concludes the analysis of cultural factors and problems related to culture-boundness.

2.1 Semantics (Basic concepts)

> Many basic facts about English have exact parallels in other languages. (This) encourages semanticists to believe that it is possible to make some very general statements about all languages, especially about the most fundamental and central areas of meaning. The fact that it is possible to translate any sentence of one language (at least roughly) into any other language (however clumsily) also reinforces the conclusion that the basic facts about meaning in all languages are, by and large, parallel.
>
> (Hurford & Heasley 1983:10)

The above quotation, apart from being optimistic about the potential translatability of all texts, also shows that the discipline of semantics (the study of meaning), so closely related to the subject of linguistics which provided the focus of the first chapter of this book, concentrates on the similarities between languages, however seemingly disparate. The concept of 'perfect translation', whereby utterances in two languages would express exactly the same proposition (*I'm cold/Ho freddo*) is relatively elusive, especially as texts become more complex, but meaning can practically always be successfully conveyed. The task of translators is to convey that meaning through the written word (or spoken word in the case of interpreters). They must decide on the meaning of the source text and relay, through words and **syntax**, that same meaning in the target text:

> A language ... is a system for making meanings: a semantic system, with other systems for encoding the meanings it produces. The term 'semantics' does not simply refer to the meaning of words; it is the entire system of meanings of a language, expressed by grammar as well as vocabulary. The text is a semantic unit ... meanings are realised through wordings.
>
> (M. Halliday 1994, xvii)

2.1.1 Reference

As seen in Chapter One during the discussion of lexical density, individual items in a text are of essentially two types: function words (grammatical items) and content words (lexical items). Function words, such as articles, prepositions, conjunctions, etc. (*the, of, however, although*), are those items that merely perform grammatical functions. Content words 'refer' to something, general or specific, that exists in the world, either concrete (*an elephant, London, Margaret's boyfriend*) or abstract (*mathematics, love, Margaret's boyfriend's idea*). It must be pointed out, however, that the whole notion of reference in semantic terms is complex and unresolved. Can a general concept such as 'beauty' be referred to in the same way as an object like a 'stone'? When does a stone become a pebble or a rock? How can the word *stone* be used to refer to all such objects when all stones are in some way different from one another? Do Americans and Indonesians refer to the same thing when they talk about *springtime*? But in spite of these valid questions, which will be discussed further in the course of this chapter, from a practical translation point of view, the notion of **reference** is a useful one. The words or expressions used to refer to 'things', even when the 'thing' is an action or event (*go, play, describe*), are known as **referring expressions**, referring to a **referent**, which is the 'thing' itself. Semantics therefore links language to the cognitive world. As language users we are able to utilise referring expressions to speak about things or events that are not present or are not happening at the time of the communication act, however complex the object or event.

Translation might then be seen as the art of matching referring expressions and functional items in two different languages. However, what makes this act a great deal more complicated than the mere switching of binary entries in bilingual dictionaries, the mere identification of an 'object' and its represention by the corresponding **sign**, is the fact that only on very rare occasions and over very limited stretches of text do the various items match unequivocably.

Returning to the quotation from Halliday above, text is a semantic unit, though made up of grammatical units: morphemes, words, groups, clauses, sentences. Morphemes, which are the smallest meaningful units in a language, may take the following forms:

1   a recognisable word: *boy*
2   a purely grammatical feature: *-ly* (for forming adverbs)

Nominal and verbal groups can range in complexity:

1   a single word: *dog, go*
2   a complex word formation:
    (nominal group) *Members of Parliament who need a swing of at least ten per cent in the run-up to the poll in order to be re-elected*
    (verbal group) *(they) were to have come*

Sentences can be of three basic types:

1   simple: *The cat sat on the mat.*
2   more elaborate in terms of coordination (**parataxis**): *He huffed, and he puffed, and he blew the house down.*
3   more elaborate in terms of subordination (**hypotaxis**): *He huffed, after having puffed, till he blew the house down.*

Moreover, the meaning of an individual unit may alter as it shifts from being, say, an isolated word to being part of a group, e.g. *heavy/a heavy smoker*, or from being a group to forming part of a clause, e.g. *a long way/ he's a long way from solving the problem*, and so on.

In fact, the various elements in a text combine in a number of ways to create **chunks** of meaning which, when bound together within the confines of the text, 'mean' something which is more (or less) than the sum of its parts. For example, the following extract is taken from Prime Minister Winston Churchill's speech following the Battle of Britain, a crucial air battle that took place during the early stages of the Second World War. His aim was to thank the pilots for their efforts and to instil a sense of national pride and purpose:

> Never in the field of human conflict was so much owed by so many to so few.
>
> (Winston Churchill, 20th Aug. 1940)

The above text can be divided into the following chunks of meaning:

Never (a general time reference in relation to the time of speaking)

in the field of human conflict (general topic background of war)

so much (gratitude) (noun phrase, object of clause in passive construction, creating sense of anticipation through deliberate ellipsis)

was owed (verb in passive voice to shift information focus to what follows)

by so many (people) (prepositional phrase incorporating elliptical subject of clause, prolonging sense of anticipation, and strengthening dramatic effect through repetition and alliteration)

to so few (airforce pilots) (prepositional phrase incorporating elliptical indirect object of clause, completing the alliterative **three-part list** *so much/so many/so few*, and contrasting strikingly with the first two items in the list)

These chunks, except for the first, consist of formations of words (wordings) which create their individual meanings. The reader or listener, however, is not delivered this 'meaning' directly. He or she has to work in order to decipher the speaker's meaning: *field* is used metaphorically, *human* and *conflict* form a collocation to stand for the single lexical item *war*, the information *(gratitude)*, *(people)* and *(pilots)* is implicit and must be retrieved from the elliptical phrases, and the marked inversion *was owed* is a function of the negative time adverbial *Never*. Yet at the time this speech was made, native English speakers (at least in Britain) would have had no difficulty in understanding what the Prime Minister meant. As usual, a crucial factor in understanding is the context, a concept that will be examined at greater length in **2.2**, but also the fact that when the various chunks are seen as a whole, as a complete text, then that text assumes a semantic character of its own and everything 'fits into place'. This particular text is an example of a carefully-thought-out piece of **rhetoric**, hence the marked syntactical construction, the carefully-chosen vocabulary, the repetition and the use of implicit reference.

As a further complication, different language communities belong to different **cultures** and within those cultures life is lived, and the world is seen, in slightly different ways. These various ways are reflected in different languages which have evolved to express the reality to which they appertain. Words do not exist before the things they are used to describe, but things can exist in one culture and not in another, and therefore be named in one language only (*briscola* – a card game, *cricket*). However, Roman Jakobson in his famous 1959 paper 'On Linguistic Aspects of Translation', explained that the meaning of any lexical item can be found in its 'translation' into some other item. He then distinguished three kinds or levels of translation:

1 Intralingual translation: translation within the same language
2 Interlingual translation: translation between two different languages
3 Intersemiotic translation: translation from the verbal to the non-verbal

By way of explanation of Level 1 he pointed out that:

> no one can understand the word 'cheese' unless he has an acquaintance with the meaning assigned to this word in the lexical code of English.

At Level 2, which is what interests us as translators, there may not always be full equivalence, but adequate interpretations practically always exist. For example, the relationship of *bread* to *pane*, *brot*, *pain*, etc. is one of equivalence in difference, the difference being clear to anyone who has breakfasted around Europe and noticed the different textures, colours, sizes and flavours of the various products that can generally be labelled in English as *bread*. Anything can be expressed, if not by one-to-one transla-tion, then perhaps by loan words (in English *spaghetti* is *spaghetti*), by specification (*nephew/nipote di zio*, highlighting a serious lexico-semantic gap in Italian) or by description (*yarder/mezzo motorizzato per il trasporto dei tronchi abbattuti* – Marolli, Dizionario Tecnico, 1979). English has no separate word for *pizza*, while Italian has no separate word for *whisky*, though both are permanent fixtures in English and Italian life, and everyone knows what the words refer to. On the other hand, both English and Italian have a term for the educational establishment children attend before primary school: *nursery school* and *asilo infantile*. However, these two expressions do not refer to exactly the same thing due, amongst other things, to the difference in the age children start school in the two countries. The fact that other similar institutions exist in both communities (play school, play group, asilo nido, scuola materna) complicates the issue, but in most cases the interlingual translation is sufficient; if in doubt, translators can resort to an intralingual explanation and gloss their target language versions: *asilo nido = asilo infantile per bambini fino all'età di tre anni = day nursery*.

To explore the semantic networks of two different languages, in order to have an idea of how complex the translation act can be, take the following simple sentence, uttered by an irate ten-year-old boy:

He ate my bacon sandwich!

Let us assume that it was uttered in the context of a scene from an English TV series that needs translating for Italian television. A basic grammatical parsing, dividing the clause into subject-verb-object, would produce *He/ate/my bacon sandwic*h, but translating each chunk would produce only potentially equivalent referring expressions. The translator would have to take care from the very first word. The Italian third person singular masculine pronoun is either *egli* or *lui*, depending on the register and whether the text is written or spoken, or it may be left out altogether. In this case the text is spoken (or rather 'written to be spoken' – it is a TV script). The referent for *He* is in fact the ten-year-old boy's elder brother, and in line with conventional Italian practice, no explicit referring expression would be used in Italian; the identification of the said brother would be evident from the verb inflection and other elements of the context and co-text. As regards the second element in the text, the third person singular of the Italian simple past tense of the verb *mangiare/to eat* is *mangiò*, but the current status of the action, and the Italian preference in these circumstances for the present perfect (passato prossimo) tense, would dictate the use of *ha mangiato*, where the inflection of the auxiliary verb indicates the grammatical person and number of the subject. In the case of the third chunk, the direct object, the first person singular possessive *my* has an equivalent in *mio/mia/miei/mie* depending on the number and person of the object or objects being possessed, but also requires a preceding definite article, in this case *il mio*. The item *bacon*, used here as a classifier to identify the type of sandwich in question, has a clear reference for a British person, both as a food in itself and as a popular form of snack when eaten between slices of bread. There is no ambiguity in the referring expressions or the referents. However, Italian culinary culture does not include the particular cut of the pig that is used for English 'bacon', though the terms *pancetta* and indeed *bacon* are used to describe other, only vaguely similar products. The English breakfast dish of 'bacon and eggs' is usually referred to in Italian, erroneously, as *uova e pancetta*. By the same token, the English word *sandwich* exists as a loan word in Italian but rarely has the same referent as its English equivalent due to the almost non-existence of 'sliced bread', as sold in Britain, in Italian bakeries. Such are the subtleties of culinary vocabulary that an expression like **sandwich di pancetta* might well have no actual referent in Italian. Thus it can be seen from this short and simple example that the matching of referring expressions and even function words across languages is not an automatic mechanism. However, common sense tells us that this utterance is eminently translatable and would not hold up work on the TV dubbing adaptation for very long. The reason for this is that the meaning can be comprehended at a higher level than the grammatically-indicated chunks. By a process of **minimal** semantic **bracketing**, which involves breaking up a text into as few meaningful 'chunks' as possible, a text can be divided into only those constituents that function as units of unequivocal meaning, what Nord (1991:20) referred to as 'translationally relevant features of the text'. In other words, if the surface meaning of single grammatically-parsable units changes when those units appear in longer word groups or expressions, then the translation of those units should be held over until an unambiguous 'chunk' of meaning emerges. For example, the temptation to translate the complete grammatical clause *We must wait for the tide/Dobbiamo aspettare la marea* must be avoided until the wider picture can be verified. The sentence may continue *We must wait for the tide of public opinion to turn* (= *Dobbiamo aspettare che l'orientamento dell'opinione pubblica segni una svolta*).

In the case under consideration here, taken as a whole, the utterance can be seen as a complaint from one boy that another has taken his food. Given the setting, it is quite feasible that the taker of the sandwich is visible on screen, even being pointed at (the actual context would clear up these matters unequivocably). Thus, in translation only the verb is necessary without the pronoun, and in the present perfect tense, particularly as the action is very recent. Finally, unless the food item in question has been seen in close-up or is particularly relevant to the plot, it is not even necessary to attempt to approximate to the original referent. In similar circumstances in an Italian setting, the boy would be eating a 'panino' and this may easily suffice as a translation (*ha mangiato il mio panino!*) or, fitting the register to the colloquial level of children and replacing the possessive with a pronoun emphasising personal involvement, *mi ha mangiato il panino!*

If the product itself is crucial to the text, the alternatives are *panino con pancetta* (understandable but a different referent), *panino con bacon* (recognisable as now sold in Italian McDonald's and similar establishments) or even *bacon sandwich* in that the two words are both Italian loans, though the collocation may not conjure up the same referent as in English. As mentioned before, the wider text, that is the entire dialogue or the entire script, as semantic units in themselves, will provide the clues for the translator to interpret the text as more than just a succession of grammatical units. It can thus be seen that a seemingly innocent item like a bacon sandwich is full of meaning potential, but what it actually <u>means</u>, in the sense of its purpose within the situation, is dictated by the <u>context</u> in which it appears.

2.2   Context

Before moving to a detailed analysis of what constitutes context, a broader macro-view will be presented, more in line with the generally accepted meaning of the word:

> The **context** of an idea or event is the general situation that relates to it, and which helps it to be understood.
>
> (Collins Cobuild English Dictionary, 1995)

Every situation in which language is used can be 'observed', as if filmed by a camera, and its features noted. These features make up the context and, although the number of permutations of language combinations at phrase, clause, sentence and text level is infinite, they are always locatable within an identifiable set of features. Various attempts have been made to explain how we are able to manoeuvre within this labyrinth of linguistic permutations with quite astonishing, computer-like rapidity. Such explanations have basically assumed that human beings are able to activate 'contexts' in order to filter out extraneous material and work within acceptable limits. They are therefore able to process text from an analysis of the situation (**top-down processing**) and not simply from the sequence of clauses and sentences as they build up (**bottom-up processing**). The most important factor in explaining top-down processing is that the <u>context</u> of discourse creates the necessary expectations for understanding the <u>content</u> of discourse.

The basic idea is that a **scenario** is activated representing the stereo-typical components of a definable situation. Anyone involved in a communicative act will practically never be faced with a totally new phenomenon. In the case of any person going about their daily business, their 'context' will be built up through a mental picture of the 'situation' in which they find themselves (buying a newspaper, taking the train, arguing with the boss) and their language 'content' will be fed by various strands of **intertextuality**. That is, the linguistic components of the communicative act will draw on words, expressions and permutations of these that have been said or heard, or read or written before in similar circumstances, either by the people themselves or by others. Consequently, the context and its linguistic content are to a certain extent circumscribed; hence the surprise that is registered by participants in **speech acts** if someone says something considered to be 'out of place', 'unexpected', even 'incomprehensible'. The translation act involves the re-enactment of a scenario at a later time (except in the case of simultaneous interpreting), and although a translation is a new linguistic act in itself, the linguistic choices made at the time of the initial act must be respected. Hence the constantly-repeated appeal to translators to make an attempt to enter into the original writer's 'scheme of things' in order to fully understand the scenario.

Various writers have in the past formulated versions of the basic scenario concept. Minsky (1975) talked of 'frames' that contain our knowledge of a given phenomenon. For example, if the topic in question is Bosnia, a frame is activated presenting data that the participants (who might consist of a single writer and a vast potential audience) can automatically conjure up in their minds – the nightly television scenes that appeared between 1991 and 1996 are an obvious image – but into which any new information can be slotted as it arises: *ethnic cleansing, arms embargo, safe corridor, rapid reaction force, contact group, peace initiative, Dayton* and so on.

Schank and Abelson (1977) went one stage further and talked of 'scripts':

> The script is a representation of a process rather than a static set of data and accommodates the notion of expectancy.
>
> (Gran and Taylor 1990:24)

The expectations referred to lead us to predict how a discourse will progress, again based on the situational context but also on the dynamics of the unfolding text. Words and expressions can be seen to govern other words and expressions in broadly predictable patterns. Returning to Bosnia, if we read that:

> This morning the United Nations special representative ...

we can be fairly certain that the clause will continue with the writer selecting from a fairly restricted paradigm of verb phrases (*left for* ..., *stated* ..., *was observed* ..., *was shot* ...?) but not *danced the tango* ..., *sang* ..., *ate a hamburger* ..., *was kissed* .... The latter selection of discarded continuations are not of course impossible, either grammatically or semantically, but would lead to a revising of the conceptualisation of the event and the activation of a different script or frame or scenario.

In a similar vein, Johnson-Laird (1980) speaks of 'mental models', Sanford and Garrod (1981) actually use the term 'scenario' and van Dijk and Kintsch (1983:11-12) speak of 'schemata' and a 'situation model' for text which they describe as:

> the cognitive representation of events, actions, and persons ...
> which integrates the comprehender's existing world knowledge
> with information derived from the text.

All this contributes to the rational structuring of the mass of linguistic and extralinguistic knowledge that comprise every act of communication and, by extension, translation.

Moving towards a more micro-based approach, the most convenient way of describing a context is to list its components. For example, Firth (1950) outlined the following elements:

> the participants, including their roles and status
> the verbal and non-verbal action of the participants
> the relevant objects and events
> the effects of the verbal action

This framework is general enough to be valid for any given textual situation. Imagine a conversation between a dentist and a patient (participants in an expert/layman relationship, the dentist enjoying, at least temporarily, superior status). The verbal action will consist of some typical obligatory elements (*'Good morning', 'Open wide', 'This won't hurt,'* etc.) as well as general chat and possible discussion of the patient's problem. The non-verbal actions will mostly consist of dental treatment of some kind, the principal objects in question being drills, instruments, basins, etc. One of the main effects of the verbal action is likely to be cooperation on the part of the patient as he/she undergoes treatment.

Hymes (1972) provided another componential breakdown of the elements that comprise any given situational context, including the following:

participants (speaker and audience)
message form
message content
setting
medium of communication
intent of communication
effect of communication
the key
the genre
the norms of interaction

This list includes the addition of components such as the form of the message (different ways of speaking can be observed in different situations), the content or topic of the text, the setting or location, the medium (for example, spoken or written), the intent or purpose of the discourse, the key or tone of the text (formal, informal), the genre or type of text, and the norms or conventions governing the particular speech act (for example, the typical turn-taking that takes place in conversations).

Michael Halliday, as we shall see below, describes context in terms of field, tenor and mode. Lyons (1977), Leech (1981) and others have described the same phenomena using their own terminology, but essentially context can be identified in terms of 'someone addressing someone else about something, somewhere, for some reason and in some way'.

Let us take as an example a debate in the British Parliament on the issue of whether or not to ban hand guns. The setting is the House of Commons, and the immediate participants are the Prime Minister and the leader of the opposition who are arguing over the issue of hand guns. There are also many other silent participants: other members of Parliament, the press, members of the general public and, potentially, millions of television viewers. There may be several functions involved, from that of defending a political position, to promoting a policy, to attacking a political opponent, even to making a good impression on national television. The medium of communication is, in the first instance, the spoken word within a debating chamber with its associated characteristics of political rhetoric aimed at an opponent and, secondly, that of the television broadcast where the non-immediate receivers of the message play a basically passive role. This set of contextual features restricts the kind of language that will be used by the participants in the unfolding of the discourse; in terms of subject matter, they will not, for example, discuss knitting patterns; in terms of style, they will not, for example, speak in verse, and in terms of register, they will not order each other to perform tasks.

As a communicative act continues, and in the case cited here it may go on for several hours, the contextual features may change; the main participants may change as other speakers take the floor, the subject matter may change as they move on to the next point on the agenda, or the passive participants may change as people come and go in the chamber or switch on and off their television sets at home. However, every stage of this act can be seen in terms of a set of features which are of fundamental importance in shaping the wording of that act. Clearly, from the translator's point of view, an understanding of the context is necessary so that he or she can relate what is said to the surrounding features and clarify any element that may seem 'out of place' or even incomprehensible in other circumstances. This accounts for the misunderstandings that arise when something is quoted 'out of context'.

For example, an expression like *'May I remind the right honourable gentleman that his tendency to be economical with the truth has cost the country dear!'* would be restricted to the kind of scenario mentioned above in terms of: a) lexical items: *right honourable gentleman*, b) collocational constructions of seemingly deviant grammar: *to cost ... dear* and c) conventionally polite register: *May I remind . . . .* These factors would have to be taken into consideration in translation, with a consequent search for similar fossilised usages, which may appear frequently in this sort of context.

2.2.1 M.A.K. Halliday and the context of situation

Bringing these linguistic and extralinguistic elements together in a scientific model of the 'context of situation', the afore-mentioned Michael Halliday sees language as a **social semiotic**, that is as a vital part of social life, enabling people to exchange meanings and thereby function in society. Halliday's **functional grammar** (**FG**) looks at how language works – how language is organised and what social functions are represented. It is more than just a descriptive or prescriptive grammar dictating what we can and cannot say or write. The cornerstone of FG is, indeed, the context of situation. Every communicative act (text of some kind) takes place in a situational and cultural 'context'. All texts are produced and received within a set of circumstances of time, place, purpose, etc. They involve various persons in various roles and are conveyed in a particular way (spoken, written, faxed, etc.). These elements combine to form the context of situation, which determines the kind of language that will be used. An understanding of the context of situation is required if a text receiver is to follow that text with ease. For example, the exhortation *'Don't forget your dinner money'* is only intelligible if the context (of a British mother speaking to a schoolchild some time during the school year before he or she goes to school) is known, and if the listener understands the English cultural custom whereby most children have their midday meals in the school.

Halliday's context of situation consists of three components: **field**, **tenor** and **mode**, which provide a helpful means of describing any socio-linguistic event:

> *Field* refers to the subject matter and the nature of the activity, i.e., what is happening, to whom, when and where, what they know, why they are doing what they are doing, and so on.
>
> *Tenor* refers to the social relationships existing between those involved in terms of power and status (e.g. father/son, manager/clerk, boyfriend/girlfriend, etc.) and thus how they feel about each other, whether they know each other well and so on. It refers also to the role structure (questioner/answerer, informer/enquirer, etc.).
>
> *Mode* concerns how the language is being used, the organisation of the text, whether it is written (faxed, e-mailed, etc.) or spoken (on the phone, recorded, etc.). Some texts are actually 'written to be spoken' (e.g. political speeches) or 'spoken to be written' (e.g. dictated letters). Mode also refers to whether a text is performative or reflective, spontaneous or well thought out.

These three elements enable the speaker/writer (subconsciously) to construct the context of situation. The translator, transposing a text at a second remove, must strive to maintain the situational and cultural context by matching the three variables in the target language version. By establishing the 'field' of a text, decisions can be made as to what terminology may or may not be adopted, how information should be presented grammatically (active/passive, stative/dynamic, etc.) and what shared knowledge should be assumed to exist between writer and reader. The 'tenor' will inform the translator as to which register to employ, in the sense of formal/informal, technical/non-technical, archaic/modern, etc., and whether the indicative (affirmative or interrogative) or imperative mood should be employed. The 'mode' points the way to the organisation of the information in terms of theme and rheme, given and new information, information focus, and so on. As Firth pointed out:

> Translation problems can be solved in the mutual assimilation of
> the languages in similar contexts of situation and in common
> human experience.
>
> (Firth 1968: 87)

If there are any elements that do not match the target culture context, they
must be accounted for. In the 'dinner money' example it would be necessary
to somehow integrate the relevant culture-specific information in languages
and cultures where children only attend school in the morning. This aspect
will be examined further in 2.4.

Of course, extended stretches of text may actually realise a sequence of
contexts of situation. As the text progresses, a series of contexts of situation
will tend to slide into one another. For example, a television advertisement
for anti-dandruff shampoo may consist of three phases:

> Phase 1: providing medical information about hair complaints
> (informative text; medical field; formal tenor/indicative mood;
> 'written to be spoken' mode of presenting factual information
> on TV)
>
> Phase 2: promoting the product (persuasive text; field of adver-
> tising; informal tenor/imperative mood; colloquial, spoken
> mode)
>
> Phase 3: showing a satisfied customer expressing his delight by
> joking with his friends (expressive text; field of collective
> enjoyment; informal tenor; conversational dialogue mode)

The value to the translator of the concept of context can be seen by
examining a practical application of some of its aspects. Juliane House, in
her highly-acclaimed book 'A Model for Translation Quality Assessment'
(1977, latest edition 1997), adopted an approach that relates context to the
act of translation.

2.2.2 A contextual model (J. House)

House devised a series of parameters designed precisely to compare source
and target texts in translation and termed them 'dimensions'. These
dimensions, based on a set of parameters first devised by Crystal and Davy
(1969), are used in an attempt to analyse a text according to its various
facets, but in this case House's model is aimed directly at translation in an
attempt to ensure that a target version can be made to match a source text

at all levels. House's situational dimensions consist of three 'dimensions of language user':

> geographical origin
> social class
> time

and five 'dimensions of language use':

> medium
> participation
> social role relationship
> social attitude
> province

The first three parameters establish the text in space, register and time, and any geo-socio-historical factors affecting language use must be identified and accounted for. The dimensions of medium, participation and social role refer to the other configurations of context of situation discussed above while 'social attitude' refers to the degree of social distance involved, going from 'frozen' to 'intimate', and 'province' is defined as referring to the 'area of operation', the field or topic in the widest sense. One of House's examples is taken from Sean O'Casey's play 'The End of the Beginning' (1977:328), and provides a useful illustration. The source text is in English, to be translated into German, and the procedure begins with a syntactic, lexical and textual analysis of this text in order to produce a 'textual profile'. The text begins as follows (without stage directions):

> DARRY I forgot. I'll have to get going.
>
> BARRY Get going at what?
>
> DARRY House-work. I dared her, an' she left me to do the work of the house while she was mowing the meadow. If it isn't done when she comes back, then sweet good-bye to the status I had in the home. (*getting into overall*) Dih, dih, dih, where's the back 'n where's the front, 'n which is which is the bottom 'n which is the top?
>
> BARRY Take it quietly, take it quietly, Darry.
>
> DARRY Take it quietly? An' the time galloping by? I can't stand up on a chair 'n say to the sun, stand thou still there, over the meadow the missus is mowing, can I?
>
> BARRY I know damn well you can't, but you're not going to expedite matters by rushing around in a hurry.
>
> DARRY Expedite matters! It doesn't seem to strike you that when you do things quickly, things are quickly done. Expedite matters! I suppose

> loitering to look at you lying on the broad of your back, jiggling your
> legs about, was one way of expediting matters: an' listening to you
> plucking curious sounds out of a mandolin, an' singing a questionable
> song, was another way of expediting matters.

House's analysis continues by tracing the following outline:

Dimensions of language user:
1 Geographical origin: Hiberno-English (strongly marked
                          phonologically and lexically)
2 Social class: Irish lower class (elements of dialectal
                          language)
3 Time: contemporary Hiberno-English

Dimensions of language use:
1 Medium: written to be acted (hesitations,
                          interjections, etc.)
2 Participation: simple dialogue
3 Social role rel.:   two interlocutors, absence of authority;
                          friends arguing
4 Social attitude: casual-intimate/mock consultative-formal
5 Province: part of one-act Irish comedy

A series of syntactic, semantic and pragmatic elements in the text are
cited as representative of the various dimensions, and House concludes that
the function of the text is to enable the reader to reconstruct a piece of
simulated reality – a domestic quarrel. The **interpersonal** component is
particularly noticeable to create emotive and humorous effects.

In the German translation, House identifies mismatches in the following
dimensions:

1 Geographical origin: No attempt made to find similar
                          geographical dialect.
2 Social attitude: The mock consultative-formal level not
                          matched, i.e. much less pretentiously
                          pompous.
3 Province: Folk-play element not represented.

She points out that for these reasons there is a violation of the interpersonal
component: the humorous element suffers through the missing interplay of
popular vernacular and deliberate pomposity. There is also a lack of
alliteration which deprives the piece of a poetic element. As a consequence,

the function of entertaining has been compromised. This is, admittedly, a case of being wise after the event, but it is hoped that the questions raised in this section regarding the importance of analysing a text in its rightful context, in order to be able to begin translating with a clear idea of what is required, have been sufficiently persuasive to encourage student translators to make the effort to ensure that the target text fits the source text contextual framework.

2.2.3 Denotation and connotation

It is now necessary to fit the semantic concepts of referent and referring expression into the concept of context. It was previously asserted that referring expressions are used to refer to referents in the real world. Sometimes the reference is direct (*'Look at this new pen I've bought'*), sometimes indirect (*'I've lost that new pen I bought yesterday'*). In either case, the transfer of the referring expression from one language to another is not complicated. However, language has developed in such a way that human communicators have the ability to use referring expressions in unstraightforward ways. Lexical items can take on various guises as they are used either **denotatively** or **connotatively**, metaphorically, figuratively, emotively, or deliberately ambiguously in the case of word play or punning. The grammar too can be metaphorically manipulated as, for example, when actions and processes are nominalised and expressed as nouns (e.g. *He hated being formal/His hatred of formality*). This kind of language use is ingrained in all languages and often calls for highly-tuned perception on the part of translators. In the first instance, however, translators can find invaluable assistance in the analysis of the context in which the language act takes place. As seen above, texts which equate referents and referring expressions unambiguously are relatively straightforward; vocabulary gaps can be filled by judicious use of a bilingual dictionary. Some texts, such as lists of instructions, can be purely functional in nature and require no effort of imagination. In fact, this text type is the most amenable to machine translation, where functional equivalents can be mechanically substituted for one another. Even more complicated categories, such as legal contracts, fall into this group, though in these cases the translator needs to be very familiar with the linguistic features and conventions of a specific sub-genre (see Chapter Three).

Even within the same language no two words can ever exactly match, whether for semantic or other reasons. In other words, there is no such thing as pure synonymy which, even if it existed, would be a pointless duplication of language resources. For example, Roget's Thesaurus gives the following 'synonyms' for *habit: wont, habitude, rule, practice, addiction, way, usage, routine, second nature, custom, convention, proprieties, stereotype, mores, etiquette, fashion, vogue, amenities, consuetude, orthodoxy, observance, tradition.* The test of true synonymy is whether two or more terms can always replace each other in any circumstance and in any context. The above list of equivalents for *habit* would fall far short of this requirement, for a variety of reasons. Some of these lexical items, in their 'habit' meaning, are associated with particular expressions: *as a rule, he has his ways.* At times such expressions are of rather restricted use: *as is my wont.* Others are associated with particular semantic fields: *drug addiction, language usage. Etiquette* and *observance* bring to mind polite behaviour and religion-based habit respectively. *Convention* applies to whole communities, *mores* is of a high academic register, *vogue* is a fashionable word of foreign origin restricted to certain groups, *tradition* has a wider range of meaning than *habit,* and *habitude* and *consuetude* are of almost zero frequency. The nearest equivalent to *habit,* i.e. *custom,* is still not a perfect substitute (cf: *smoking is a bad habit/*custom, It is the custom/*habit in this country to throw confetti at weddings*).

In view of such differences in shades of meaning and usage, it would be more appropriate to speak of near-synonyms rather than synonyms in cases of this type. However, even near-synonymity suggests that the items in question do contain many common components of meaning, and that it is merely one, or possibly more than one, distinguishing characteristic that differentiates them. As seen above, at times the distinguishing feature may be a question of frequency of use, or of collocation with particular terms, or of belonging to a particular semantic field. But it may also be a question of connotation.

All words have a value attached to them, which may or may not be immediately apparent in all contexts. As Sinclair (1996:75) explains, each lexical item, which is 'a single, independent, meaningful choice of words' must contain an element of **semantic prosody** and this is instrumental in integrating that item with the surrounding co-text, providing the pragmatic meaning in each context. The values that are attached to lexical items are intrinsically denotative values. The term 'denotative' describes the way lexical items refer to a 'referent' in the real world, as explained above, whether concrete or abstract. In semantic terms, it would be more accurate to say that lexical items themselves refer to an **extension** of an entity. The extension of an entity is any past, present or future example of that entity. For example, the word *rat* refers to countless millions of different individual animals that have existed, now exist or will exist in the future. But in spite of the fact that these animals are all different in some way (colour, size, etc.) the word *rat* denotes them all; it is an extremely useful example of linguistic shorthand. However, the denotative meaning of *rat* only covers the core **prototype** meaning – roughly a four-legged animal, distinguished by a long tail, whiskers, etc. (the kind of image provided by children's drawings of rats) – while in the wider world people often associate a whole range of other features with the word *rat*, for example disease, evil and other decidedly unappealing characteristics. Experimental researchers, on the other hand, might associate rats with scientific advance. Thus, words can easily assume what is called a connotative value depending on the context in which they are used, and the purposes and ingenuity of the user. In the utterance '*I would stay clear of that rat Jones!*', the listener would not conjure up an image of a rodent interlocutor, but of a mutual acquaintance reputed, at least by the speaker, to have a deceitful or vindictive nature. The reason for the ease in understanding such an utterance is the fact that words can have a connotative meaning in addition to their denotative meaning. At times the connotation may be embedded, e.g. '*He is a child*' referring to a grown man, where the properties alluded to transcend the denotative 'infant human', or it may derive from external association, even of relatively recent origin. '*Did you see Wimbledon?*' will not be a question regarding merely a south London suburb, but a reference to the international tennis championships.

Translation then can be seen from yet another perspective, namely the matching of 'values' and the assigning of the relevant label in the language in question. To return to the 'rat', in its denotative sense *rat* has its Italian equivalent in *ratto* or *topo*, which refer to the same basic 'extension', and therefore these items can be considered interlingual near-synonyms in the sense that they can usually replace one another in translation. But not always! The deceitful person referred to earlier could not be referred to as a *ratto* or a *topo* in Italian but rather, perhaps, as a *verme*, at least maintaining the zoological connection.

The lesson for translators is clear, namely to be sure to have understood the connotative features of any word or expression. Going back to the list of near-synonyms of *habit*, it can be seen that the value attached to each individual item in the list is slightly different in each case and can change with every separate use of the same term. For example, the word *routine* implies habitual action and is therefore included in the list, but has a component of 'rigid regularity' that is missing from *habit* and the other near-synonyms. By the same token, the word *routine* can be used purely denotatively in its own right with the meaning of 'regular practice', e.g. *parliamentary routine*. On the other hand, when it is used in expressions like '*I need a break from the usual routine*' a further connotational component of monotony and predictability can be felt. In terms of translation, in the first instance, a solution such as *la solita vita parlamentare* would be appropriate, whereas in the second instance a term more expressive of the connotative element might be '*. . . il solito tran tran*'. The actual word *routine* has come into the Italian language in the form of a loan, and would be appropriate in certain contexts but, as can be seen, other near-synonyms are at times more suitable.

Proper names, especially fictional proper names, may contain connotative elements (see **1.2.1**) designed to be humourous or instructive, and provide the only real occasion when they need to be translated. One is reminded of *Mr Plod the policeman* in Enid Blyton's 'Noddy' stories where the verb *plod/camminare col passo pesante* evokes the typical friendly policeman's way of walking, the previously-mentioned *Mock Turtle* in Lewis Carroll's 'Alice in Wonderland' or Dickens' *Mr Gradgrind* in 'Hard Times', where the metaphorical connotations of the verb *grind* conjure up the image of an austere and disciplinarian figure.

Political correctness

A current example of how connotation can affect meaning, and consequently translation strategy, is the emergence of the concept of **political correctness**. According to the principles of this concept, certain terms are to be avoided because their connotations give offence to certain members of society, for example, those belonging to a minority group of some sort, and are to be replaced by inoffensive terminology. Apart from the apocryphal, and deliberately comical, extremes attributed jokingly to exponents of political correctness by their enemies (for example, the overtly euphemistic *vertically challenged* for *short*, and *temporarily able* for *fit*), many terms have gained credence in modern language use and have effectively transplanted previously suspect items. In particular, the general use of masculine pronouns has been largely replaced by the use of twinning (*he or she, he/she, s/he, him/her*, etc.), by pluralising the referent in question, or by dispensing altogether with pronouns. For example, instead of *the translator must be* *careful when he translates connotational meaning*, the plural version *transla-tors must be careful when they translate connotational meaning* or the pronounless *the translator must be careful when translating connotational meaning* are preferred. Most publishing companies now give instructions to their authors, and by extension to translators, as to how to avoid offensive lexis or grammar.

In terms of English/Italian, there are areas where this kind of reasoning finds a direct equivalent, e.g. *il traduttore* to refer to all 'traduttori' (where the use of the plural would solve the problem in the same way), but as Italian generally dispenses with pronouns in anaphoric reference, the *he/she* question hardly arises. There is now a steadily-growing tendency to neutralise female equivalent nouns such as *actress, manageress*, etc. and refer to males and females as *actors* and *managers*, just as 'doctors' and 'accountants' are not marked for gender. The problem in translation terms is that the issue within the English-speaking world is to do with the sexist connotations of such distinctions, and is aimed exclusively at combatting discrimination against women, while in Italian the lexical rules are not based on convention but on grammatical gender. While *manager/ess* is neatly taken care of in Italian by a genderless *dirigente*, and *attore* could feasibly stand for *attrice* too, some terms in Italian are grammatically feminine and cover both females and males (*stella (del cinema)*, even *persona*), while others are grammatically masculine (*capo, architetto*).

But apart from these more complex questions, the negative connotations of many terms have been recognised and adapted, a process that has been transferred across languages, sometimes with a time-lag, and this needs to be monitored. For example, hardly anybody today refers to *underdeveloped countries* or *paesi sottosviluppati*, nor do we speak of *mongols* or *mongoloidi*. During this century the words *cripple* and *lunatic* have given way to *physically handicapped* and *mentally handicapped*, but even these have now been largely replaced by *disabled* (even 'differently abled'), and *mentally ill*. The reason for these changes was that *cripple* first and *handicapped* later displayed connotative features of disgust and loathing. It was indicative how children, capable at times of thoughtless cruelty, would use these words to insult weaker members of the group. For the moment *handicap-pato* remains in Italian, possibly because, being a calqued expression, it does not have the same connotations as *handicapped*, but *portatore di handicap* is already current. Such changes can catch the translator unawares and cause him or her to be guilty of anachronism. The *blind* in many contexts must be referred to as '*non-vedenti*', and, as a recent TV documentary indicated, a person arrested and taken to the police station to be put *in cella*, is now housed in a '*custody suite*'.

Lexical cohesion/Semantic fields

As we saw in Chapter One, the concept of word association – the way words are related to one another – can be discussed in terms of lexical cohesion, specifically in terms of repetition and reiteration:

Repetition
1 the repetition of actual words, often in preference to their substitution by pronouns because of the enhanced rhetorical effect
2 the repetition of grammatically-related items (*go, went, going*, etc.)

Reiteration
1 Synonymy: the question of (near) synonymy has been dealt with above.
2 Antonymy: antonymy associates words in terms of pure opposites, e.g. *male/female* (one is either male or female), gradable opposites, e.g. *good/bad* (one can be quite good or very bad, for example) and converse terms where the use of one term cannot be divorced from direct association with the other, e.g. *husband/wife*.
3 Hyponymy: hyponymy involves the inclusion of one term in a superordinate category, e.g. *dog* is a hyponym of *animal, pianist* is a hyponym of *musician*, and so on. The superordinate categories group together lexical items that exclude one another in terms of paradigmatic choice, e.g. in terms of makes of *car*, if your vehicle is a *Fiat* it cannot at the same time be a *Volkswagen*.
4 Semantic field: semantic fields group associated vocabulary items together. For example, in the strictest sense, it would be possible to make a list of all the words associated with the fruit and vegetable section of a supermarket. At a wider level, the term 'semantic field' could be usefully extended to cover all the words and expressions associated with 'supermarkets', from the products on sale, to the typical decor, to the various ranks of staff, etc. Although this larger supermarket list would be quite long, it would also be relatively predictable; we would expect it to contain terms such as *baked beans, spaghetti, housewife, checkout attendant*, etc. and not to contain terms like *elephant, rock-singer* or *existentialism*. All texts are created within a broad semantic field or a series

of semantic fields, and the choice of vocabulary within a text will be largely restricted by those fields.

Lexical items in all the various relations thus far discussed form chains of cohesion throughout a text, and provide the text with a degree of texture and a level of predictability that facilitate comprehension. Mary Snell-Hornby (1988:70f) provides an excellent illustration of this phenomenon in her analysis of W. Somerset Maugham's 'The Pacific' (1921):

> The Pacific is INCONSTANT and UNCERTAIN, like the SOUL OF MAN. Sometimes it is *grey* like the **English Channel** off **Beachy Head**, with a heavy swell, and sometimes it is rough, capped with *white crests*, and BOISTEROUS. It is not so often that it is calm and *blue*. Then indeed, the *blue* is ARROGANT. The *sun shines* FIERCELY from an unclouded sky. The trade wind gets into your blood and you are filled with an impatience for the unknown. The billows, magnificently rolling, stretch widely on all sides of you, and you forget your VANISHED YOUTH, with its MEMORIES, cruel and sweet, in a restless, intolerable DESIRE FOR LIFE. On such a sea as this Ulysses sailed when he sought the Happy Isles. But there are days also when the Pacific is like a lake. The sea is flat and *shining*. The **flying fish**, a *gleam of shadow* on the *brightness* of a mirror, make little **fountains** of *sparkling* **drops** when they **dip**. There are **fleecy clouds** on the **horizon**, and at *sunset* they take **strange shapes** so that it is impossible not to believe that you see a range of **lofty mountains**. They are the **mountains** of the COUNTRY OF YOUR DREAMS. You sail through an UNIMAGINABLE **silence** upon a magic sea. Now and then a few **gulls** suggest that **land** is not far off, a **forgotten island** hidden in a wilderness of waters; but the **gulls**, the MELANCHOLY **gulls**, are the only sign you have of it. You never see a **tramp**, with its FRIENDLY **smoke**, no **stately bark** or **trim schooner**, not a **fishing boat** even: it is an empty desert, and presently the emptiness fills you with a vague FOREBODING.

In a single paragraph of text she identifies four distinct lexical fields (The Pacific, Man, Light and Seascape) which themselves are cohesive within the overall semantic field of a poetic description of the sea. For example, in terms of 'The Pacific', she traces the lexical items Pacific, heavy swell, rough, capped/crests, calm, billows, rolling, such a sea as this, Pacific, lake, sea, mirror, magic sea, wilderness of waters, empty desert, emptiness. As regards 'Man', she identifies INCONSTANT, UNCERTAIN, SOUL OF MAN, BOISTEROUS, ARROGANT, FIERCELY, VANISHED YOUTH, MEMORIES, DESIRE FOR LIFE, COUNTRY OF YOUR DREAMS, UNIMAGINABLE, MELANCHOLY, FRIENDLY,

FOREBODING. 'Light' is represented by *grey, white crests, blue, blue, sun shines, shining, gleam of shadow, brightness, sparkling, sunset*. Finally 'Seascape' is described in terms of the **English Channel, Beachy Head, flying fish, fountains, drops, dip, fleecy clouds, horizon, strange shapes, lofty mountains, mountains, silence, gulls, land, forgotten island, gulls, gulls, tramp, smoke, stately bark, trim schooner, fishing boat.**

Clearly, translators have to be attuned to the range of vocabulary at their disposal in order to navigate within the semantic field in question. In the limited cases of specific interest groups (quizmasters, weather forecasters, air-traffic controllers, etc.), the range will be restricted and circumscribed in both source and target language and therefore more easily accessible, but very often the components of the semantic field as viewed from the source language culture may differ slightly from those of the target language culture. Furthermore, the less specific and more general the wording, the more scope there is for lexical choice and semantic wandering. It is, in fact, easier to find an equivalent in the one-to-one lexical transfer of a technical term (*alloplastic adjustment/adattamento alloplastico*) than is the case with a vaguer, many-to-many potential transfer. Steiner (1997) points to the difficulty encountered in translating into German the high-frequency, high-vagueness words *equipment* and *reliable* in an advertisement for Rolex watches. He also points out (1997) that in the German translation he analysed, words referring to the semantic field of adventure (wearing a Rolex en route to the South Pole) were translated with semi-equivalents expressing even more general meanings than in the original. All such considerations, of course, highlight the elements that create the distinctiveness of different languages, but various concepts borrowed from cognitive psychology (frames, scripts, scenarios, mental models, etc., see **2.2**) may help the translator in such cases.

De Beaugrande and Dressler (1981:90) brought together the various notions of frames and other similar concepts in their general discussion of 'schemas' to refer to what is basically a mental image of a semantic field. For example, if the subject of a speech act is a professional football match, then the participants in that act will activate a mental picture of all it entails. Some of the features in any given 'frame' will be universal; in this case the ball, the twenty-two players, the referee, the cheering, etc. Consequently, in translation terms, a matching of certain referents can take place: *la palla, i giocatori, l'arbitro*, etc. The mental image of the proceedings and the surrounding circumstances, backed by the homogeneous lexical strings used in the speech act, keep participants 'on track' and thus provide a blueprint for the translator as well, but certain elements in the respective English and Italian 'frames' will diverge. Part of the English speaker/writer's scenario would contain such culture-specific items as rows of raised scarves, glossy programmes produced by the club, and bawdy songs. The Italian scenario would include showers of ticker-tape, coloured flares and drums. Thus the translator, in dealing with a text concerning this scenario, would need to know how far his or her 'frame' already matched that of the source text 'frame', tying in with the previously-mentioned Juliane House's translation assessment model, consisting of a series of parameters or 'dimensions' which effectively represent the components of the context of situation in question.

So, whichever route is taken, the activation of frames or schemas, the reconstruction of the context of situation, or the matching of House's dimensions, the translator's indispensable objective is still to make every attempt to recreate the context surrounding the text to be translated, within the cultural confines of both source and target languages.

2.3   Pragmatics

The discipline of **pragmatics** cannot be totally separated from either semantics or linguistics, given that it deals with 'meaning within meaning' and with 'speech acts', but it merits a separate heading because of its essential feature of examining 'speaker meaning' as opposed to 'sense' (dictionary meaning) or 'sentence meaning'. Longman's Dictionary of Language Teaching and Applied Linguistics (1992) defines pragmatics as:

> the study of the use of language in communication, particularly the relationships between sentences and the contexts and situations in which they are used. Pragmatics includes the study of:
> a) how the interpretation and use of utterances depends on knowledge of the real world
> b) how speakers use and understand speech acts
> c) how the structure of sentences is influenced by the relationship between the speaker and the hearer.

Thus, it can be seen that pragmatics is basically that branch of semantics that attempts to go beyond the surface, or even connotative, meaning of utterances and sentences to test what actual meaning lies behind them. Intralingually it examines speech acts from the point of view of the intentions of the participants, and analyses how successful communication can be achieved, given the enormous potential of language to create ambiguity, polysemy, obscurity, generality and specificity, irony and emotivity, and the powerful resources it contains to produce word play of every kind.

In order to put some order into this potential chaos, the philosopher Grice (1975) formulated his now well known 'Cooperative Principle' in which he suggested that efficient communication depended on the recognition of a number of maxims:

1 Do not say too little or too much (quantity maxim)
2 Tell the truth or what you know (quality maxim)
3 Only say what is relevant (relevance maxim)
4 Be perspicuous, brief and orderly (manner maxim)

The fact that observation of the world tells us that speakers do not always stick rigidly to these principles (they are verbose, they lie, they prevaricate), does not detract from the fact that in statistical terms they generally do stick to them, and what is more, listeners expect this cooperative behaviour from their interlocutors, and are therefore able not only to understand the surface elements of the communication, but also the 'unsaid' element through deciphering **implicatures** as to what is meant. Grice uses the term 'implicature' to refer to what speakers actually mean by what they say. For example, consider the following dialogue:

A: Are you coming to the match?
B: Ah, I went last week.

There is no immediately logical connection between the two utterances. Certainly, B knows which match is being referred to through A and B's shared knowledge, but he replies obliquely. However, given that A expects B to be cooperative in his reply, A is able to understand that an implicature is being used, and that B is indirectly explaining that he cannot go to the match because he went last week. Perhaps this week he is duty bound to spend time with his family.

While it must be added as a rider that Grice's principles, and attendant implicatures, are based on the use of the (spoken) English language, there are presumably similar sets of parameters at work in other languages, and in the written mode. Where they might not always match is where there is most chance of translation not delivering a completely successful message. To take a seemingly simple example of where pragmatic function can create difficulty, we will take the case of the **attitudinal disjuncts** in fact and infatti, and see how they function as discourse markers. Naturally there is a tendency to consider their functions as being broadly similar in English and

Italian, though intuitively translators know this is not so. Bruti (1996) distinguishes the pragmatic and discursive functions of the two items, pointing out how *in fact* is used to reformulate, to correct, to anticipate further clarification and generally to aid progression of the discourse, while the purpose of *infatti* is to express acquiescence, compliance and agreement and occasionally to attract attention, and is not primarily involved in discourse progression. Thus a suitable translation for:

> I don't remember much about it. In fact I can't remember anything about it.

might be

> Non ricordo molto in proposito. Anzi, non ne ricordo niente.

Similarly, the translation of:

> A: Va preso un po' alla volta.
> B: Ah sì infatti.

should reject *in fact* in favour of, for example:

> A: It should be taken a bit at a time.
> B: Yeah, right.

2.3.1 Knowledge of the world

Before knowledge of the world can be easily defined or usefully discussed, it must be decided what world is being referred to. For meaningful communication to take place, and this includes the act of translation, the participants in the communication act must inhabit the same '**universe of discourse**'. This term refers basically to the fact that people need to identify with the same sets of parameters regarding the world they live in. As Hurford and Heasley (1983:59) put it:

> the universe of discourse for any utterance is ... the particular world, real or imaginary (or part real, part imaginary) that the speaker assumes he is talking about at the time.

When one hears expressions like '*they are speaking at cross purposes*' or the metaphorical '*I don't think we're speaking the same language*' between, say, an adolescent girl and her mother, one of the problems is probably that the interlocutors are clinging to partially different universes of discourse. Western businessmen were surprised that their counterparts in one developing country did not believe that the Americans had managed to land a man on the moon (Apollo was considered to be an elaborate propaganda coup), and consequently they had different views regarding scientific advance and the role of the USA in the world. More importantly, it could be said that in important areas the two sets of interlocutors inhabited different universes of discourse, one in which it was believed that man had set foot on the moon and one in which the moon remained unexplored.

People can inhabit different universes of discourse permanently or temporarily. Small children inhabit a world in which Father Christmas exists, a world which adults are called upon to temporarily enter; atheists inhabit a world in which God does not exist, complicating efforts at communication with believers; in general, different peoples' cultural values can put them in a particular universe of discourse, at least some of the time. But for the purposes of translation, the same universe of discourse must reign between the source and target writer. In terms of translation between Europeans, for example, a broadly similar universe of discourse can usually be assumed, but when it does not, and the more diverse the cultures of the two language communities the more possible this eventuality becomes, translation becomes seriously difficult. Particularly at the level of 'on-the-spot' interpreting, international incidents can arise from 'not speaking the same language'.

The anthropologist Malinowski's notion of 'context of culture', expressed in the 1923 paper 'The problem of meaning in primitive languages', was formulated as a means of successfully translating the language of Pacific islanders into English. Malinowski stressed the idea that in order to under-stand the meaning of a foreign language, it was necessary to have a sound knowledge of the immediate environment of a speech act (which he, like Halliday years later, called the 'context of situation') allied to a sound knowledge of the wider cultural environment.

The ideas of Edward Sapir (1929) and his pupil Benjamin Whorf (1956) followed this anthropological line, and further emphasised the role of culture in interpreting language (and languages). The so-called 'strong' Sapir-Whorf hypothesis rather stretches this idea to the limit by suggesting that language controls our way of thinking, and that people from different cultures have different views of the world, imposed on them by language.

> ... no two languages are ever sufficiently similar to be considered as representing the same reality. The worlds in which different societies live are distinct worlds, not merely the same world with different labels.
>
> (Sapir 1929:214)

As a prototypical psycholinguistic theory, the Sapir-Whorf hypothesis thus suggested that translation between languages was impossible in that the language we speak governs our thoughts, and therefore our perceptions of the world, in a different way from the speakers of any other language. In other words, and to adopt a current metaphor, there is not a level playing field between the speakers of different languages, and therefore they cannot play the same game. Although the fact that countless successful translations have been made certainly challenges this thesis, what we can gain from the hypothesis is that language can influence thought to a certain extent, and that the languages of different cultures will present the world in different ways.

Indeed, even between languages and cultures which are geographically and politically close, lexical items can carve up the world in slightly different ways; the earlier example of the *bacon sandwich* (**2.1.1**) is a case in point. Even such deceptively simple items as *Good evening/Buona sera* do not refer to the same time spans, and do not have the same frequency of use or register when used as a greeting; many Italian visitors have caused amusement in England by using 'Good evening' in informal company.

Referring to cultures where people are generally fairer-haired, the word *blonde* generally refers to a higher degree of 'blondeness' than the word *biondo*, which, indeed, often needs to be translated as *fair*. The difficulty in interpreting the Italian adjective *parecchio(i)*, that is in quantifying it and finding an English equivalent, is not helped by consulting the dictionary, which offers such diverse options as *several, a lot (of), a number of, quite a few*, which are confusing to the English translator who perceives substantial differences between them.

In simple terms, then, in order not to say 'Good evening' to someone in the middle of the afternoon, in order not to mistake a fair-haired girl for a blonde girl, and not to over- or undervalue a quantity of items, translators need to know both language worlds very well. Of course, this knowledge goes much deeper than what is illustrated by these examples but, by the same token, these little matters can also falsify or trivialise a translation.

2.3.2 Speech acts

The speech act theory developed first by Austin (1962), and which still enjoys authoritative status, referred first of all to an utterance of any kind as a **locutionary** act. The act that is performed, representing the intention of the person formulating that utterance, and known as the **illocutionary** act, may or may not be immediately apparent from the words that are spoken or written. For example, the student who says *'May I have a handout, please?'* at the beginning of a lecture is clearly making a request, but the student who simply says *'I haven't got a handout'* is not just providing information for whoever wants to listen, but also expressing a desire to the lecturer that he or she would like a handout in order to follow proceedings. If, as would be expected, the lecturer then provided him or her with said handout, the speech act would be deemed to have reached a satisfactory solution. The resultant effect of a speech act is known as the **perlocutionary effect**. Searle (1969) then went on to attempt to actually categorise speech acts by dividing them according to their performative function, i.e. whether the speaker is stating, praising, assessing, threatening, preaching, etc. These functions may not be immediately apparent from a literal interpretation of the wording of a text; there may be an underlying message, an indirect, pragmatic meaning. Considered in terms of rank, these meanings can be recognised at various levels:

1 a single lexical item
2 an individual speech act
3 an exchange
4 a concatenation of speech acts
5 an entire text

The 'hidden' pragmatic meaning may be identifiable at each individual level or only following a consideration of the relations subsisting between the various levels. Consider the following sequence from Oscar Wilde's 1893 play 'A Woman of no Importance':

> HESTER WORSLEY: ... Let all women who have sinned be punished.
> LADY HUNSTANTON: My dear young lady.
> HESTER WORSLEY: It is right that they should be punished, but don't let them be the only ones to suffer ... You are unjust to women in England. And till you count what is a shame in a woman to be an infamy in a man, you will always be unjust, and Right, that pillar of fire, and Wrong, that pillar of cloud, will be made dim to your eyes, or be not seen at all, or if seen, not regarded.
> LADY CAROLINE: Might I, dear Miss Worsley, as you are standing up, ask you for my cotton that is just behind you? Thank you.
>
> (*enter Mrs Arbuthnot*)
>
> LADY HUNSTANTON: My dear Mrs Arbuthnot. I am so pleased you have come up. But I didn't hear you announced.

MRS ARBUTHNOT: Oh I came straight in from the terrace, Lady
Hunstanton, just as I was. You didn't tell me you had a party.
LADY HUNSTANTON: Not a party. Only a few guests who are staying
in the house, and whom you must know. Allow me. Caroline, this is
Mrs Arbuthnot, one of my sweetest friends. Lady Caroline Pontefract,
Lady Stutfield, Mrs Allonby, and my young American friend, Miss
Worsley, who has just been telling us how wicked we are.
HESTER WORSLEY: I am afraid you think I spoke too strongly, Lady
Hunstanton. But there are some things in England ...
LADY HUNSTANTON: My dear young lady, there was a great deal of
truth, I dare say, in what you said, and you looked very pretty while
you said it, which is much more important, Lord Illingworth would tell
us.

(Wilde 1982:103)

As with all Oscar Wilde's works, the discourse contains a great deal more meaning, at all levels, than first meets the eye. At the level of individual speech act, the locution *My dear young lady* appears twice, on each occasion uttered by the same speaker, Lady Hunstanton. However, on neither occasion is meaning restricted to the literal affectionate statement, and the purpose of the utterance differs on the two occasions of its use. In the first instance it expresses mild (and mock) shock at Hester Worsley's preceding comments. The preceding discourse (co-text) is, of course, crucial to an understanding of what follows, but it is not always sufficient. In this case the young American woman, Hester, has just completed a scathing criticism of the idle, snobbish and selfish behaviour of the English aristocracy, culminating in an indirect plea for women's rights. The mildness, and the falseness, of Lady Hunstanton's reaction reflect her total disdain for the views of this impertinent foreigner.

The second occurrence of *My dear young lady* follows a slight backtracking on the part of Hester: *I am afraid you think I spoke too strongly, Lady Hunstanton.* On this occasion, the caricatured upper class English lady is merely being condescending, having not been influenced even minimally by the American's diatribe. In terms of translation into Italian, the literal *Mia cara signorina* is not very convincing in either case, and the translation in any case may have to be different on the two occasions. In the compendium volume of Wilde's works (d'Amico 1994:435), while the first instance is translated with *Mia cara ragazza*, the second is a much more peremptory *Ragazza mia*.

Hester's complaint that *You are unjust to women in England* seems to be in direct contradiction with her earlier demands for punishment, but the ongoing text reveals that it is merely her unorthodox approach to women's equality that creates the apparent incompatibility. That this attitude should be so much in contrast with that of her interlocutors is of course a deliberate ploy on Wilde's part to ridicule both. And this brings us to one of the most important features the translator must bear in mind when dealing with expressive, particularly literary, texts. Apart from the pragmatic meaning that can be imputed to the characters themselves in a play or novel, treating them as if they were autonomous beings, there is the further complication of the author's purpose in writing the text. Hester's pompous manner and pretentiously elaborate prose is tailored to her role in the play; Wilde wanted to set her up as a foil to the aristocratic English whom he would later satirise. Translators must respect the pedantic register and the exaggerated style in their syntactic and lexical choices.

Another interesting aspect emerges here at the level of exchange. In much ordinary conversation, exchanges in dialogue are to a large extent predictable through the conventional use of **adjacency pairs**. The term 'adjacency pairs' describes the way utterances often appear in complementary couplets in conversation. The most obvious examples are greetings:

> A: Good morning.
> B: Good morning.
>
> A: How are you?
> B: Fine thank you.

The typical question/answer and enquiry/response frameworks of discourse also provide many pairs:

> A: What time is it?
> B: Two o'clock.
>
> A: Do you mind if I sit here?
> B: Not at all.

Many more examples could be cited and are typical of casual conversation, but the interesting thing about all Wilde's texts is that at times no obvious pairing can be discerned in exchanges. It seems on occasion that the participants in the discourse carry on their own parts of the dialogue regardless of the responses of the other interlocutors. This is a device used by Wilde to make certain characters seem pompously arrogant, or frustratingly absent-minded, or simply uninterested in the views of others.

The response of the meekly polite Lady Caroline, who follows the portentous words of Hester Worsley with *Might I, dear Miss Worsley, as you are standing up, ask you for my cotton that is just behind you?* is designed to demonstrate the unfeeling desire of the upper classes to avoid any contact with the harsh reality of the real world. This is further suggested by Lady Hunstanton's complete ignoring of Hester and her turning to the newly-arrived Mrs Arbuthnot.

Wilde also takes this opportunity to leave us in no doubt as to who is in charge of this genteel gathering, as the host's disapproval is apparent in *But I didn't hear you announced.* The pragmatic haughtiness transcends the simple affirmation. In fact, Lady Hunstanton's generally hypocritical attitude towards, for example, Mrs Arbuthnot, is revealed in her choice of the expressions *I am so pleased* and *one of my sweetest friends*, where the pleasure and the sweetness have no real force.

At the level of the single lexical item, the choice of *wicked*, which might be considered an example of hyperbole with its connotations of evil and malice, is again used deliberately to make Hester Worsley sound exaggeratedly critical. Indeed, it is this choice of word which sparks Hester's partial contrition. The **coefficient of intensity** (a measure of the relative force of words, see Snelling 1992:121) of the item *wicked* in this context was clearly understood as having a high value by the translator who provided ... *stava dicendo che siamo tutti dei mostri*, using a noun of equal force.

However, in cases of this type, it is really only when the concatenation of speech acts, some of which seem at first sight inappropriate, are considered as a whole, that the translator can gain a holistic picture of the register, style and lexicogrammatical resources needed. Lady Hunstanton's last speech in this extract is indicative. It is essential to be aware that Wilde wishes to satirise the Victorian upper classes by highlighting their negative characteristics through subtle caricature. At times, however, the characters become almost likeable because they are humorous, and this element must also transpire. One aspect that emerges from many of Wilde's works, and which is illustrated in many of his famous aphorisms, is the curiously lax attitude of the English aristocracy towards immorality, sloth, and vice in general, and their total indifference to the plight of the lower orders. Hester Worsley's attack on such haughty indifference is answered by *there was a great deal of truth in what you said* which, of course, Lady Hunstanton does not believe for a moment, and the key to understanding this is in the *I dare say* which Wilde skilfully inserts into the sentence. But then Hester is completely humiliated by Lady Hunstanton's gratuitous comment that *you looked very pretty while you said it*, which ridicules the American's protofeminist ideas, and is then compounded by *which is much more important*. The flippant incongruity of this last remark is a hallmark of Wilde's irreverent style. The fact that an aristocratic male buffoon Lord Illingworth is credited with such a crass observation simply accentuates the insult (for Hester Worsley) and the humour (for the audience).

This short extract sets the tone for the whole play, and only a complete 'pragmatic' reading of the text can bring out the many humorous, satirical, seriously critical and stylistically elegant facets put into it by Wilde. It is the translator's task to transpose this reading into a target text that recreates, as far as possible, the various pragmatic meanings at every level necessary.

2.3.3 The interpersonal element

Pragmatics is concerned with the use of language in social interaction, and thus the interpersonal component in communication is very important in determining lexicogrammatical choice. Questions of register come into play depending on the social status, personality, age, sex and education level of the participants in a discourse. What lexicogrammatical choices are appropriate is governed by pragmatic social norms that dictate, for example, that it is generally unwise to say '*Alright mate?*' to a job interviewer (who would be expecting a respectful manner), inappropriate to say it to one's grandmother (because of her age, sex and relational standing), insensitive to say it to someone who has just received bad news, though perfectly acceptable to use it to address a good friend. Similarly, the good friend would be surprised to hear himself greeted by '*Good afternoon, I trust you are well*'.

Such considerations are of a broadly universal nature, though the social norms of different cultures can differ in various ways. Many languages have a built-in politeness mechanism in the use of pronouns (*tu* and *Lei* in Italian) whereas English has to use other devices, such as a widespread use of the adverbial *please*, or the use of the tentative *may* and *might* or conditional forms. Cf:

> Posso farti una domanda?/Can I ask you something?
> Posso farLe una domanda?/May I ask you a question?
> Vieni!/Come on!
> Venga/Please come this way; Would you step this way?

The fact that the pronoun distinction does not exist in English also raises the question of how to translate the verb phrases *dare del tu* and *dare del lei*. In conversation, the invitation *Puoi darmi del tu, sai* has often been translated by some variation of *Please call me George/Bill/Mary*. Conversely, the instruction *Devi dare del lei al Signor X* might become *Remember to be polite to Mr X*.

It is also true that certain social niceties are more acceptable in some cultures than others. In Italian society, where cuisine is afforded a great deal of importance, it is normal when invited to dinner to offer profuse compliments on the food that has been prepared. Total silence would also not be appreciated in an English context but the praise, regardless of the excellence or otherwise of the meal, would be more muted (note the lack of an equivalent for *Buon appetito!*). On the other hand, the ubiquitous **phatic** 'pleases' and 'thank yous' that are so common in English speech are not always necessary in equivalent Italian situations.

A further pragmatic consideration concerns what are known as the **felicity conditions** that must be fulfilled before a speech act can be successful. For example, for an instruction such as *Please put litter in the bin provided* to be effective, the speaker/writer must have the necessary authority (e.g. a council notice), there must be a need for litter to be put in the bin (e.g. to keep a picnic ground tidy) and a reason for the receiver of the message to act accordingly (e.g. a sense of civic pride). It may be that in translating from one language to another the felicity conditions for a communicative act may differ. For example, a sign in an English pub that says *No underage drinking* relies for effective communication on the fact that the local police have the authority to make such a stipulation, the fact that drinks can be obtained from the establishment in question, and the fact that potential offenders are aware of the legal age limit for drinking alcohol. If the sign were to be translated into Italian (a quite feasible possibility), the last felicity condition would probably not be satisfied and extra information would be required to explain that the age limit is eighteen years.

2.4   Cultural constraints

Much mention has already been made, in this chapter and previously, of the influence of cultural factors on language, and consequently on translation, but in this section the question will be examined further. Culture is such a wide subject that it interests scholars from many different areas ranging from anthropology and ethnography to philosophy, sociology, psychology and, what concerns us here, linguistics and translation studies. Man is a tribal animal, and since the days when movement, and consequently communication with other tribes, was restricted by physical limits and lack of knowledge of the existence of other communities, especially those more distant in terms of both distance and way of life, human beings' ways of living and thinking have become ingrained. The linguistic implications of this state of affairs should be clear; languages developed within specific sets of circumstances. Still today, in many of the less-charted areas of the world, hundreds of mutually unintelligible languages exist within relatively restricted areas, reflecting and maintaining cultural distances.

Through a process that can be described in terms of an increasing density of communication, one dominant language can, over time, establish itself over one or more nations (e.g. Italian, English). In these circumstances intracultural and intercultural differences can be understood, mediated or simply tolerated through the mutual understanding afforded by a single code. A common language has a powerful unifying function and force, and in turn helps to mould what we recognise, as outsiders, as a distinct culture. Even the individual words of a language are often expressly linked to the culture (cf: *pizza* and *cricket*, above).

As O'Connor and Seymour (1990:131) point out, 'We learn what things mean from our culture and individual upbringing'. Thus, anyone communicating in their native language will express themselves in language that reflects their cultural upbringing, and therefore their view of the world, as suggested by Malinowski, Sapir and Whorf. This ranges from the use of particular lexis to refer to culture-bound phenomena (*darts league, carol-singing, A-levels, polenta, passeggiata, fuori corso*) to set expressions which are rooted in the (ancient or modern) folk history of the culture (*Boxing Day, taking coals to Newcastle, in bocca al lupo, Buon appetito*) to different ways of viewing the same reality. Ulrych (1992:72) points out how colours would not appear to be perceived in the same way by English and Italians (cf: *'yellow' egg yolk/il rosso dell'uovo*) to the relative emphasis given to certain qualities or characteristics (Steiner notes in the afore-mentioned translation of the Rolex advertisement that the German version puts the accent on reliability whereas the English original stresses the adventure aspect). Even where equivalents are proposed for terms such as those cited above, for example in bilingual dictionaries, cultural shades of meaning distinguish them. For example, *una passeggiata* can be described in physical terms as *a walk*, but the phenomenon to which the Italian term usually refers is not an English habit, for meteorological as well as traditional reasons. *Carols* in the sense of Christmas songs or hymns exist in Italian, but the act of going from door to door singing them does not.

Katan (1996:19) describes culture as:

> ... a shared mental model or map of the world. The model is a system of congruent and interrelated beliefs, values, strategies and cognitive environments which guide the shared basis of behaviour. Each aspect of culture is linked in a system to form a unifying context of culture which identifies a person and his or her culture.

Translators find themselves in the position of having to straddle two cultures, and in order to successfully make the linguistic jump from one to the other, they should have a thorough knowledge of the potential of both systems to express experience, entities or events. The translator should therefore ideally be bilingual and bicultural. Although it is by no means a foregone conclusion that such persons will have the other skills required to translate, it is interesting to note that one of the characteristics of true bilinguals is that they are always unquestioningly accepted as members of both cultural communities.

It is the ability to move effortlessly between the two cultures that would enable a translator to see the symbolism and the humour in an English comedy situation featuring a Pakistani man in work clothes looking round a door and saying *'There's trouble at mill'*, and would prevent him from translating *mill* with *mulino*. The expression in question has become fossilised in the language; it is associated with early industrial unrest in the factories of the Industrial Revolution (the cotton and woollen 'mills'), but is now used metaphorically for humourous effect when a troublesome situation arises. The fact that the speaker is a Pakistani is an ironic reference to the fact that, since the Second World War, many of the workers in such factories have been immigrants from the Indian sub-continent. Thus the expression *'There's trouble at mill'*, for historico-social reasons, can be aptly described as 'culture-bound', and it is this phenomenon of cultural specificity that does so much to impede cross-cultural communication.

2.4.1 Culture-bound language

Any discussion of culture-bound language must cover the whole range of human experience, from geographical names to institutional terms to culture-specific terminology referring to ways of life, social organisation, local customs, material artefacts and so on. However, it must first be stressed that the culture-bound element in language must be seen in relation to the vast areas of language use that are of a more universal nature. If the whole of language was culture-bound, then reciprocal understanding and translation would indeed be almost impossible, but common sense tells us that much of the language we use has universal application. For this reason we are able to identify (or miss!) culture-bound elements within larger stretches of relatively inter-cultural text.

The geographical names of places, rivers, mountains and so on can be learned, but (often dialectal) terms describing geographical or other natural phenomena that are more locally defined (*moors, cwms, dales, fells, fens; lande, Carso, masi, sacche*) are trickier and may have to undergo a reduction from the specific to the generic (*moor/brughiera, dale/vallata, maso/farm*) unless a suitable matching can be negotiated (*heath/landa?*).

The category of institutional terms is intended here to refer to those national or government institutions that may differ to varying degrees in form or function from country to country due to historical or political reasons. Sometimes, or on some occasions, such terms are simply transcribed (*Foreign Office, Serie A*), though they may need what Newmark (1984:76) calls a translation couplet in apposition: *cassa integrazione (Italian redundancy fund), by-election (elezione suppletiva in Gran Bretagna)*. Literal, transparent translations are often possible, especially when similar institutions exist in the source culture and where the influence of the European Union is to be seen in the standardisation of such translations, e.g. *La Camera dei Comuni* or *the Italian Senate*. However, such translations are also attempted even when there is no real equivalent in the target language: *Il Cancelliere dello Scacchiere* for *Chancellor of the Exchequer, the Northern League* for *La Lega Nord*.

At times, however, the above practice is risky because of the existence of a conceptual gap: Italian bureaucracy, for example, provides terms like *certificato di residenza* and *stato di famiglia*, which have no equivalent in English because the referents do not exist. The transparent translation *certificato di residenza/residence certificate* has little meaning in English contexts (*family status certificate* has even less), but if, as will presumably be the case, it occurs in an Italian or other congruent context, it might well suffice. If it is not clear from the context, then a note of explanation must be provided, preferably in the text but, if necessary, in a footnote. A peculiarly English institution is the Christmas pantomime with its associated terminology (*dame, principal boy, pantomime horse*, etc.), not to mention the names (*Widow Twanky, Buttons, Mother Goose*) where the conceptual gaps will need to be filled with acceptably understandable translations (*Mamma Oca/Mother Goose*) or explanatory phrases (*principal boy/donna che fa la parte dell'eroe*).

However, the most serious culture-based problems that beset translators are to be found among the many lexical items and expressions that contain, always or on some occasions, a potentially incomprehensible or misleading cultural aspect. Many authors have written on this subject and many individual lexical items have been singled out for analysis: Nida (1964) on *lamb* as a non-universal symbol of peace, Susan Bassnett (1991:19) on *butter* and its (dis)similarity to *burro*. A virtually endless list could be provided. Consider the cultural implications of the following supposed translation equivalents: *breakfast/prima colazione* (what is eaten?), *party/festa* (what goes on?), *barrister/avvocato* (what are their duties?), *geometra/surveyor* (who goes by this name?), *villetta a schiera/terraced house* (who lives in it?). But what is perhaps more important for the translator is a list of strategies for dealing with such terms, once a cultural feature has been identified. As with institutional terms, they can be transcribed (*baseball*, *pizza*), translated literally or transparently (*pallacanestro*, *Neapolitan*) or provided with a couplet – *porcini (edible mushroom)* – or even a triplet: *tiramisù (pick-me-up, Italian cream and coffee dessert dish)*.

If such expedients are not available, however, other solutions must be found, for example the use of a cultural equivalent. Care must be taken, however, as to whether the specificity of the source text term precludes the target language cultural equivalent in the context in which it is found. For example, referring to the Italian *ACI (Automobile Club Italia)* as the *automobile association* is acceptable if the reference is simply to an unspecified organisation of this type, for example in a story (*Hanno dovuto telefonare all'ACI/They had to phone the automobile association*), but not in a text dealing specifically with the particular organisation in question. Where the specificity is important, a descriptive element may be required; in the above case, simply the *Italian automobile association*.

Where still no solution can be found, the translator may have to resort to: 1. paraphrase, 2. annotated explanations or even 3. deletion, if the term's omission does not detract from the essential meaning:

1 The boys were out playing conkers/I ragazzi erano fuori a giocare con le castagne d'India
2 The boys were out playing conkers/I ragazzi erano fuori a giocare a 'conkers' (un gioco inglese nel quale i bambini stanno uno con una castagna d'India a penzoloni da un filo, mentre l'altro cerca di rompere la castagna dell'avversario con la propria facendola roteare nell'aria)
3 The boys were out playing conkers/I ragazzi erano fuori a giocare

To conclude this section, it can be pointed out that, particularly over the last decade, translation scholars have been giving more attention to cultural influences on translation, as is shown by a number of chapter headings: Snell-Hornby (1988:39) 'Translation as a Cross-Cultural Event'; Bassnett (1991:13) 'Central Issues: Language and Culture'; Nida (1996) 'Changes in Language and Culture'. Nida's chapter deals with such cultural issues as the introduction of new terminology through, for example, technology: *CD ROM*, *airbag*, *digital television*. There is an established trend to transfer such technical terms intact, or create literal 'loan' translations, into languages other than English such as the Italian *CD ROM* and *TV digitale*. In some countries, such as France, there has been quite understandable opposition to this process, but it continues unabated. Perhaps even more insidious for native language purity is the trend towards adopting loan translations of expressions that already exist in a different form in the receptor language. The example of the influence of dubbed English-language films and television series leading to the use of such expressions as *Buon pomeriggio* in Italy on the model of *Good afternoon* has already been mentioned. Similar processes have been identified in other languages. But in view of the growing interest and the undoubted assistance this will provide for translators, we can now agree with Katan (1996:159) that:

> the process of translation is now being understood as an exercise, not only in understanding texts, but in understanding cultural frames.

Chapter Two: Suggested further reading

Austin, J.L. 1962. *How to Do Things with Words*. London: Oxford University Press.

House, J. 1981 (new edition 1997). *A Model for Translation Quality Assessment*. Tübingen: Gunter Narr Verlag.

Katan, D. 1996. *Translating across Cultures*. Trieste: SERT, Università di Trieste.

Leech, G.N. 1981. *Semantics*. Harmondsworth: Penguin Books.

Leech, G.N. 1983. *Principles of Pragmatics*. London: Longman.

Lyons, J. 1977. *Semantics* (2 vols). Cambridge: Cambridge University Press.

Palmer, F.R. 1976. *Semantics*. Cambridge: Cambridge University Press.

Chapter Three

Language Variety: Text Types and Genre

Chapter Three looks at the different kinds of language translators can encounter in their work. There are various ways of categorising text, and this is reflected in the division of the material into various typologies. Starting from the fundamental distinction between spoken and written language, this Chapter then examines **sociolinguistic** varieties ranging from geographical and social dialects to age and gender based 'lects'. A separate account of traditional text types based on subject area (literary, technical, legal, etc.) and respective sub-types (novel, medical text, etc.) is followed by a more technical consideration of the concept of genre.

OVERVIEW OF CHAPTER

1 Written and spoken language

The two basic varieties are considered with reference to lexical density, hypotaxis/parataxis, nominalisation and intertextuality.

2 Sociolinguistic varieties

Geographical, social, generational and gender-based varieties of language are discussed in this section.

3 Text types

Texts are here categorised according to the broad subject matter they deal with. The particular typological breakdown adopted in this section covers literary, technical, legal, commercial, journalistic and advertising texts.

4 Genre

Recent approaches to genre have attempted to categorise texts in terms of identifiable situations that are distinguished by a series of obligatory features, some of which are specific to that situation. Such 'genres' can be very restricted in dimension (greengrocer's shop service encounter, international fisheries conference, etc.), these being sub-genres of wider varieties (general service encounters, international meetings) and so on.

3.1   Introduction and definition

The terms 'language variety' and 'text type', although rather wide-ranging and open to various interpretations, have long been used in approaches to the general categorisation of text, and will be discussed here in terms of their continuing relevance to translation. More recently, and at a higher level of specificity, the concept of 'genre' has emerged in linguistic studies as a more sophisticated measure of text identification, and this too will be examined. This chapter will therefore analyse the question of language variety from several angles, starting and ending with attempts to establish exactly what 'genre' is from a textual point of view, and how it can be useful for translators. Intuitively, people know that a genre is a 'type', but the word has a more specific meaning in the field of applied linguistics. Threadgold, in the Encyclopedia of Language and Linguistics, Vol. 3 (1994:1408) explains that:

> Genres in most analyses are considered to have specific forms
> which organise the matter or substance of which the genre is made.
> The form may impose a subject matter, a manner or mode, or a
> typical text structure.

More specifically, Longman's Dictionary of Language Teaching and Applied Linguistics (1992:156) refers to

> a particular class of speech events which are considered by the
> speech community as being of the same type. Examples of genres
> are: prayers, sermons, conversations, letters, novels. . . . They have
> particular and distinctive characteristics.

This is becoming more useful to the translator as a breakdown of genre-based texts, but while it is true that a conversation can be distinguished from a letter, which in turn can be distinguished from a novel, by virtue of particular characteristics appertaining to each, it is also true that conversations can be of many 'types', as can letters and novels. Furthermore, a novel may contain a letter or a conversation, a letter may relate a conversation and a conversation may contain discussion of or quotations from a novel. Consequently, we will have to go beyond the dictionary definitions if we wish to find a really useful parameter for categorising texts.

However, before continuing the discussion on genre definition (see **3.5**), it must be pointed out that texts have long been divided into categories in a number of ways, depending to some extent on the nature of the task requiring their division. For example, sociolinguists, who study language in relation to social factors, adopt a breakdown based on (inter)national varieties, in turn based on different peoples, races and individuals speaking variations of the same basic language, or on gender, age, or social class lines.

Alternatively, it has been common practice within the international English teaching community, including the specialist schools of translation and interpreting, to divide texts according to subject area and talk about broad 'text types': literary texts, technical texts, legal language, commercial English, advertising copy, etc. This tendency has given rise to a plethora of acronym-labelled sub-types of language: LSP (Language for Special Purposes), LMP (Language for Medical Purposes), BE (Business English) and so on.

At a further remove, texts can be categorised as to their function, their style or their 'register'. The latter term is used here in the narrow sense of formal/informal, high/low, or specialist/general (a more technical definition of register will be discussed in **3.5.1**). As regards style and register, more or less subtle distinctions may be identified, based on levels of formality, colloquial usage or technicality. The classifying of texts according to their function, on the other hand, is connected to whether they are designed to narrate, to describe, to explain, to entertain, to threaten, etc. For example, many characteristics of narrative text can be observed and identified:

> the use of first and third person pronouns as referring expressions
> the use of the agentive subject
> the concentration on the specific rather than the generic
> the use of the past tense
> the use of chronological linking devices

More specifically, Simpson (1992:60) discusses narrative structure in terms of Labov's various phases of narrative:

> abstract beginning
> orientation
> complicating action

resolution
evaluation
coda

(from Labov 1972)

The reader's attention is drawn to the fact that a story is beginning, and a course of action is described involving various characters, in a certain setting, etc. (orientation). The key action takes place affecting the situation (complicating action). A problem is solved or an event is finalised (resolution) and an explanation is given (evaluation). The story is rounded off, often referring back to the beginning (coda). The linguistic features often connected to the various phases are listed:

the past progressive verb form for orientation
the simple past in the middle phases
explicatory modals for the evaluation
a general timeless statement for the coda

Yet more parameters could be conceived, as for all other functions, but it can already be seen that the isolation of text varieties in the linguistic sense is not a straightforward matter. But before examining individually the various approaches to classification in more depth and considering their individual merits, the fundamental and clearly analysable difference between the major categories of written and spoken language will be briefly examined.

3.2   Written and spoken language

In terms of the spoken/written divide, the translator is most usually concerned with the written variety of language. The interpreter, who preceded the translator historically, deals with the spoken genre, although more often it is the 'written to be spoken' type that emerges in conference situations. This section will therefore distinguish, in particular, the most important features of written text.

From its very beginnings, written language had a purpose, or set of purposes and has come to differ from spoken language in a variety of ways. Halliday (1985:44) explains the genesis and subsequent development of written language as follows:

Writing evolved for a range of distinct social functions; it was not primarily a new way of doing old things with language. In other words it came into being precisely so that new registers could be created: so that there could be a 'written language' that was not the same as the spoken. Again, this is not to imply that there will be one clearly defined 'written' variety; what emerges is a new range of functional variation, which leads to the emergence of configurations of semantic and lexicogrammatical patterns that then come to be recognised as characteristic of writing.

Firstly, it can be seen that the concept emerges of 'register' as variety, and this will be analysed further in **3.5**. The question that must be asked now is: what are the characteristics of written text? Written language, as we have seen, is more lexically dense than spoken language (see **1.2.2**) though less grammatically intricate, it has an organised clause structure featuring frequent hypotaxis (main and subordinate clauses in sequence) and a high proportion of nominalisation. Information is often bound up in complex noun groups with long strings of pre-modifying nouns and adjectives and post-modifying prepositional phrases, often connected by verbs of the **copular** variety, which are low on dynamism (see **1.1.3**) and carry little of the meaning in a clause. Sentences are complete and uninterrupted. It will be seen later that these properties have a particular relevance in technical, legal and journalistic writing. The following, for example, is a sample of an Italian newspaper article demonstrating how much information can be packed into what is essentially a single sentence:

> Una volta ancora l'approccio iniziale non è stato molto diverso: la Lega essendo contrassegnata dal presupposto, venato, checché se ne dica, di razzismo che riduceva essenzialmente l'immigrazione ad un fatto criminale; il Pds, apparendo frastornato tra la percezione della insofferenza crescente per la contiguità con gli extracomunitari di una gran parte della sua base popolare, e il permanere, soprattutto nella militanza tardosessantottina, di remore ideologiche intrise di terzomondismo facilone e malriposto; i cattolici di sinistra – a cominciare dall'Ulivo – assumendo un ruolo, percepito dalla maggioranza dell'opinione pubblica come provocatorio, come sostenitori attivi di un ineluttabile quanto felice esito di una società multirazziale, portatrice di vantaggi economici e valori civili; infine la Chiesa, promuovendo un caritevole modello missionario, universale e illimitato, che dovrebbe, peraltro, propiziare l'evangelizzazione cattolica con nuovi afflussi di fedeli e di vocazioni ecclesiali.
>
> (La Repubblica 16/11/95)

The written language, compared to the spoken, contains more low-frequency items as found, for example, in technical and bureaucratic discourse. The spoken variety makes easy recourse to the device of intonation in order to frame meaning, whereas the written language relies more on word order and logical information presentation achieved through theme/rheme and given/new information patterns (see **1.1.4**). There is much use of the passive voice and impersonal constructions of the *It is said that . . . / Si dice che . . .* type.

It is much easier to recognise certain language 'standards' in written text, in the sense that the phenomenon of intertextuality, or how texts relate to other previously-produced texts, is easy to establish because of their physical existence. Models exist and are being constantly reproduced, and these models have often stood the test of time. Texts can be read and re-read and consequently valued and re-valued many times, distancing themselves often quite radically from their original contexts of situation.

Even in an age of recorded speech, most spoken language is there one minute and gone the next. It is tied to the context in which it is produced, except for the minimum amount of spoken language that is recorded and used at a later juncture. And in a very obvious sense, most spoken language is produced 'to be spoken' and therefore consists of all the hesitations, repetitions, reformulations, and general ungrammaticalities that are missing from the written mode.

3.3   Sociolinguistic varieties

> Sociolinguistics studies the ways in which language interacts with society.
>
> (Crystal 1981:252)

Society, any society, consists of an ever-changing variety of individuals and groups. When individuals can be seen to belong to recognisable multiple units, social groups can be identified. These social groups may be very large (the English, women, young people) or much more restricted (Londoners, animal rights activists, basketball players), and these groups may overlap considerably. And whatever other social characteristics distinguish such social groups, language is a very important component: it is usually possible to associate some particular (socio)linguistic features with them. Within the English-speaking world (a very wide social group), a great many linguistic features can be seen to be common to all speakers but, for example, the British and the American varieties differ in a number of ways:

distinctly different lexical items (*elevator/lift*, *autumn/fall*,
    queue/line)
variations in pronunciation (*lever*, *tomato*, even *cigarette*)
spelling (*honour/honor*, *programme/program*)
grammar (*Have you got ...?/Do you have ...?*, *travelling/traveling*)

The same phenomenon can be observed between other English-speaking communities: reading 'Long Walk to Freedom', the autobiography of Nelson Mandela, the British English reader is struck by the author's constant use of the term *fellow* across a whole range of registers and to refer to very different individuals. The term is rather outmoded in British English, though still current in the South African variety. Clearly, translators must be aware of the national linguistic group they are translating from and, more importantly, writing for. Very often, for example, medical texts may be sent to both English and American journals (e.g. The Lancet, The New England Journal of Medicine) to be considered for publication. In theory, the former would require spellings such as *sulphuric acid* and *fibre-optic* and the latter *sulfuric acid* and *fiber-optic*. Both are of course correct and thus acceptable, but translators should at least be consistent if they begin in either the English or American mode. Such differences between the various international types of English should be recognised though not exaggerated. The area of common language usage is, in fact, vast.

As well as the above-mentioned lexicogrammatical areas, stylistic differences can also be recognised. The ironic component so prevalent in the English journalism of The Economist, for example, seems to be less prevalent in equivalent publications such as Time and Newsweek. Conversely, American commercial rhetoric can often be much more dynamic than its staid English counterpart.

A much more apparent discrepancy exists between native English and the **interlanguage** spoken by hundreds of millions of non-native speakers around the world. 'Interlanguage' refers to the English (or any other language) spoken by learners, and can, by definition, be located anywhere along the spectrum that ranges from beginner's hesitancy to near-fluency. Many interlanguage speakers provide work for translators, either translating their own imperfect texts into other languages (an Egyptian businessman wanting to market his products in Germany, where English is a much more readily-translated language than Arabic), or correcting their own attempts at text production (an Italian doctor writing for The Lancet). Clearly, when dealing with interlanguage, which has become an extremely widespread phenomenon, translators must be prepared to deal with varying levels of inaccuracy.

International language variation gives way to national variation, in the form of local dialects and accents. In the case of Britain, though not necessarily elsewhere, such dialects and accents are simultaneously associated with social class, that is the lower the socio-economic grouping, the stronger the local speech variation. The traditional class-consciousness of the British therefore stereotypically associates 'Cockney' dialect with the poorer areas of east London. The translator must be attuned to this, particularly when translating direct speech, for example in novels, films or the tabloid press. For example, the classic novelist D.H. Lawrence and, more recently, Alan Sillitoe, both made extensive use of the Nottingham dialect, albeit fifty years apart, in their works. Translation into standard Italian would rob (and has robbed) such books of their authentic 'working-class' flavour. In the film 'My Beautiful Launderette', which features the middle-class Pakistani community in London, language is a key element. In fact, the most refined English is, ironically, spoken by some of the Asian characters, while the local white underclass articulate badly in broad 'Cockney', underlining a message about the changing ethnic roles in London society. The dubbed Italian version of this film neutralised the dialectal differences, thereby losing a crucial element in the overall semiotic framework. The answer to this problem may lie in simply using a restricted code, that is a limited number of verbal items in the target language to match the inarticulateness and limited range of lexis in the source language, rather than try to force some target language dialect. The classical origin of practically all Italian vocabulary, for example, already creates a sense of register difference in the translation of 'sub-standard' English language: *'It don't work'/'Non funziona'*. The street talk of south London delinquents is at one end of a spectrum that ranges from ritualistic through formal to informal to casual to intimate to taboo language (see Nida 1996:28). It is low authority speech indicating a low level of education and expertise.

The generation gap, rightly or wrongly often blamed for lack of understanding between parents and children, has a linguistic component. The language of youth, often fickle and fleeting, sometimes leaves its mark by adding new terms and expressions to the language. The translators of popular songs, for example, should pay heed to this phenomenon. Younger still, the language of children is characterised by easily-recognisable, if not easily-defined, features. In Roddy Doyle's novel 'Paddy Clarke ha, ha, ha', the author recounts the story of children in 1968 Dublin as seen through the eyes of a small boy:

> We were coming down our road. Kevin stopped at a gate and bashed it with his stick. It was Missis Quigley's gate; she was always looking out the window but she never did anything.
> - Quigley!
> - Quigley!
> - Quigley! Quigley Quigley!
> Liam and Aidan turned down their cul-de-sac. We said nothing; they said nothing. Liam and Aidan had a dead mother. Missis O'Connell was her name.
> - It'd be brilliant, wouldn't it? I said.
>
> (Doyle 1993:1)

The paratactic style of short sentences, the taunting chant, the spelling, the choice of lexis (*brilliant*) all make it clear to the reader that the teller of the story is a child, even though this has not been made explicit at this stage of the novel. This age-based variety of language must of course be captured in translation. The names in this story (*Liam, Aidan, Missis O'Connell*) also point to it being set in Ireland, so it can now be seen how two varieties, one generational and one geographical, overlap in this context. If it is also pointed out that the area of Ireland in question is the notoriously under-privileged north Dublin, then the social factor also comes into play, with its dialectal component.

The rise in importance of feminist thinking and women's studies has led to various attempts to isolate women's language and men's language. One of the most well known authors on the subject, Deborah Tannen (1992) claims that the basic difference between the ways men and women speak is based on the fact that the former use language primarily to preserve their independence and negotiate status, while the latter use it to make connections and reinforce intimacy. This defining of the fundamental motives behind '**genderlect**' helps us to understand why men often seem overbearing to women, and often downright boring in their insistence on imparting information to uninterested ears, and why men at times find women's conversation trivial or unnecessarily personal.

> Intimacy is key in a world of connection where individuals negotiate complex networks of friendship, minimize differences, try to reach consensus, and avoid the appearance of superiority, which

would highlight differences. In a world of status, independence is key, because a primary means of establishing status is to tell others what to do, and taking orders is a marker of low status. Though all humans need both intimacy and independence, women tend to focus on the first and men on the second. It is as if their life-blood ran in different directions.

(Tannen 1992:26)

On the strength of this divide, it might be thought that men's and women's language differs only in terms of content or style, but the two varieties can also be distinguished by certain lexicogrammatical choices. Coates (1989:94) points to women's greater use of minimal responses such as *'Mm'* and *'Yeah'* and their consequently lower propensity to interrupt during conversation, and to a greater use of **epistemic modality** in the form of adverbials and verb forms such as *'perhaps'*, *'I think. . .'*, *'sort of'*, *'probably'* and the like. She explains that:

> women exploit the polypragmatic nature of epistemic modal forms. They use them to mitigate the force of an utterance in order to respect addressee's face needs.

Goodwin (in Cortese 1992:168) also speaks of variations in syntactic forms while discussing the language of boys and girls' disputes:

> Boys make their accusations directly in forms such as 'Boy, you broke my skate board'. Girls by way of contrast frame their accusations as reports about offences heard from an intermediary.

Although most of these writers tend to suggest that the two sexes could narrow the gap between their respective speechways with a little good will, and that there are signs that this is happening, these sex-based genres still differ sufficiently to provide two more varieties for translators to bear in mind.

3.4   Text types

As mentioned in the Introduction, the appellation 'text types' usually brings to mind a classification very commonly used in language teaching and translation training, and which fulfils a need to categorise the vast amounts of material students are called upon to translate, that is, the labelling of texts as either literary, technical, journalistic, etc. Baker (1992:114) takes the concept of text types a little further, as an overlapping notion with genre, and refers firstly to a classification

> based on the contexts in which texts occur and (which) results in institutionalised labels such as 'journal article', 'science textbook', 'newspaper editorial' or 'travel brochure'.

Indeed, all these more specific text types will be featured in Part Two of this book, and the concept of 'genre' in the next section, but for the moment we will consider a typology of six broad categories.

3.4.1 Literary texts

The fact that any literary text of note requires careful attention for its own sake, and contains (perhaps conceals) a series of pragmatic, stylistic and ultimately linguistic features that make it unique, might warn against attempting to discover any general underlying characteristics of the type that could be useful to translators. However, the type is easy enough to isolate in broad terms. First, we must consider Bühler's 1934 distinction between three basic functions of language:

> the referential or **informative** function (Darstellungsfunktion): the function of providing information about the facts and events of the real world, for example in a newspaper article
> the **expressive** function (Ausdrucksfunktion): the function of providing an expressive outlet for speakers/writers, allowing them to exploit their creative skills, for example in a poem
> the **vocative** or persuasive function (Appellfunktion): the function of persuading or influencing others, for example in a political speech

Literary text comes very close to the top end of the 'expressive function of language' spectrum and, when faced with a literary work, translators must know that they bear a heavy responsibility to examine every sentence in terms of its denotative and possibly connotative meanings, and weigh its significance in terms of a whole chapter or a whole book. Many different varieties, styles and even functions of language may interact with one another in the unfolding of a play, novel or short story, and may display evident features of the age in which they were written. Apart from all manner of word play, metaphorisation and use of figures of speech, the source text author may also resort to linguistic idiosyncrasy in the form of symbolism, rhetoric or bizarre description.

Walter Benjamin (1923) suggested that tampering with the expressive nature of literary language was so difficult that trying to translate it could not produce a satisfactory version in a target language, but might lead to an understanding of what he called a 'pure language' hanging in the air above all terrestrial languages, and between the two texts. Many scholars have accepted this notion to varying degrees but others (see T. Parks, 1995) have rejected it. Umberto Eco (1995:138), for example, many of whose works have been successfully translated, questions the existence of a pure language (which he refers to as a 'no language's land' between source and target texts). However, the concept of a 'no language's land', if slightly adapted, can be useful in explaining how a translation, particularly a literary translation, is not complete until all the linguistic, pragmatic and stylistic aspects have been properly understood and accounted for.

By way of illustration, ten extracts have been chosen from the ten short stories contained in Margaret Atwood's 1991 book 'Wilderness Tips', accompanied by annotations relating to the particular use of language employed, and the meanings contained therein:

> The waitresses are basking in the sun like a herd of skinned seals ...
>
> (True Trash:1)

Use of simile providing a denigratory image of the women, who are in fact being spied upon by a group of 'macho' boys.

> On the thirteenth of November, day of unluck, month of the dead, Kat went into the Toronto General Hospital for an operation.
>
> (Hairball:33)

Creation of morphologically unusual lexical item in *unluck*.

> How did Selena get here?
>
> (Isis in Darkness:51)

The story opens with a question regarding an as yet unintroduced person.

> Julie broke up with Connor in the middle of a swamp.
> Julie silently revises: not exactly in the middle, not knee-deep in rotting leaves and dubious brown water. More or less on the edge; sort of within striking distance. Well, in an inn, to be precise. Or not even an inn. A room in a pub. What was available.
> And not in a swamp anyway. In a bog.
>
> (The Bog Man:79)

A state of sad mental confusion is portrayed by the futile attempt *to be precise* and is further illustrated by the tortured metaphor which doesn't quite work, the lexical repetition and the squalid nature of the metaphor itself.

> 'You bring back much wampum', says Cappie. 'Do good in war, my braves, and capture many scalps'
>
> (Death by Landcape:110)

The girls in the story are at a north American summer camp and knowledge of this institution is important to understand their conversation; in this case they are using stereotypical native American language, and pretending to be boys.

> It was the aunts who brought most of the food for the Sunday dinners. They would arrive with roasts, lemon meringue pies, cookies, jars of their own pickles.
>
> (Uncles:128)

A certain gastronomical familiarity is required here to know the substance and the importance of the listed foodstuffs, all typical of north American cuisine, and their place in the folk culture.

> This was how she understood men and their furtive, fumbling, threatening desires, because Jane herself had been a consequence. She had been a mistake, she had been a war baby. She had been a crime that had needed to be paid for, over and over.
>
> (The Age of Lead:157)

This short extract contains examples of **phonological equivalence** in the alliterative *furtive, fumbling*, **syntactic equivalence** in the repetition of the compound verb structure *she had been ...*, and **semantic equivalence** in the negative things she had been.

> This man has a name, of course. His name is Charles. He's already said 'Call me Charles'. Who knows what further delights await me? 'Chuck' may lie ahead, or ' Charlie'. Charlie is my darling. Chuck, you big hunk. I think I'll stick with Charles.
>
> (Weight:174)

The major factor here is that of the level of formality, attaining the right register. The extract begins neutrally with the woman's private thoughts, then becomes (self) mocking with the ironic *Who knows what further delights await me?*. But the major difficulty for the translator lies in how to deal with *Chuck* and *Charlie*, both diminutive forms of *Charles*, the former particularly north American. The fact that *Charlie is my darling* and *Chuck, you big hunk* are stressed indicate that they stand for something outside the immediate context, and indeed it is important to know that the first is an old popular song and the second a deliberately ironic dig at the 'macho' connotations of the name *Chuck*.

> 'Geology is destiny', says Pamela, as if to herself … 'This lake is full of hidden rocks. It can be dangerous. But I'll take care of you.'
> Is she flirting with him? Can a crag flirt?
>
> (Wilderness Tips:204)

The story relies heavily on the symbolism of a lake and its natural surroundings. The metaphorical *crag* is a little forced in English but needs to have a similar effect on a target audience.

> The paper Marcia writes for is housed in a bland, square, glass-walled, windowless building, put up at some time in the seventies, when airlessness was all the rage.
>
> (Hack Wednesday:227)

The premodifier **syllable gradation** in *bland, square, glass-walled, window-less building* (1,1,2,3), that reaches a crescendo in *windowless*, adds to the negative impact of the adjectives, reinforced further by the postmodifiers with their ironic air.

The above examples, all from the same volume, have been used to stand for countless other examples of texts produced in the history of literature in all languages, basically to stress the fact that literature involves the creative use of language, the creating of something special with and through language. It therefore requires a similar sensitivity and effort of imagination on the part of the translator. Parks (1995:37) talks of how literature

> declares its difference (*from other texts, including other literary texts*) and in so doing both surprises and challenges.

He goes on to say (ibid:38) that

> a translator should be sufficiently familiar with the literature of the source language and above all with its standard usages as to be aware of those differences, and should concentrate his efforts on reproducing the same kind of difference, which is to say the same kind of identity in relation to other texts, as far as possible, in the target language.

While most other text types can be described by recourse to a considerable amount of intertextuality (features that recur frequently in texts of the same type), it is the lack of intertextuality in its most creative parts that distinguishes literature from those other forms, and that provides the greatest challenge to translators.

3.4.2 Technical texts

The term 'technical' is suitably all-embracing as to include the scientific disciplines (medicine, physics, astronomy, chemistry, etc.), fields of applied technology (computers, engineering, etc.) and even less obviously 'scientific' subjects such as geography, economics, architecture and the like. It is, however, sufficiently self-explanatory as to exclude literature, most journalism, advertising, commerce and the law, which will be dealt with separately in this chapter. The meaning of the term in translation circles is sufficiently well-understood for course titles to include the description 'technical' without fear of ambiguity.

Technical writing (and its translation) is as old, historically, as literary writing and thus has a long and extensive tradition. It is formal and impersonal, and the formality is intrinsic to the conventionalised structures which will be illustrated below. It is impersonal inasmuch as science and technology should maintain an objectivity that precludes the giving of opinions in the first person or overt demonstrations of emotion. As Newmark (1993:146) points out, referring specifically to the instructions for a coffee machine:

> There are no cultural or connotational difficulties, no metaphors,
> ... few idioms, no colloquialisms.

All technical texts will also, to some extent, be specialised in that they are produced to deal with a specific task in hand. They are, in general, informative in function though may also contain expressive elements: Giambagli (1992:64), after referring to the importance of standardised formulae and technical terminology, lists 'testo libero' as a major component of technical text, where the writer (and translator) can feel much less bound by rules or conventions. Darwin's 'Voyage of the Beagle' and Hawking's 'Brief History of Time' are technical texts that actually became best-sellers.

The grammar of scientific language may intuitively be considered complex by the layman, influenced by the technical nature of the content. Yet the language of everyday communication and non-technical texts is often more grammatically intricate. It is also true that at first sight it is the obscure, specialised and, more importantly, unfamiliar vocabulary that makes the technical text seem so complex. However, more than technical terms and syntactic considerations, it is the nominalised nature of the discourse that creates its specificity and its relative impenetrability. As is pointed out in Quirk et al. (1985:1351), technical language has a higher proportion of complex noun phrases, a lower proportion of names and pronouns, and fewer simple noun phrases as clause subject:

> <u>Two or more atoms joined to form a molecule</u> are represented by ...
> <u>The pictures radioed back by Mariner 9 as it orbited Mars</u> showed a host of ...
> <u>The appearance of the Milky Way</u> tells us ...
>
> (from Yates 1988)

Many of the modern characteristics of technical discourse were first developed in the seventeenth century. During this period of scientific enlightenment, it was decided by the scientific community that English ought to equip itself with the requisite terminology if it were to replace the classical languages, relegating the latter to the providers of affixes and a few core terms. It was at this time that the move towards concision and nominalisation began, accompanied by an increase in the use of copular verbs to connect ever more elaborate nominal groups. Gotti (1996:27) shows how Newton's 'Treatise on Optiks', published in 1704, demonstrates this shift:

> ... sentences are quite long, with very lengthy noun phrases preceding and following the verb. Moreover, the verbs (in these cases 'are' and 'is composed of') start to assume the copular function usual in modern scientific English, where the verb merely links the very long nominal phrases coming before and after it. Each sentence is structurally simple, with few or no subordinate clauses, complying with the modern preference for coordination rather than subordination in sentence structure.

In fact, noun groups dominate technical discourse and can often be seen to be arranged in predictable patterns around relational processes (that is, basically the copular verb *to be* in the present tense, either alone or in participle phrases) or the passive form of a restricted number of verbs (the passive is typically used to relate the theme of the clause to the related event or process):

(NG = noun group)

NG *is* NG

NG *is correlated/contrasted/mixed/with* NG

NG *is caused/complemented/restricted by* NG

NG *is composed/consists of* NG

NG *is due to* NG etc.

But it is the nominalisation itself that particularly distinguishes technical grammar (and written language as a whole) from the grammar of the spoken language (see **3.2**), often on the basis of what Halliday (1994:353) calls **grammatical metaphor**. This starts from the premise that the verb system provides the lexis to describe processes, actions or states:

1 When you instal a new flywheel housing, you must position it...
2 Manufacturers have drastically changed the materials they select.
3 The most common cause of engine trouble is contaminants in the system.

(adapted from Johnson 1988:10,5,18)

Technical texts, however, often nominalise processes and actions, so that the above examples might be expressed as:

1 The flywheel housing installation position must be ensured...
2 Major shifts in material selection can be observed
3 System contamination-based engine trouble is...

Notice that in the case of 2, a **material process**, where something happens, has been transformed into a **mental process** (*observed*). Such nominalisations may also be connected by the metaphorical use of a verb:

Successful growth requires constant sunlight.

The processes involved – '(plants) growing successfully' and 'the sun shining constantly' – have been compressed into noun phrases linked by a single verb (*require*). This kind of transformation does not necessarily cause translation difficulties as similar processes exist to a certain extent in both English and Italian but, as observed in Chapter One, the **noun strings** so typical of technical English have to be unravelled in Italian in a different way. In fact, the mechanism by which English creates its own particular form of noun-only strings to form extended nominal groups provides scientific language with compact, meaning-dense nominalisations that form the stepping stones of scientific discourse. They form the theme element of clauses, the 'points of departure' in the information structure. Typically, they gather together data provided in previous clauses and pack it up in a noun group of 'given' information before the discourse goes on to provide new material in theme patterns described by Lemke (1990:203) as 'webs of semantic relations'.

a) Later-model computers are provided with the capability of handling numerous input devices directly. These multitask computers treat the incoming data in much the same way as the earlier computers did. Incoming data is received from the various input devices and is lined up.

(Johnson 1988:81)

b) Energy occurs in several forms. A familiar example is the energy a moving body possesses by virtue of its motion. Every moving object has the capacity to do work.

(Johnson 1988:29)

In a), the theme/given pattern is evident, but also in b) the point of departure is *energy*, picked up again in the succeeding clause by *A familiar example* (of energy), while body and motion are neatly subsumed in *Every moving object* in the third sentence.

The greater nominal content of technical writing inevitably means that the lexical density of such texts is higher than in the more prevalently verbal non-technical texts. Lexical density can measure either the proportion of lexical words to function words or the proportion of lexical words to the number of clauses in a text.

The gaseous products of volcanic activity include water vapour, carbon dioxide, nitrogen, hydrogen and various sulphur compounds. The most prominent constituent is water vapour.

(Yates 1988:111)

This short extract contains seventeen lexical words compared to six function words in two clauses and a comparison can be made with a non-technical, narrative text of similar length, also containing direct speech:

On the school bus going home she whispered in my ear, "That was because of us, wasn't it! – what happened to that woman."

(Oates 1994:5)

The non-technical text contains seven lexical words and sixteen function words in three clauses.

As Halliday (1988:164) pointed out with his 'crack growth rate' example, a sort of evolution can be plotted from the spontaneously verbal to the totally nominalised, as the strings of nouns and qualifiers compress the knowledge of entities and processes into single units:

a) glass cracks more quickly the harder you press it
b) cracks in glass grow faster the more pressure is put on
c) glass crack growth is faster if greater stress is applied
d) the rate of glass crack growth depends on the magnitude of the applied stress
e) glass crack growth rate is associated with applied stress magnitude

Whereas in a) the sentence can be parsed as:

(Noun Group + Verb Group + Adverb Group) +
(Adverb Group + Noun Group + Verb Group + Noun Group),

by e) the parsing is reduced to:

(Noun Group + Verb Group + Noun Group),

the first noun group being a four-noun string, the second a string consisting of one adjectivised verb and two nouns. Pinchuck (1977:166) also explains how the sources of vocabulary for technical discourse are varied and go beyond the noun and noun group to also include compounds (*sphygmo-oscillometer*), derivatives (*inelasticity*), new applications of words in the general lexicon (*force*), neologisms (*digital TV*), borrowings and loans (*software*).

At the macro level, the fact that technical texts conform to certain conventionalised patterns has been demonstrated by various authors (Trimble 1985, Widdowson 1978, 1979). Indeed, the presence of pre-existing schemes makes the author's (and the reader's) work much easier. All doctors are familiar with the typical structure of a medical trials paper:

Introduction
Objectives
Materials and Methods
Discussion and Results
Conclusion

Similar, though less explicit, stages have been identified for other types of technical text. For example, in the field of economics, a typical pattern has been observed and presented as a series of moves (Salvi 1996):

1 establish field
2 summarise previous research
3 introduce present research
4 conclude

Specialist readers expect information to be presented in this way. They expect the typical formulae of analysis/prediction, cause/effect, comparison/ contrast, etc., to be contained within these structures. Fortunately for the translator, such pre-existing patterns are seen to be fairly universal, though it must be said that small variations can be observed; in the case of the above breakdown of economic texts, for example, the 'conclusion' in English is seen to be typically much shorter and less comprehensive than in Italian. But in spite of these particularised reservations, a series of broad characteristics help to give a sense of intertextual coherence to technical text, and it is extremely important to recognise and then maintain the appropriate register across languages. While it is also true to say that marked differences of a lexical and syntactic nature can be identified within one single scientific text (e.g. a school text book that ranges from expository discourse to experimental reports to quotations from world-famous scientists to 'question and answer' format to statistical presentation), the important thing to discover is whether these differences form a recognisable pattern and therefore together form a recognisable text type consisting of a number of variously-defined sub-text types. (This point will be taken up again in **3.5** in the discussion of macro and micro genres.)

3.4.3 Legal texts

The overriding consideration in the legal language of any idiom is that it be flawless and therefore not betray the fundamental rights of any person or group. The consequent scrupulous attention paid to making sure that legal text is hermetic and unambiguous is one of the main reasons for its at times seemingly impenetrable, syntactically complex nature, full of apparent redundancy. For translators this is both a blessing and a curse in that they cannot make mistakes, but the guidelines are rigid; there is little or no room for creative interpretation. In a sense, the language of law lies across foreign tongues and the job of translators is to shift elements of legal linguistics across foreign languages without necessarily conforming to reciprocal lexical or grammatical patterns. The fact that legal systems differ between nations and cultures (cf: English common law and Italian constitutional law) can make any kind of matching approximate:

> English law is the historical source of the common law group of
> legal systems ... The Common Law legal family is altogether
> different in its characteristics from the Romano-Germanic family.
>
> (Garzone, Miglioli, Salvi 1995:3)

But once equivalents are found, then consistency is paramount.

Each (legal) language displays particular uses of lexis, grammar and rhetorical style which can (and must) be 'matched' with items that would not be considered to 'match' in other contexts: the translation of *statement of defence* involves neither the term *dichiarazione* nor *difesa*, as might be expected in other circumstances, but *replica del convenuto*. In terms of grammar, the use of elaborate hypotactic constructions is universal. There is, for example, widespread use of conditional clauses introduced by *if/ should/where (qualora/dovesse/laddove)*, reflecting the cautious nature of legal decision making. The present (and present perfect) tenses are prevalent, in addition to the **deontic** *shall/dovrà, dovranno* where the obligations of law are concerned.

> Upon receipt of any order by the agent for goods the said agent shall immediately transmit the above mentioned order to the principal ...
>
> (Strutt 1992:119)

Stylistically, there is much repetition or partial repetition, a resort to capital letters and other emphatic devices to stress the importance of the key figures in a legal text:

> All rights reserved. No part of this publication may be reproduced, stored in a retrieval system, or transmitted, in any form or by any means, electronic, mechanical, photocopying, recording, or otherwise, without the prior permission of the publishers.
>
> Senza il permesso scritto dell'Editore, sono vietati la produzione anche parziale, in qualsiasi forma e con qualsiasi mezzo elettronico o meccanico (compreso fotocopie e microfilm), la registrazione magnetica e l'uso di qualunque sistema di meccanizzazione e reperimento dell'informazione.
>
> (in Ulrych 1992:265)

The tone is archetypally impersonal, often ritualistically conventional:

> In accordance with Article 3, sub-section (d), clause 13a ...
>
> circolare Murst prot. 1433 dd. 10/6/1997

The syntactic format of a legal text is similarly rigidly organised in paragraphs, with appropriate punctuation consisting of a frequent use of colons, semi-colons, numbers and spacing.

But it is perhaps in the realm of lexis that most people identify a particular variety of language in legal text. The first items to come to mind may be the archaic terms so typical of English juridical jargon:

whereas/permesso che
whereby/per cui, per la qual cosa
thereby/a causa di ciò, in merito
henceforth/d'ora in avanti
hereinafter/d'ora in poi, ai sensi del (presente contratto)
hereto/qui, a questo
in witness thereof/in fede di ciò
the aforesaid/di cui sopra

Most of these have a conjunctional function, along with other items of formal, not yet archaic terminology:

whilst
nevertheless
although

Many terms are used exclusively, or predominantly, within a legal context:

to sue/citare, far causa
warrant/ingiunzione, mandato, ordine
summons (n)/mandato di comparizione
binding/vincolante
to enact/emanare
default/inosservanza, inadempimento

Others can be seen to belong to the legal and other sectors (e.g. commerce, science):

mortgage/ipoteca
merger/fusione
patent/brevetto

Moving from vocabulary items to more extended locutions, similar observations can be made. Formulaic expressions of a ritualistic or **performative** nature are used, even to link various parts of the discourse:

given that/dato che
in the event of/nel caso di
it is hereby certified/certifica
I, the undersigned, .../Il sottoscritto ...

In spite of the formal nature of the language, a number of verb + preposition constructions are also to be found in English legal documents:

to lay down (regulations)/formulare
pertaining to/in riferimento a, riguardo a
to provide for/provvedere, prevedere

The distinction between English legal discourse and ordinary English discourse is greater than that between Italian legal language and ordinary Italian. The balancing of registers is thus more complex than in, say, scientific text. For example, a number of fossilised expressions are to be found, along with expressions of foreign or classical origin:

> ordinary care and skill /diligenza del buon padre di famiglia
> without let or hindrance/senza (alcun) impedimento
> malice aforethought/premeditazione
> force majeure/forza maggiore
> inter alia

All the examples listed above are, however, unambiguous and are retrievable on demand (either mentally or from a dictionary or data bank). The translator must also be aware, however, of the many lexical collocations inherent to legal language:

> to claim damages/chiedere risarcimento
> to commit for trial/rinviare a giudizio
> to draft a bill/redigere un progetto di legge

Another particularly common phenomenon in legal text is the frequent use of twinned terms, which may be nouns, verbs, adjectives, adverbs and even prepositions, which do not usually find their equivalents in similar twinnings:

> rights and privileges/diritti
> aid and abet/essere complice
> whereupon and wherefore/al che
> goods and chattels/ogni sorta di beni mobili
> null and void/nullo

In spite of the previously-mentioned universality of legal language, each individual language also contains examples of culture-bound terminology that can create translation problems. Examples (also used outside strictly legal circles, for example in detective stories) include terms referring to juridical rank, where the ranking systems differ: *barrister* (British English), *attorney*, *prosecutor* (both British and American English with different shades of meaning), *avvocato*, *procuratore*, *pubblico ministero*. Viezzi (1996:99) tackles the translation problems that can arise with *attorney*:

> 'Attorney' is a term to be handled with care as it has different
> meanings (and, as has already been mentioned, it also has different
> meanings on the two shores of the Atlantic). When used alone, the
> term is a contraction of the complete form 'attorney-at-law' and

refers to anyone practicing the legal profession. In the United
States the attorney-at-law 'may exercise all the functions of the
English barrister, attorney, and solicitor' (Walker 1980:93). The
attorney is therefore 'un avvocato'. The use of the word
'procuratore' to refer to an attorney-at-law is not unjustified,
though, as in Italy a 'procuratore' ('procuratore legale' in its
complete form) is someone who, with some limitations, may
'rappresentare la parte in giudizio in cause civili ... e penali'
(Vocabolario della lingua italiana 1986).

While legal language would appear to be freer than most text types from the
influence of time and fashion, the economic and political progress of
Europe towards ever greater unification is resulting in a wider spread of
Euro legal language, and this trend can be expected to continue, with vast
amounts of legal documentation being translated into all the languages of
the member countries. An example in English and Italian:

Policy of the Community
Title I – Common Rules

CHAPTER I – RULES ON COMPETITION
Section I – Rules Applying to Undertakings

Article 85

1. The following shall be prohibited as incompatible with the common
market: all agreements between undertakings, decisions by associations
of undertakings and concerted practices which may affect trade between
Member States and which have as their object or effect the prevention,
restriction or distortion of competition within the common market, and in
particular those which:

a. directly or indirectly fix purchase or selling prices or any other trading
conditions, etc.

Politica della Comunità
Titolo I – Norme Comuni

CAPO I – REGOLE DI CONCORRENZA
Sezione I – Regole Applicabili alle Imprese

Articolo 85

1. Sono incompatibili con il mercato comune e vietati tutti gli accordi tra
imprese, tutte le decisioni di associazioni d'imprese e tutte le pratiche
concordate che possano pregiudicare il commercio tra Stati Membri e che

abbiano per oggetto e per effetto di impedire, restringere o falsare il gioco della concorrenza all'interno del mercato comune ed in particolare quelli consistenti nel:

a. fissare direttamente o indirettamente i prezzi d'acquisto o di vendita, ovvero altre condizioni di transazione, ecc.

Furthermore, the law is polymorphic and legal texts must be subdivided into a series of subtypes which may have an informative, technical, scholarly or pragmatic register (see analysis of specific genre 'contract' in Part Two). British English legal language differs from American (cf: French and French Canadian) and all legal texts contain in any case a host of elements appertaining to the standard language. Nonetheless, the above brief over-view of some of the micro-elements of the broad text type should suffice to show its level of specificity and where translators should be looking in their efforts to transpose the dictates of one law into another.

Strutt's 'Longman Business English Usage' (1992:119), referring to the need for students of business and commerce to be familiar with legal terminology, actually provides an example of a typical text 'translated' intralingually:

Upon receipt of any order by the agent for goods the said agent shall immediately transmit the above-mentioned order to the principal who (if such order is accepted by the principal) shall execute the same by supplying the goods direct to the customer.

When the agent gets an order for goods he/she must send it off to the principal who will then supply the goods if he/she wants to.

This may be a useful academic exercise, but the translator would then have to translate the demystified version into suitably arcane legal target language. The example does, however, lead the discussion neatly into the next section dealing with commercial language.

3.4.4 Commercial texts

Although commercial or business language, like the other categories discussed in this section, overlaps considerably with other areas, particularly the legal field (contracts, commercial litigation, etc.), it displays sufficient specificity to be considered as a broad separate classification. Indeed, much effort has gone into presenting commercial language as a separate entity in the field of language teaching. The market offers a great many textbooks, course books and multimedia applications facilitating the study of this text type as a distinct discipline. Official examinations in this broad subject have been established by bodies such as the Cambridge University Local Examinations Syndicate (the Certificate in English for International Business and Trade) and the London Chamber of Commerce (English for Business, English for Commerce).

Essentially, the commercial English that differs from other categories is to be found in the stylised 'sub-types' that permit communication in the business world, namely commercial letters, faxes, memos, reports and the like: the practical language of buying and selling. For example, the layout of the standard business letter is as follows:

24 High St.
Newcastle
NE46 4AB

29 March 1998

Mr J. Smith
28 Broom St.
Hexham
NE71 25V

Dear Mr Smith (or) Dear Sir/Madam
re. late payments

....
....
....
....

Yours sincerely (or) Yours faithfully (if person not known)

Ena Brown
Sales Manager

(adapted from Mellor & Davison 1994:143)

Within the letter itself, a number of typical constructions can be identified. If it is a reply it will begin with *Thank you for your letter of* ... and any correspondence will probably end with *I look forward to hearing from you* or *Please acknowledge receipt* ... . In between, typical strategies include the following:

I am writing to you to .../Le scrivo per ...
We wish to inform you that .../Desideriamo informarLa che ...
I should be very grateful if you could (confirm, send, etc.)/Le sarei grato
  per (la conferma, l'invio, ecc.)

I feel I must point out .../Faccio notare che ...

A meeting will be held ... to discuss/Si terrà una riunione al fine di discutere

Our company is planning to expand .../La nostra società intende espandersi ...

Please let us know if you require further information/Se avete bisogno di ulteriori informazioni, fatecelo sapere.

Some typical extracts from Italian business correspondence are provided by Codeluppi (1997):

Vi trasmettiamo in allegato .../Please find included ...

Vogliate cortesemente inviarci il Vs. catalogo e il listino prezzi/Would you be so kind as to send us your catalogue and a price list

I nuovi prezzi entrano in vigore .../The new prices come into force ...

Siamo disposti a soddisfare la Vostra richiesta .../We are ready to meet your request ...

The overt politeness is reinforced, particularly in English which lacks the polite *Lei* or *Voi* form, by a more than casual use of the conditional tense and set expressions such as *I should be very grateful ...*, *I look forward to hearing from you ...*, etc. The *Dear Sir/Madam, Yours Sincerely, Distinti saluti* set of conventions are obligatory elements, examples of what the individual cultures have ritualised.

With modern improvements in communication technology, a practice has developed recently of sending letters in the form of faxes before they are sent by post: theoretically, there should be zero difference in the two modes of communication. However, when a fax is sent in lieu of a letter it may betray certain differences in form and style. Not enough evidence has been accumulated yet to identify fax-writing (or e-mail-writing) as fully-fledged types or 'genres' within the wider text type of correspondence, but observation suggests that faxing leads to a less formal approach than letter-writing and to a tendency to write in note form rather than in extended prose. Electronic mail messages tend to be low on formal or phatic content. In this sense, they represent a half-way stage between a letter and a memo.

The memo is much shorter and to the point than a letter, its purpose being to communicate a particular message as efficiently as possible, though maintaining a level of politeness. A memo from an office manager to a company's representatives, informing them that a new supply of company-headed writing paper, note pads and ball-point pens embossed with the company's name and address has arrived, and is to be given to customers, would look like this:

> To: all representatives
> From: Miss J. Treadgold, Office Manager
> Subject: Ordering of company-headed stationery
> Date: 1/1/98
> The supply of company-headed writing paper, note pads and ball pens embossed with the company's name and address will be available from next Tuesday from my office. These are to be distributed to customers.
>   All representatives should decide how many of these items they require. I need to have all orders on my desk in writing by next Monday at the latest.

(Mellor & Davison 1994:3)

A memo usually imparts instructions or complaints and contains linguistic strategies such as:

> With reference to .../In riferimento a ...
> It has come to my attention that .../Mi è stato fatto notare che ...
> Please make sure that .../Vogliate assicurarvi che ...
> I would like you to take care of the following .../Vogliate occuparvi delle
>   seguenti ...
> Please note .../Ricordate che ...

The business report, finally, is a stylised example of a text type which follows a certain logical development. This can be summarised as the setting out of a task (usually commissioned by some person, typically the boss), a description of procedure, and a presentation of results and concluding remarks, usually presaging suggestions for improvement or future development. The language of a report must be neutral and restricted to factual presentation, often in an itemised way: *a) ... b)* ..., etc. In many ways the reporting methodology resembles that required for scientific experimentation, with much use of the passive voice, copular verbs and nominalisation. For example:

> The product was tested in four different areas. The test assessments were the following:
> Area 1:...
> Area 2:...

All the above examples are merely illustrative and serve to show that the writer of commercial texts has to work within certain prescribed limits. Most of the examples are taken from English, though Italian has its corresponding formulae. Rather than translation in the narrowest sense, what is required in this field is a sensitivity to the norms so as to be able, as a translator, to know that *I acknowledge receipt* is *Accuso ricevuta* and *I look forward to hearing from you* is best served by *In attesa di una Sua gentile risposta*. These equivalents admit of little variation or deviation. More than in many other fields, the translator can simply look at the original and then rewrite it according to the target language commercial norms, at times overriding more apparently equivalent lexical choices and grammatical structures.

3.4.5 Journalistic texts

The term 'journalistic' may still raise a few eyebrows amongst linguistic purists but most new dictionaries carry it, and as a term it is useful in distinguishing textual material which is actually written by journalists (news reports, editorials, special features) from all the other linguistic elements that make up a modern newspaper. Advertising, horoscopes, weather reports, crossword puzzles, business reports, racing results, cartoons, film reviews, agony aunt columns, obituaries and letters to the editor are but a few examples. Though of little direct interest to translators, they represent very distinct 'types' in their own right, bringing us closer to the concept of genre. Fries (1995:320), for example, shows how obituaries, news reports and letters to the editor differ already in their theme patterning quite apart from lexicogrammatical distinctions. He explains how an obituary is characterised by theme **iteration** where the progressive themes refer in turn to the deceased, the service, the funeral, the burial, and so on. He also points out that such differences exist between news reporting and editorials, showing that genre distinctions are observable even among the truly 'journalistic' material. Well-written editorials and features will display many of the creative characteristics of literary text, and in the tabloid variety of newspaper, amusing (though often predictably banal) word play and colloquiality accompany most articles. Consider the following extracts from articles dealing with an incident that occurred at Glyndebourne opera, found respectively in a quality newspaper and in a popular newspaper (see Grundy, 1993:67-8):

> Kurt Streit, the American tenor, needed stitches to his face after he allegedly became too friendly with his leading lady and her boyfriend hit him, it was disclosed yesterday.

Mr Streit, who plays Ferrando in Trevor Nunn's Glyndebourne production of Mozart's Così Fan Tutte, embraced the soprano Amanda Roocroft, 24, who plays Fiordiligi, as part of the plot.
But her boyfriend, David Ellis, 22, a singer in the chorus … was watching from the wings.
A confrontation with Mr Streit during the after-show party … ended in blows.

HE'S TOO COSÌ WITH MY GIRL
Passion and jealousy spilled over into real life after a rehearsal for the posh Glyndebourne opera. Humble chorus singer David Ellis watched in the wings as girlfriend Amanda Roocroft's embrace with star Kurt Streit lingered a little too long.
The grand finale came at an opening party for Così Fan Tutte, Mozart's masterpiece about unfaithful women and jealous men.
Ellis punched the hunky American tenor when he kissed Amanda farewell at the restaurant party in Nether Wallop.

The quality paper maintains a sober approach and assumes a certain knowledge of opera characters and directors on the part of the readership. The popular paper merely describes Glyndebourne opera as *posh*. It plays on the Italian word *così* through its graphic similarity with the English *cosy*, and adopts the colloquial *hunky*, more commonly ascribed to handsome film stars, to describe a singer.

However, the most representative genre within the blanket text type 'journalism' is the informative news report: Crystal and Davy (1969:173) point out that 'the central function of a newspaper is to inform'. And the most striking characteristics of this kind of journalistic text, at least in the English language press, are those elements that are clearly visible every time a newspaper is read. The different fonts, colours and letter sizes that distinguish: 1 major headlines from minor headlines (leads), 2 leads from the various other sub-headings, and 3 all the various headlines from the main text, make newspaper layout easily recognisable among most other written text forms. The format adopted is also important in terms of the pragmatic presentation of information. Using the visual metaphor of an inverted pyramid, the most important items of information in any newspaper report are presented first, in the various headlines and in the opening sentences of the text. It is understood that many readers often progress no further than these initial stages in their perusal of the news, and that the later stages are often liable to be trimmed by editors. This strategy has the advantage of concentrating information into easily-accessible 'chunks', but it is also open to the more dubious practice of overloading a headline with copious data that is misleading in terms of the whole context of an article. The translator, therefore, needs to be aware of these conventions, which may not be mirrored in languages other than English. In fact, White (1997:3), while showing that 'the contemporary lead-dominated news story of English language journalism' is so much the norm as to be 'the way news writing is most usually taught in journalism training programs', analyses an article from the French daily Figaro. His conclusion is that the French article

> demonstrates that the 'standard' generic structure of the hard-news report as taught in English-language journalistic training programs may not apply so universally or so naturally across cultures. The 'Figaro' report (of the IRA attack on the British Tory Party conference) is clearly not an example of the lead-dominated, 'inverted pyramid' structure promulgated by English-language journalistic training texts.

However, English journalism continues to adopt this strategy, and various kinds of 'shorthand' have been devised to create headlines and leads. This encapsulating of information in limited spaces may owe something to journalists' traditional note-taking techniques, where brevity was, and remains, a very important factor, though editors seem to have perfected the style.

Any seemingly redundant grammatical items may be removed. For example, the article:

> Channel rail link decision this week
>
> (The Independent 15/3/93)

copular verbs:

> Fresh fruit the pick of the bunch this week
>
> (The Times 29/7/94)

connectives:

> The company facing death by bureaucracy
>
> (The Daily Telegraph 29/8/94)

possessives:

> Mother tells of baby's death at hospital
>
> (The Independent 23/3/93)

The concentration of information in the various headline forms does however conform to certain patterns. Downing (1997) studied to what extent headlines and leads availed themselves of **finite verb** structures and to what extent they used nominalisations, the latter being a particularly efficient way of encapsulating and condensing information. One conclusion, however, backed by numerous examples, was that it is extremely common to find finite verb structures in headlines, with nominalisations of the same information only in the leads:

> *Headline*: Planners compete to rebuild bombed city
> *Lead*: The multi-million pound rebuilding ...
>
> *Headline*: America closes tourism office
> *Lead*: The decision to close the United States Travel and Tourism Administration ...

Either way, the concentration of information at the beginning of the article/report has repercussions on the theme/rheme structure of the journalistic text. White's study, mentioned above, shows how the news story departs from the classic, chronological narrative that presents information according to the following pattern:

> theme A + rheme A,
> theme B (= rheme A) + rheme B,
> theme C (= rheme B) + rheme C
> etc.

Rarely does a text progress consistently smoothly in this way, but there is a general tendency in narratives to present information in more or less this linear fashion. The news story, on the other hand, follows an orbital pattern, that is most clauses in the text refer back directly to the headline and lead. In this way a **hypertheme** is created in the headlines, stressing even further the importance of those initial stages.

The tabloid press exploits this strategy to an even greater extent than the quality press, possibly owing to the fact that many readers are not looking for lengthy news items, but also to the fact that it is a convenient way of creating sensationalism. The less detailed the study of a news item, the easier it is to make it seem exciting, usually at the expense of any semantic rigour. Apart from the information density, the kind of language found in tabloid headlines and leads is distinctive in that it transcends the **common core** of language, which is largely found, on the other hand, in the main text. Thus the headlines contain the kind of lexis that has 'marked associations' (Carter 1996:10), creating the sensational effects that help to sell the papers. Witness the now notorious examples from The Sun, aimed respectively at the Argentine government during the Falklands/Malvinas War and at the European Community President: *Up your Junta!*; *Up Yours Delors!*

Having seen that French news reporting does not necessarily follow the English model, and this is even truer of more diverse cultures, it would be instructive to observe how news is reported in the Italian press. In fact, many of the characteristics of the English model can be observed in Italian newspapers, though not always to the same extent, and there are also some net differences. Firstly, the headlining system is often more elaborate, consisting of an 'occhiello' (or pre-headline), a headline proper and a sub-headline, though these fulfil much the same function as the English model.

A more marked difference can be identified in terms of projection, or the reporting of speech. Newspapers regularly quote direct or indirect participants in the events they report, but this phenomenon takes on a particular guise in the headline system. Speech is reported by journalists for three basic reasons according to Bell (1991:207):

1 a quote is valued as a particularly incontrovertible fact
2 to distance and to disown, to absolve the journalist
3 to add to the story the flavour of the newsmaker's own words

and the tripartite Italian headlining system gives ample scope for this device. It is consequently statistically more common in Italian reports. However, it is often far from clear whether the quote is genuine or not: very often the writer simply interprets the participant's words or feelings. In the following 'occhiello' the quotation does seem to be directly attributable to Lega Nord leader, Umberto Bossi:

> Il leader della Lega si corregge dicendo che 'in ogni accordo bisogna dare per ricevere qualche altra cosa'.
>
> (Corriere della Sera 28/2/94, in Ondelli, 1995:263)

However, in the following case from the same source, the attribution of the quote is much less certain, in spite of the inverted commas, and seems to be more of an interpretation of events:

> Tornati in libertà, i capi della rivolta di ottobre in Russia rilanciano la sfida al Cremlino.
> 'ELTSIN, NON HAI PIU' FUTURO!'

Whether genuine or contrived, in both languages it is a way of creating interpersonal communication between writer and reader by exploiting many of the characteristics of the spoken language. Unlike the examples above, when English journalists use this method, they tend to postplace the speaker:

> It's time for IRA truce, says Adams.
>
> (Daily Telegraph 30/8/94, in Ondelli, 1995:264)

Alternatively, they quote single key words:

> IRA dismisses truce as 'unworkable'.

The more widespread use of quoting in Italian also reveals itself, for example, in the common use of the first person pronoun, the use of the first names of important persons, and the use of questions to create a kind of dialogue:

> Sono gay, prego Dio di farmi morire
> Helmut, l'inamovibile
> E adesso chi governa?

English journalists, at least those of the quality press, seem to be more reticent about reaching such a high degree of intimacy.

The Italian informal 'dialogue', at least in headlines, is marked by grammatical features such as cleft sentences, the use of the generic third person plural, the *che* exclamative, the *Cosa?* interrogative and the use of general lexical items such as *cosa*, *storia*, *affare* and the ubiquitous verb *fare*. It is also marked by a more than casual frequency of colloquial terms, though the main text then continues in much more sober tone.

In Britain, as mentioned before, it is the tabloid press that exploits the more colloquial and 'oral' mode in its presentation of news, though to a greater degree and to a much baser level than the Italian dailies. Italy has its equivalents to the English popular press in a series of weekly magazines (Novella 2000, Intimità, etc.) which adopt the same sensationalising approach, and many of the scandalous contents of this popular press, both English and Italian, are quite frequently to be found translated. The same salacious style should be maintained and arranged around the usually revealing photographs that accompany such texts. At a more serious level, the journalistic registers found in Corriere della Sera or The Guardian, apart from the differences outlined in this section, show much similarity, and it is this register that must be recognised and maintained.

3.4.6 Advertising texts

Advertising text, by its very nature, deals with a vast range of subject matter but also conforms to a number of stylistic and lexicogrammatical patterns. In terms of function, the informative role of advertising is becoming ever more peripheral in an era of conspicuous consumption. An advertisement is designed mainly to attract attention, not to impart knowledge. Indeed, some products (e.g. cigarettes) are now advertised with zero wording. However, where wording appears, notwithstanding how banal it may seem, it will usually have involved considerable cost in terms of advertising consultancy fees. The thought that goes into successful publicity suggests that a substantial expressive element can be imputed to advertising discourse along with the obvious vocative, persuasive component. The well-reputed British Sunday newspaper The Independent on Sunday considers advertising text sufficiently interesting to run a weekly column reviewing the best 'ads'.

While the message may be simple, it is likely to contain, for example, some form of **mnemonic** pattern provided by phonological equivalences such as alliteration, rhyme, **onomatopoeia** and so on, or striking repetition or reiteration of some description.

DRINKA
PINTA
MILKA
DAY

BEANZ
MEANZ
HEINZ

FRESCHISSIMA, LIMPIDISSIMA, ... LEVISSIMA

If the texts are a little longer, they can be expected to display the features associated with spoken language (low lexical density, use of generic terms, repetition, verbalisation), even if they are written. Another of the important characteristics of spoken language is that it is more rhythmic; it is also easier to access and more interpersonal. Advertisements may even contain extended stretches of typically spoken language such as stories or anecdotes. Being more verbal in nature, this broad language type is more dynamic and more likely to attract attention. The verbs are usually of the everyday familiar type, in English often of Anglo-Saxon derivation.

> Buy now ... Pay September
> Venite anche voi
> Be among the winners (*dynamic* be).

As clearly demonstrated by these examples, the persuasive nature of advertising language means that the imperative mood will be chosen with a higher than usual frequency.

In line with the spoken mode, incomplete sentence structures are common:

non-finites:

> How to relieve tension.
> Acquario di Genova. Tante code da ammirare, nessuna da fare.

disjunctive grammar:

> Tomorrow in the Daily Telegraph. A-Z of Science.
> Con Panorama le videocassette.

verbless clauses:

> The taste of real coffee. Rich. Smooth. Mellow.
> (see Leech 1966)
> Honda Accord. Spirito di Ricerca.

Texts are essentially organised in terms of logical relations in one of two ways – parataxis or hypotaxis. As mentioned earlier in **3.2**, hypotactic sentences consist of notions organised hierarchically in terms of main and subordinate clauses. Paratactic sentences, more typical of the spoken mode, keep each clause on an equal footing through the use of conjunctions or punctuation, thereby simplifying the presentation of information and ideas. The parataxis evident, for example, in the 'coffee' example above is a typical device of advertising copy. Other grammatical features include a widespread use of deictics, especially the personal pronouns and possessives *you, your,* etc., in order to engender a sense of shared knowledge:

> Is your hair thinner than it was a year ago?
> La tua prima Mitsubishi

There is also an extensive use of adjectives to describe products and, by logical extension, much use of comparatives and superlatives to show how such products compare favourably to others:

> The ultimate word processor.
> The new, longer, wider Peugeot 106.
> Freschissima, limpidissima ...

The previously-mentioned financial commitment involved in advertising also suggests that advertising copy should contain something special, something worth paying for, and this calls for a degree of creativity. Some of the most successful advertising slogans, however deceptively banal, are often the result of many hours of creative endeavour:

1 Guinness is good for you
2 The United Colours of Benetton
3 La più amata dagli italiani

In the case of 1, the *g* alliteration highlights the deliberate ambiguity in the meaning of the word *good* (delicious and healthy). Example 2 exploits the iconic side of the medium as it is always accompanied by a creative, eye-catching, and often controversial, photograph, whereas 3 picks up on a slogan first used to describe a beautiful woman and relies on shared knowledge and intertextuality to transfer the image to kitchen furniture.

The above examples merely highlight the importance of the use of some creative kind of word play in advertising: metaphor, **simile**, idiom, **metonym**, **pun**, invention, etc.

Amica è un viaggio fuori e dentro di te.
Speak freely. Vodaphone's new digital tariff.

Purely lexically speaking, advertising relies a great deal on lexical cohesion in order to provide a cohesive and, more importantly, coherent message to its audience. A more elaborate advertisement for Mitsubishi cars demonstrates this aspect:

My mother wanted me to have piano lessons.
My father wanted me to go to Harvard.
My teacher wanted me to become a lawyer.
My wife wants me to stay at home.
. . .
Mitsubishi Motors.

The lexical cohesion consists of simple repetition (*wanted me to . . .*) and more subtle reiteration in the grouping of the various authoritative figures *mother, father, teacher, wife*(!) and the connecting semantic field of bourgeois pursuits.

In conclusion, the main characteristics that stand out in any discussion of advertising discourse are those relating to the expressive potential of the general text type. This puts the translator in a similar position to that regarding literary texts. However, the fundamental difference is that an advert exploits the interpersonal, spoken mode, is short and generally with little co-text. The text usually appears outside of any pre-established context (except in the case of a series of advertisements for the same product) and will generally be of brief existence. The translator needs to know the product being advertised and the potential buyers very well. This last point is very important in view of the fact that the public are targeted by advertisers. If a person is unmoved, or even irritated, by a single advertisement, then probably he or she has not been targeted. The level of sophistication in the business today means that few advertisements turn out to be total failures. Having established the qualities (real or imagined) of the product and the make-up of the readership, translators can then attempt a creative translation. Here, they are on their own, but an examination of similar texts in similar locations (be they billboards, glossy magazines, or television) in the two languages will show definite similarities in approach, and suggest that potential exists for successful transfer. This is not to say, however, that there are no important stylistic differences between languages associated with what appeals more to potential buyers within each individual culture. For example, English advertisements rely very heavily on humour (English humour), and thus there is much evidence of word play and intertextual allusion. Italian advertisers can be seen to place more attention on the aesthetic attributes of products in line with the Italian predilection for style and handsome presentation. This has consequences on translation options extending from macrostructural considerations (topic emphasis, description or parody?, length of exposition) to register problems regarding the degree of formality, solemnity and technicality to adopt. The same product can be advertised in different ways using different linguistic devices, but at this point the 'translation' would benefit from a joint approach involving the translator and the advertising consultant. Translators can do what they can with the words of the text, advertisers will do what they will with the result.

3.5   Genre

Having now looked at two broad ways of categorising texts, based on sociolinguistic considerations and general subject area respectively, it may still be argued that for certain purposes, including translation, these typologies are still too generic. Adopting now the term 'genre' in a more refined sense, it is possible to identify genres, sub-genres, and what Hatim (1990) calls 'genrelets' at much greater levels of **delicacy** (specific detail) than the text types so far discussed. In other words, if those text types are considered macro-genres, then there exists a whole complex network of sub-divisions of sub-types of those macro-genres. For example:

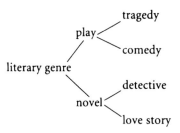

Hasan (1989) isolated a number of (sub) genres within the area of spoken language; one example was that of a '**service encounter**' consisting of a typical exchange at a greengrocer's shop (1989:59). She points out that this subgenre of a broad macrogenre (shopping) has a number of obligatory and optional features. The obligatory features include, for example, the Sale Request (*'Can I have ...?'*, *'Have you got ...?'*), which would also be general to all shopping genres, while optional features include such items as *'See you tomorrow'* and *'Can you change a £50 note?'*. It is, in particular, the obligatory features that allow us to identify a genre, though the optional elements are by no means necessarily random and form an important part of the generic structure. In the case of the above service encounter, a number of obligatory features common to the superordinate genre, such as the Sale Request, and a number of obligatory features more specific to the sub-genre in question (fruit and vegetable terminology) together map out the genre 'service encounter/greengrocers'.

Another example from the same source involves a legal document, a 'deed of transfer'. This can be considered a sub-type (a genrelet) of the genre 'contracts', itself a sub-genre under the general heading of legal language. The deed of transfer is described as a verbal regulation of social interaction through legal documentation. It is a means for an individual to address society through a pre-arranged method – a formula used for very specific purposes, and performative in nature (it transfers a property). Because of a number of pre-established (obligatory) features, a document of this kind forms an easily-recognisable genre.

As with the example of literary genres and sub-genres, and the above example of 'deed of transfer' within the wider legal language category, the field of journalism can also be represented in terms of a system network:

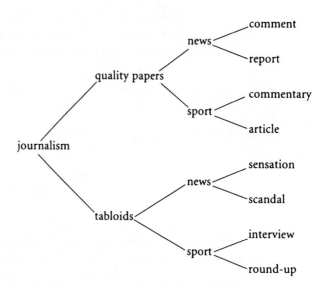

Working backwards, it can be seen that a sensational scoop (*Prime Minister sells off furniture at 10 Downing Street*) can be traced back through the system till it is encompassed by the broad genre of journalistic language or newspaper text. Thus, this sub-genre must contain some of the features of journalistic language before it can 'enter' the system labelled 'tabloids'; it must then take on some of the features of tabloids before progressing to 'tabloid news', and thence to 'sensational scoop' and so on. The broad genre can then be looked on as a starting point for a text, providing it with some basic features, which become in turn tuned to a greater specificity, the further into the system the text is located.

However, there will be more than one broad genre. In the above example, apart from being a journalistic text, the sensational scoop also belongs to the broad genre of written language (as opposed to spoken, written to be spoken, spoken to be written, etc.), and to the informative text type, perhaps with a dash of expressivity in the colourful portrayal of the news. These broad genres are mapped onto one another to create a set of features that can be easily recognised when they appear on the front page of The Sun or The Daily Mirror. This genre is therefore a hybrid, as many genres turn out to be.

Macro and micro genres may also be based, as suggested in **3.1**, on parameters such as function, style or 'register', as well as subject matter. However, the term 'register' now also requires a more refined definition. Several writers, in particular Halliday, have in fact equated register with genre, and this concept will now be analysed in this light.

3.5.1 Register

Register is one of the most important components of Halliday's functional grammar theory, and he describes it as the functional variation of language – 'variety according to use' (1985:43). The three variables of field, tenor and mode that make up the context of situation determine the register. It will be recalled (**2.2.1**) that field, tenor and mode refer respectively to 'what is happening', 'who is participating' and 'what role the language is playing' in any communicative situation. In other words, register refers to what a person is doing with language at any given moment (making a speech, telling someone how to cook eggs, encouraging a football team, writing a business memo, etc.) and it can be deduced that, at least theoretically, there are as many registers as there are distinct activities. The various contexts of situation contain the semantic potential to specify registers, and it is here that the similarity with Hasan's genre formulation is apparent.

At times, genres and their linguistic manifestations are very tightly circumscribed, for example in the case of the highly-restricted language of air-traffic controllers and football results announcers, but generally all (con)texts contain a high degree of intertextuality in that many grammatical structures, lexical items and stylistic configurations are common to all or many varieties, as all texts have to interact symbiotically in some way with the wider community. In order to qualify for genre status, we have seen that a text must include a minimum number of obligatory elements which distinguish it as a recipe, a car salesman's patter, a sermon, the rules of a boardgame, or whatever – elements that are recognised by participants in the social action.

Genres can also be interpreted by what they omit, in the sense that participants are so conditioned by the 'obligatory elements' that they can supply them when they are actually missing in the discourse. We do not need to know the particular participants or other elements of the immediate context of situation such as the time or the place of the drawing up and the signing of, for example, a deed of transfer, to be able to recognise it as a genre type. We would be able to recognise the obligatory elements from the template version of the document before the details are filled in. For example, an English gas bill looks very much like an Italian gas bill. It is the 'mode' element that is therefore important initially in the recognition of this type of text (the layout and presentation) suggesting that there is some connection between form and function; similar kinds of document used in similar situations (forms to be filled out in order to sanction some legal right) are recognised as such whatever the actual wording. Clearly, inter-personal features (the cold bureaucratic formality) and extralinguistic factors (the presence of a lawyer in an office, the presentation of the document in an official envelope, etc.) reinforce the genre as a 'social occasion'.

An indication of how easy it is to recognise genres is provided by the concept of the comic 'spoof', where an actor or comedian, or any so-minded individual, may imitate a particular genre situation such as the Queen addressing the public (*'My husband and I ...'*), a footballer answering questions (*'La palla è rotonda ...', 'Noi andiamo avanti per la nostra strada, ...'*), or a headmaster scolding a child, etc. Seen in this light, it can be said that genres in effect make up society, even to the extent of delimiting genre-based communities where textual and non-textual features combine. Linguistics and rhetoric help define social institutions – the 'Oasis' fan club, l'assemblea dei condomini, the Freemasons, each of which use a form of discourse containing obligatory features. Of course, these obligatory features may change over time through additions and elimina-tions. Young people's 'street' talk would be a good example of this dynamic element in the modes of discourse and patterns of communication of genre-specific language.

Consider the following extracts from an Italian magazine for teenage girls:

> E adesso a parlare è lei, GERI, la più discussa, la più desiderata (dai maschietti) la più osé delle Spice.
>
> Trova il tuo LOOK – TRUCCO DA GIORNO
> Questa settimana la protagonista del nostro 'prima e dopo' è Stefania, una Mag-girl di 15 anni.
>
> LA POSTA DI SUSY E PATTY
> Hi, sfolgoranti girls, eccoci di nuovo tutte insieme!
> Racconta gli attimi 'happy' vissuti con il pop che non dimenticherai mai!
>
> (Magazine 6/3/97)

Firstly, the subject matter of the magazine is predictable (pop personalities, clothes, boyfriends, etc.) but so also are questions of style. The syntactic equivalence in *la più ..., la più ..., la più ...* is dynamic. The cataphoric introduction *lei* is sufficient to grab the attention of an audience who have no difficulty in identifying *Geri* or the *Spice (Girls)*. The use of the intimate second person singular pronoun and first names is in line with teenage talk and the *nostro* shows that the magazine is very much a part of their world.

The slang *Mag-girl* forms part of the identity process. *Susy* and *Patty* (carefully-chosen names) show the penchant for using English terms, those in current use and others used for the occasion in inverted commas, which befits any discussion of pop music. These lexicogrammatical and stylistic elements are obligatorily found in virtually every issue of this magazine and others like it. Bex (1996:133) explains how the writer manages to maintain this genre style:

> In the construction of a given text my linguistic choices are constrained by the genre with which I want it to be associated.

In order to be in a position to translate such material, it is important to have knowledge of equivalent target language publications. This requires a greater degree of specialised background research than simply considering the characteristics of journalistic text.

It requires a sensitivity to what is known as the **discourse community**: it is possible to recognise sequences of language within the speech patterns of well-defined groups that transcend chance occurrence. Swales (1990) referred to such groups as 'discourse communities', that is, the people involved in a common task or event and the language they use in accomplishing that task or acting out that event. Everyone naturally belongs to many discourse communities at different times, and to varying degrees, and thus is constantly, and subconsciously, in contact with a wide range of genres. This range may however be limited by social or political factors. For example, the 'house mortgage agreement' genre would not be available to citizens in a society that did not allow private property, hence the difficulty of translating such documents into Russian or Chinese, at least until fairly recently. Swales (1996:47) also points out that people can be initiated into a discourse community, as for example when a new lecturer at a university is gradually introduced to the genres of 'writing research papers', then 'writing article reviews' and then, perhaps, 'writing job evaluation letters'.

The following are extracts from student compositions on secondary school reform:

> The Italian Minister of Education, Mr Berlinguer, has recently proposed a substantial change in the education system.
>
> But why should countries change their education system?
>
> On the other hand, the British system has always preferred early specialisation.

Again, a certain number of predictable features are identifiable: this kind of essay very frequently begins with a thematic noun phrase (e.g. the name of a person) or a time adverbial (e.g. *Recently ...*, *Over the last few years ...*) setting the scene. The rhetorical question is a much-used device, as is the comparison and contrast technique exemplified by *On the other hand*. Certain discourse markers appear with a much more than casual frequency (*However, Nevertheless, Indeed, Similarly*), as do expressions like *It must be remembered that ...*, *In spite of the fact that ...*, and negative adverbial phrases requiring inversion beginning with *Never ...*, *Only ...*, and so on. However, if the subject of the composition were some other controversial topic (the legalisation of soft drugs, the arguments for and against euthanasia, the role of referenda) these features would not change appreciably, except for the vocabulary. At this point it is possible to draw some boundaries and speak of the genre of 'student compositions on argumentative topics'.

It would also seem clear that the rationale behind the isolating of the student composition genre lies not only in the choice of grammatical constructions and lexis but on the text's function, the fact that the text is argumentative as opposed to informative or descriptive or narrative or aesthetically creative, and thus at a more abstract level. Bloor (1996:59) actually goes so far as to isolate three sub-genres of student writing, claiming that 'first year reports', 'final year project reports' and 'student newsgroups' display a sufficient number of distinct obligatory features to meet the requirements of genrehood, at the same time showing how new configurations can develop into genres. For example, she isolates a genre (1996:81) which she calls 'academic writing in computer science', pointing to its specificity in the following terms:

> The format and style of the writing is distinctive with respect to degrees of formality and lexical innovation, and it also appears that specific new genres are evolving in on-line communication ...
> many features are influenced by the spoken language and by input from members of other, highly influential, discourse communities that embody aspects of youth culture. This accounts for a high degree of informality incorporating graphic features, humour, and slang – features not traditionally associated with writing in an academic institution.

To show how the isolation of a macrogenre such as 'school composition' is insufficient to cover the various subgenres immediately associated with it,

Christie (1995) provides a breakdown of the literary essay based on compositions written by Australian secondary school pupils on Carson McCuller's 'To Kill a Mockingbird':

Stage One: Reconstruction of event
'Atticus was sitting on a swing'

Stage Two: Interpretation of characters' motives
'he thinks that Jem killed Ewell'

Stage Three: Judgement on character
'he's a recluse; she's so sweet'

Stage Four: Judgement on significance of event
'That's a beautiful moment'

Stage Five: Judgement on significance of book
'one of the things that moves me incredibly is how unfair life is'

Stage Six: Judgement on life
'life is about growing up, learning new things'

The approach is different to the argumentative composition while maintaining some features of the superordinate genre. It indicates the interface between two conceptions of genre based respectively on the style and the function.

Rega (1992:71) illustrates another kind of interface in showing how the 'microlingue' of economic language (budget reports, stock market bulletins, etc.) intertwine with the genres 'academic paper', 'newspaper article' and so on, which can then be categorised again in terms of description, exposition, etc. Hatim and Mason (1990) pare down even further this kind of genre depiction by expounding a model of context that brings together the communicative, pragmatic and semiotic values of a text. They first distinguish text types as, for example, argumentative, expository or instructive, but then investigate this breakdown further to identify sub-genres at this more abstract level. For example, an argumentative text may be based on 'through-argument' where an initial point is presented and defended, or on counterposition where an initial point is demolished. We can thus formulate different sets of parameters for categorising texts to set alongside or integrate with those based on subject matter and sociolinguistic factors. For the translator, the mapping of all the features so far considered will be automatic if he or she has an understanding of the equivalent genre in the target language. Otherwise it will have to be constructed, and it is here that the teaching of approaches to genre and text analysis are so important.

Going back over the various ways of isolating the different kinds and levels of text type or genre, but particularly to the equating of genre and register in the Hallidayan sense, once the salient characteristics of a genre-based text have been recognised and understood, 'we can translate different registers into a foreign language' (Halliday, 1994:137). Unlike sociolinguistic distinctions such as dialects, which are different ways of expressing the same thing, registers/genres are vehicles for saying different things. To use a blatantly obvious example, it is crucial for the translator to understand and recognise the vehicles used to express, for example, condolences to bereaved relatives, both in English and Italian, and to be able to distinguish them from those used to express birthday greetings.

If the translator can move from genre to genre, and within those genres from genrelet to genrelet at ever increasing levels of delicacy, even within the same extended text, then the lexicogrammatical, semantic and pragmatic considerations that were the focus of Chapters One and Two should fit into place. Human language has evolved to deal with the manifold areas of human endeavour and exchange, and it is the translator's job to provide the fine tuning that is needed to transfer a genre-based text in the source language as accurately and sensitively as possible into an equivalent text in the target language. If all the elements, obligatory or otherwise, of the genre are respected, translators will do their job well and provide a true rendering of meaning across a linguistic and cultural divide.

Chapter Three: Suggested further reading

Baccolini, R., Bollettieri Bosinelli, R.M. & Gavioli, L. (eds) 1994. *Il doppiaggio: trasposizioni linguistiche e culturali*. Bologna: CLUEB.

Beccaria, G.L. 1973. *I linguaggi settoriali in Italia*. Milan: Bompiani.

Cortelazzo, M.A. 1990. *Lingue speciali. La dimensione verticale*. Padua: Unipress.

Cortese, G. (ed.) 1996. *Tradurre i linguaggi settoriali*. Turin: Libreria Cortina.

Garzone, G., Miglioli, F. & Salvi, R. 1995. *Legal English*. Milan: EGEA.

Halliday, M.A.K. 1985. *Spoken and Written Language*.
    Oxford: Oxford University Press.

Hatim, B. & Mason, I. 1990. *Discourse and the Translator*. London: Longman.

Nida, E. 1996. *The Sociolinguistics of Interlingual Communication*.
    Brussels: Editions du Hazard.

Pinchuk, I. 1977. *Scientific and Technical Translation*. London: André Deutsch.

Swales, J.M. 1990. *Genre Analysis*. New York: Cambridge University Press.

Tannen, D. 1992. *You Just Don't Understand*. London: Virago.

Trimble, L. 1985. *English for Science and Technology*.
New York: Cambridge University Press.

Ventola, E. & Mauranen, A. (eds) 1996. *Academic Writing*.
Amsterdam & Philadelphia: John Benjamins.

Widdowson, H. 1979. *Explorations in Applied Linguistics*.
Oxford: Oxford University Press.

Part Two

Practice

The Process of Translating and 'The Rolling Translation'

Introduction

From even a cursory skimming of the lexicogrammatical, semantic, stylistic and cultural material discussed in the preceding chapters, the reader should be left with the clear impression that language activity does not take place in a vacuum, and that any language act must be considered in all its linguistic and extralinguistic aspects before being translated. However, any text taken individually must be considered on its individual merits, and text analysts or translators may wish to apply some of the above considerations and discard others depending on the text and context they are dealing with. The actual methodology adopted in the analysis of a text will then depend on the emphasis and the amount of detail they wish to apply.

The methodology outlined in this section will deal with translating both into and out of the translator's native language. In both cases, the translator is encouraged to create a 'pre-translation picture' of the text, a 'traduzione interna' (Arcaini 1986), by judiciously analysing its various features and by blending the relevant elements into one another to create a target text. That the above is as much a psychological task as a linguistic one has been demonstrated in recent years by work on the cognitive processes involved in translation. In the 1980s, with the advent of 'thinking aloud protocols' (TAPs), it became possible to track the thought processes of translators while they worked. Translators were encouraged in experiments to speak out loud the ideas that came into their heads while translating. One of the major exponents of this methodology, Hans Krings, published an article in 1987, The Use of Introspective Data in Translation, outlining the rationale, design and analysis of such 'thinking-aloud techniques'. From the didactic point of view, the value to students and teachers springs from the following observation:

> many processes automated in highly proficient professional
> translators still take place on a conscious level in learners.
>
> (Krings 1987:161)

Indeed, Krings' findings are extremely enlightening, albeit applied to specific texts and, to some extent inevitably, in artificial conditions. They regard the following areas:

1 decision-making processes – the evaluation of competing potential translation equivalents ('equivalent retrieval strategies') and the rationale behind the final decision
2 assessing the relative importance of morphosyntactic, lexicosemantic and pragmatic considerations
3 the role of intuition

(ibidem)

The kind of analysis pursued in the following pages is based to some extent on similar ideas, but attempts to follow the <u>silent</u> thinking strategies of translators as they work through a first reading, a pre-translation examination and a stage by stage transposing (or rolling) of the text from L1 to L2, whether from second to native language or vice-versa. Another of Krings' findings was that the kind of problems encountered (though not necessarily the number) did not differ appreciably with regard to translation direction. The approaches to both are now discussed in more detail.

Italian/English translation

In the specimen texts that follow, where the translation is into the author's mother tongue, in this case English, the steps in the process will be presented mechanically in the form of a 'rolling translation' as translators gradually mould their native language into the required shape, by sifting through the layers of meaning in the foreign language source text. From a largely literal, first draft version, the text will be analysed from the point of view of its lexicogrammar and the necessary modifications to be made in line with contrastive linguistic, lexical and terminological considerations. The text thus rolls onwards before being subjected to a deeper analysis of its more semantic, pragmatic, stylistic and cultural features, where appropriate. And so the target text takes shape as it rolls towards completion, that is to the complete satisfaction of the translator after having thoroughly analysed the source text from the point of view of the various parameters available. Of course in the case of trained translators, the 'rolling' is a largely automatic exercise as the various levels coalesce in their minds, and as they subconsciously superimpose those various levels on one another, bringing to bear their knowledge and experience to the task in hand as they simultaneously deal with linguistic and extralinguistic factors. As Nida (1996:109) says:

> Translators who are certain of the meaning of a passage in the source language find that a correct translation in the target language develops almost without thinking.

However, this is not the norm among trainees. Fraser (1996:71), reporting on the observation of both professional and student translators, points out that 'language learners checked only how they had actually solved what they perceived as (usually lexical or syntactic) problems, and failed to pay attention to text-level features'. Moreover, it is also true that while translators turn over differing solutions in their minds, they often write them down and cross them out again, a process which the idea of the rolling translation is designed to simulate. When they are not written down on paper or computer screen they are often 'written' mentally or voiced silently or aloud. Indeed, the above-mentioned Thinking Aloud Protocols (TAPs) were an attempt by translation researchers to tap translators' thought processes by getting subjects to voice out loud their thoughts and decisions as they translated. Thus the formal preparation of successive versions and their systematic manipulation, in an attempt to emulate professionals in their (probably) silent thought processes, and consequently to channel the students' energies in the same direction, can be justified, at least as a useful convenience for illustrative purposes. It can also be useful in showing how continuously modifying a target text can help to eliminate inelegant and inappropriate expressions. It can be instrumental in identifying and eradicating that type of 'translationese' that Baker (1995) is attempting to isolate in her study of corpus-based translated texts (see **1.2.3**).

Even the totally artificial and seemingly absurd 'literal' version has its uses and students seem to appreciate it as a starting point. It is, in any case, not totally literal, as the basic contrastive grammatical rules are observed, e.g. adjective position, use of the article, etc, but it shows how easily the source text can influence the translator, and how the false lexical and grammatical 'friends' are constantly lying in wait. It stands as a warning against the temptation of settling too soon for the easy answer. It should also be seen as a mental springboard from which translators create their text through rejecting this clearly inadequate version, thinking of other solutions and asking the following questions:

Does that sound right?

Would I use that word if I were writing this as an original text?

Is this term appropriate, given the formal/informal, technical/non-technical register?

I know this is grammatically correct, but do English-speaking people actually say this?

How is this concept expressed? I've heard it said or seen it written so many times!

There are several possibilities here, but which collocates best with the co-text?

This is much shorter/longer than the original, but that's how it would be expressed, isn't it?

This is not an exact equivalent, but surely this is what is meant?

It is then a question of mentally going through different versions until the right combinations start to 'click' and the text resembles an English original. Some back-checking may be in order if the translator's mind has travelled too far from the original, but this should be considered an integral part of a single process as the target version coalesces through a number of virtual stages.

English/Italian translation

Where the translation is out of the author's mother tongue, in this case from English into Italian, the methodology adopted dispenses with the iconic representation of the 'rolling' approach. Nonetheless, the source text is thoroughly analysed just the same, thereby sensitising learners to the fact that a text exists within certain semantico-linguistic limits and attuning them to the benefits of pre-translation analysis. The importance lies in being able to observe, identify and understand the various components pertinent to a given source text in order to create a target text 'in its image', thereby not neglecting any relevant facet.

Analyses of both kinds of translation may be followed by 'official' or previously-made translations of the text in question, for purposes of contrast and comparison. This practice is adopted particularly in cases of translations (and originals) which naturally appear together, e.g. instructions for use, compact disc notes. Students are then encouraged to try out their own translational skills, both on texts which are continuations of the works analysed and other material from the same fields.

TEXTS FOR ANALYSIS AND TRANSLATION

The texts have been arranged in the following categories:

1 Literary, Journalistic and Film Texts

The literary text, by its very nature, whether it is fictional or non-fictional, requires particularly careful scrutiny by the translator and merits its own section. Indeed, there is a copious literature on the subject of literary translation, much more extensive than that on any other category. The non-fiction element includes biographical, academic and historico-political works. Journalism is included in this category as a non-fiction genre often containing elements of an expressive and creative nature. Film scripts also fit into the same broad category though, as will be seen, they present their own translation modalities. English texts for translation into Italian are alternated with Italian texts for translation into English.

2 Technical and Scientific Texts

The importance of technical and scientific translation is to be found in its pre-eminent position in the working world of the translator rather than in its aesthetic merits. The everyday bread and butter of professional translation typically includes drafts for medical or other scientific conferences, manuals, technical instructions, academic literature, scientific journal articles, and so on. The majority of this material needs to be translated from Italian into English, and this is reflected in the proportion of Italian texts provided for analysis. However, in the case, for example, of instruction manuals, there is a constant need for translation into Italian, and two such texts are presented first.

3 Legal, Commercial and Promotional Texts

The third category groups together legal, commercial and promotional material in that these text types often merge together in specific sub-genres. For example, a contract is often an amalgam of legal and commercial discourse, advertising texts are both promotional and commercial, and European Union documentation may be legal and promotional. Business correspondence, tourist information and CD notes complete the section.

Chapter One

Literary, Journalistic and Film Texts

1.1 Literary texts

The general distinguishing features of the literary genre are discussed in Part One, Chapter Three, but the translator needs to bear in mind one other important factor if faced with a literary text. When dealing with fictional literature there are, in effect, two contexts of situation to consider with two sets of participants and circumstances. Firstly, we have a communicative act involving the author and his/her potential audience over time. In the case of major authors this can be a gigantic and highly varied audience, ranging from schoolchildren to literary critics to film producers. Then, secondly, there is the actual situation portrayed, though with varying degrees of authenticity. The more accomplished the work, the nearer it comes to being that mirror of life to which art aspires, and the more necessary it will be for translators to understand that context of situation. The cheap detective novel, or love story, or station newstand thriller, whose setting in time and place is of minor importance and whose characters seem interchangeable with those of thousands of others of the same genre, can fit into a well-established 'schema' in translation as the context of situation becomes standardised and predictable. More important works of literature require greater attention, however, as the context will be crucial to creating atmosphere and will change considerably and unexpectedly as the discourse progresses. The first text presented for analysis is indeed an extract from a classic work of English literature.

1.1.1 'Martin Chuzzlewit' by Charles Dickens

'I think, young woman,' said Mrs Gamp to the assistant chambermaid, in a tone of expressive weakness, 'that I could pick a little bit of pickled salmon, with a little sprig of fennel, and a sprinkling of white pepper. I takes new bread, my dear, with jest a little pat of fresh butter, and a mossel of cheese. In case there should be such a thing as a cowcumber in the 'ouse, will you be so kind as to bring it, for I'm rather partial to 'em, and

they does a world of good in a sick room. If they draws the Brighton Old
Tipper here, I takes *that* ale at night, my love; it bein' considered wakeful
by the doctors. And whatever you do, young woman, don't bring more than
a shilling's worth of gin and water-warm when I rings the bell a second
time; for that is always my allowance, and I never takes a drop beyond!'

Having preferred these moderate requests, Mrs Gamp observed that
she would stand at the door until the order was executed, to the end that
the patient might not be disturbed by her opening it a second time; and
therefore she would thank the young woman to 'look sharp'.

(1986:480)

Source text analysis

In the case of the above text, the macro context of situation is that of the
nineteenth-century Dickensian novel and all that we now know about this
very particular genre. The modern translator of Dickens needs to be aware
of the social history of the period, many insights into which can be
gleaned from reading Dickens himself, and also the author's formidable
character-forming gifts. The more bizarre Dickensian characters, such as
the one portrayed here, are the product of a deep-rooted and highly
observant knowledge of the seedier side of Victorian London allied to a
fertile imagination. The function is expressive, though indirectly informative, and the style is highly literary in that every word is well thought out,
even when it is misspelt, colloquial or seemingly banal. The style is also
unmistakably Dickens, an illustration of the idiolect of the genius. The
term 'idiolect' refers to the personal language system that is identifiable in
all human beings, the way individuals express themselves. In the case of
great writers, the creative elements that form part of that idiolect are
visible on the printed page. Naturally, these put a tremendous burden on
the translator, and also warn against the practice of translating long works
in collaboration with others or as a team effort. A single translator can
pick up certain quirks and tell-tale markers in the original, and see that
they fit into the target text pattern.

Bearing this in mind, the translator can turn to the micro context of
situation of each section of the novel. The short extract here features the
incorrigible Mrs Gamp in the protagonist's role and a passive chambermaid.
The role relationship is very definitely that of superior to inferior bolstered
by respective strengths of personality. The setting is a dingy boarding house
where Mrs Gamp is purporting to look after (or look over) a seriously ill

man, and is ordering her evening's refreshments before settling down to this arduous task. The environment is fairly sordid and there are hints of drunkenness but the essential humour of the situation transpires. The text is in the written mode but the language in the first paragraph is the spoken variety and in the second that of the erudite scribe.

The first paragraph hangs together with the main theme *I* clearly setting the tone and establishing the centre of attention. The personal pronoun, together with the patronising addressing of the maid (*young woman ... my dear ... you ... my love ... young woman*) provide the main cohesive force and establish the role relation: the *you* should be a *tu* in Italian. The clause structure is largely paratactic in keeping with the spoken mode. Dickens uses punctuation and conjunctions (*and, for* – in the sense of *because*) to achieve this, and provides balance in the hypotactic clauses through a pattern of request cum justification: *In case there should be ... will you be so kind, If they draws ... I takes, whatever you do ... don't bring ...*

Dickens clearly devised an idiolect for Mrs Gamp though some of her idiosyncrasies are more obvious than others. Glaring mispronunciations like *cowcumber, jest* and the typical Cockney *'ouse*, and grammatical aberrations such as *If they draws, they does* and *I takes* are accompanied by attempts to 'speak properly' that do not quite work. The use of the set expression *will you be so kind* is a reasonably successful effort but the opening (*I think ... that I could pick a ...*) is a little unusual. She begins sentences in a haughty manner (*If there should be such a thing as ...*), only to fall down later in the above-mentioned travesties of pronunciation and morphology, and the invention of words such as *wakeful*.

There are one or two common contrastive grammar traps to note. *Mrs Gamp observed that she <u>would stand</u> at the door* requires a conditional perfect in Italian. The verb *thank* in *would thank the young woman to look sharp* is unusually employed as a projecting verb acting like *told* or *asked*.

The syntactic equivalence in the repeated expressions *a little bit of, a little sprig of, a sprinkling, a little pat, a mossel* (a variation on *morsel*) is reflected in the semantic equivalence of small quantities of food leading to *not more than a shilling's worth of gin* (note the saxon genitive on *shilling*). The mock 'moderateness' of Mrs Gamp's requests is anticipated by Dickens himself when he explains that the maid is addressed in tones of *expressive weakness*. There is also phonological equivalence here, intended or otherwise, in the repeated 'i' sound and in the plosive repetition of *pick a little bit of pickled salmon*.

At a lexical level, one question that must be tackled before the translation is complete is whether and how to translate the name *Mrs Gamp*. She is a major character in English literature and her name, which also means 'umbrella', is occasionally used to describe an unkempt and maladroit individual. Certain terms date the piece, including *chambermaid* and *ale*. *Brighton Old Tipper* is a type of beer sold at the time, as explained in an endnote in the original, and the *gin and water-warm* habit is also identifiable with dissolute nineteenth century ladies.

Stylistically, the second paragraph is totally different. The lexically-dense written mode comes to the fore as Dickens reports on the end of the scene. The main ingredient here is irony as the author deliberately heightens the tone to make Mrs Gamp seem all the more ridiculous, though not undeserving of a certain sympathy. The irony lies in the high register vocabulary choice (*Having preferred these moderate requests, until the order was executed*), the classic British irony of understatement (*these moderate requests*), and the false assignment of considerate feelings to Mrs Gamp herself (*to the end that the patient might not be disturbed*). The surface representation belies the pragmatic message; the irony must come through in translation too.

By way of illustration, an accredited 1927 translation of 'Martin Chuzzlewit' by Silvio Spaventa Filippi is provided below:

> Credo, cara ragazza – disse la signora Gamp alla cameriera assistente, in un tono di manifesta debolezza, – ch'io potrò prendere un pezzetto di salmone salato, con un pizzico di gambo di finocchio e una impolveratura di pepe bianco. Pane fresco, cara, con una piccola tavoletta di burro e un pezzetto di cacio. Se mai ci fosse in casa qualche cetriolo, sarete così gentile da servirmelo, perché i cetrioli mi piacciono molto, e fanno un mondo di bene nella camera d'un malato. Se qui si spilla la birra di Brighton, portatemela, amor mio; stasera prendo appunto la birra di Brighton, che tiene svegli, come dicono i dottori. Comunque, figlia mia, non mi portate più d'uno scellino di gin con l'acqua bollente, quando sonerò un'altra volta il campanello: non ne bevo mai più di tanto, neppure una goccia di più!
>
> Formulate queste modeste domande, la signora Gamp aggiunse che avrebbe atteso sull'uscio l'esecuzione degli ordini, per non disturbare, aprendo una seconda volta, l'infermo: e perciò raccomandò alla cameriera di far presto.
>
> (trans. Filippi 1927)

In line with the above analysis, it can be seen how Filippi manages to recreate phonological and syntactic equivalences, archaisms and lexico-grammatical incongruences, though not always in the same places. For example, the alliteration *pick a little bit of pickled salmon* is captured, merely requiring the shifting of the 'p' plosives from *pickled* to *pezzetto*. The sentence structure follows the English pattern reasonably closely, deviating mostly in the subordinate clause in the second paragraph: *to the end .../per non disturbare, ...* . The odd term *mossel* in mossel of cheese is translated by a similar nominal group *pezzetto di cacio*, but the deviance is shifted to the second noun. An attempt is made at Mrs Gamp's idiolectal quirks with the word *impolveratura* rather than *spruzzatina*, the term more usually associated with *sprinkling*. The latter is a case of compensation. Filippi introduces an unusual item in the Italian translation before Dickens does in the original, but then uses congruent items later for certain Mrs Gampisms. He also compensates with outdated vocabulary, using a modern equivalent for *ale* while adopting the more old-fashioned *sonerò* for the current English, albeit grammatically erroneous, *I rings*.

No attempt is made to alter the grammar (as in *I takes*) or morphology (as in *'ouse* and *'em*). Certainly, there is a danger in Italian of descending too far into localised dialect with the graphic representation of spoken language, which would perhaps transmit the wrong signals, though somewhat colloquial usage such as *tiene svegli* is used. Interestingly, Filippi has Mrs Gamp address the chambermaid as *Voi* while keeping all the condescending endearments.

Mrs Gamp's attempts at a more elevated style are also maintained, cf: *In case there should be such a thing .... will you be so kind as to .../Se mai ci fosse ... sarete così gentile da ...* . The most glaring example of idiolect in the discourse is the riotous *cowcumber*, Mrs Gamp's fanciful term for 'cucumber'. Though recognising the afore-mentioned danger of using dialectal expressions in Italian because of their unfamiliarity over areas of Italy where that dialect is not spoken, the northern term *cucumero* might have proved appropriate here. On the other hand, *the Brighton Old Tipper* is such a problem that *la birra di Brighton* is probably as much as could be hoped for.

Filippi sees fit to add the instruction *portatemela* in that sentence, leading to the need to alter the punctuation and repeat the untranslated name, perhaps for reasons of greater clarity. However, he commits the only error in the translation shortly thereafter – Mrs Gamp drinks 'Brighton Old Tipper' *at night*, not *stasera*.

The change in register in the second paragraph is handled nicely, beginning, in fact, with the rendering of *expressive weakness* in the first paragraph: *manifesta debolezza* captures the irony perfectly. The second paragraph begins appropriately (*Formulate queste modeste ...*) and the pompous *until the order was executed* picks up the same words: *l'esecuzione degli ordini.*

The conditional *would stand* is duly transformed into a conditional perfect *avrebbe atteso*, while the rather unusual conditional at the end (*would thank*) is wisely changed to the past tense: *raccomandò*, the perfect choice of verb. The final *far presto* is less colloquial than *look sharp*, but is enough to create the register contrast.

In this comparison of the source text analysis and Filippi's translation, the differences observed are as important as the similarities. There can be as many versions of this text as there are translators willing to translate it. The important thing is that nothing is left to chance, that the pre-analysis prepares the translator to make his or her own, very personal, choices.

The text continues as follows, and is offered for practice:

A tray was brought with everything upon it, even to the cucumber; and Mrs Gamp accordingly sat down to eat and drink in high good humour. The extent to which she availed herself of the vinegar, and supped up that refreshing fluid with the blade of her knife, can scarcely be expressed in narrative.

'Ah!' sighed Mrs Gamp, as she meditated over the warm shilling's-worth, 'what a blessed thing it is ... to be contented! What a blessed thing it is to make sick people happy in their beds, and never mind one's self as long as one can do a service! I don't believe a finer cowcumber was ever grow'd. I'm sure I never seen one!'

She moralised in the same vein until her glass was empty, then administered the patient's medicine, by the simple process of clutching his windpipe, to make him gasp, and immediately pouring it down his throat.

'I a'most forgot the piller, I declare!' said Mrs Gamp, drawing it away. 'There! Now he's comfortable as can be, *I'm* sure! I must try to make myself as much so as I can.'

The following practice text, from another classic of English literature, is to be found at the beginning of Henry Fielding's novel 'Tom Jones':

In that part of the western division of this kingdom, which is commonly called Somersetshire, there lately lived (and perhaps lives still) a gentleman whose name was Allworthy, and who might well be called the favourite of both Nature and Fortune; for both of them seem to have contended which should bless and enrich him most. In this contention, Nature may seem to some to have come off victorious, as she bestowed on him many gifts; while Fortune had only one gift in her power; but in pouring forth this, she was so very profuse, that others perhaps may think this single endowment to have been more than equivalent to all the various blessings which he enjoyed from Nature. From the former of these, he derived an agreeable person, a sound constitution, a solid understanding, and a benevolent heart; by the latter, he was decreed to the inheritance of one of the largest estates in the country.

1.1.2 'Se torno a nascere' by Luca Goldoni

The concept of the 'rolling translation' is now presented in the following treatment of a short passage for translation from Italian to English. The extract is taken from Goldoni (1987:119).

> Stamattina alle prime ore dell'alba un reparto di 'berretti verdi' di Bodrato e un commando di 'berretti rosa fucsia' di Forlani hanno circondato e attaccato con logica di annientamento l'intera area-Zac. Subito dopo i comandanti delle due formazioni hanno indetto una riunione ristretta per concordare una strategia comune in vista del congresso delle 'Brigate Libertas' che si terrà in autunno. Gli schieramenti dipenderanno in parte dall'esito del congresso delle 'Brigate Garofano' che dovrebbe iniziare alla fine del mese. Il comandante di queste ultime, Craxi (il leggendario partigiano Pedro), ha intanto precisato la sua clamorosa denuncia: secondo Pedro il commissario politico della 18a Eni, Hermes (Roberto Mazzanti), avrebbe venduto agli arabi l'80 per cento del materiale paracadutato dagli americani durante gli ultimi due mesi.

The text, first published in 1981 and revised several times since then, falls into the often best-selling political satire genre. It presents a number of difficulties to the translator, while certainly not qualifying for any kind of lofty literary status. The first stage in the process represents little more than an academic exercise, but provides a starting point. It is a literal word-for-word translation, taking account of only the very basic tenets of contrastive Italian/English grammar, e.g. the saxon genitive and adjective position:

> This morning at the first hours of the dawn a unit of Bodrato's 'green berets' and a commando of Forlani's 'fuchsia pink berets' have surrounded and attacked, with the logic of annihilation, the entire Zac area. Immediately after the commanders of the two formations have called a restricted meeting to agree a common strategy in view of the 'Brigate Libertas' congress which will be held in autumn. The formations will depend in part on the outcome of the 'Brigate Garofano' congress which should begin at the end of the month. The commander of these last, Craxi (the legendary partisan Pedro), has meanwhile made clear his clamorous denunciation: according to Pedro the political commissioner of the 18th ENI, Hermes (Roberto Mazzanti), would have sold 80% of the material parachuted by the Americans during the last two months to the Arabs.

The text then needs to be examined on a lexicogrammatical, terminological, linguistic and text-linguistic, cultural, historical, semantic, and pragmatic level, as well as requiring considerable text-internal and text-external knowledge (co-text and context). The content pre-dates the revelations of the 'Tangentopoli' investigations but anticipates them in no uncertain terms. The broad genre is political satire, but as in this particular case it is a satirical attack on the Italian political system, and as the allegorical scenario which forms the particular context of situation is that of guerilla warfare redolent of the partisan campaigns of the Second World War, the foreign reader (we shall assume British English for the moment) needs guidance.

Lexicogrammatical analysis

Looking at the text from the translator's point of view, in the first sentence it must be decided how long a period of time is being considered in the expression *alle prime ore dell'alba – ore/hours* or simply the time around the dawn? Opting for the latter, the expressions *at the first light of dawn* or the condensed *in the early dawn* would seem to be appropriate.

Reparto is *unit* and *commando* is *commando* according to all the dictionaries, but wait! The English reader is, in fact, more familiar with the term *commando* being used to describe individual members of a *(commando) group/force/unit*. Indeed, the latest Oxford and Longman dictionaries seem to recognise this by defining *commando* as: *(member of a) group of soldiers* . . . .

The time marker *stamattina* dictates the use of the simple past tense in English for the translation of *hanno circondato e attaccato*. Ditto *hanno indetto/called* a little further on.

The syntagm *con logica di annientamento* seems fairly formal, but surely it means they were *bent on annihilation*, whereas *immediately thereafter* restores some formality to the pseudo-seriousness of the text.

Formazioni: units? groups? forces? All part of the divergence but all a bit weak. *Outfits* is colloquial but, there again, this is not a serious bulletin.

Riunione ristretta is commonly used in Italian where the more important members of a group meet first before a general assembly. Here, something like a *meeting of the high command* or *officer's meeting* seems to be meant.

Concordare in this context ideally requires the prepositional verb *agree on*, though this is not mandatory.

. . . che si terrà in autunno: generally speaking, a passive voice form in the corresponding tense is required to render the Italian impersonal *si* construction, namely *which will be held*, but in this case an alternative construction, which also has collocational force in this particular environment, is available: *to be held*. The time marker requires the article in English, and this is mandatory: *in the autumn*.

The term *schieramenti* would seem to have the force of *alliances* in this text but, if this is too risky, then *alignments* can be brought in.

As for *. . . che dovrebbe iniziare*, this is not an occasion for the use of *should* either in its weak or its deontic (obligation) form. This near-certainty is expressed well by the *to be to* construction: *is to begin*. All the various versions of *Questo/i/a/e ultimo/i/a/e* can be translated by *the latter*.

English has no verbalised form of the adjective/noun *precise/precision*. However, in this case the verb *precisare* is attached to the noun *denuncia*, and this collocation is the key to translation (see below).

Denuncia: the non-transparent translation is, possibly, *accusation* and 'accusations' are *made* (see above).

The adjective *clamorosa* has its equivalent in *sensational* (cf: newspaper headlines). *Clamorous* means 'making loud demands or protests'.

The possessive adjective is unnecessary in English in *Craxi made a claim*.

In the final clause, there is a didactically splendid example of the Italian use of the unreal conditional to express allegation. Indeed, the English stock equivalent is *is alleged to have*.

Paracadutato is best devalued to *dropped*. The context should be clear from the co-text – from the sentence preceding this passage we learn that the above scenario is being played out against a wider fiction of the Russians invading Italy.

Following this lexicogrammatical fine tuning, the translation should roll on as follows:

> This morning in the early dawn a unit of Bodrato's 'green berets' and a commando-group of Forlani's 'fuchsia pink berets', bent on annihilation, surrounded and attacked the entire Zac area. Immediately thereafter the commanders of the two outfits called a meeting of the high command to agree on a common strategy in view of the 'Brigate Libertas' congress to be held in the autumn. The alliances will depend in part on the outcome of the 'Brigate Garofano' congress which is to begin at the end of the month. The commander of the latter, Craxi (the legendary partisan Pedro), has meanwhile made a sensational accusation: according to Pedro the political commissioner of the 18th ENI, Hermes (Roberto Mazzanti), is alleged to have sold 80% of the material dropped by the Americans during the last two months to the Arabs.

Textual, cultural and semantico-pragmatic analysis

From a text-linguistic viewpoint, many of the cohesion devices (linking mechanisms) are common to both languages and do not create translation problems. It is, however, important to maintain the extended military metaphor (and the cohesive key words) wherever it arises, and this requires a certain amount of 'world knowledge' regarding the subject in question as well as the ability to click into the military 'schema' and ally it to the more local Italian political 'schema' of the recent past. The politician *Bodrato* represented one tendency of an already faction-ridden party within a long-established coalition, and his group is given the label of the well-known, John Wayne-associated American fighting force, the 'green berets', thus setting the scene for Hollywood-style rivalry. The *fuchsia berets* of political ally Forlani shift the allegory from American to Italian soil with a clear reference to the Italian parachute regiment. The attack is against the *area-Zac*, a newspaper invention referring to those members of the Christian Democrat party who followed the moderate Zaccagnini. The illocutionary intent (see Part One) of the *berets* is presumably two-fold: to create a mildly absurd 'tag' and to maintain an Italian military connection to counterpoise the American. *Fuchsia-pink* as a translation fulfils one of these objectives but not the other. Perhaps *the red white and green berets* (incidentally picking up on the 'green' of the Americans) would provide the recognition signal. The *area-Zac* is more tricky, in that the politician himself was not well-known outside Italy even when he was alive. Reducing to sense and referring to *Zaccagnini and his supporters/the Zaccagnini-led fringe, block, faction*, etc., seems safe, perhaps with a footnote on all three politicians mentioned.

In the second sentence, the transparent translation of *comandanti* with *commanders* upsets the canons of military hierarchy. To avoid risking confusion between non-corresponding rank equivalents, a safe solution would be *commanding officers*.

The *Brigate Libertas* and *Brigate Garofano* have a triple role in illocution. They are part of the ongoing military metaphor, but this time hark back clearly to the resistance movement and the various 'brigate' (not to mention the fortuitous association with the infamous Brigate Rosse), and they bring in the two major power contenders within the government at that time: the Christian Democrat party (whose motto was 'Libertas') and the Socialist Party (whose emblem was a carnation). The English reader is well-acquainted with the concept of political *congressi* (*conferences*, however) and one component in the translation would be admirably covered by *the Christian Democrat Party Conference* and *Socialist Party Conference*. But the military/resistance allusions? Replace *Party* with *Forces* or *Movement* or *Regiment* or *Brigade*?!

The next use of *comandante*, this time referring to the former Socialist Party leader Bettino Craxi with his reputation for autocratic leadership, might veer the translator towards a more forceful term, but even *leader* would cover both semantic components: Craxi was a (political) head, and *resistance leader* is a collocation.

The names *Pedro* (and *Hermes*?) can be left, as they are explained in the text. *Commissar* for *commissario* is technically incorrect but adds to the image of intrigue and foul play.

The last obstacle, however, is a real challenge: *the 18a Eni*. ENI is the nationalised energy conglomerate, notorious for being a fount of illicit earnings for the political parties who fought over its management. It is here styled as a military division involved in just such an enterprise. *The 18a* can remain (though of course the number is irrelevant). In terms of 'equivalent effect' a more general, suspicion-inducing political body might be sought, one that an English reader (though not necessarily American or non-British) would recognise as such. What about *quango*?

The translation has now rolled to the following possible conclusion:

This morning in the early dawn a unit of Bodrato's 'green berets' and a commando-group of Forlani's 'red, white and green berets', bent on annihilation, surrounded and attacked Zaccagnini and his supporters. Immediately thereafter the commanding officers of the two outfits called a meeting of the high command to agree on a common strategy in view of the Christian Democrat Movement Conference to be held in the autumn. The alliances will depend in part on the outcome of the Socialist Movement Conference which is to begin at the end of the month. The leader of the latter, Craxi (the legendary partisan Pedro), has meanwhile made a sensational accusation: according to Pedro the commissar of the 18th Quango, Hermes (Roberto Mazzanti), is alleged to have sold 80% of the material dropped by the Americans during the last two months to the Arabs.

This translation, as it stands, is a suggestion. It is open to criticism and further analysis. Time, insight and a fresh approach would doubtless provide other, better, solutions. I am still not happy, for example, with *outfits* and one or two of the more adventurous ideas, but this is not the point. It is the method of analysis and the concept of working through the components that is important.

The text continues as follows and is offered for translation practice:

Radio Londra anche stamattina, nella sua emissione delle ore 7, ha trasmesso i consueti messaggi speciali in codice: 'Le tangenti volano basse', 'Le poltrone sono finite', 'Le convergenze a volte sono parallele'. Decodificando quest'ultimo messaggio, il comandante unico delle formazioni scudo-crociate Pablito (Flaminio Piccoli) ha deciso di rompere gli indugi e di dare attuazione al piano 'Blue Light': parlando dalla torretta di un'autoblinda ad almeno ventimila partigiani confluiti in una località della Val di Fiemme, Pablito ha illustrato i dettagli dell'operazione auspicando che 'alla tattica dello scontro sia da privilegiare la strategia del confronto e delle larghe intese'.

'Sono due anni che elaboriamo strategie' ha gridato un comandante di distaccamento 'e non abbiamo ancora fatto deragliare neppure un treno'. Al che, Pablito, un po' pallido ed emozionato, ha scandito: 'Sono in grado di annunciare che da qualche ora un nostro commando è impegnato in una rischiosissima azione di cui non posso ancora fornire i particolari'

The next text, also offered for practice, is taken from another mildly satirical work; Beppe Severgnini's 'L'Inglese: lezioni semiserie' (1992:28):

Il successo della lingua inglese riempie di stupore. Quando Giulio Cesare sbarcò in Britannia circa duemila anni fa, l'inglese non esisteva. Mezzo millennio più tardi, una lingua semi-incomprensibile chiamata 'Englisc' era parlata dallo stesso numero di persone che oggi parlano il dialetto lodigiano. Mille anni dopo, al tempo di Shakespeare, l'inglese era solo l'idioma di sette milioni di indigeni confinati su un'isola, nemmeno tanto grande, all'estremo nord-ovest dell'Europa.

Oggi è la lingua del pianeta. La prima vera 'lingua internazionale', con buona pace dei fanatici dell'esperanto, o di buffi idiomi artificiali come Interlingua, Novial e Interglossa. Mai, nella storia, si era verificato un fenomeno del genere: il greco, il latino, il turco, l'arabo, lo spagnolo, il francese, il tedesco e il russo si sono succeduti come lingue internazionali, ma nessuna ha mai raggiunto la stessa penetrazione. Per quasi quattrocento milioni è lingua madre; per altrettanti è seconda lingua. In India il primo ministro Nehru dichiarò nel 1947: 'Entro una generazione l'inglese non verrà più usato'. Si sbagliava: oggi gli indiani che parlano inglese sono più numerosi degli inglesi stessi, e 'l'Indian English' viene considerato indispensabile per tenere unito uno Stato dove si parlano quasi duecento idiomi diversi (nel 1984, quando Rajiv Gandhi in seguito all'assassinio della madre Indira si rivolse al paese per invitare alla calma, lo fece in inglese). Almeno mezzo miliardo di individui, infine, parlano inglese come lingua straniera: si va dalla quasi perfezione di un uomo politico svedese ai suoni misteriosi emessi da un venditore di souvenir del Cairo.

1.1.3 'The Secret Diary of Adrian Mole' by Sue Townsend

'The Secret Diary of Adrian Mole' was a phenomenal best-seller in the United Kingdom, due to its incisive humour and uncanny accuracy in portraying British social mores and private conflicts. That these are ingredients for translational disaster was borne out by the fact that in Italy the book has passed practically unnoticed. The difficulties involved were undoubtedly connected to the pragmatic, stylistic and connotative features that were the key to the understanding of the book, which as a popular best-seller did not present particularly serious difficulties at a purely linguistic or philosophical level.

As noted previously in **1.2.1**, the book takes the form of a diary and is thus conveniently divided into the days of the year. The following entry is for Saturday, August 15th. This analysis was first presented at the F.I.T. Conference in Belgrade in 1990.

> My father, Stick Insect and Maxwell House saw me off at the station. My father didn't mind a bit that I chose to go to Scotland instead of Skegness. In fact he looked dead cheerful. The train journey was terrible. I had to stand all the way to Sheffield. I spoke to a lady in a wheelchair who was in the guard's van. She was very nice, she said that the only good thing about being handicapped was that you always got a seat on trains. Even if it was in the guard's van.
> My mother and creep Lucas met me at Sheffield. My mother looked dead thin and has started dressing in clothes that are too young for her. Lucas creep was wearing jeans! His belly was hanging over his belt. I pretended to be asleep until we got to Scotland.
> Lucas mauled my mother about whilst he was driving.
> We are at a place called Loch Lubnaig. I am in bed in a log cabin. My mother and Lucas have gone to the village to try to buy cigarettes. At least that is their story.   (1982:110)

Source text analysis

From the point of view of syntax, the text could be described as elementary, the sort of text provided for practice in the early stages of a translation course. One or two points arise, however. There is a phrasal verb (*to see off*) which would probably require moving up or down a level to a single verb form or to a verb phrase, depending on the target language. For example, in Italian: 1 *salutare (alla partenza)*, 2 *veder partire*, 3 *accompagnare alla stazione*. Notice that the single verb form 1 really requires the adverbial adjunct to avoid ambiguity, 2 is little used and 3 assumes that the 'seeing off' involved prior transportation to the station. The participle use following the preposition *about being handicapped* is often tricky to fit into similar sentences in other language systems. Italian, for example, would most comfortably adopt an infinitive.

There is an interesting succession of tenses in the second paragraph where the simple past is followed by the present perfect and in the next sentence by the past continuous. This sequence mirrors the perspectives of the boy as he recounts the scene, and Italian in this case would be best served by the succession: present perfect *mi è sembrata*, present perfect *ha cominciato* and imperfect *portava*.

In terms of information structure, the subject/theme combination so typical of English is maintained throughout. It is particularly evident due to the fact that Adrian does not construct complex, hypotactic clause sequences. Nor should the translator. In this way the focus on new information provides an effortless narrative flow with constant anaphoric reference, giving cohesion to the text. This is easy to translate – as mentioned previously, it is the culture-bound coherent element that may prove difficult.

From a lexical point of view, the first sentence provides some fascinating examples of proper names. The context tells us nothing. Prior knowledge is required to understand that *Stick Insect* is the name Adrian gives to his father's extremely thin lover. The translator must work through the image to create 'equivalent effect' (e.g. *Manico di Scopa* in Italian). *Maxwell House* is a much more interesting case (see Part One **1.2.1**, also for a discussion of the vocabulary item *to maul*).

The semantic notion of the universe of discourse places participants in a communicative event so that the concept of 'cross purposes' can be avoided. The first universe of discourse to be considered is that contained in the text itself, which is a communicative event between a fourteen-year-old boy and himself. If this is understood, then later comments on style and pragmatics will be seen in a clearer context. The boy's perspective, so different from that of an adult or objective observer, is enshrined in language use.

The denotative terms *train journey, lady in a wheelchair, guard's van* can, as it were, be translated straight out of memory (and by activating the correct frame or script or scenario, see Part One) or the dictionary. This is not the case with connotative terms; the two holiday options *Scotland* and *Skegness* are not chosen casually. The former indicates a typical choice of the middle-class Briton, looking to get away from 'day trippers', showing an ecological interest and an appreciation of natural beauty and perhaps physical exercise. Skegness is strictly for the masses, and along with other British towns such as Wigan and Scunthorpe is a source of mild humourous contempt for the bourgeoisie. In common with other provincial holiday towns such as Blackpool and Great Yarmouth, it epitomises the genuine, though rather vulgar, seaside-resort syndrome so much associated with the English working-classes. Adrian Mole, aged thirteen and three-quarters, already a vicarious social climber, would not be seen dead in Skegness. However, it is very probable that the 'world knowledge' of the average reader of a translated version of 'Adrian Mole' would not stretch as far as Skegness, and thus the whole connotative effect would be lost. One solution is to affix a rather clumsy term in apposition (e.g. *the popular holiday resort, Skegness*) and then translate that, or add something to the text to bring out the connotative meaning. In Italian, the mention of Skegness could be gratuitously followed by *quel postaccio sul Mare del Nord*.

The fact that his mother's lover was wearing *jeans* shocked and appalled Adrian – the simple lexical item *jeans* again takes on other connotations. The idea is that a man of his age and position (i.e. a surrogate parent) should not be wearing an item of clothing associated with the younger generation. It is quite possible that trends in fashion and national attitudes towards the generation gap may have to dictate the choice of term here.

Closely connected to this semantic appraisal of the text, the pragmatic load is first carried in the second sentence (*My father didn't mind a bit*), where Adrian is almost on the point of understanding that his father is pleased not to have him around and to be left in peace with his lover. This theme runs through to the last paragraph, where the illocutionary intent of the simple sentence *I am in bed in a log cabin* is a cry for help. The translator must consider whether the pseudo-log cabin syndrome sums up the same kind of socially-conscious, 'trendy' holiday arrangement, so alien to fourteen-year-old boys, in the culture of the target language.

Stylistically, the first feature that stands out is the short, 'staccato' style of paratactic clauses, with its succession of 'punchy' past tenses, designed to reflect the diary entry style of an adolescent. There can be no justifiable reason for altering this. The childish character of the writing is also exemplified by the repeated use of the adjective *dead* as an intensifier, viz: *dead cheerful*, *dead thin*. A similar age-related register should be found in the target language. The choice of the colloquial *belly* fits into this same register.

However simple the style is meant to be, it is a literary work and thus warrants examination in terms of non-casual language use within the text itself. Text analysis techniques would point to such phonological equivalences as <u>Sco</u>tland and <u>Sk</u>egness where the matching consonant clusters may not be coincidental. Italian *Scozia* maintains the equivalence and therefore simple equation is called for.

The syntactic and semantic equivalence of *My father/My mother* as subjects of the opening sentences of paragraphs one and two respectively should be noted. More interestingly, the inversion of *creep Lucas/Lucas creep* is effective, particularly as in both cases the syntagm is deviant, as the noun *creep* should be preceded by an article.

Looking at the structure of the text, the second paragraph ends abruptly and is followed by a single, short sentence expressing Adrian's disgust at Lucas's behaviour. The flow of discourse is effectively halted, a punctuation device that should be maintained, before the final paragraph completes the day with Adrian's ironic observation *At least that is their story*. The translation comment finishes with this idiomatic expression, one of the more easily translatable elements in the text. In Italian it can be verbalised into the substitution *Questo perlomeno è quello che mi hanno raccontato*.

The above represents the thought processes brought to bear on the text. Although the analysis is not divided into sections with numbers and sub-headings, it does inevitably follow a certain superimposed order as it deals with the linguistic, semantic, pragmatic and stylistic aspects. It is nevertheless recognised that the translator may not approach the analysis according to this prescribed order of events. Reiterating what was said in the introduction, the presentation is designed to be illustrative rather than a precise set of instructions.

The official translation (Brera 1991:132) of this passage is now presented for comparison:

> Il papà, Stick Insect e Maxwell mi hanno accompagnato alla stazione. Papà se ne frega che abbia scelto di andare in Scozia invece che a Skegness. Sembrava spudoratamente allegro. Il viaggio in treno è stato tremendo. Ho dovuto restare in piedi fino a Sheffield. Ho chiacchierato con una signora sulla sedia a rotelle nel ridotto del controllore. Era molto simpatica, diceva che l'unico vantaggio di essere handicappati è che si trova sempre il posto a sedere in treno!
>
> La mamma e Lucas il lascivo mi aspettavano a Sheffield. Lei era molto dimagrita. Si è messa a vestirsi da ragazzina. Il lascivo era nientemeno che in jeans! Aveva la pancetta a balconcino sopra la cintura. Ho fatto finta di dormire fino in Scozia.
>
> Lucas sfruculiava mia mamma anche mentre guidava.
> Siamo in un posto che si chiama Loch Lubnaig. Sono a letto in una capanna di legno. La mamma e Lucas sono andati in paese a cercare delle sigarette. Questo almeno è quello che mi hanno raccontato.

The text continues as follows and is offered for practice:

Sunday August 16th
There is a loch in front of the cabin and a pine forest and a mountain behind the cabin. There is nothing to do. It is dead boring.
Monday August 17th
Did some washing in a log cabin launderette. Spoke to an American tourist called Hamish Mancini; he is the same age as me. His mother is on her honeymoon for the fourth time.
Tuesday August 18th
Rained all day.
Wednesday August 19th
Sent postcards. Phoned Pandora, reversed charges. Her father refused to accept them.
Thursday August 20th
Played cards with Hamish Mancini. His mother and stepfather and my mother and her lover have gone to see a waterfall in the car. Big deal!
Friday August 21st
Walked two and a half miles into Callander to buy Mars bar. Played on Space Invaders. Came back, had tea. Phoned Pandora from log cabin phone box. Reversed charges. She still loves me. I still love her. Went to bed.
Saturday August 22nd
Went to see Rob Roy's grave. Saw it, came back.

The text now proposed for translation practice is the beginning of Chapter Seven of Tim Parks' best-seller 'Italian Neighbours':

July? Dog-days. The heat that is, and Vega.
We had settled down in the flat, bought a few 100-watt bulbs, only to realise what an attraction they were to the moths and mosquitoes. We had got used to the tock-tock of midnight ping-pong from across the street, discovered that something of a breeze could be created by opening all the windows of the flat simultaneously and waggling one of the communicating doors, eaten our

way through mountains of water-melons (to every season its antidote), and dedicated a shelf of the fridge to bowls of sliced peaches swimming in Valpolicella.

We had even made our first tentative peace with Lucilla, offered our help around the house should she ever need it, assured her we would take no part in the court case pending in which Marta and Maria Rosa were to be accused of having dashed to *il Professore*'s bank security box only moments after his heart attack and burnt the will naming Lucilla as his sole heir.

'But who was *il professore?*'

'Why Umberto! Patuzzi! A wiser man never lived. A real *professore.*'

1.1.4 'Essere di paese' by Gina Marpillero

This autobiographical novel written by a Friulian housewife captures the meaning of the pregnant Italian expression 'essere di paese' within a historical framework set between the two world wars. The opening lines to several early chapters have been chosen for translation analysis.

> L'infanzia ha avuto per me due fasi importanti, ma delle quali ho un ricordo tutto di riporto. Personalmente non ho l'impressione di averle mai vissute, se non per sentito dire. I due periodi sono: la morte di mio padre e la 'profuganza'.
>
> Della 'profuganza' come la chiamava mia madre, ho vaghi ricordi.
>
> I miei fratelli erano ormai grandi. Paolo era sempre sotto le armi, in Marina, ma nello stesso tempo aveva fatto la maturità scientifica e si era iscritto al Politecnico di Milano in ingegneria meccanica. Mario finiva ragioneria a Udine e Berto faceva le medie a Tolmezzo.
>
> La donna che è rimasta importante nel mio ricordo è la Cristina, detta Cristinon per la sua esagerata grassezza.

The broad context of situation throughout this book is the ever-present 'paese' and the author's recounting of her experiences therein. Village life exists in every country and common factors link them all. Similarly, the concept of the 'paese' is common to all Italy, but the particular location involved in this work is Friuli and there are sound historico-sociological reasons, as well as the evident geographical considerations, for bearing this fact constantly in mind. However, to begin with, picking up again on the 'rolling translation' approach, a literal version is provided, though the most obvious grammatical modifications have already been effected, i.e. adjective position, pronoun position (itself affecting verb/subject order: *come la chiamava mia madre/as my mother called it*), no article with the possessive, the use of *have* as auxiliary.

> The childhood has had for me two important phases, but of the which I have a memory all of bringing back. Personally I have not the impression to have ever lived them, if not for heard say. The two periods are: the death of my father and the 'profuganza'.
>
> Of the 'profuganza' as my mother called it, I have vague memories.
>
> My brothers were by now big. Paolo was still under the arms, in the navy, but in the same time had done the scientific 'maturità' and he had enrolled at the Polytechnic of Milan in mechanical engineering. Mario was finishing accountancy at Udine and Berto was doing the middle school at Tolmezzo.
>
> The woman who has remained important in my memory is Cristina, said Cristinon for her exaggerated fatness.

Lexicogrammatical analysis

Firstly, the question of the use of the article with abstract nouns must be addressed. The article must be removed from *childhood* but the noun cannot be left unqualified or it will refer to childhood in general. Picking up the *per me* following the verb, the possessive *My* can be used, though the transparent use of the verb *to have* would then be weak. *My childhood* can thus be followed by, for example, the substitute verb *consisted of* in the appropriate simple past tense form (the author was already elderly in 1980).

If it is decided to maintain the original construction *(ma) delle quali* and the nominalised *ho un ricordo* and therefore *of which I have a … memory*, the tricky *tutto di riporto* might be rendered by *only an indirect* or, more adventurously, *totally second-hand*. Alternatively, the verbalisation *which I only vaguely remember* may be sufficient. The nominal *ho l'impressione* would certainly be better verbalised into *I don't feel* with a *that* clause replacing the perfect infinitive: *that I have ever experienced them*.

There is then a 'set expression for set expression' situation: *se non per sentito dire/if not through hearsay*.

The *'profuganza'* is certainly a special lexical item, whose origin only becomes clear in the second extract. As we discover, it belongs to the author's mother's idiolect and fills a lexical gap in Italian, as no abstract noun based on *profugo/refugee* exists. The potential solutions are threefold: 1 use a synonym-based abstract term on the divergence principle (see Part One **1.3.2**) such as *refuge, exodus, flight*, 2 leave the term in 'Italian' and supply an explanation in apposition or in a footnote, or 3 invent a similarly imaginative term in English: *refugisation? refugeehood?*

It is advisable to stick to the original syntactic structure in *Della 'profuganza' come la chiamava mia madre, ... ho vaghi ricordi* in order to maintain the information focus, though the *ho vaghi ricordi* could be amplified by the addition of *only: I have only vague/hazy memories.*

The *fratelli ... grandi* are indeed *brothers* (there are no females apart from the author) but their bigness lies in their being *grown up.*

The armed forces requires an article in English: *the army, the air force,* and in this case (*Marina*), *the navy.*

Note *nello stesso tempo/at the same time*, but perhaps *simultaneously* would fit better.

Another truly lexicogrammatical problem is the name *Cristinon*. The name is dialectal (Friuli) but is indicative of the ease with which Italian can allocate attributes through affixes. The *-one* suffix indicates large size and so poor Cristina earned her nickname. However, the co-text does not suggest that any malice was intended by this appellation, and thus English devices such as *Fatty* would be inappropriate, though *Tubby* might be inoffensive enough. In any case, building a term around the actual name is beyond the reach of English grammar. The *esagerata grassezza*, on the other hand, could be toned down by way of compensation to simply *because of her size/ample figure.*

Applying the above considerations the translation becomes:

> My childhood consisted of two important phases, but of which I have a totally second-hand memory. Personally I don't feel that I have ever experienced them, if not through hearsay. The two periods are the death of my father and the 'profuganza'.
>
> Of the 'profuganza' as my mother called it, I have only vague memories.
>
> My brothers were by now grown up. Paolo was still under the arms, in the navy, but he had simultaneously done the scientific 'maturità' and had enrolled at the Polytechnic of Milan in mechanical engineering. Mario was finishing accountancy at Udine and Berto was doing the middle school at Tolmezzo.
>
> The woman who has remained important in my memory is Cristina, known as Tubby because of her ample figure.

Cultural and semantico-pragmatic analysis

Starting with the title, what does the expression *essere di paese* conjure up for the Friulian? For the person who actually comes from the 'paese' it means 'home' and a strong attachment to the place of one's birth, however 'old-fashioned' this may appear to others in terms of tradition, mentality and prospects in the modern world. To those from the 'città' it may suggest a certain lack of sophistication, but as Italians in general attach great importance to remaining close to their origins, the overall impression of being from the 'paese' is positive. Indeed, the author exalts her background. Consequently, the translation must strive to maintain the sociological nuances while making the concept sound reasonably appealing. Componential analysis is thus required to identify the various ingredients of 'paese' life and relative feelings about it. Perhaps *Where I Belong* is an overstatement but it is a step in the right direction.

Looking now at *'profuganza'* from a pragmatic point of view, and seeing it as part of an affectionate portrayal of the author's mother, it becomes clear that some kind of inventive word play would be suitable (e.g. *our refugeehood*), but the solution must be left to the individual translator's ingenuity.

The idiomatic expression *sotto le armi* is often translated in bilingual dictionaries as simply *in the army*. In this case, *Paolo was still in the navy* (NB *sempre/still*) might suffice, but if a similar register of expression is desired in English then there are a number of options: *in uniform, in the forces, at sea*.

In the case of *aveva fatto la maturità scientifica*, the translator must choose between the generic and the specific, and therefore make decisions as to how much specificity is warranted. Remaining generic, sufficient information may be provided by *he had finished secondary school*. However, the fact that he went on *to study mechanical engineering at Milan Polytechnic* (an acceptable transparent equation) can be bolstered by knowing that Paolo *passed his final exams at the technical school*. As the concept of enrolling at university does not fit an English scenario (though it does an American), it is sufficient to note that *he went to Milan Polytechnic*. On the same lines, *ragioneria* can be described as *commercial school*, while the American system can provide a useful term for *le medie* in *junior high school* (cf. British English *middle school*).

The translation rolls on:

My childhood consisted of two important phases, of which I have only an indirect memory. Personally I don't feel that I have ever experienced them, if not through hearsay. The two periods are the death of my father and our 'refugeehood'.

Of the 'refugeehood' as my mother called it, I have only vague memories.

My brothers were by now grown up. Paolo was still in uniform, in the navy, but he had simultaneously passed his final exams at the technical school and had gone to Milan Polytechnic to study mechanical engineering. Mario was finishing commercial school in Udine and Berto was at junior high school in Tolmezzo.

The woman who has remained important in my memory is Cristina, known as Tubby because of her ample figure.

And so the translation rolls to a (temporary) halt. Much has been covered but translators can never be totally satisfied until all the linguistic, semantic and stylistic angles have been tested to their satisfaction. They may want to revise their efforts several more times.

The chapter regarding Cristinon continues as follows and is offered for practice:

Era in servizio da noi, ma più che altro per servire la mucca. Teneva pulita la stalla, mungeva, portava fuori il letame con il 'gei' (la gerla, che si portava sulle spalle). Era una gerla esclusivamente adibita a questo trasporto, essendo tutta incrostata di letame. Anche il sacco che si metteva sulle spalle doveva essere usato solamente in questa occasione, perché aveva un forte odore ed era alle volte macchiato dal liquido che usciva dal letame. Il sacco si metteva a punta sulla testa come il cappuccio di un frate, piegando uno dentro all'altro i due angoli chiusi.
C'era, poi, da buttar giù il fieno, attraverso il 'golar' una specie di botola che andava dal fienile direttamente nella stalla.
Tutti i lavori che si riferivano al mantenimento della mucca erano della Cristinon. Falciare l'erba, girarla e voltarla e quando era diventata secca, ovverosia fieno, portarla a casa sulla testa, con quel sistema in vigore tutt'ora dalle nostre parti.

1.1.5 Mozart letter: CD notes

The notes accompanying compact discs can often reserve surprises in the form of rare genrelets. In the Deutsche Grammophon (1980) recording of 'The Magic Flute', the sleeve note consists of a letter from Mozart to his wife which appears in German, English, French and Italian. The original German was translated into English by E. Anderson and the Italian version by G. Cervone was taken from Anderson's work 'Letters of Mozart and his Family' (1966). The Italian version is thus a translation of a translation, suggesting that the translator be on his/her guard for traces of 'translationese'. The English text is presented below:

Mozart to his wife at Baden

Saturday night at half past ten o'clock   Vienna 8-9 October 1791

Dearest, most beloved little Wife,
Although Saturday, as it is post-day, is always a bad night, the opera was performed to a full house and with the usual applause and repetition of numbers. It will be given again tomorrow, but there will be no performance on Monday. So Süssmayr must bring Stoll in on Tuesday when it will be given again for the *first time*. I say for the *first time*, because it will probably be performed several times in succession ... I am taking *Mamma* tomorrow. Hofer has already given her the libretto to read. In her case what will probably happen will be that she will *see* the opera, but not *hear* it ... I went into a box ... There everything was very pleasant and I stayed to the end. But during Papageno's aria with the glockenspiel I went behind the scenes, as I felt a sort of impulse today to play it myself. Well, just for fun, at the point where Schikaneder has a pause, I played an arpeggio. He was startled, looked behind the wings and saw me. When he had his next pause, I played no arpeggio. This time he stopped and refused to go on. I guessed what he was thinking and again played a chord. He then struck the glockenspiel and said 'Shut up'. Whereupon everyone laughed. I am inclined to think that this joke taught many of the audience for the first time that Papageno does not play the instrument himself ...

Analysis

The text is that of a letter written by an (already famous) husband to his wife. The context therefore involves two intimate participants, the purpose of the text producer being that of creating a sense of relaxation for the imparting of information. The time is the late eighteenth century in central

Europe and the letter deals with the topic of the first performances of 'The Magic Flute' and Mozart's movements around these events.

The current setting for the text is a compact disc sleeve produced two hundred years after the event; consequently one might expect to detect certain epoch markers in the style and lexis (assuming they were picked up in the original translation).

The original letter was written by hand and contains a number of recognisable features associated with the informal register of personal letter writing. The translation from the German is grammatically correct and flows reasonably well but it is difficult to tell to what extent the rather staccato rhythm reflects Mozart's style of writing or some inevitable mechanism inherent to German/English translation. The Italian translation, in any case, must be based on the English; the rest is speculation.

Although Mozart betrays emotive features in this letter (pleasure at his work's reception, tinged with a certain apprehension with regard to certain aspects), the text consists largely of a recounting of events, indicative of a superficial, rather infantile state of mind (Will his wife approve? Does he care?). Our world knowledge of Mozart includes a suspicion of a certain impishness in his character, mixed with his undeniable genius. Indeed, there are signs of more serious intent, such as his consideration in the last sentence.

The text we are confronted with uses italics for emphasis and intimate terms, though it is doubtful whether the original displayed these distinctions in any way. The discourse is coherent in that it sticks to one topic and to the terminology of a particular semantic field, and is cohesive in spite of omissions from the original indicated by dots.

Before looking at the Italian translation and the solutions sought for individual items, it may be useful in this case to examine the information structure of the text, given the inherent unpredictability of the writer and the genrelet 'letters to one's spouse'. The opening sentence starts with a subordinate clause and a minor theme, setting up *Saturday* as the main theme to be compared further on with *Monday* and *Tuesday*. The theme of the main clause (*the opera*) is the macro theme of the whole text and is extensively referred to anaphorically (*it . . . it . . .* etc.), providing straightforward narrative style cohesion.

Lexical cohesion is inherent in the semantic field of opera but, in line with English stylistic conventions, also provides for repetition of terms, e.g. *performed–peformance–performed, arpeggio–arpeggio*.

So, an important marker as it introduces unheralded new participants, is followed by the introduction of the personalised theme *I*, to be repeated many times as the immodest Mozart unfurls his tale. However, the staccato *I went into a box* also heralds a change in the discourse as the story begins.

The *I* is no longer theme in the clause *He was startled*, though the passive form still emphasises the doer and the sentence ends with the information focus on *me*.

The alternation of the themes *he* and *I* set up the game metaphor, as Mozart 'plays' with the performer. This alternation also interweaves with a series of time themes (*when ... this time ... then ... whereupon*) which are crucial to the structure of the discourse.

The projected clause *Shut up* is unexpected in its context in the tale but consonant with the intimate letter genre and with the letter's writer.

Whereupon everyone laughed is an incomplete English sentence but its dry succinctness sets up very effectively the last sentence with its anaphoric reference to the whole preceding text (this joke) and its justifying moral.

The Italian version is as follows:

> Mozart alla moglie a Baden
>
> Sabato sera alle dieci e mezza   Vienna 8/9 ottobre 1791
>
> Mia carissima, ottima mogliettina,
> sebbene il sabato sia sempre un giorno sfavorevole, essendo il giorno della posta, pure l'opera è stata rappresentata a teatro completo col successo e i bis consueti. Sarà rappresentata ancora domani, ma non lunedì. Perciò Süssmayr deve condurre qui Stoll a vederla martedì, quando sarà di nuovo rappresentata *per la prima volta* – dico *per la prima volta* poiché verrà probabilmente data più volte di fila ... Domani ci porto *Mama*; Hofer le ha già dato da leggere il libretto. Nel caso di *Mama*, andrà probabilmente a finire che lei *vedrà* l'opera, ma non l'*ascolterà* ... Sono andato ... in un palco ... ho provato tanto piacere e vi son rimasto sino alla fine. Durante l'aria col Glockenspiel di Papageno mi sono portato dietro la scena, ché sentivo oggi un grande desiderio di recitarla io stesso. Allora, per scherzo, nel momento in cui Schikaneder aveva una pausa, ho suonato un arpeggio. Lui si è spaventato, ha guardato dietro le quinte e mi ha visto. Quando c'è stata la seconda pausa non ho fatto niente. Lui si è fermato e non dava segno di voler continuare. Ho capito il suo pensiero e ho suonato di nuovo un accordo. Allora ha dato un colpo al Glockenspiel dicendo: *tappati la bocca*. Allora tutti si sono messi a ridere. Penso che con questo scherzo molti hanno capito per la prima volta che non era Schikaneder a suonare lo strumento ...

The extended date and time provided at the top of the letter (*Saturday night at half past ten o'clock/Sabato sera alle dieci e mezza*) is one epoch marker, having a rather quaint sound to it for today's ears. Otherwise the format is that of an informal letter; the colloquiality is particularly noticeable in the expression *bad night* and the invitation to *Shut up*. The latter is captured register-wise with *tappati la bocca*, though *giorno sfavorevole* might be considered too congruent for *bad night*. *Night* in any case refers to 'sera' and therefore *una serataccia* may have been more appropriate.

The intensifiers and diminutives in the opening greeting (*Dearest, most beloved little wife*) give free rein to the range of Italian devices available to express every nuance of intimacy or dimension: *Mia carissima, ottima mogliettina*.

The lexical item *full house* is a set expression equation: *tutto esaurito*. Italian terminology (*libretto, arpeggio, aria*) is to be expected in a text concerning opera, as are German names and the term *glockenspiel*, given the geographical context.

As regards grammar, considerations are based on the proviso 'even given Italian syntax conventions, … '. The first sentence is conventional with two subordinate clauses, a main clause and circumstantial information. There is no need for anaphoric pronouns in Italian because of the gender markers, though the opposite is the case with the possessive pronoun (*nel caso di Mama*), where *nel suo caso/in her case* is potentially ambiguous.

The shift *the libretto to read/da leggere il libretto* is of little significance, but indicative of Italian flexibility (the inversion of noun and verb is also possible).

Where Schikaneder <u>has</u> a pause surprisingly gets shifted back to <u>*aveva una pausa*</u>; generally it is English that prefers a past tense when recounting past events.

The extensive range of Italian reflexive verbs provides *si è spaventato*, even more immediate and effective than the English passive *he was startled*.

The substitution of the personal pronoun *he* with *Quando <u>c'è</u> stata la seconda pausa* removes the opportunity to play on the *he/I* alternation.

The focus on *arpeggio–arpeggio–chord* at the end of their respective clauses is interrupted in the Italian by a *niente* in place of the second *arpeggio*, once again reflecting the Italian aversion to repetition.

I guessed what he was thinking is nominalised to *Ho capito il suo pensiero*, a mechanism that works more frequently in this direction.

The Italian *molti hanno capito* is kinder to the audience than the English, where Mozart (through the joke) *taught* the audience.

Finally, the substitution of the player *Schikaneder* for the opera character *Papageno* in the last sentence is consonant with the Italian translator's choice of tense *non era*; he is thinking of that particular performance whereas the English version appears to consider the work in the abstract.

1.1.6 'Danubio' by Claudio Magris

The following extract from Claudio Magris's 'Danubio' is in fact the opening paragraph of a geo-literary *tour de force*. The book uses the course of the River Danube from its source to the sea as a vehicle to examine the vast cultural heritage of the countries the river passes through. As the book is not fiction, the context of situation of the text is simply that of an author introducing his work. As regards the interpersonal relationship, the readership is unknown in terms of numbers but will almost certainly be largely restricted to educated readers. The text is informative and expressive, written in high register Italian but highly readable as the discourse flows like the river it describes:

> 'Carissimo!
> L'assessore di Venezia, sig. Maurizio Cecconi, sulla base del progetto allegato ci ha avanzato la proposta di organizzare una mostra sul tema 'L'architettura del viaggio: storia ed utopia degli alberghi'. La sede prevista è Venezia. Del finanziamento si interesserebbero diverse istituzioni ed organizzazioni. Se Lei vorrà dimostrare interesse per una collaborazione …'
> Il caloroso invito, recapitato qualche giorno fa, non si rivolge ad un destinatario preciso, non nomina la persona o le persone che apostrofa con trasporto; lo slancio affettuoso patrocinato dall'Ente Pubblico trascende le individualità particolari e abbraccia il generale, l'umanità o almeno una larga e fluida comunità di colti e intelligenti. L'allegato progetto – steso da professori delle università di Tübingen e di Padova, articolato secondo una logica rigorosa e corredato di bibliografia – vuole portare all'inesorabile ordine del trattato l'imprevedibilità del viaggio, l'intrico e la dispersione dei sentieri, la casualità delle soste, l'incertezza della sera, l'asimmetria di ogni percorso. Lo schema è la bozza di uno statuto della vita, se è vero che l'esistenza è un viaggio, come si suol dire, e che passiamo sulla terra come ospiti.
>
> (1986:11)

A literal translation at this level of language, making the usual elementary modifications, reveals the complexities involved.

'Dearest!
The councillor of Venice, Mr Maurizio Cecconi, on the basis of the
attached project has advanced the proposal to us to organise an
exhibition on the theme 'The architecture of travel: history and utopia of
the hotels'. The site foreseen is Venice. Of the financing several
institutions and organisations would interest themselves. If you will like to
show interest for a collaboration ... '
The warm invitation, which arrived a few days ago, does not turn itself to a
precise receiver, it does not nominate the person or the persons who it
apostrophises with transport; the affectionate rush sponsored by the
Public Board transcends the particular individualities and embraces the
general, the humanity, or at least a wide and fluid community of cultured
and intelligent. The attached project – laid down by professors of the
universities of Tübingen and Padua, articulated according to a rigorous
logic and furnished with bibliography – wants to take to the inexorable
order of the treatise the unpredictability of travel, the intricacy and the
dispersion of the paths, the casuality of the stops, the uncertainty of the
evening, the asymmetry of every route. The scheme is the proof of a
statute of the life, if it is true that the existence is a journey, as it is used to
saying, and that we pass on the earth as guests.

This version is, of course, purely illustrative but gives us a base to roll from.

Lexicogrammatical analysis

The introduction is original in its form, starting with the vocative
Carissimo! requiring an equally arresting opening in English, typically *My
dear friend!*. From the grammatical point of view, a number of contrastive
elements are worth considering. The Italian nominalisation *ha avanzato la
proposta di* could easily be accommodated in English through verbalisation
(*has proposed*), and the oblique object *ci* can be dispensed with. On the
other hand, *di organizzare* can be nominalised to *the organisation of*.

Titles of books, films, etc., including exhibitions, require capital letters
for the lexical words in English.

Starting from *gli alberghi/hotels*, a number of definite articles require
removal as they do not refer to specified or qualified referents (cf:
l'umanità/humanity, *dei sentieri/of paths*, *della vita/of life*). In other instances, the Italian definite article or zero article needs to be replaced by an
indefinite English article: *del trattato/of a treatise*, *con bibliografia/with a
bibliography*.

The lexical item *previsto/foreseen* takes on a rather different meaning in contexts such as this; it has the force of suggestion or proposal. Similarly, the verb *interessare* takes on the meaning of 'look after' in *si interesserebbero* and the intention is more certain than the conditional tense would suggest.

The future tense in the conditional clause *Se Lei vorrà* ... must be transformed into a present *If you wish* ..., or indeed a conditional in the stylised formula *If you would like* ... . The text then talks of una *collaborazione*, a common Italian juxtaposition of indefinite article and abstract noun, requiring replacement in English with a nominalisation of some kind or a verbalisation: *an interest in collaboration, interested in collaborating*.

The *non si rivolge* in the seventh line illustrates that neat Italian impersonal formula that requires the passive voice in English (*is not addressed to* ...). And it is not addressed to a *preciso destinatario*. The transparent translation is too fancy, a more generic *particular person* will suffice. *Nominare* is a partial false cognate (to nominate = to appoint) and is best translated by *name*. The noun *trasporto* is used here in the sense of enthusiasm or *zeal*.

The noun *slancio* is one of those common yet slippery words whose meaning is clear but not easy to pin down lexically, in that it changes from context to context. Its association with the adjective *affettuoso* steers us towards solutions such as *this spurt of affection*, while combining the components of the two items might give us *this effusive message*. *Le individualità* can be reduced to the (generic) *individual*. The adjective *larga*, whose usual accepted translation equivalent is *wide*, belies its status as a false friend, as in this case *large* is more appropriate.

In any case the *warm invitation* is addressed to a *comunità di colti e intelligenti*, indicating the Italian facility for nominalising adjectives. English can respond similarly with the generic adjective and the article (*the educated and the intelligent*), provide a general noun for the adjectives (*educated and intelligent people*) or take advantage of a collective noun and refer to *the educated community*.

The phrasal verb *drawn up* is to be preferred to the more literal *laid out* in the translation of *steso*. The participle *articolato* is another slippery customer, though playing safe in this instance, the translator could opt for *organised* or *constructed*.

The question of re-ordering arises again in the typically Italian *vuole portare all'inesorabile ordine del trattato l'imprevedibilità del viaggio,* ... . Whatever the constraints of theme and rheme, which in Italian put the information focus on the long list of paratactic noun phrases, English syntax cannot be bent and pushes the prepositional adverb phrase to the end of the sentence: *It is designed to bring the unpredictability of travel ... etc ... etc ... to the inexorable order of a treatise.* So be it! The last two items on the list must be linked by the conjunction *and*. The set expression *come si suol dire* at the end of the first passage also exemplifies the impersonal *si* construction, but in this case a corresponding active set expression in English is called for: *as they say.*

This is the current state of the translation, remembering that this is really still a mental abstract:

> 'My dear friend!
> The councillor of Venice, Mr Maurizio Cecconi, on the basis of the attached project has proposed the organisation of an exhibition on the theme 'The Architecture of Travel: the History and Utopia of Hotels'. The site suggested is Venice. Of the financing several institutions and organisations will look after it. If you wish to show an interest in collaboration ... '
> The warm invitation, which arrived a few days ago, is not addressed to a particular person, it does not name the person or the persons who it apostrophises with such zeal; this effusive message sponsored by the Public Board transcends the particular individual and embraces the general, humanity, or at least a large and fluid community of the educated and the intelligent. The attached project – drawn up by professors at the universities of Tübingen and Padua, constructed according to a rigorous logic and furnished with a bibliography – it is designed to bring the unpredictability of travel, the intricacy and the dispersion of paths, the randomness of stops, the uncertainty of the evening, the asymmetry of every route to the inexorable order of a treatise. The scheme is the draft of a statute of life, if it is true that existence is a journey, as they say, and that we pass over the earth as guests.

Cultural, semantico-pragmatic and stylistic analysis

The apparent amplification of *Carissimo* to *My dear friend* is merely an example of balancing the coefficient of intensity (see Part One **2.3.2**) to refer to the power a single word contains. For example, a strong or intensified adjective, as in the case considered here, may need compensating in translation by two, three or more correspondingly weaker items.

The *assessore di Venezia* poses the problem of how to deal with administrative terminology under different constitutional systems. Furthermore, it is not clear from the Italian exactly what post this *councillor* holds. Normally an 'assessore' has a particular responsibility (all'istruzione, al commercio, etc.) and can be referred to as an officer (Education Officer, Tax Officer, etc.), but simply *di Venezia* does not allow this option.

The title *Mr* for *sig.* is based on the model *Mr Prodi*, etc., but as the context here is totally Italian there is an argument for leaving the title in the original: *Sig. Maurizio Cecconi*.

The theme structure of the text begins with the human participants and then moves to the important subject matter (*l'invito, il progetto, lo schema*) in a progression that English can follow comfortably, but the clause *Del finanziamento si interesserebbero diverse istituzioni ed organizzazioni* highlights a significant element of comparative linguistics. The choice for the translator is between opting for standard English syntax norms, fronting and thematising the subject (*Several bodies …*) or maintaining the theme/rheme structure and information focus with, perhaps, *The financing will be taken care of by …* .

Translating the rather inflated *apostrofare* with *apostrophise* maintains the right rhetorical register.

L'Ente Pubblico in question is not specified (cf: *Ente di turismo/Tourist Board*) and therefore *the Local Authority* would be safe.

Stylistically, repetition is more acceptable in English than in Italian and thus, in the last sentence, *esistenza* is better rendered by *life* in spite of its appearance six words previously.

Putting these few touches to the translation, we arrive at the following:

> 'My dear friend!
> The Venice councillor, Sig. Maurizio Cecconi, on the basis of the attached project has proposed the organisation of an exhibition on the theme 'The Architecture of Travel: the History and Utopia of Hotels'. The site suggested is Venice. The financing will be taken care of by several bodies. If you would like to show an interest in collaboration … '
> The warm invitation, which arrived a few days ago, is not addressed to a particular person, it does not name the person or the persons who it apostrophises with such zeal; this effusive message sponsored by the Local Authority transcends the particular individual and embraces the general, humanity, or at least a large and fluid community of the educated and the intelligent. The attached project – drawn up by professors at the universities of Tübingen and Padua, constructed according to a rigorous logic and furnished with a bibliography – is designed to bring the unpredictability of travel, the intricacy and the dispersion of paths, the randomness of stops, the uncertainty of the evening, and the asymmetry of every route to the inexorable order of a treatise. The scheme is the

draft of a statute of life, if it is true that life is a journey, as they say, and that we pass over the earth as guests.

Finally, as the translation rolls to a halt, it is instructive to take a look at the highly-reputed official translation of 'Danubio' by Patrick Creagh for Farrar, Straus & Giroux:

> 'Dear friend!
> Sig. Maurizio Cecconi, alderman of the city of Venice, has proposed that we organise an exhibition based on the enclosed prospectus, entitled 'The Architecture of Travel: Hotels, their History and Utopia'. The proposed location is Venice. A number of institutions and organisations appear willing to underwrite it. If you are interested in working with us ... '
> This cordial invitation, which arrived a few days ago, is addressed to no one in particular, and does not name the person or persons apostrophised with such rapture. The affectionate outburst sponsored by the municipality transcends the individual to embrace the general: humanity at large, or at least a vast and fluid community of the cultured and intelligent. The proposal attached has been drawn up by professors at the universities of Tübingen and Padua, drafted according to a rigorous logic, and furnished with a bibliography. It aims to reduce the unpredictability of travel, the intricacy and divergence of paths, the fortuity of delays, the uncertainty of evening and the asymmetrical quality of any journey, to the inexorable order of a treatise. The whole scheme is a first draft of a Statute for Living − if life is a journey, as they say, and we pass across the face of the earth as guests.

The reader can see how the professional translator has rolled the text around in his mind to come up with his particular version, and can admire such solutions as *A number of institutions and organisations appear willing to underwrite it, This cordial invitation ... is addressed to no one in particular* and *The affectionate outburst ... .* The muted *Dear friend* for *Carissimo* also shows a sense of fine tuning; the coefficient of intensity of the Italian intensified adjective is not as strong as the English superlative. For example, the adjective *bellissimo* often requires a simple *beautiful*, while *bello* may merit no more than a *nice*.

This author finds less convincing the use of *alderman of the city of Venice* and *the municipality*, in that the first term refers to an office that no longer exists within the British civic hierarchy, and the second lacks specificity, but such quibbles are the stuff of translation debate, and if readers/translators feel that further rolling is required, then they should be encouraged to continue.

The text continues as follows and is offered for practice:

> Certo, nel mondo amministrato e organizzato su scala planetaria l'avventura e il mistero del viaggio sembrano finiti; già i viaggiatori di Baudelaire, partiti alla ricerca dell'inaudito e pronti a naufragare in questa sortita, trovano nell'ignoto, nonostante ogni disastro imprevisto, lo stesso tedio lasciato a casa. Muoversi, comunque, è meglio che niente: si guarda dal finestrino del treno che precipita nel paesaggio, si offre il viso a un po' di fresco che scende dagli alberi sul viale, mescolandosi alla gente, e qualcosa scorre e passa attraverso il corpo, l'aria si infila nei vestiti, l'io si dilata e si contrae come una medusa, un po' di inchiostro trabocca dalla boccetta e si diluisce in un mare color inchiostro. Ma questo blando allentamento dei nessi, che sostituisce l'uniforme con un pigiama, è l'ora di ricreazione nel programma scolastico, più che la promessa del grande disssolvimento, del folle volo in cui si varca il confine. Velleità, diceva Benn, anche quando si sente lo spietato azzurro spalancarsi sotto l'opinabile realtà. Troppi aruspici compiaciuti e perentori ci hanno insegnato che la clausola 'tutto compreso' dei tariffari turistici include pure il vento che si leva. Ma rimane, per fortuna, l'avventura della classificazione e del diagramma, la seduzione metodologica; il professore di Tübingen ingaggiato dall'assessore, consapevole che la prosa del mondo minaccia l'odissea, l'esperienza concreta e irripetibile dell'individuo, si rincuora citando a pagina 3 Hegel, grande allievo del seminario teologico della sua città, e ripetendo con lui che il metodo è la costruzione dell'esperienza.

1.2   Journalistic texts

There is not, and never has been, any strict ruling as to what kind of texts should be used in translation courses at university, college or school level, and any wide-ranging investigation would doubtless throw up a vast range of the most varied and interesting material. However, for a variety of reasons perhaps connected with didactic continuity, tradition, ease of access of materials, fashionable trends or, indeed, proven value, a number of broad 'genres' figure frequently amongst course materials. Among these, pages of literary text, business correspondence and, more recently, technical texts and advertising script form a very large proportion and are dealt with elsewhere in Part Two. It will be the concern of this section to comment on the translation of another genre much favoured in the classroom, and that is the language of newspapers and magazines – journalistic texts.

Newspaper and magazine articles are indeed favoured by many translation teachers, and with good reason, in spite of the comparative infrequency with which such texts are actually translated in real time in the real world. Such texts, in fact, provide a never-ending, up-to-the-minute source of important, interesting and stimulating information offering translation students an infinite range of linguistic, semantic and pragmatic elements to test their translating skills. And such texts are, in fact, translated, though not necessarily in the time-honoured way. Consider how Italy's La Repubblica regularly reports what foreign newspapers have to say in its *Opinioni dal mondo* section. On Wednesday 13th November 1996, the Italian daily paper reported from The Independent, Le Monde and Time. As regards the English newspaper, the comment on an article about Italian treasury bills (BOT) took the following form:

> L'Independent analizza quella che definisce 'una vera e propria svolta sui mercati finanziari': la corsa ai buoni del tesoro italiani, che presentano rendimenti interessanti se rapportati all'inflazione. Il mercato 'prende sul serio gli impegni italiani nonché l'inaspettato entusiasmo che percorre il paese per la moneta unica europea'. Se tutto andrà bene, 'l'Italia avrà nel 1997 un deficit pubblico non superiore al 3,3% del PIL, mentre la Gran Bretagna sarà intorno al 3,5. Anche sull'inflazione, tutto lascia prevedere che l'Italia si troverà meglio piazzata sul Regno Unito, che così scivolerà al fondo della classifica del G-7'.

As can be seen, the translation proper is restricted to the parts in inverted commas while the rest of the article is 'interpreted' in report form.

Certainly, the kind of article that is most likely to be translated is one that deals with national issues in one country about which other nations might be interested or curious. For example, in 1996 the 'Tangentopoli' revelations in Italy and the ramifications of the outbreak of 'Mad Cow Disease' in Britain provided material that was duly translated into most other European languages.

1.2.1 Italian national newspaper (Corriere della Sera)

The first article chosen in this section regards a legal decision on the phenomenon of absenteeism, a subject that could well interest readers in other countries and therefore be a candidate for translation.

RISARCISCA I DANNI IL DIPENDENTE ASSENTEISTA

ROMA – Il dipendente pubblico che si assenta arbitrariamente dal servizio per svolgere altre attività, è tenuto a risarcire il danno arrecato all'erario. Il danno va quantificato in base agli emolumenti illecitamente percepiti. Il principio è stato sancito dalla Corte dei conti nel condannare un addetto alla portineria di un presidio ospedaliero di Isernia a risarcire 200 mila lire, equivalenti a quanto illecitamente percepito in due giorni di lavoro.

All'impiegato i giudici contabili hanno contestato di essersi arbitrariamente assentato dal suo posto di lavoro pur avendo timbrato il cartellino di presenza. Nel tentativo di farla franca, il dipendente aveva prodotto un certificato medico attestante una visita odontoiatrica.

Nella stessa sentenza, i giudici hanno però bocciato la richiesta del pm contabile di introdurre il principio che si debba anche tener conto degli oneri conseguenti agli effetti negativi che l'assenza ingiustificata ha prodotto sulla qualità del servizio.

Il collegio ha riconosciuto la possibilità che possano determinarsi anche questo tipo di danni che però non sono esattamente determinabili.

Literal translation

PAY BACK THE DAMAGES, ABSENTEE DEPENDENT

ROME – The public dependent who absents himself arbitrarily from the service to perform other activities, is held to pay back the damage caused to the public expenditure. The damage goes quantified on the base of the emoluments illicitly perceived. The principle has been sanctioned by the Court of accounts in condemning an adept at the door of a hospital praesidium of Isernia to repay 200 thousand liras, equivalent to how much illicitly perceived in two days of work.

To the employee the accountant judges have contested of being arbitrarily absented from his place of work though having stamped the card of presence. In the attempt to make it frank, the dependent had produced a medical certificate attesting an odontoiatric visit.

In the same sentence, the judges have however failed a request of the accountant public ministry to introduce the principle that one must also keep count of the burdens consequent to the negative effects that the unjustified absence has produced on the quality of the service.

The college has recognised the possibility that they can determine themselves also this type of damages that however are not exactly determinable.

Linguistico-pragmatic analysis

The translator is faced here with a newspaper article on a legal topic, suggesting a subtle mixture of two different registers, and will therefore tread a fine line throughout in handling these two genres, given the added difficulty of non-matching legal terminologies. To begin with the headline, *dipendente assenteista* can be condensed to *absentee*, a common term in English labour terminology. The translator must then decide what to do with the important subjunctive *Risarcisca* in the Italian text. The form denotes obligation and *must* would presumably come to mind. The re-ordering process would then have to be completed with a translation for *danni*. The term *damages* has to be considered because of its legal (and monetary) flavour, but would a person in this situation have to pay 'damages'? To avoid the risk of using this term inappropriately, one solution available to the translator is to rely solely on the verb and announce that *Absentees must pay*. All will be revealed in the text, and this is in line with the English newspaper headline practice of exploiting ellipsis. If not satisfied with this loophole, the translator could remain a little more neutral and opt for *Absentees must pay compensation*.

The translator would probably decide to make the singular *dipendente pubblico* plural and talk of *Public employees*. The verb *remain* collocates well with *absent* and provides the verbalisation. Translators will treat the adverb *arbitrariamente* with care; they should ask themselves when being absent causes disapproval – it is of course when one is absent *without permission*. Translating *dal servizio* with *from their place of work* may seem an over-translation but this will be compensated later in the text where *posto di lavoro* appears. This shows how important it is to have an overall view of the text before beginning to translate, fully vindicating the efficacy of the pre-translation analysis.

In the search for a suitable verb to collocate with *employment*, the phrasal verb *take up* might spring to mind. The use of *l'erario* in Italian brings to mind taxes and public expenditure; a term used in this metonymic way in English is *the Treasury*. In the second sentence, to avoid the *danno* problem again, the translator may use the device of shifting from the specific to the generic and refer to *The sum*. The highly latinate *emolumenti illecitamente percepiti* requires some delving into the semi-legal terminology of journalism – perhaps *unlawfully received payments* sounds suitably solemn. The English legal term *ruling* seems very fit for this text and could be used in two or three instances, for example, to translate *principio*. The *ruling* would then be *confirmed* by the *Corte dei conti*. This latter body belongs more to continental European law, but the European Union and the data-banks produced for that organisation provide useful translations in such cases – here the *State Audit Court*.

The translator would be well aware of the legal false friends *condanna* and *sentenza*, and would make the lexicogrammatical changes necessary (*nel condannare/in sentencing*). For the purposes of the article, a lexical condensation of *un addetto alla portineria di un presidio ospedaliero* to *a hospital porter* is justified, in that the important element is simply that he was a state employee. Playing safe, the translator may be satisfied with *pay* for *risarcire* in the third instance of use. It is usual practice to convert a sum of money in one currency into the target language equivalent and put it in brackets: *200,000 lira (approx. £70)*.

In paragraph two, an initial re-ordering is required to conform to English syntax and place the subject at the beginning of the sentence. On the basis of *the State Audit Court*, *i giudici contabili* would logically become *Audit Court judges*. Although *contestato/charged* is not a constant translation couplet, it is what fits best in this context.

It is a well-known fact that English employees 'clock in' when they get to work, though the translator may have a few qualms about the register of this expression. An alternative could be *stamped his time card*. A similar register problem is posed by the expression *farla franca*. Knowledge of colloquial Italian or a decent dictionary would provide the translator with *to get away with (it)* as an equivalent English expression on all levels, yet it doesn't work. The translator would have to reach the conclusion that an English newspaper of the Corriere della Sera category would not use that expression (though The Sun would!), and find a more sober version like *to avoid detection*. The technical-sounding *visita odontoiatrica* translates into a more mundane-sounding *dental appointment*.

In the third paragraph, the translator would see the need to change the preposition in the opening phrase while keeping the adverbial in theme position: *Nella stessa sentenza/By the same ruling.* The *pm* (pubblico ministero) is an Italian figure best translated generically by *(public) prosecutor.* The rest of this long sentence (... *di introdurre il principio che si debba anche tener conto degli oneri conseguenti agli effetti negativi che l'assenza ingiustificata ha prodotto sulla qualità del servizio*) needs dissecting and re-arranging, though it may seem somewhat strained in English whatever re-ordering process is applied. Using such legal terminology as *incurred, deleterious* and *unwarranted,* the sentence could end up as *to apply the principle that expenses incurred as a result of the deleterious effects on the quality of the service by the unwarranted absence also be considered.* Note the shifting of the passive infinitive verb form *be considered* to the end of the sentence.

Il collegio refers essentially to *the Court,* another acceptable use of metonym. And so the translation has rolled on to a point where an English readership can reconstruct the event:

ABSENTEES MUST PAY COMPENSATION

ROME – Public employees who remain absent from their place of work without permission in order to take up other employment must pay compensation to the Treasury. The sum will be calculated on the basis of the unlawfully received payments. This ruling was confirmed by the State Audit Court when sentencing a hospital porter in Isernia to pay 200,000 lira (approx. £70), the sum unlawfully received for two days of work.

The Audit Court judges charged the employee with being absent without permission despite having clocked in (stamped his time card). In an attempt to avoid detection, the man had produced a medical certificate showing a dental appointment.

By the same ruling, however, the judges rejected the Audit Court prosecutor's request to apply the principle that expenses incurred as a result of the deleterious effects on the quality of the service by the unwarranted absence also be considered.

The Court recognised the possibility that such expenses could also occur but that they are not precisely calculable.

The following article dealing with Italian internal affairs is also taken from the Corriere della Sera (6/12/96) and is offered for practice:

Una donna alla vicedirezione del Sisde, era prefetto a Lodi

LODI – Dalle sponde dell'Adda alle rive del Tevere, dalla Prefettura di Lodi alla vicedirezione del Sisde. Per Annamaria Sorge Lodovici, 56 anni, senese, primo prefetto del neonato capoluogo della Bassa, il soggiorno a Lodi è durato un solo, intenso anno. Al suo arrivo, il 6 novembre '95, qualcuno aveva sorriso di fronte al prefetto in gonnella con pochi collaboratori, due stanze, un tavolo e quattro sedie rimediate nella cadente ex pretura.

Da toscanaccia volitiva, annunciò: 'Qui a Lodi servono almeno dieci persone. Se non arrivano presto, andrò io a Roma a prendermele'. Ieri ha assunto il nuovo incarico a Roma, dove affiancherà il direttore del Sisde, Vittorio Stelo, con cui aveva già collaborato a Siena, Genova e Firenze. La scorsa settimana, nell'annunciare il trasferimento, Annamaria Sorge aveva nascosto a fatica la commozione: 'L'incarico è prestigioso – aveva commentato -, ma la soddisfazione è pari al rammarico che provo nel lasciare Lodi. Mi dispiace andarmene ora che c'è ancora molto da fare. E' un distacco brusco, che può sembrare perfino prematuro. La città e la sua gente mi rimarrano nel cuore'. Un mese fa le era toccata anche l'emergenza maltempo, con l'Adda a spasso per le campagne e i paesi.

Autoritaria al primo approccio, le bastavano un paio di battute per far capire che era pronta più ad ascoltare che a pontificare, decisa al punto di vedersi affibbiare l'etichetta (maschilista) di uomo in gonnella, forse per l'abitudine di girare per la città senza scorta, quasi in incognito. Dava retta a tutti, anche a chi, magari in modo inopportuno, la fermava per strada. Due giorni dopo l'arrivo a Lodi le era piombata una vera grana tra capo e collo: il caso del sindaco leghista Alberto Segalini, pescato con un mazzo di banconote prelevate dalla cassa del centro estetico in cui lavorava come chirurgo plastico.

The next practice article is from La Repubblica (20/4/96):

Presa la 'talpa' di Falcone

PALERMO: Era un agente della scorta di Giovanni Falcone, ma faceva la 'talpa' per Cosa nostra. M.C., che protesse il magistrato fino a un anno prima della strage di Capaci, è stato arrestato. Secondo l'accusa il poliziotto forniva notizie alla famiglia mafiosa Ganci. Un pentito afferma che M.C. avrebbe fornito a Cosa nostra notizie su un confidente, poi ucciso ...
Una storia semplice, quella di M.C., 34 anni, palermitano della zona di Cruillas, una famiglia normale, una vita apparentemente normale, una carriera normale. L'ha raccontato A.N., uno dei tanti pentiti, uno che conosceva tanti segreti della Noce, il quartiere dei Ganci. 'Il poliziotto ci passava alcune notizie ... è stato lui ad esempio a indicarci pure il nome di quel confidente che abbiamo poi ucciso ...', rivelò al capo della 'mobile' insieme ai particolari di una rapina miliardaria alle Poste.

1.2.2 English national newspaper (The Observer)

The following article is taken from The Observer Review (12/11/95), a long-standing vehicle for general interest features and creative journalism:

A breath of fresh Eire

The time: a balmy October evening. The place: the National Film Theatre. An audience of several hundred people, most of them English, are sitting spellbound, listening to a small man talking animatedly about film, cultural hegemony, the information society and the future. 'We don't have to lie down,' he says, 'before a culture that is driven by greed.' There is a collective sigh of approval. 'It is surely wrong,' he continues, 'that all the images of the world should come from one place.' A ripple of agreement runs through the audience, like a breeze running over a field of ripening corn.

The man is Michael D. Higgins, Ireland's Minister for Arts, Culture and the Gaeltacht, and he is explaining what has to be done if Europeans are not to be reduced to passive consumers of whatever the American multimedia industry chooses to pump down the information highways of the future. In the discussion which follows the formal part of the NFT programme, one senses a kind of wistful astonishment in his English listeners.

> And one can see why: for they are looking at a representative of a
> species which, after 15 years of Thatcherism, they thought had become
> extinct: a Minister for arts and culture who knows and cares a great deal
> about both.

The pun in the title, playing on the homophones *Eire/air*, prepares the
reader for a well-written article on the subject of culture. The paronomasia
(pun-making), however, also contains an important reference to Ireland, a
vital part of the context of situation, and which should be captured in the
translation. *Una boccata di pura Irlanda* captures both the *air* and *Eire* (for
this and other suggestions for the translation of this text, I am indebted to
Prof. E. Argenton of the University of Trieste).

The official translation of the article, taken from Internazionale (12/1/
96), is provided at the outset for the purpose of comparison:

Official version

Una boccata di pura Irlanda

Tempo: una mite serata d'ottobre. Luogo: il National Film Theatre. Un
pubblico di parecchie centinaia di persone, in maggioranza inglesi, ascolta
rapito un uomo di bassa statura cha parla animatamente di cinema, di
egemonia culturale, di società dell'informazione e del futuro. 'Non
dobbiamo inchinarci', afferma, 'di fronte a una cultura dominata dall'avidità'.
Si sente un generale sospiro di approvazione. 'E' senza dubbio sbagliato',
continua, 'che tutte le immagini del mondo provengano da un solo posto'.
Questa volta un mormorio di assenso attraversa la sala, simile alla brezza
che pettina un campo di spighe mature.

Ed è facile capire perché: si trovano di fronte un esemplare di una
specie che dopo quindici anni di thatcherismo tutti credevano estinta: un
ministro dell'arte e della cultura che conosce e si preoccupa molto di
entrambe.

L'uomo è Michael D. Higgins, ministro irlandese dell'Arte, della Cultura e
del Gaeltacht, e sta spiegando cosa bisogna fare per evitare che gli
europei si riducano a essere consumatori passivi di tutto ciò che l'industria
multimediale americana decide di pompare nelle autostrade
dell'informazione del futuro. Nel dibattito che segue alla parte ufficiale del
programma, si percepisce una specie di preoccupato stupore da parte del
pubblico inglese.

A number of translation couplets in a relationship of total equation can
be identified immediately: *October evening/serata d'ottobre, cultural hege-*

mony/*egemonia culturale*, information society/*società dell'informazione*, sigh of approval/*sospiro di approvazione*, passive consumers/*consumatori passivi*, the American multimedia industry/*l'industria multimediale americana*, information highway/*autostrada dell'informazione*, etc. Others require fairly limited modifications: *an audience of several hundred people/un pubblico di parecchie centinaia di persone*, *the discussion which follows/il dibattito che segue*, *one senses/si percepisce*, *a representative of a species/un esemplare di una specie*.

At a grammatical level, a number of changes are required to conform to contrastive syntactic structures. The article in the noun phrases *The time* and *The place* is best eliminated in Italian to provide a note-like *Tempo* and *Luogo*, followed in all cases by a colon. The relative clause that is implicit through the use of the *-ing* form in *talking animatedly* requires the explicit *che* clause in Italian: *che parla animatamente*. Mr Higgins points out that '*It is surely wrong that all the images of the world should come from one place*'. The fact that he is expressing an opinion calls for the subjunctive mood in Italian: '*E' senza dubbio sbagliato che tutte le immagini del mondo provengano da un solo posto*'. The two passive infinitive forms in *he is explaining <u>what has to be done</u> if Europeans <u>are not to be reduced to</u>* cannot be accommodated as such by Italian syntax. In the first case, the convenient verb *bisognare/to need to, to have to* can be used, and in the second case a subjunctive, dictated by the use of an infinitive clause of purpose: *sta spiegando cosa bisogna fare per evitare che gli europei si riducano a . . . .* .

At a lexical level, a componential analysis of the adjective *balmy* includes such components as temperate, soft, warm, and calm. As the description in question is of an October evening in Ireland, the 'warm' and 'soft' attributes may have to be tempered. *Mild* seems a good solution. Although the words *film* and *cinema* are current in both languages, their exact meanings diverge slightly, enough to make *film* more suitable in English, and *cinema* more suitable in Italian, in this context. In the case of the unusual collocation *wistful astonishment*, an intuitive sense of the meaning of *wistful* may need corroboration. A study of both monolingual and bilingual dictionaries establishes that the adjective contains a definite sense of '*desiderio*', perhaps tinged with a little '*malinconia*'. As *desideroso* and *malinconico* would tend to lie too far in those respective directions, the use of *ansioso stupore* may be an appropriate choice. Neither the English nor the Italian text give any assistance with *Gaeltacht* and equivalent effect is therefore achieved. The metaphorical element contained in *And one can see why* can be normalised, like all metaphors if they do not work as successfully in the target language, to *Ed è facile capire perché.*

Turning finally to the major difficulties to be found in this text, it is, predictably, the more figurative use of language that could give rise to debate among translators. The audience are said to be *sitting spellbound, listening to . . . .* The official version (OV), through a process of reordering and reduction, provides the concise *ascolta rapito.* However, the subject matter is not particularly mysterious or entrancing, and the fact that the people are sitting down may be important, so an appropriate descriptive tone might be achieved through *se ne sta seduto, affascinato, ad ascoltare . . .* Higgins uses the expression 'We don't have to lie down before a culture . . .', OV opts for the more common figurative image provided by *inchinarci.* An alternative could be *chinare il capo di fronte a . . . .*

The most figurative sentence in the text is definitely *A ripple of agreement runs through the audience, like a breeze running over a field of ripening corn.* The efficacy of the English sentence lies in the choice of metaphors *ripple* and *breeze,* allied to the repetition of the verb *run* and the image of the *corn.* The twin images are of a gathering murmur from a group of people and a field of corn swaying in the breeze. In the OV, *un mormorio di assenso* captures the murmur, but the rest of the sentence does not refer specifically to the people and uses the rather unusual metaphor *pettina.* The *audience* and the field of waving corn are better represented by *un mormorio di assenso serpeggia tra il pubblico, simile ad una brezza che fa ondeggiare un campo di spighe mature.* The OV translation *pump down/pompare* seems a little forced; perhaps *immettere a forza* might be better.

The following article, dealing with the danger of subsidence in a former salt mining town, is also taken from The Observer (18/1/98) and is offered for practice:

Town that grew too fat on salt is falling into hole no one will fill

The people of Northwich in Cheshire are used to a bit of subsidence, the legacy of centuries of salt mining that began with the Romans, peaked with the Victorians, and ended in 1928.

But nobody told them that one day the whole town is likely to collapse into mines so cavernous that they were used for a huge banquet held for Tsar Nicholas in 1844. That is the fate awaiting them as history prepares to exact a cruel revenge on the town that grew fat on salt.

A series of reports by consultant engineers have warned that the town will sink into the mines within three to 13 years.

Disaster is imminent, say the reports, because the thin salt pillars left by mining companies are crumbling. The pillars hold up 300ft. of earth, and hundreds of houses and businesses on the surface.

Vale Royal borough council says it will cost £16 million to fill the total of around 90 mines with a soda ash-concrete mix and make them safe. But no one knows where the money will come from. 'It would be easier to move the entire town,' one official admitted ruefully.

1.2.3 In-flight magazine

The text chosen for analysis in this section is taken from Arrivederci, the Alitalia in-flight magazine for October 1996. Such glossy publications typically contain general interest articles supplemented by numerous colour photographs, usually written in at least two languages. The text featured here was written by Alberto Sordi, the famous film actor, and tells of the impression he gained of the Lombard town of Vigevano during the filming of Mastronardi's novel, 'Il maestro di Vigevano'.

Il mio maestro di Vigevano

Ho scoperto Vigevano nel 1963, girando il film di Elio Petri 'Il maestro di Vigevano'. E' la storia di un uomo povero, che conduce una vita miserabile e si mette nei guai. Ha una moglie molto graziosa, interpretata da Claire Bloom, che qualcuno ricorderà accanto a Charlot in 'Luci della Ribalta'. E vuol mettersi a lavorare anche lei per realizzare i sogni impossibili con lo stipendio del marito. Ma lei doveva essere compiacente con certi industriali, e qui nascono i guai che annienteranno il marito. Io volevo adattare il mio personaggio al mio vero maestro delle elementari. Si chiamava Mangano e portava le scarpe a punta come arma per dare calci nel sedere agli scolari distratti. Ma l'autore del libro da cui è tratto il film, Lucio Mastronardi, era contrario e allora noi ci attenemmo scrupolosamente al suo testo. Mastronardi era di Vigevano. Sullo sfondo del libro c'è il 'boom economico' che aveva invaso la sua cittadina. E' il paese delle calzature, si esportano in tutto il mondo e Mastronardi lo ricorda nel suo esordio letterario. Era malato di nervi: si suicidò. M'è rimasta nella memoria la sua attenzione ai dettagli della vita di provincia, che a me piace molto. Ho vissuto i due mesi del set a Vigevano. Da allora non vi sono più tornato perché non è un luogo di transito.

(Arrivederci, anno VII, no. 80 ott. 1996)

Literal translation

My teacher from Vigevano

I discovered Vigevano in 1963 filming the film of Elio Petri 'Il maestro di Vigevano' (The Schoolmaster from Vigevano). It is the story of a poor man, who conducts a miserable life and puts himself in trouble. He has a very pretty wife, interpreted by Claire Bloom, who someone will remember alongside Charlie Chaplin in 'Limelight'. And she wants to put herself to work, her too, to realise the dreams impossible with the salary of her husband. But she had to be pleasant with certain industrialists, and here the troubles are born which will annihilate her husband. I wanted to adapt my character to my real primary school teacher. He was called Mangano and he wore shoes with points like a weapon to give kicks in the bottom of distracted students. But the author of the book from which was taken the film, Lucio Mastronardi, was contrary, and so we kept scrupulously to his text. Mastronardi was of Vigevano. On the background of his book there is the 'economic boom' which had invaded his town. It is the town of shoes, they export in all the world, and Mastronardi records it in his literary debut. He was ill with nerves: he committed suicide. It has remained in my memory his attention to details of the life of the province, which I like a lot. I lived the two months of the set in Vigevano. Since then I have not returned, because it's not a place of transit.

The OV translation, which accompanies the Italian text column for column, is inserted at this point as reference will be made to it in the commentary.

Official version

My teacher from Vigevano

I discovered Vigevano in 1963 while on location for Elio Petri's 'Il maestro di Vigevano' (The Schoolmaster from Vigevano). The movie recounted the miserable life of a poor man who got into trouble. He had a lovely wife, played by Claire Bloom, the actress who played a memorable role in 'Limelight' starring Charlie Chaplin. In the movie she wanted to work in order to buy things she could never afford on her husband's meager wages. But that meant being charming with certain businessmen, and this ultimately led to her husband's undoing. I wanted to base my character on my real grade school teacher. His name was Mangano and he wore pointed shoes which he put to good use kicking distracted students in the rear. But Lucio Mastronardi, the author of the book the movie was based on, was against the idea, so we kept very close to his text. Mastronardi was from Vigevano. His story was set against the backdrop of his hometown's economic boom. The town's business was making shoes which were exported all over the world, as Mastronardi recorded in that first book of his. He had mental problems, and eventually committed suicide. I will always remember his detailed description of life in a provincial town, which I still find appealing. For the two months of shooting, I lived in Vigevano. I haven't returned, since it's not a place one passes through on the way to anywhere else.

Lexicogrammatical and semantic analysis

In the opening sentence, we are introduced to Petri's film (and Mastronardi's novel), *Il maestro di Vigevano*. The title of the article plays on this terminology with *Il mio maestro* . . . . If there is a reason to change this term (see OV), it is to make the distinction between Sordi's primary school 'teacher' (the Italian equivalent of which is, however, *maestro*) and the character in the novel/film, a distinction that does not appear necessary. It may be that, as the OV translator was using American English (cf: *on location, movie, meager*), the term *schoolmaster* would have clashed with the co-text (**grade schoolmaster*). The participle form *girando* can be maintained with *while filming*. The economic use of the saxon genitive (*Elio Petri's 'Il maestro di Vigevano'*) is typical of the film commentary genre. However, the omission of the noun *film* or *movie* at this point means that it has to be used at the beginning of the next sentence: *The film tells the story* . . . . The present tense is normal in this kind of recounting, though the past tense would then be used in the subordinate *of a man who lived a miserable life and got himself into trouble*. The *got himself* reflects the self-responsibility of *mettersi*. In the next sentence, the active *che qualcuno la ricorderà* can be subjected to passivisation: *will be remembered* (da qualcuno) *for her role in* . . . . The sentence can then end with another example of the saxon genitive form: *Chaplin's 'Limelight'*. At the beginning of the following sentence, the addition in the OV of *In the movie* (or *In the film*) is necessary to orient the reader. Again, in terms of the coefficient of intensity, *vuol mettersi a lavorare* is best rendered by *she wanted to go out to work*. The OV paraphrases *realizzare i sogni impossibili*, though the metaphor can be kept with *to fulfil the dreams that were impossible on her husband's salary*. The term *salary* (cf: OV *wages*) is correct, in spite of the meagreness, as it is the pay of a schoolmaster.

The next sentence contains the deliberately euphemistic reference to how the wife was to behave with certain businessmen (*doveva essere compiacente*) and this must be maintained, for example, *she had to be nice to certain businessmen*. The connotation is stronger than the literal sense in this passage whereas the opposite is true of what follows: *nascono i guai che annienteranno il marito*. The OV *and this ultimately led to her husband's undoing* shows a careful reading of the actual meaning of the text.

The OV goes into paraphrase again when describing Sordi's teacher's shoes *which he put to good use kicking distracted students in the rear*. The use of *students* for primary school children is further evidence of the American English employed (cf: *pupils* in British English). Keeping closer to the original, one could translate *he wore pointed shoes as a weapon to kick the backsides of those pupils who weren't paying attention*, which also renders *distratti* better. The OV quite rightly translates *era contrario* with *was against the idea*, as the English adjective has less autonomy than the Italian. The verb/adverb combination *attenemmo scrupolosamente* can be matched by *stuck closely*.

The next three sentences are distinguished by some punctuation and organisation of ideas that do not easily translate. Some adaptation is required: *Mastronardi was from Vigevano and his story is set against the background of the economic boom that the town had experienced. Vigevano is* <u>the</u> *shoe-manufacturing town, exporting all over the world, and Mastronardi recalls this in his literary debut.*

Era malato di nervi requires careful handling in terms of politically correct language. *He had psychological problems* renders the idea and the OV addition of *eventually* in *he eventually committed suicide* is helpful both semantically and rhythmically in such a short clause. In the next sentence, the opening notion *M'è rimasta nella memoria* can be kept in this position by altering the perspective slightly (see OV *I will always remember*). The expression *la sua attenzione ai dettagli* exists in English, and thus *his attention to detail in describing provincial life* is an acceptable option. The final clause in the sentence (*che mi piace molto*) should refer clearly to *provincial life*, for example, *which I like so much*. In the case of the OV choice of *which I still find appealing*, it is not clear whether it is the author's 'detailed description' or 'provincial life' which Sordi finds 'appealing'.

The final sentence seems straightforward, e.g. *I've never been back ...* , but *since it's not a place one passes through on the way to anywhere else* (see OV), although a set expression in English, is perhaps too long, and *since it's not a place one passes through* would be sufficient.

The translation has thus rolled to an (at least temporary) conclusion:

> I discovered Vigevano in 1963 while filming Elio Petri's 'Il maestro di Vigevano' (The Schoolmaster from Vigevano). The film tells the story of a man who lived a miserable life and got himself into trouble. He had a lovely wife, played by Claire Bloom, who will be remembered for her role in Chaplin's 'Limelight'. In the film she wanted to go out to work to fulfil the dreams that were impossible on her husband's salary. But she had to be nice to certain businessmen and this ultimately led to her husband's undoing.
>
> I wanted to base my character on my real primary schoolmaster. He was called Mangano and he wore pointed shoes as a weapon to kick the backsides of those pupils who weren't paying attention. But Lucio Mastronardi, the author of the book the movie was based on, was against the idea, so we stuck closely to his text.
>
> Mastronardi was from Vigevano and his story is set against the background of the economic boom that the town had experienced. Vigevano is <u>the</u> shoe-manufacturing town, exporting all over the world, and Mastronardi recalls this in his literary debut.
>
> He had psychological problems and eventually committed suicide. I will always remember his attention to detail in describing provincial life, which I like so much. During the two months of filming I lived in Vigevano. I've never been back since it's not a place one passes through.

The text continues as follows and is offered for practice:

> Io ero nel pieno del mio successo, venivo da 'Un americano a Roma', 'Lo scapolo', 'Il marito', 'Il seduttore'. Ma c'era attorno a me una curiosità composta, limitata a espressioni di ammirazione, alla richiesta di un autografo. Vigevano è abitata da gente operosa, laboriosa, vorrei dire seria, che non scende a compromessi con le frivolezze. E in questa oasi tranquilla, nelle pause di lavorazione andavo a passeggiare nella piazza centrale dove si concentra la vita della cittadina, straordinaria, con la chiesa della Madonna della Neve dove andavo a messa la domenica.

Ricordo il castello di Grazzano: l'intero paesino è di proprietà della famiglia Visconti. Che sorpresa nel vedere che tutti vivono in costume. Si mangia pure bene: minestroni, pasta e fagioli, carne ai ferri e come vino il 'Franciacorta'. Più volte il sindaco di Vigevano organizzò pranzetti ufficiali in mio onore. Mi raccontavano la storia della città. Ci sono tre momenti fondamentali: Vigevano in età romana, poi nella seconda metà del 1100 si schierò con la Lega Lombarda. Infine svolse la sua parte nel Risorgimento.

1.3   Film translation

1.3.1 Film dubbing

Film dubbing, the least studied of all the branches of translation

(Viaggio 1992)

If subtitling, the other system widely used for translating films and TV series, is included in this observation, it can be seen that a large and important sector of modern life has received insufficient attention. In England most foreign films are subtitled; in Italy they are dubbed. There are historical and pragmatic reasons for this difference that need not concern us here, but the current situation is very relevant. In recent years, the two university faculties of translation and interpreting in Italy (at Forlì and Trieste) have begun studying the phenomenon of film translation in conjunction with professionals in the field. Various conferences have been held, for example, in the afore-mentioned Forlì and Trieste, and research projects launched which have already produced interesting results. Certain features of this genre have already been identified, and it is hoped that in the future a real contribution can be made to the study and development of this constantly-expanding branch of translation practice.

At one of the first of the conferences mentioned above (see Bollettieri Bosinelli et al. 1994), it was pointed out by Gianni Galassi (1994:63), a leading professional in the field, that the actual translation of the script is merely an initial stage in the process of adaptation that has to be carried out before actors take on the task of actually dubbing the original film. Various factors come into play along the way: the matching of verbal with non-verbal elements (the images on the screen, the gestures and physical location of the actors, lip synchronisation in close-ups), commercial considerations of length, suitability, etc. and, crucially, the handling of the many-headed beast of cultural transfer. This latter problem, however, though huge, is one that can be addressed at the level of initial translation. Students at both Forlì and Trieste have been encouraged to work on just such problems, finding where translations do or do not work and suggesting solutions. Very often they discover that cultural barriers and functional breakdowns, rather than linguistic inaccuracies, are the real obstacles to successful film translation. For example, references to people or entities known only in the source language culture have to be adapted.

This is often the case when characters from other areas of public life, sport or the media emerge in film dialogue. For example, a well-known trade union leader, a cricketer or a character from a British soap opera would probably be unknown to an Italian audience. However, if the characters themselves are only important in terms of what they represent, then equivalents can be found among Italian political figures, football heroes or more internationally known 'soap' stars. In terms of the cinema, in Woody Allen's film 'Annie Hall', Annie refers to her grandmother as 'Grammy Hall' in a conversation with the character Alvy. Alvy responds facetiously by asking her if she grew up in *a Norman Rockwell painting*. The problem in translating this is to capture the tone of Alvy's quip. Norman Rockwell is well known in the United States as a painter of scenes of typical all-American life. The allusion is to Annie's naivety in the 'sophisticated' world of Alvy. The solution lies in finding an equivalent personage (though not necessarily a painter) who would conjure up the same image for an Italian audience, but that could feasibly be cited by an American. The Italian translator changes the reference from a Norman Rockwell painting to *le illustrazioni di Mary Poppins*. This wholesome fictional character is internationally known and generally considered to represent traditional values and standards, the kind of image abhorred by the New York intelligentsia. The irony is thus conveyed with no significant loss of meaning.

In terms of function, if the function of a line of dialogue is to be humorous or frightening or seductive, or whatever, it is this function that must be conveyed, if necessary at the expense of linguistic fidelity. In the following example, the function of the exchange is to create humour through ambiguity:

INGA: Werewolf!
FRANKENSTEIN: Werewolf?
IGOR: There!
FRANKENSTEIN: What?
IGOR: There wolf, there castle!

(from Mel Brooks' 'Young Frankenstein')

In this case the OV translation is arguably even more humorous than the original, and the same ambiguity is maintained:

INGA: Lupo ulula!
FRANKENSTEIN: Lupo ululà?
IGOR: Là!
FRANKENSTEIN: Cosa?
IGOR: Lupu ululà, castello ululì!

Oreste Lionello (1994:46), the actor who has successfully dubbed Woody Allen into Italian for many years, points out that although even a film translation should be as faithful as possible, in line with the norms governing all translation practice, it is essentially false, indeed its dignity lies in its falseness, its second-handness. Thus the new script has to stand up on its own and this may imply considerable latitude with respect to the original. The specimen text that follows consists of a number of extracts from Spike Lee's successful though controversial film 'Do the Right Thing', translated into Italian by Mario Paolinelli and dubbed under the direction of Pino Colizzi. This film holds the dubious record of containing the highest number of expletives ever heard in a motion picture, as it traces a day in the life of the black community in a suburb of Brooklyn. The problem of translating this kind of language, together with many other socio-linguistic elements, was the subject of an exhaustive thesis (Crescenzi 1993), elements of which will appear in the following analysis. The film begins with the voice-over of a local radio disc-jockey, Mister Senor Love Daddy, with all the sociolinguistic ingredients that this particular genrelet implies.

MISTER SENOR LOVE DADDY:
Wake up! Wake up! Wake up! Wake up! Up ya wake! Up ya wake! Up ya wake! Up ya wake! This is Mister Senor Love Daddy, Your voice of choice. The world's only twelve-hour strong man on the air, here on We love Radio, 108 FM. The last on your dial but first on ya hearts, and that's the truth Ruth! Here I am, am I here? Y'know it. It ya know. This is Mister Senor Love Daddy, doing the nasty to ya ears, ya ears to the nasty. I'se play only da platters dat matter, da matters dey platter and that's the truth Ruth. From the heart of Bed-Stuy you are listening to We love Radio. Doing the ying and the yang, the hip and the hop. The stupid fresh thing, the flippity flop. I have today's forecast for you: hot! The color for today is black. That's right, black. So you can absorb some of these rays and save that heat for winter. So you want to get out there and wear that black and be involved. Also the day's temperature is going to rise above 100

degrees. So that's a jerri curl alert. That's right. Jerri curl alert. If you have a jerri curl stay in the house or you will end up with a permanent plastic helmet on your head forever! All right! We're going to say hello to Mister and Missus, that's Mister and Missus. And Happy Birthday to Big Red, Little Red and Miss Annie Mae who is 100 today and if you care to stay out of this heat, you might live to be that old yourself.

Analysis

The analysis attempts, in retrospect, to follow the thought processes of the translator, and of those involved in modifying the text at a later stage, in the production of the final script for 'Fa' la cosa giusta', which appears at the end of this section.

The initial succession of *Wake up*s and *Up ya wake*s has been rendered by a probably indefinite number of *in piedi*s sandwiched between *sveglia*s and *che aspetti fratello*s. The *Svegliati, in piedi/in piedi sveglia!* which respectively open and close the line reflect the idiolectal habit Love Daddy has of reversing his locutions (*Wake up! Up ya wake!*). This quirk is repeated several times later in the text, and therefore also needs to be established straight away in translation. The addition of a couple of *che aspetti fratello*s establishes the recognition of black dialect, a device often used in Italian to translate, for example, the ubiquitous *man* in expressions like '*Hey, man, what you doin', man!*'.

Any attempt to translate *Mister Senor Love Daddy* would be wasted time; the name is internationally understandable, especially to the target audience for this film, and creates the right atmosphere. The phonological equivalence so evident in the easy rhyme *your voice of choice* is recreated with *la voce che vi piace* which in fact achieves an alliterative effect with the initial *v* of *voce* and *vi* and the repeated tʃ sound. The four-word noun string *twelve-hour strong man* needs syntactic and semantic attention, but the translator wisely rejects the usual grammatical solution of prepositional phrases and thinks of meaning; what is Love Daddy offering? The answer to this question is that *vi assicura 12 ore di trasmissione*. *Strong man* becomes *asso*. Again *We love radio* should be transparent enough to be understood and, in any case, functions as a proper name with all the protection that is its due. The substituting of *lunghezza d'onda* for *dial* maintains the semantic field of radio, which is all that is important: the function is stronger than the word. The assonance in *è vero, lo giuro* goes some way towards emulating the phonological equivalence in *that's the truth Ruth!*.

Here I am, am I here? reiterates the previously-analysed idiolectal element, immediately further reinforced by *Y'know it. It ya know.* The translator can be seen to wrestle with the problem (*Eccomi da voi ma sono qua? Sì che sono qua, sapete che ci sono*) even though exact reversal is impossible. The pronunciation element, which is phonetically transcribed in English (*Y', ya*) must be dealt with at another level, in the accents and intonation of the actors. Similarly, the punctuation devices used by the translator differ from those found in the original, but this is of minimal importance in such a high-speed oral delivery.

The next example of Daddy's verbal idiosyncrasy is devoid of semantic value (*doing the nasty to ya ears, ya ears to the nasty*), but maintains the idiolect. The translator has already lost some of the force of this quirk, probably inevitably, in the last example, so in this case he probably decided simply to achieve some kind of phonological effect (*le orecchie vi delizia, sì, che nelle orecchie vi starnazza*) cleverly catching the double significance of *nasty* (theoretically unpleasant but, in this context, the opposite) by providing both *delizia* and *starnazza*. Daddy then surpasses his own linguistic inventiveness with *I'se play only da platters dat matter, da matters dey platter*, roaming into the territory of caricature with the 'd' sound replacing the 'th' – the clichéd identifying feature of black speech. The translator plays safe by merely reverting to the reversal technique (*il meglio della musica, della musica il meglio*) though why he continues to play safe with the repeated *and that's the truth Ruth/credeteci che è tutto vero* is not clear.

The translator's strategy for dealing with the culture-bound element *Bed-Stuy*, an example of an abbreviated place name well known to an American audience as a black neighbourhood of Brooklyn, New York, is to leave it out; this strategy is always available if the name in question is not important to the understanding of the text. He could, on the other hand, have substituted *Brooklyn* as a sufficiently-known place marker. The enigmatic *ying, yang, hip, hop* and *flippity flop* warrant no translation effort, except perhaps into English for many readers.

The events of the film take place against a backdrop of a sweltering city day and the images on the screen are already eloquent as to the fact that the weather is *hot!/caldo!* though the cultural question has to be addressed in recording the temperature as being *38 gradi* (centigrade)/*100 degrees* (fahrenheit). The question of wearing black is dealt with straightforwardly, and the *jerri curl* converts nicely to *(bi)godini*. The play on words with *permanent* works equally well in Italian and in English. Daddy repeats *Mister and Missus* in his *saluti*, while the translator introduces *signorine* –

no harm done. And the names *Big Red*, etc., remain the same as the translator brings Love Daddy's first verbal assault to an end.

> MISTER SENOR LOVE DADDY:
> Svegliati, in piedi in piedi in piedi in piedi in piedi che aspetti fratello, che aspetti fratello in piedi sveglia! Qui è Mister Senor Love Daddy, la voce che vi piace, l'unico asso al mondo che vi assicura 12 ore di trasmissione qui su We love Radio 108 FM, l'ultima sulla lunghezza d'onda ma la prima nei vostri cuori e sento che questo è vero, lo giuro. Eccomi da voi ma sono qua? Sì che sono qua, sapete che ci sono, sì, Mister Senor Love Daddy è qui che le orecchie vi delizia, sì, che nelle orecchie vi starnazza e vi passa solo il meglio della musica, della musica il meglio e credeteci che è tutto vero. Sui 108 FM siete all'ascolto di We love Radio che manda in onda lo ying lo yang con l'hip e l'hop oppure l'ultima follia in corso, il flippity flop. Ed eccovi le previsioni del tempo di oggi: caldo! Il colore giusto di questa giornata è il nero, proprio così il nero, così potrete assorbire un po' di questo calore e metterlo da parte per l'inverno, perciò uscite con qualcosa di nero addosso e siate dei nostri ma c'è di più, oggi la temperatura supererà i 38 gradi perciò allarme rosso di godini, sì avete capito bene, allarme di godini, se ne avete in testa restate in casa o vi ritroverete in testa un casco di plastica permanente. E ora passiamo ai saluti, ai signori e alle signore e perché no, anche alle signorine e buon compleanno a Big Red, Little Red e alla signorina Amy May che oggi compie 100 anni e se state attenti a tenervi fuori da questo caldo forse anche voi arriverete alla sua età.

Another extract highlights the use of taboo language (the OV is on page 218). The most aggressive character, Buggin' Out, accuses a white boy, Clifton, of standing on his new shoes:

> BUGGIN' OUT: You almost knocked me down, the word is excuse me.
> CLIFTON: Excuse me, I'm sorry.
> BUGGIN' OUT: Not only did you knock me down but you stepped on my brand new white Air Jordans I just bought and all you can say is excuse me?
> CLIFTON: Are you serious?
> BUGGIN' OUT: Yeah I'm serious. I'll fuck you up quick two times. Who told you to step on my sneakers? Who told you to walk on my side of the block? Who told you to live in my neighbourhood?
> CLIFTON: I own this brownstone.
> BUGGIN' OUT: Who told you to buy a brownstone on my block in my neighbourhood on my side of the street? Yo, what are you living in a black neighbourhood for anyway? Motherfuck gentrification!

CLIFTON: As I understand this is a free country and a man can live
 wherever he wants.
BUGGIN' OUT: A free country! I should fuck you up for saying that stupid
 shit alone.

The first line of the dialogue is intimidatory, and the translator intensifies this aspect by adding the condescending *bello*. The reference to *una spalla* can be attributed to the image on the screen. The maintaining of *Jordan* suggests that the translator considered this make of shoes sufficiently well known in Italy as to require no assistance. Again the screen action would help.

As Buggin' Out gets more excited, his language becomes increasingly expletive-ridden and he drops into the use of the so-called f-word. Like his contemporaries, he uses this lexical item as virtually any part of speech and with such frequency that it often lacks any kind of semantic content. With the expression *I'll fuck you up quick two times* he is presumably threatening violence. The translator keeps this function and the accompanying vulgarity with *ti tiro quel culo due volte*. In the three questions that follow, the Italian version lacks some details but it can be seen on examination that the syllable count of the words used is very similar, a not insignificant consideration.

The culture-bound term *brownstone* is left out and the essential information provided with *questa è casa mia*. Buggin' Out rages on and ends his tirade with the most offensive expletive: *motherfucker*. It must be said, however, that the term has achieved such frequency amongst certain speech communities that its force has diminished, and in this case its purpose is merely that of a strong intensifier; *strafottuta* gives the idea.

Interestingly, *fottere* and its derivatives are frequently used to translate the various forms of *fuck* in films because of the phonological similarity, even though these terms are not used in this way in the community at large. *Fottere* is one example of a number of terms that have gained in significance through their use as dubbing devices.

Gentrification on the other hand is a culture-bound term describing the trend of upwardly-mobile young people moving into run-down areas to buy property cheaply, renovating that property and making it marketable at a higher price, a practice which does not meet with the approval of the local populace. Buggin' Out's inability to articulate clearly his protest to a presumed member of the white bourgeoisie prompts the translation *bianca borghesia bianca del cazzo!*.

Clifton's response is met with more swearing, faithfully translated at least in terms of illocutionary force. The issue at stake (the *free country/paese libero*) is very important to an understanding of the film, and the pragmatic element of anger at society should be given priority.

BUGGIN' OUT: Per un pelo non mi sbattevi per terra bello, si dice scusa.

CLIFTON: Sì, scusami mi dispiace.

BUGGIN' OUT: Non solo mi hai distrutto una spalla ma hai anche pestato le mie Jordan nuove di zecca appena comprate, non sai dire altro che scusa amico?

CLIFTON: Fai sul serio?

BUGGIN' OUT: Faccio sul serio amico e quant'è vero ti tiro quel culo due volte. Chi ti ha detto di sporcarmi le Jordan? Chi ti ha detto di camminare qui? Perché sei nel mio quartiere?

CLIFTON: Ma io sto qui, questa è casa mia.

BUGGIN' OUT: E chi cazzo ti ha detto si venirla a comprare nel mio quartiere, nel mio isolato, sul mio lato della strada? E poi perché sei venuto a vivere in un quartiere nero, strafottuta bianca borghesia bianca del cazzo?!

CLIFTON: A quanto mi risulta questo è un paese libero, le persone possono abitare dove vogliono qui.

BUGGIN' OUT: Un paese libero! Dovrei romperti il culo per averla detta questa frase da coglione!

The extract that follows is provided for practice. Following the destruction of the Italo-American Sal's pizzeria at the end of the film, Mookie the pizza-boy exchanges a few acrimonious words with his former boss before Mister Senor Love Daddy has the last word:

SAL: You're a Rockefeller Mookie, you're a fucking Rockefeller. You got your fucking pay. Leave me alone now.

MOOKIE: Sal, my salary is 250 a week all right? I owe you fifty bucks.

SAL: Keep it.

MOOKIE: You keep it.

SAL: You keep it.

MOOKIE: You keep it.

SAL: I don't believe this shit.

MOOKIE: Believe it.

SAL: Are you sick?

MOOKIE: It's hot as motherfucker but I'm alright though.

SAL: They say it's even gonna get hotter. What are you gonna do with yourself?

MOOKIE: Make the money, getting paid. I gotta go see my son if that's alright with you.

MISTER SENOR LOVE DADDY: Hey Mook, it's the Mook man. I see you walking down the block. Go on home to your kid. Now the news and the weather. Our Mayor has commissioned a blue ribbon panel and I quote 'to get to the bottom of last night's disturbance. The City of New York will not let any property be destroyed by anyone.' End quote. His Honor plans to visit our block today. Maybe he should hook up with our own Da Mayor*, buy him a beer. Your Love Daddy says 'register to vote'. The election is coming up. There is no end in sight from this heatwave, so today the cash money word is chill, that's right, chill. When you hear chill call in at 505 L-O-V-E and you win cash money honey. This is Mister Senor Love Daddy coming at you from what's last on your dial but first in your hearts and that's the quintessential truth Ruth! The next record goes to Radio Raheem. We love you brother.

* a drunken old man, a character in the film

1.3.2 Subtitling

In the case of film translation from English to Italian, for reasons which can be traced back to the early days of the cinema during the fascist period in Italy when the use of foreign languages was banned, dubbing is the technique practically always employed. In Britain, on the other hand, where the demand for film and television translation is very limited, due to the fact that most material used is produced already in the English language, dubbing has never become established as it has elsewhere in Europe and other parts of the world. Foreign films are generally subtitled for an English audience. Subtitling involves the translation of the spoken language to the written language within the time restrictions presented by moving images on the screen, and as such would seem to be governed by a series of parameters not met with in other types of translation. Certainly, it has its specificity, particularly as regards the problem of condensing rapidly-spoken dialogue into easily-readable chunks on the screen, and yet a thorough study of the subtitling technique carried out in Trieste (Sandrelli, 1996) shows remarkable affinity with general translation practice. The vehicle used to demonstrate the basic tenets of subtitling translation is Nanni Moretti's Italian film 'Caro Diario'. The text that follows is from the opening scene.

A: Ormai ho paura di rimettermi in gioco, sono un vigliacco. Ma cosa è successo in tutti questi anni? Ditemelo voi … Io non lo so più.

B: Ti si stanno imbiancando le tempie.

C: Incominciano a pesare le sconfitte.

D: Una serie ininterrotta di sconfitte.

A: La nostra generazione … Che cosa siamo diventati? Siamo diventati pubblicitari, architetti, agenti di borsa, deputati, assessori, giornalisti … Siamo tanto cambiati, tutti peggiorati. Oggi, siamo tutti complici, tutti compromessi.

E: Eh, ma perché tutti? Questa fissazione di dire tutti complici, tutti compromessi … Siamo tutti complici …

D: Non c'è niente di concreto nella mia vita … Quando è l'ultima volta che abbiamo fatto una passeggiata? Ormai noi due stiamo insieme solo per abitudine.

C: Tu ti vergogni di me. Che mal di testa. Anche gli Optalidon non sono più gli stessi. Ti ricordi il tintinnio rassicurante del vecchio tubetto? Ora è tutto cambiato; ora è veramente tutto cambiato.

D: Sai una cosa, Antonio? Sei peggiorato. Non riesci più a provare un sentimento autentico.

A: Siamo invecchiati, siamo inaciditi, siamo disonesti nel nostro lavoro. Gridavamo cose orrende, violentissime nei nostri cortei … e ora guarda come siamo tutti imbruttiti.

Literal translation

A: By now I have fear to put myself again in play, I am a coward. But what is happened in all these years? Tell me it you … I do not know it more.

B: They are getting white your temples.

C: They begin to weigh the defeats.

D: An uninterrupted series of defeats.

A: Our generation … What are we become? We are become publicists, architects, agents of the stock exchange, deputies, aldermen, journalists … We are a lot changed, all worsened. Today, we are all accomplices, all compromised.

E: Eh, but why all? This fixation to say all accomplices, all compromised … We are all accomplices …

D: There is nothing of concrete in my life … When is the last time that we have made a walk? By now we two are together only for habit.

C: You shame yourself for me. What headache. Even the Optalidon are
    not more the same. You remember the reassuring tinkling of the old
    tube? Now it is all changed; now it is truly all changed.
D: You know a thing, Antonio? You are worsened. You don't succeed
    more to prove an authentic sentiment.
A: We are aged, we are acidified, we are dishonest in our work. We
    shouted horrendous, very violent things in our processions ... and now
    look how we are all uglified.

As mentioned before, subtitling does have its own specificity and a
number of strategies are adopted that may not be found in other branches
of translation, but the basic tactics will be recognisable to all those with any
experience of translation in general. For example, compare the Malone
strategies for translation (Part One **1.3**) with Gottlieb's list of ten designed
for subtitlers (Gottlieb 1992:166-168). Gottlieb speaks of

1 expansion: the adding of explanatory material
2 paraphrase: the necessary changing of some elements between
    source and target language
3 transfer: complete and faithful translation
4 imitation: intact transposition of the source language
5 transcription: the attempt to reproduce sounds that are unusual to
    both languages, e.g. animal cries
6 dislocation: the use of different linguistic means to maintain the
    same effect
7 condensation: a more concise rendering of the source language text,
    without actually eliminating material completely
8 decimation: the actual elimination of part of the original discourse
9 deletion: total elimination
10 resignation: the finding of a solution that does not fulfil the
    linguistic or semantic requirements of the source language but that
    is dictated by extraneous factors

All these strategies are to be found in the handling of Moretti's film, and
the intuitive reasoning that perhaps items 7, 8 and 9 would be particularly
useful in its translation into subtitles was partially borne out in the OV
(i.e. the translation used in the film). Roughly 25% of the text was
translated in this way. However, what is interesting is that more than 65%
of the source text was 'transferred' in a linguistically and semantically
faithful manner, as is indicated by the short extract used here for
demonstration purposes:

A: I'm afraid to re-think my life. I'm a coward. What happened? Tell me. I don't know anymore.

B: Your temples are turning white.

C: The weight of defeat.

D: A series of defeats.

A: What has our generation become? Publicists, architects, brokers, congressmen, journalists. We all changed for the worse. Sold out, compromised, co-opted.

E: Why all? This fixation with us 'all' being sold out and co-opted!

D: When did we last take a walk? We stay together out of habit.

C: You're ashamed of me. What a headache! Even Optalidons … are different now. Remember the rattle of pills in the old tube? Everything has really changed.

D: Know what, Antonio? You've worsened. You have no real feelings.

A: We're old, bitter, dishonest. We used to shout awful, violent slogans! Look how ugly we've gotten!

Translation analysis in terms of Gottlieb's strategies

The expression in the first clause is decidedly Italian, and its exact meaning in the context is not easy to ascertain; the action takes place in a film within a film, but is designed to set the scene of a perplexed existence. The meaning is presumably something like 'I'm worried about jumping back into the fray'. The OV paraphrases this expression to such an extent that this meaning, if it is the meaning, is lost. But then *I'm a coward* is entirely faithful. This is followed in the next caption by an example of decimation as the translator gets rid of *in tutti questi anni*, a vague time reference. *I don't know anymore/Io non lo so più* is straightforward enough.

The literal *Your temples are turning white* may err too much on the side of direct transfer; imagining this exchange in English, *your hair* would seem a more likely choice of vocabulary. Then there is a first example of condensation and the tension that exists between a more spontaneous *The defeats are beginning to weigh on me* and the need not to overload the reader's attention span, a trend continued in the next phrase where the addition of *endless* (for *ininterrotta*) seems to beg for space.

The condensation continues in the next speech as the initial noun phrase is blended into the verb phrase that follows, then there is decimation as *assessori* are left out of the list of professions, with no detriment to the discourse. The blending process of condensation is seen again in the next clause, while what follows is an unusual case of expansion. The choice of the item *sold out* is particularly appropriate in terms of the register one would expect from the character and in its semantic components. However, *compromised* and *co-opted* seem less convincing; the former smacks of false friendliness. Other expressions a translator might mentally scan are *caught up*, *part of it* and *involved*. In any case, the terms are re-used in a condensed form by E before, in the case of D's speech, a line is actually deleted: *Non c'è niente di concreto nella mia vita* .... However, the translation then continues as a direct transfer until the decimation of *rassicurante* and *Ora è tutto cambiato*. Neither is a serious loss. The meaning of the adjective is fairly implicit and the next sentence repeats the message: *Everything has really changed*.

The pronounless *Know what ... ?* is well translated, but it is doubtful whether an English speaker would use the expression *'You've worsened'* in preference to *'You've got worse'*. Certainly, the condensation resulting in *You have no real feelings* is justified.

Old, *bitter* and *ugly* translate the participles *invecchiati*, *inaciditi* and *imbruttiti* into more acceptable English than a literal version, and of course the removal of the repetition of the pronoun and verb provide breathing space. Some necessary decimation in this relatively long speech does not affect comprehension.

Kovacic (1995) has pointed out that a visible fault in subtitle translation is that of concentrating on the ideational meaning of the text, in the Hallidayan sense of the informative, newsworthy elements, as opposed to the interpersonal elements that trace a character's thought processes or establish power relations between characters. In other words, the subtitles merely chronicle events rather than examine deeper processes. For this reason, devices such as the correct sociolinguistic choice of lexis *sold out*, and the deliberate lack of the pronoun in *Know what ... ?* have an importance that goes beyond their surface meaning.

The text continues as follows and is offered for practice:

NANNI: Voi gridavate cose orrende e violentissime e voi siete imbrutitti. Io gridavo cose giuste ed ora sono uno splendido quarantenne!
Sì la cosa che mi piace di più è vedere le case, vedere i quartieri e il quartiere che mi piace di più di tutti è la Garbatella. E me ne vado in giro per i lotti popolari. Però non mi piace vedere solo le case dall'esterno, ogni tanto mi piace vedere anche

come sono fatte dentro e allora suono ad un citofono a faccio finta di fare un sopralluogo e dico che sto preparando un film. E il padrone di casa mi chiede: 'Di che parla questo film?' E io non so che dire ... che cos'è questo film: è la storia di un pasticciere trotzkista ... un pasticciere trotzkista nell'Italia degli anni '50. E' un film musicale. Un musical. Però! Mica male il musical sul pasticciere trotzkista nell'Italia conformista degli anni '50.

E andando in Vespa mi piace anche fermarmi a guardare gli attici dove mi piacerebbe abitare. Mi immagino di ristrutturare appartamenti, su in alto, che vedo dalla strada, ma ... appartamenti che i proprietari non hanno ... nessuna intenzione di vendere ... E un giorno poi, un attico che mi sembrava più accessibile di altri io e Silvia siamo anche saliti a vederlo. Abbiamo chiesto quanto costava e ci hanno risposto dieci milioni a metro quadro. Come dieci milioni a metro quadro? Eh, dice sì, ma non si può fare un discorso di tanto a metro quadro perché Via Dandolo è una via storica, ha detto il proprietario. Garibaldi qui ci ha fatto la resistenza ...

Non lo so, non riesco a capire, sarò malato ma io amo questo ponte, ci devo passare almeno due volte al giorno.
(*ad un automobilista*) No, sa cosa stavo pensando? Io stavo pensando una cosa molto triste, cioè che io, anche in una società più decente di questa, mi ritroverò sempre con una minoranza di persone. Ma non nel senso di quei film dove c'è un uomo e una donna che si odiano, si sbranano su un'isola deserta perché il regista non crede nelle persone. Io credo nelle persone, però non credo nel maggioranza delle persone. Mi sa che mi troverò sempre a mio agio con una minoranza ...
AUTOMOBILISTA: Va be, auguri.

NANNI: In realtà il mio sogno è sempre stato quello di saper ballare bene. 'Flashdance' si chiamava quel film che mi ha cambiato definitivamente la vita, era un film solo sul ballo, saper ballare e ... invece ... alla fine ... mi riduco sempre a guardare, che è anche bello, però è tutta un'altra cosa.
(*ad un ragazzo*) Sa qual è il mio sogno? Il mio sogno è sempre

stato quello di saper ballare! Io non sono stato più lo stesso dopo che ho visto ... quel film 'Flashdance' con Jennifer Beals. Quella ballerina laggiù è Jennifer Beals?

RAGAZZO: No.

NANNI: Come li invidio! Lei è Jennifer Beals?

RAGAZZO: No.

NANNI: Spinaceto: un quartiere costruito di recente. Viene sempre inserito nei discorsi per parlarne male, 'Va be, ma qui mica siamo a Spinaceto! Ma dove abiti, a Spinaceto?' Poi mi ricordo che un giorno ho letto anche un soggetto che si chiamava 'Fuga da Spinaceto', parlava di un ragazzo che scappava da quel quartiere, scappava da casa e non tornava mai più. E allora andiamo a vedere Spinaceto.

(ad un ragazzo su un muretto) Eh, Spinaceto, pensavo peggio, non è per niente male!

RAGAZZO: Ma infatti! Lo sai che ci stavo pensando?!

NANNI: Ciao!

RAGAZZO: Ciao!

Chapter Two

Technical and Scientific Texts

The characteristics of technical and scientific texts are discussed in Part One, Chapter Three, but a brief comment will be added here. Generally speaking, technical and scientific texts are more straightforward than other texts from the pragmatico-cultural point of view; science and technology transcend cultural mores and represent a universal point of reference for mankind. Translation difficulties lie more at the level of lexicogrammar and style, and this will be reflected in the analyses presented in this section. The language is usually considered to be more formal than in standard discourse, but this is an oversimplification. Broadly speaking, texts dealing with academically scientific material tend to use a more formal register based on varying levels of subject-specific graeco-latin terminology, which helps to distinguish this register from the standard. However, this tendency can vary greatly, ranging from the language of school text books to that of articles in highly specialised journals and the learned works of established experts in the field. More strictly 'technical' texts, such as manuals and specialist magazines aimed at a wider public, are often much less formal and display user-friendly features more akin to standard language. Pinchuk (1977:167) makes the distinction between 'scientific language' and 'workshop language', stating that:

> The scientific language draws on a humanistic education, while workshop terms are non-literary, practical, colloquial and sometimes humorous.

It is also a commonplace, based on truth, that Italian technical and scientific language is that bit more formal than English, though this is partly due to the fact that ordinary Italian is by its very nature more Latinate and elaborate of expression.

2.1   Scientific texts

2.1.1 School text book

In line with the principle of 'gradual approximation' outlined by Widdowson (1978:91) with a view to gradually weaning students of English onto ever more complex technical reading exercises, the first text provided in this section is relatively simple, taken from a scuola media textbook (Bonnes & De Re, 1989), to be followed by more demanding material more representative of the real world of work. The short extract in question deals with 'le centrali nucleari'.

> Nelle centrali nucleari i reattori realizzano la fissione nucleare controllata e vengono impiegati per produrre energia elettrica.
>
> Il funzionamento di una centrale nucleare può essere così schematizzato: l'energia prodotta dalla fissione, che si libera sotto forma di calore, viene ceduta dal reattore a un fluido refrigerante. Questo allora si trasforma in vapore e alimenta una turbina. La turbina mette in moto un generatore che a sua volta produce l'energia elettrica. Il meccanismo del funzionamento di una centrale nucleare è dunque molto semplice, ma i rischi connessi all'uso dei combustibili nucleari richiedono che essa funzioni nelle condizioni di massima sicurezza.
>
> Purtroppo non esistono centrali nucleari sicure al 100% e proprio per questo l'impiego dell'energia nucleare ha suscitato e suscita numerose polemiche.
>
> Le centrali nucleari, infatti, sono in grado più di tutte le altre di soddisfare la sempre maggiore richiesta di energia e consentono di risparmiare altre fonti a più rapido esaurimento, come il petrolio, ma nello stesso tempo possono causare danni gravissimi.

The context of situation of this text is clearly circumscribed; it is a school book written to be read by secondary school pupils, the roles of the participants being informer and learners. The material is technical but the text is organised cohesively and coherently in line with the canons of written discourse for scholastic purposes. The information is structured chronologically (and logically), there is much lexical cohesion, and the text is accompanied by a coloured diagram.

Literal translation

Nuclear centres

In the nuclear centres, the reactors realise the controlled nuclear fission and are used to produce electric energy.

The functioning of a nuclear centre can be so schematised: the energy produced by the fission, which liberates itself under form of heat, is ceded by the reactor to a refrigerating fluid. This then transforms itself in steam and feeds a turbine. The turbine puts in motor a generator which at its time produces the electric energy. The mechanism of the functioning of a nuclear centre is therefore very simple, but the risks connected to the use of nuclear combustibles require that it function in the conditions of maximum security.

Unfortunately nuclear centres do not exist safe at 100% and right for this the employment of nuclear energy has provoked and provokes numerous polemics.

The nuclear centres, in fact, are able more than all the others to satisfy the always major request of energy and consent to save other founts at more rapid exhaustion, like petrolium, but, in the same time they can cause very grave damages.

With texts of a technical nature, a literal translation can be more immediately useful than is the case with many other text types, given the lack of potentially ambiguous and allusive semantico-pragmatic elements in such a denotative and univocal genre. However, translators into English would have to bear in mind a number of lexicogrammatical conventions if they were to translate it for similar use.

Lexical analysis

The translator must provide the key vocabulary item equivalents by searching through his/her own knowledge stock or consulting the relevant literature. In this case, given the limited complexity of the text, dictionaries should suffice. The translator can be expected to know certain automatic transparent equivalences (*reattori/reactors, fissione nucleare/nuclear fission, turbina/turbine, massima sicurezza/maximum security*), others that are not so transparent (*centrali nucleari/nuclear power stations, energia elettrica/ electric power*), and others that are not transparent at all (*realizzano/produce, si libera/is released, vapore/steam, alimenta/feeds, richiesta/demand*).

Other terms may require consultation. The equivalents of *funzionamento* are a transparent *functioning* or an Anglo-saxon *working* (even *running*), and although old English terms are not usually considered to be of a technical register, in this case *working* would probably be chosen (but see below). The use of *illustrated* for *schematizzato* would be dictated by the presence of the diagram. Familiarity with semi-technical language in fields such as these, which figure quite prominently in the media from time to time, should produce familiarity with terms such as *cooling* for *refrigerante*. On the other hand, *mette in moto* referring to the *generator* may require a little thought as to the various contenders for the translation: *activates? starts up? puts in motion?* In the end, the term which may strike the translator as most appropriate in this case, even though it does not feature prominently in most technical dictionaries, is *works*. This term may recall a chain of events in a process: *the steam works the turbine, which works the generator, which works the wheel*, etc. These mnemonic devices should not be undervalued in attempting to gauge whether something 'sounds right'. The dictionary can be relied on to provide the translations of *combustibili/ fuels, petrolio/oil, polemiche/controversy* and *consentono/enable*. With most of the lexis under control, the translation rolls on towards completion, but the translator will not be entirely satisfied with the grammar, or with how this information is expressed.

Nuclear power stations

In nuclear power stations, reactors produce controlled nuclear fission and are used to produce electric power.
The working of a nuclear power station can be thus illustrated (*a diagram also accompanies the text*): the energy produced by fission, which is released in the form of heat, passes from the reactor to a cooling fluid. This is then transformed into steam and feeds a turbine. The turbine works a generator which in turn produces electric power. The working mechanism of a nuclear power station is therefore very simple, but the risks connected to the use of nuclear fuels require that it function in conditions of maximum security.
Unfortunately 100% safe nuclear power stations do not exist and just for this the use of nuclear energy has provoked and is provoking a great deal of controversy.
Nuclear power stations, in fact, are able more than any other to satisfy the ever greater demand for energy and enable us to save other resources nearer to exhaustion, like oil, but at the same time, they can cause very great damage.

Grammatical analysis

The Italian text begins with an adverbial and makes *i reattori* the subject, while it would be more in keeping with English style and perspective to subjectivise and thematise the *nuclear power stations* themselves. English technical texts also make use of noun groups including the definite article used in the generic sense (*the nuclear power station*) though this option would be second choice here. The simple present tense passive form *vengono impiegati/are used* must be maintained in keeping with one of the cardinal features of the type/genre, but the paratactic structure of the original, which may have been adopted to make for easy reading, could easily give way to a hypotactic main clause + relative + subordinate phrase: *Nuclear power stations contain reactors which are used to produce electric power through controlled nuclear fission.*

In the second sentence, *The working of a nuclear power station* would probably not entirely convince the translator, in spite of having opted for *work*. Experimenting with alternative ways of expressing the same concept, it is easy to imagine the nominalisation *How a nuclear power station works* coming to mind. The sentence continues with another passive (*can be illustrated*) and the Italian *così* begs the convention *as follows*. The noun *l'energia* loses the article in English, while it may be expedient to forfeit the passive *viene ceduta dal reattore* in favour of an equally genre-dependent present tense *passes from the reactor*. Again, this movement is clear from the non-verbal support of the diagram.

In the next sentence, the translator has a choice of sticking to the Italian temporal adverb *allora/then* or changing the perspective to a place adverb: *Here*. In fact little changes, in that in either case the adverbials are vague and each contains a component of the other, though the thematising of *Here* is quite common practice in English, especially in the presence of a diagram. The Italian *si trasforma* would undergo an effortless change to the passive voice, but the ensuing verb chain may again be changed from the paratactic to the hypotactic by the forming of a clause of purpose (*to feed a turbine*) followed by two relative clauses. In the final sentence of the second paragraph, in the phrase *i rischi connessi all'uso dei combustibili nucleari*, the transparent *connected* might be replaced by a more common collocate: *involved*.

The beginning of the penultimate paragraph would have to produce the string *100% safe nuclear power stations*. The Italian *proprio per questo*, however, would really need expanding to *for this very reason*, which would be the appropriate choice of expression in the circumstances. The double use of the verb *suscitare* in the two tenses invites care in finding the right equivalent (*provoke? raise? create?*). A common collocation of a certain authority is *give rise to*, and this would fit the two occasions here presented in the present perfect and present continuous tenses respectively. The plural adjective and noun in Italian *numerose polemiche* should not deflect the translator from naturally opting for a non-count *great deal of controversy*.

The last paragraph begins by posing the interesting question of the respective discursive functions of *infatti* and *in fact*, which has been the subject of a good deal of academic debate. In the case of *Le centrali nucleari, infatti* the *infatti* reiterates the positive tone of the beginning of the discussion, whereas if the translator into English inserted *in fact*, he or she would run the risk of distorting the meaning by suggesting that what was coming was in direct contrast to all that had come before. An emphatic *indeed* would be more appropriate, allied to the adjectival phrase *better equipped*. The noun *demand* attracts the collocation *ever-growing*, and the translator would be justified in equating *fonti* with *risorse/resources*, as supported by the mention of *oil*. The phrase *nearer to being worked out*, though semi-colloquial, is a current alternative for *a più rapido esaurimento* and, finally, the superlative *gravissimi* cannot be underplayed, hence *immeasurable*. The translation has rolled home:

Nuclear power stations

Nuclear power stations contain reactors which are used to produce electric power through controlled nuclear fission.

How a nuclear power station works can be illustrated as follows (*a diagram also accompanies the text*): energy produced by fission, which is released in the form of heat, passes from the reactor to a cooling fluid. Here it is transformed into steam to feed a turbine, which works a generator which in turn produces electric power. The working mechanism of a nuclear power station is therefore very simple, but the risks involved in using nuclear fuels require that it function in conditions of maximum security.

Unfortunately 100% safe nuclear power stations do not exist and for this very reason the use of nuclear energy has given rise in the past and is still giving rise to a great deal of controversy.

Nuclear power stations are indeed better equipped than any other to satisfy the ever-growing demand for energy and enable us to save other resources which are nearer to being worked out, like oil, but at the same time they can cause immeasurable damage.

The text goes on to discuss 'La fusione nucleare' and is offered for practice:

LA FUSIONE NUCLEARE

L'enorme energia degli atomi può essere utilizzata anche in modo diverso dalla fissione nucleare.

Fin dal 1920 i fisici avevano avanzato l'ipotesi che energia potesse essere ricavata non spezzando gli atomi, bensì combinando nuclei più piccoli in nuclei di maggiori dimensioni. E' il processo della fusione nucleare, il 'motore' delle stelle. Ma è possibile realizzare qui sulla Terra la fusione per ottenere grandissime quantità di energia? Questo processo avviene solo ad altissime temperature, pari a milioni di gradi, e l'energia sprigionata è enorme e difficilmente controllabile. L'uomo è riuscito a ottenere le temperature necessarie al processo di fusione utilizzando la più grande fonte di energia che conosca: una bomba a fissione nucleare. Nel 1952 l'energia sprigionata da una bomba atomica innescava un processo di fusione in un ordigno bellico statunitense, la bomba H, nella quale atomi di deuterio e di trizio, cioè atomi di idrogeno più pesanti perché contenenti nel nucleo rispettivamente anche un neutrone oppure due neutroni, 'fondono', cioè si uniscono tra loro, trasformandosi in elio.

The next text offered for practice is from a university text book on statistics, 'Statistica Applicata' by Franco Giusti (p.9):

Problemi di esecuzione delle rilevazioni statistiche
Collettivi statistici, unità statistiche, rilevazioni statistiche: richiami

La statistica è la disciplina che studia i *fenomeni collettivi* di qualsivoglia natura (fisici, biologici, demografici, socio-economici, ambientali), la cui misura richiede la disponibilità di una *massa* di osservazioni individuali; essa mira all'acquisizione ed alla classificazione dei dati singoli, nonché alla loro sintesi, all'elaborazione ed all'analisi per la scoperta di regolarità di massa, per la formulazione di ipotesi e teorie circa i meccanismi di regolazione dei fenomeni stessi, e per la loro verifica.

L'insieme delle unità portatrici delle singole manifestazioni del fenomeno collettivo è detto *collettivo statistico*: ma come sinonimi si utilizzano anche i termini *universo, popolazione, massa*; ad esempio: il collettivo delle nascite in Italia in un determinato anno, il collettivo dei prezzi all'ingrosso del grano che si formano in un dato giorno nei vari mercati, le aziende agricole esistenti in un determinato momento, gli studenti iscritti a una certa data all'Università 'La Sapienza'.

I casi individuali che formano oggetto di osservazione sono denominati *unità statistiche*: esse vengono enumerate e classificate sulla base di determinati *caratteri* o *caratteristiche* posseduti – qualitativi o quantitativi, di stato o di flusso – i quali forniscono le connotazioni delle unità ai fini dell'indagine: ad esempio, se si studia il collettivo delle abitazioni rispetto all'affitto, per ogni unità enumerata occorrerà acquisire anzitutto l'informazione sull'affitto, ma anche le misure di altri caratteri, coerenti con le finalità della ricerca, quali la dimensione dell'abitazione in termini di superficie o di numero di vani, la dotazione di servizi, la localizzazione, e così via.

2.1.2 Magazine article

The following portion of text is taken from the National Geographic magazine (Vol. 171, No. 4, April 1987, pp. 501-536) and displays the typical style of that publication, that is, a layman's 'chatty' approach to a scientific topic. The subject is pollution, the author Noel Grove, the title 'Air – an atmosphere of uncertainty':

> Where our air is concerned, in Casmalia as in the rest of the world, we live in an age of uncertainty. As damage from our aerial soup concerns us more and more, an alarmed public clamors for answers and action. Both are slow in coming.
>
> For example, the Carcinogen Assessment Group (CAG), an arm of the Environmental Protection Agency, was formed in 1976 to determine what chemical substances pose high cancer risks. Out of the thousands of commercial substances released to the atmosphere, 'we've reviewed the data on about 200 of them,' said Dr. Roy E. Albert, former CAG chairman, 'those that have been identified as possibly carcinogenic and worthy of further study.' His voice grew steely. 'The record of EPA regulation is

abysmal. But research is expensive, and the funding we are now getting for research is inadequate.'

Yet the air pollution picture is not totally bleak. Continuing research offers some hope of improvement. In late 1986 two scientists reported a chemical process capable of eliminating nitrogen oxides from diesel exhaust gases and coal-fired boilers. The hot gases, passed over a nontoxic chemical called cyanuric acid, break down into harmless nitrogen and water. If later research supports the findings, a giant step could be taken toward eliminating a major contributor to acid rain and man-made ozone.

The following translation (Chigine, 1994:98) will be used as reference for the commentary:

Per quanto riguarda la nostra aria, in Casmalia come nel resto del mondo, viviamo in un'epoca di incertezza. Mentre i danni prodotti dalla nostra zuppa aerea ci preoccupano sempre più, un pubblico allarmato chiede a gran voce risposte e interventi; ma entrambi arrivano lentamente.

Ad esempio, il Gruppo di valutazione carcinogena (CAG), un braccio dell'EPA, venne costituito nel 1976 per stabilire quali sostanze chimiche ponessero alti rischi di cancro. Delle migliaia di sostanze chimiche in commercio rilasciate nell'atmosfera, 'abbiamo riesaminato i dati su circa 200 di esse', disse il dott. Roy E. Albert, il precedente direttore della CAG, 'quelle che sono state identificate come possibili carcinogene e meritevoli di ulteriori studi'. La sua voce divenne dura: 'I risultati ottenuti dall'EPA sono ancora molto scarsi. Ma la ricerca è costosa e i fondi che abbiamo ora sono inadeguati per la ricerca.'

Eppure il quadro dell'inquinamento atmosferico non è completamente tetro. Il proseguimento della ricerca offre qualche speranza di miglioramento. Alla fine del 1986 due scienziati presentarono una relazione su un processo chimico in grado di eliminare gli ossidi di azoto dai gas di scarico dei diesel e dalle caldaie a carbone. I gas caldi, fatti passare su una sostanza chimica non tossica chiamata acido cianurico, si scompongono in azoto non nocivo e acqua. Se ricerche successive dovessero confermare questi risultati, un passo da gigante potrebbe essere fatto per l'eliminazione di una delle sostanze che più contribuisce alla pioggia acida e all'ozono antropogenico.

As mentioned above, this short extract is a portion of a wider article in which it has already been explained that Casmalia is a small town in California. The translation of *an age of uncertainty* with *un'epoca di incertezza* is interesting in that the more transparent translations of the two terms *age* and *epoca*, namely *età* and *epoch* respectively, do not collocate comfortably with *incertezza* and *uncertainty*. The original metaphor *aerial soup* requires an original metaphor in response: *zuppa aerea*. The single verb form *clamors* (the spelling of which identifies the text as American) is best translated with a more elaborate verb phrase: *chiede a gran voce*. The transparent translation of *action* with *azione* would not be as effective as the use of *interventi*, so common in such Italian contexts (cf: *interventi finanziari, interventi politici*, etc.) and very rarely translatable with *intervention(s)*. The short, and effective, sentence that ends the paragraph in English requires some imaginative punctuation in Italian too.

At the beginning of the second paragraph, the initials *CAG* do not match the translated name of the group in question, but this little inconsistency is not as important as the translation of *Carcinogen Assessment Group*, particularly of the word *assessment/valutazione*, and the providing of the abbreviated form of the actual organisation. The organisation represented by the initials *EPA* (the Environmental Protection Agency) appeared earlier in the text. Depending on the kind of organisation concerned, a *chairman* is usually either a *presidente* (e.g. *Chairman of the Board, chairman of a football club*) or a *direttore* (as in this case). Note the translation of *worthy of further study* with *meritevoli di ulteriori studi*. The following sentence (*His voice grew steely*) is indicative of that original informal style alluded to earlier. The style seems more in tune with Hollywood than serious scientific research, and *La sua voce divenne dura* may capture this register to a certain extent. The slight informality continues in the direct speech: the overstated adjective *abysmal* is matched by *scarsi*.

The components of doom and gloom contained in the adjective *bleak* are captured in *tetro*. The typically English noun string is in evidence in *diesel exhaust gases*, requiring two prepositional phrases in Italian: *gas di scarico dei diesel*. Similarly, chemical compounds are often grammatically represented by noun strings: *nitrogen oxides/ossidi di azoto*. The lexical item *coal-fired boilers*, on the other hand, exemplifies the use of the compound adjective and again requires a prepositional phrase: *caldaie a carbone*. The phrasal verb in the next sentence (*break down*) is translated by an Italian reflexive verb (*si scompongono*). The common collocation *a giant step* finds its equally common equivalent in *un passo da gigante*. Neologisms in the scientific field require accurate translation: *acid rain* is now well-known as *pioggia acida*; *man-made ozone* is less familiar, but the translation must be *ozono antropogenico*.

The text continues as follows and is offered for practice:

Perhaps the most controversial environmental issue of the decade is acid rain, but that too is clouded in mystery. 'We are in the infancy of understanding the full effects on an atmosphere acidified by burning fossil fuels,' Dr. Chris Bernarbo, an air-quality expert, told me. 'In order to really understand it, we must conduct years of research.'

The federal Clean Air Act of 1970, amended in 1977, expired in 1981. As of this writing it continues on extensions, outdistanced by the growing knowledge about air pollution.

We live on a forgiving planet, with mechanisms to deal with natural pollutants. Decay, sea spray, and volcanic eruptions annually release more sulfur than all the power plants, smelters, and other industries in the world. Lightning bolts create nitrogen oxides just as automobiles and industrial furnaces do, and trees emit hydrocarbons called terpenes. Their release triggers a bluish haze that gave the Blue Ridge its name.

For millions of years the ingredients of such substances have been cycling through the ecosystem, constantly changing form. They pass through plant and animal tissues, sink into the sea, return to earth, and are vaulted aloft in some geologic event to begin the cycle again.

2.1.3 Scientific journal material

The text chosen to represent scientific journal material is taken from the Italian publication Sapere (April 1996), and deals with an ethological approach to child abuse (p.27). The text is designed for an educated but not specialist readership:

Un modello etologico (di Massimo Bardi)

Il maltrattamento infantile è un fenomeno così vasto e eterogeneo che sarebbe illusorio cercare motivazioni semplici e facilmente isolabili per la sua manifestazione. Negli anni '70 due scuole di pensiero si contrapponevano nel tentativo di spiegare l'eziologia: quella che proponeva un modello fondato su psicopatologie interne al maltrattatore (disturbi emotivi, bassa autostima, nevrosi, esperienze infantili fortemente disturbate, dipendenza da droghe ed alcolici ...) (Spinetta e Rigler, 1972; Steele, 1977) e quella invece che poneva l'attenzione sulle condizioni ambientali esterne all'adulto (stress, malattie, isolamento, disoccupazione, povertà, ignoranza, appartenenza a classi sociali disagiate ...) (Gelles, 1973; Strauss et al., 1979). Negli stessi anni, inoltre, studiosi del comportamento animale cercavano di collocare l'infanticidio e il maltrattamento in generale in un quadro evolutivo più ampio, interspecifico, elaborando i modelli di investimento parentale (Trivers, 1974) e di utilizzo dell'infante come mezzo per incrementare la possibilità di lasciare discendenti propri (Hrdy, 1979).

Da questo sforzo congiunto si è evidenziato un elemento comune, un filo conduttore che lega i tanti casi del variegato 'mondo' del maltrattamento, e questo filo ci dice che l'amore dei genitori per i propri piccoli, il rispetto e il senso di tenerezza e protezione che un adulto esprime nei confronti dei piccoli conspecifici in condizioni 'normali' (cioè nella maggior parte dei casi), non sono meccanismi 'istintivi', riflessi condizionati, trattamenti 'dovuti', ma sono risposte comportamentali che vanno conquistate prima e rafforzate di volta in volta. In altre parole, per essere buoni genitori e adulti sensibili e responsabili nei confronti dei piccoli, occorre da un lato avere appreso come esserlo, dall'altro trovarsi in circostanze esterne adeguate. Ovverosia occorre essere motivati a prestare loro cure e attenzioni: adulti scarsamente o per nulla motivati sono proprio quelli più propensi a maltrattare, e minore è la loro motivazione, maggiore è la frequenza e l'intensità del maltrattamento.

Il livello motivazionale del curatore dipende da una serie di stimoli (sia propri, ovvero interni allo stesso, che ambientali, cioè esterni), i quali in sintesi possono essere raggruppati in quattro categorie fondamentali:

1 – stimolazioni ormonali e genitali al momento del parto
2 – stimoli da parte dell'infante (attivi e passivi)
3 – ontogenesi ed esperienza (processi neurali – ricordo)
4 – interazione sinergica fra i primi 3 fattori.

Literal translation

An ethological model

Infantile maltreatment is a phenomenon so vast and heterogeneous that it would be illusory to look for simple and easily isolatable motivations for its manifestation. In the seventies two schools of thought counterpoised each other in the attempt to explain the etiology: that which proposed a model founded on psychopathologies internal to the maltreater (emotive disturbances, low autoestimation, neurosis, strongly disturbed infantile experiences, dependence from drugs and alcoholics ...) (Spinetta e Rigler, 1972; Steele, 1977) and that which instead put the attention on the environmental conditions external to the adult (stress, illnesses, isolation, unemployment, poverty, ignorance, appertaining to disadvantaged social classes ...) (Gelles, 1973; Strauss et al., 1979). In the same years, furthermore, students of the animal behaviour tried to collocate infanticide and the maltreatment in general in a more ample, interspecific evolutive picture, elaborating the models of parental investment (Trivers, 1974) and of utilisation of the infant as means to increment the possibility of leaving proper descendants (Hrdy, 1979).

From this conjoined effort a common element was evidenced, a conducting wire which ties the many cases of the variegated 'world' of maltreatment, and this wire tells us that the love of parents for their proper little ones, the respect and the sense of tenderness and protection which an adult expresses in the confrontations of the conspecific little ones in 'normal' conditions (that is in the major part of the cases), are not 'instinctive' mechanisms, conditioned reflexes, 'due' treatments, but are behavioural responses which go conquered first and strengthened time in time. In other words, to be good parents and sensible and responsible adults in the confrontations of the little ones, it occurs from one side to have learned how to be it, from the other to find oneself in adequate external circumstances. Or really it occurs to be motivated to lend their cures and attentions: adults scarcely or for nothing motivated are properly those more likely to maltreat, and minor is their motivation, major is the frequency and the intensity of the maltreatment.

The motivational level of the curer depends from a series of stimuli (both proper, or internal to the same, or environmental, that is external), the which in synthesis can be grouped in four fundamental categories:

1 – hormonal and genital stimuli at the moment of the birth
2 – stimuli on the part of the infant (active and passive)
3 – ontogenesis and experience (neural processes – memory)
4 – synergic interaction among the first 3 factors.

Linguistic and semantic analysis

The phenomenon of *maltrattamento infantile* is unfortunately so wide-spread and so often reported in the media that the (semi) technical English term for it should be on the tip of any translator's tongue – and that term is *child abuse*. The adjective *widespread* (for *vasto*) is that which collocates best with *phenomenon*, and the translator might consider that *eterogeneo* would be better translated by *varied* in this 'science for the layman' introduction. It is indeed to some extent illusory to believe that a literal translation of *sarebbe illusorio* (*it would be illusory* ...) sounds sufficiently English to be

correct, but turning over the concept in the mind and trying out a few other
semantically valid versions, the translator may feel that a more spontaneous
solution such as *there is little point in ...* may be more appropriate, even in
terms of register in the early part of this article. The adjective *identifiable*
(like the verb *identify*) should always be lurking in the translator's mind
when texts contain *isolabili* (*isolare*) or *individuabili* (*individuare*). In the
case of *motivazioni* the translator may stop to consider the use of
motivation(s), the latter being the term used in psychology, but may equally
be swayed by the dictionary information that, in the plural, *motivazioni* can
be translated by *reasons*. Similarly, in the case of *manifestazione*, the medical
register would suggest *manifestation*, but would not rule out *appearance*,
and many translators would find the latter more appealing.

In the second sentence, the translator would have to find a way of dealing
with the common Italian reciprocal verb construction *si contrapponevano*
most succinctly by inserting an adjectival participle before the noun phrase:
<u>*opposing*</u> *schools of thought*. The noun *tentativo* could then be effortlessly
verbalised into *attempted*. The translator would then have to consider the
question of scientific register in *eziologia/etiology*, bearing in mind that the
Italian term would be understood by a wider public than the English direct
equivalent; most educated English readers would be better served by *causes*.
The *two schools of thought* are distinguished in Italian by *quella che .../
quella che ...* . After deciding that *that which* is ugly in English, the
translator would probably soon recall the grammatical convention that
replaces *that* with the pronoun *one*: *one ...*/*while the other ...* . With the
verb *proporre* (here *proponeva*) the translator should naturally test whether
propose is the suitable translation, and consider whether it is more or less
suitable than a near synonym like *put forward*. The verb group *based on* (for
fondato) is much more familiar in English than *founded on* in this kind of
context (cf: *basically* for *fondamentalmente*) and would be there at the
forefront of the translator's thinking. The *interne a/esterne a* pair would
require a little thought, and some degree of basic re-ordering would almost
certainly be needed, possibly eventually resulting in something like *the
psychopathological condition of abusers themselves*. The difficulty of translating *patologie* with a straight *pathologies* is mentioned on page 262. As
regards the bracketed list, the translator may risk reducing *esperienze
infantili fortemente disturbate* to *troubled childhood*: the co-efficient of
intensity (see Part One, **2.3.2**) of *troubled* is high and equals the combined
intensity of *fortemente disturbate*. The suffix *-hood* in *childhood* gives the
word enough scope to cover the whole concept of *esperienze infantili*, and

troubled childhood is, in any case, a familiar collocation. The choosing of *pointed to* for *poneva l'attenzione* would be the result of the same reasoning that resulted in the translation of *proponeva* with *put forward*, and the translation of *invece* would seem to be irrelevant. Logic might suggest the use of *surrounding* for *esterne a*. The second bracketed list ends with *appartenenza a classi sociali disagiate*, a convenient Italian noun phrase which sends the translator off in a useless search for a noun to cover *appartenenza*. The final decision must be for a nominal group, to maintain continuity with the other items in the list – perhaps *low social status*. The preposition in the Italian adverbial *Negli stessi anni* has to change to <u>At</u> *that time*.

The *inoltre* in the last sentence of paragraph one seems as redundant as the *invece* in the previous sentence. *Studiosi* are *scholars*, but the latter term is not usually followed by the prepositional phrase *of . . .*, and thus, while not wishing to dispense with what is indeed the correct term, the translator may expand slightly to *scholars studying animal behaviour*. Translators may hark back to the basic English grammar book explanations of tense usage with the translation of *cercavano*. As the action is taking place simultaneously with another action, the text book would tell us to use the past continuous tense *were trying*. The choice of *general abuse* in preference to *abuse in general*, which might be a better way of expressing this concept in other circumstances, would derive from the translator's trying that particular option and abandoning it because of the clash with the prepositional phrase beginning with *in* that follows. The adjectival item *interspecifico* would alert the translator to what might be sectorial jargon, a supposition confirmed by the appearance of *conspecifico* a little further on, but there is no reason to translate these terms with anything but *interspecific* and *conspecific*. The same logic pertains to *investimento parentale*. As the language register becomes a little more technical, *means/mezzo* and *possibility/possibilità* would be preferred to *way* and *chance*. The final *propri* at the end of the paragraph is another case of potential redundancy, especially if *lasciare* is replaced with *having*.

The first long sentence in the second paragraph should keep translators occupied for a while, as they wrestle with the various conflicting constructions that will present themselves as they try to create sense, fluency and style at the same time. What might happen is the following: *joint effort/sforzo congiunto* is adopted as a modern collocation and *elemento comune* and *filo conduttore* are conflated into *common thread*, thereby maintaining at least some of the metaphorical effect and avoiding the need to repeat a near synonym after the verb. There is no finite verb form based on *evidence* in English, but *emerged* would come naturally. The metaphors in *i tanti casi del variegato 'mondo' del maltrattamento* can be maintained, but the preposition *of* would be weak; the grammatical metaphor *all the cases that make up the variegated 'world' of abuse* makes things clearer. There is every reason to introduce the English Saxon genitive construction in *parents' love* and *an adult's respect*. The Latin initials in *i.e., in most cases/cioè nella maggior parte dei casi* suit the register. The Italian *risposte comportamentali che vanno conquistate prima* is deontic, in that it implies obligation: *behavioural responses which have first to be mastered*.

No translator should fall to the false friend *sensibile*, which is of course *sensitive*, but *nei confronti di* may need moulding into *in dealing with*, a different translation of the same prepositional phrase that appeared a few lines previously. As it is not a key expression in the text, it may undergo varied treatment. The standard expression to translate *da un lato/dall'altro* is *on the one hand/on the other*.

Note the force of the adverbial *how* in . . . *to have learned how*. To translate *circostanze esterne adeguate* translators have to remember the range of contexts in which words such as *circostanze* and *adeguate* appear, and thus remind themselves of how much licence they have. The addition of *esterne* should point in the direction of *(surrounded by) the right environment*.

In the final sentence of the paragraph, the dictionary translation of *ovverosia* is *that is (to say)*, but this expression is frowned upon as a sentence opener. The translator might opt for a more conventional *This means that . . . .* The second 'occurrence' of *occorre* (a neat way of explaining the false friendliness of this term) prompts the deontic *need to be motivated*, while the *prestare loro cure e attenzioni* can be dealt with by the all-embracing *look after + properly*. The translator can avoid tortuously succinct solutions to the neat Italian *scarsamente o per nulla motivati* by repeating the verb: *hardly motivated or not motivated at all*. The translator would have *prone to* ready as the translation of *propensi a*, but if the word that follows is *abuse*, the meaning would be ambiguous between verb and noun (is the adult or the child the victim?). Hence *likely to*.

The final paragraph introduces the term *curatore* which, after some deliberation, the translator may decide to translate with *parent*, as this is the 'curatore' in question, though *caregiver* has emerged of late. The prepositions that follow, respectively, *dipende* and *depends* are *da* and *on*.

A certain amount of contraction would probably follow. The use of *ovvero* and *cioè* suggest repetition, and thus the bracketed information could be reduced to *(both internal and external)*. The adverb *conveniently* would replace *in sintesi* reasonably elegantly. Point 1 (*al momento del parto*) has a conventional equivalent in *on giving birth*.

The translation has thus rolled linguistically and semantically to a conclusion; being of a technical nature, the text presents no significant pragmatic or cultural difficulties:

An ethological model

Child abuse is such a widespread and varied phenomenon that there is little point in looking for simple and easily-identifiable reasons for its appearance. In the seventies two opposing schools of thought attempted to explain the etiology: one put forward a model based on the psychopathological condition of abusers themselves (emotional disturbances, low self-esteem, neurosis, troubled childhood, drug and alcohol dependence …) (Spinetta e Rigler, 1972; Steele, 1977) while the other pointed to the environmental conditions surrounding the adult (stress, illness, isolation, unemployment, poverty, ignorance, low social status …) (Gelles, 1973; Strauss et al., 1979). At the same time, scholars studying animal behaviour were trying to place infanticide and general abuse in a wider interspecific evolutionary framework, developing models of parental investment (Trivers, 1974) and use of the infant as a means of increasing the possibility of having descendants (Hrdy, 1979).

From this joint effort a common thread has emerged linking all the cases that make up the variegated 'world' of abuse, a thread that tells us that parents' love for their children, an adult's respect and sense of tenderness and protection towards conspecific children in 'normal' conditions (i.e., in most cases), are not 'instinctive' mechanisms, conditioned reflexes, or 'due' care, but are behavioural responses which have first to be mastered and then reinforced over time. In other words, to be good parents and to be sensitive and responsible adults in dealing with children, it is necessary on the one hand to have learned how, and on the other to be surrounded by the right environment. This means parents need to be motivated to look after children properly: adults who are hardly motivated or not motivated at all are those more likely to abuse, and the lesser their motivation, the higher the frequency and the intensity of the abuse.

The motivational level of the parent depends on a series of stimuli (both internal and external), which can be conveniently grouped into four basic categories:

1 – hormonal and genital stimuli on giving birth
2 – stimuli on the part of the infant (active and passive)
3 – ontogenesis and experience (neural processes – memory)
4 – synergic interaction among the first 3 factors.

The text continues as follows and is offered for practice:

1) Stimolazioni ormonali e genitali alla nascita
L'insieme dei cambiamenti che avvengono nella fisiologia di una madre durante la gestazione e nel momento del parto sono fondamentali per prepararla psicologicamente alla futura presenza del figlio, sono essenziali cioè affinché si generi l'accettazione prima e l'attaccamento poi – imprinting – nei confronti del neonato. Non a caso madri che vivono una gravidanza difficile, con problemi di salute o soggette a notevoli stress ambientali (isolamento sociale, problemi economici, scarsità di risorse ...), o che subiscono un parto particolarmente difficile e travagliato, sono significativamente più prone al maltrattamento rispetto a quelle che hanno gravidanza e parto regolari (Lynch, 1976; Montagu, 1993).

2) Stimoli da parte dell'infante (attivi e passivi)
I neonati vengono alla luce dotati di un repertorio di moduli comportamentali che li rendono in grado di comunicare con il proprio curatore, moduli che, nel loro insieme, costituiscono una fonte stimolatoria di fondamentale importanza nella regolazione della relazione diadica madre-figlio, e quindi nella motivazione materna. Tali stimoli possono essere passivi, cioè indipendenti dalla volontà del piccolo (dimensioni, proporzioni e forma del corpo – soprattutto quella del cranio – colore, odore, temperatura corporea) e attivi, ovvero da lui controllati (riflessi, moduli locomotori, vocalizzazioni, espressioni facciali, stimolazioni tattili).

Lineamenti arrotondati, occhi grandi, corpo piccolo e gracile; riflessi di prensione e di ricerca del capezzolo, incerti moduli locomotori, stimoli auditivi (pianto ed altre vocalizzazioni), sono tutti tratti comuni agli infanti che suscitano tenerezza negli adulti, e quindi stimolano il comportamento parentale (Hinde, 1977; Montagu, 1993; Pryce, 1992). Ogni qual volta si manifesta una deficienza nella interazione fra curatore e il piccolo abbiamo come immediata conseguenza una mancata soddisfazione dei bisogni di quest'ultimo, e quindi, in sostanza, un atto di maltrattamento. L'origine di tale deficienza si può localizzare a livello del curatore, a livello del piccolo o a livello del contesto ambientale.

3) Ontogenesi ed esperienza

Benché negli adulti di primati esista un insieme di comportamenti parentali universali, e quindi innati, è risultato evidente che un genitore debba apprendere come si cura un figlio. Persino in specie filogeneticamente più 'primitive', come le scimmie del Nuovo Mondo, è stato dimostrato che i curatori hanno bisogno di una istruzione nel difficile campo dei comportamenti parentali. Tale apprendimento avviene in due fasi distinte: esperienze fatte nella propria infanzia e esperienze fatte con prole propria.

Esiste un buon accordo fra i ricercatori nel sostenere che uno sviluppo disturbato possa condurre ad elevati gradi di inadeguatezza parentale; in particolare, una delle caratteristiche che molti genitori maltrattanti hanno in comune è proprio quello di essere stati, a loro volta, maltrattati da piccoli. Vari sono i modi in cui esperienze infantili fortemente negative possono condurre gli adulti ad una inadeguata motivazione parentale. Essi, infatti, possono apprendere comportamenti antisociali (aggressività, uso della violenza, tendenza all'isolamento …) attraverso l'esposizione alla violenza, oppure possono acquisire una incapacità di provare empatia e attrazione verso il piccolo perché cresciuti in un ambiente 'freddo' e ostile, o anche perché le esperienze infantili negative possono condurli all'uso di droghe o di alcolici o generare seri problemi psichici.

Un comportamento parentale adeguato si può acquisire anche con l'esperienza che si ha con prole propria: madri multipare sono generalmente madri migliori di quelle primipare nelle maggioranza delle specie studiate.

2.2   Instructions

2.2.1 Television operating instructions

It is a commonplace among translators that Italian translated texts are always more lengthy than their English originals, given stylistic differences, the more formal restraints of the written language and the potential in Italian for periphrasis, that is, the use of more elaborate wording than is absolutely necessary. This generalisation, which like all generalisations holds true in many cases, becomes less universally applicable when extended to more informative text types. For example, in the case of manuals, instruction leaflets and the like, the source of so much multilingual translation these days, such conventional wisdom can no longer be taken for granted. Very often in this kind of translation Italian can be more succinct and to the point, rejecting the more chatty, and therefore more lengthy, approach adopted by increasingly more consumer-friendly instruction writers in English. That the opposite also remains true (Italian can be more verbose) indicates that any prediction is hazardous. In the following text, a set of instructions on how to operate a Philips television, the translator must be true to his or her brief, which is presumably to make those instructions as clear as possible for the Italian purchaser of the TV set. The translator must have an understanding of the expectations of the consumers, and this even refers to syntactic questions related to theme/rheme development and information focus. In other words, the translator should be sensitive to how Italian users like to have information presented. How can the mental image of the instruction be made clearest in that particular language? The context of situation is again a distance relation between the anonymous writer and a wide potential public. Notwithstanding the lack of personal acquaintance between the participants, certain interpersonal elements traceable to the friendly approach are present. The translator into Italian must evoke the Italian context of situation and consider the interpersonal parameters generally associated with that situation, i.e. how formal or informal the register should be.

Congratulations on your purchase of a new colour television. We are pleased that you have chosen a Philips. It is a very modern set with many facilities and the best way to get to know them is to read through the Operating Instructions carefully. If the set has already been adjusted by your dealer, the main section of interest to you is 'Operating your TV' (see page 4).

Operating the TV
Switching on
Press the mains switch (on the TV). Programme number 1 appears in the window and the station stored on it appears on the screen.

Programme selection
To select programme numbers 0 to 9 press the relevant digit button.
To select a programme number consisting of two digits press button -/--.
Two bars will then appear in the window (on the TV).
It is possible to return to programme nos. 0 to 9 by pressing button -/--.

Picture and sound

○ Brightness
◑ Colour saturation
◁ Volume

This change is **not** permanent. When the **green** button is pressed the picture and sound setting stored on this button is restored and this is also the case when the TV is switched on after being switched off.

Muting
Press button ☒
The sound is switched on again by pressing the green button or by pressing button ☒ again.

Opening the set
The rear cover of the set may only be removed by a service technician.

Linguistic, semantic and cultural analysis

With reference to the earlier discussion of interpersonal relations in the Italian context of situation, the Italian translator may want to avoid the false friendliness in the first sentence by condensing the meaning into one clause and getting straight into the more familiar aspects of the genre in question; the field and tenor elements of the context of situation would be that of bare instructions imparted by an impersonal technician to an unknown public with a very specific objective. The next sentences set a fairly informal tone using Anglo-saxon-based conversational verbal expressions such as *to get to know* and phrasal verbs (*read through*), which can be conveniently dealt with in Italian by the simple verb forms *conoscer(lo)* and *leggere*. Generally speaking, in texts of this nature, English too would adopt the Latinate near-synonyms of more colloquial verb forms, phrasal verbs, etc., but current usage favours a more user-friendly approach, suggesting a more familiar use of language, at least in the opening stages. As Italian has only the Latinate option it will in any case tend to sound more formal, though the translator can 'show willing' by adopting, for example, a superlative *-issimo* form of a more conversational nature: *modernissimo*. In the fourth sentence, the item *adjusted* provides an example of a very economical kind of English verb containing a range of implicit senses (cf: *to arrange, to set, to involve*); here it covers the whole idea of being *predisposto per la ricezione delle trasmittenti*. And this is an example of where translators have to ask themselves how much information their readership requires, whether translating *adjusted* with *predisposto* alone would be pragmatically or stylistically acceptable. It is not made explicit who the pronoun/possessive *you/your*, used three times in this sentence, refers to, but the English reader would almost certainly feel it was him or herself, as in more blatant advertising discourse. The translator is faced with a choice between various options, and might choose just one or more than one: the impersonal article *Impiego del televisore* or the plural *voi/vostro*. The personal *tu* form would not be chosen here – the genre register would not allow it – though this would be acceptable in advertising also in Italian (see Part One, **3.4.6**).

If the gerundive *Operating the TV* is translated by the nominal *Impiego del televisore*, then the pattern can be repeated: *Switching on/Accensione del televisore*.

Programme number 1 appears in the window and the station stored on it appears on the screen demonstrates how translators are called upon to give serious thought to how their readers mentally process information, influenced by the syntactic patterns of their language. English thematises the logical subject in the first clause, and also in the second to create a pattern of syntactic equivalence which also puts the information focus on the places to look for. This arrangement would be less effective in Italian, though the translator might mentally work through it initially before shelving it in favour of something like *Nella scala appare il programma numero 1 e sullo schermo la trasmittente memorizzata su questo numero*. Italian, it would seem, prefers to set the scene in theme position and put the focus on the subject; placing the subject to the right of the verb is an extremely common syntactic option, particularly in written Italian.

The pairing *stored/memorizzato* is becoming standard in the field of telematics, though this process of standardisation is not as rapid or clear-cut as might be desired (cf: *save* = *salvare/memorizzare/archiviare* in computerspeak).

More nominalisation is possible in the next section with *To select/Per la selezione dei* … naturally repeated in the sentence that follows. The same question of theme progression then emerges in *Two bars* … . The English writer then curiously provides the information that the *window* in question is *(on the TV)*, perhaps to prevent less perceptive readers from gazing at the outside world. It is unlikely that the Italian term *scala* could create such ambiguity. *It is possible* … can be reduced in English to the meaning of 'To return to programme nos. 0 to 9, press button -/--'. This would provide the Italian *Per tornare ai numeri dei programmi da 0 a 9 compreso ripremete il tasto -/--*. This process of intralingual translation (see Part One, **2.1.1**) prior to interlingual translation should be attempted whenever the target language seems to be straining unduly to contain a source language concept.

Interestingly, in the section *Picture and sound*, English relies on non-verbal communication by merely displaying the three symbols for *Brightness*, *Colour saturation* and *Volume* and hoping that users will understand that which Italian makes explicit: *mediante i tasti + e − potete aumentare o diminuire il livello della saturazione, della luminosità e del volume*. In translating the pared-down sentence *This change is not permanent*, there is room for an adjectival support such as *di carattere permanente* – Italian is not naturally brusque. The longer sentence that follows displays that uneasy mix of conversational style and technical instruction discussed previously. The Italian translator would be wary of copying this, either syntactically or stylistically; the initial passive constructions don't bend into Italian and *and this is also the case when* ... betrays the expected register. The *switched on after being switched off* seems unnecessarily clumsy though certainly delivers the message unequivocably. This is a case in point where one might expect the translation into Italian to be tighter than the English; the translator must think how to translate the entire chunk and not be misled by smaller units. The Italian OV of this sentence in the instruction manual goes: *Premendo il tasto verde o riaccendendo il televisore otterrete l'immagine ed il suono nuovamente al livello preregolato*, which is neater than the English.

The next section features a relative neologism deriving from the adjective/verb *mute* (cf: *muted sound*). Italian has an adjective *muto*, but is not in the business of creating this kind of technical terminology. It is quite possible, however, that the English term *muting* (the creation of neologisms on the basis of existing lexis and grammar is very much an English language phenomenon and shows no sign of abating) will eventually come into Italian as a loan word, its relative transparency facilitating comprehension. For the moment, though, it will have to be paraphrased into something like *Interruzione del suono*. The English *Press button* ⊠ assumes total familiarity with what is implied by the term *muting*; the Italian readership may need a word or two more of explanation: *Mediante il tasto* ⊠ *potete disinserire il suono. The sound is* ... pays no heed to the stylistic nicety of avoiding repetition, which the Italian translator would be sensitive to, even in a technical text. An adverbial equivalent to *again/nuovamente* can be alternated with the prefix to the verb <u>ri</u>*premete*, which itself can alternate with *premete*. These small considerations make the text more readable to an Italian audience and thus more assimilable.

The last section (*Opening the set*) is again illustrative of the need to shift perspective for a translation into genuine Italian. The item in theme position in the English text tells us what the sentence is going to be about (*the rear cover of the set*) and the typical use of the passive puts the focus on who the agent is. Italian may shift the emphasis by thematising the important adverbial *solo* and focus on the thing that can only be opened in certain circumstances. The information can be the same but languages often have different ways of presenting it, ways that are ingrained in the linguistic tradition of a speech community.

As mentioned in Part One, **2.3.1.**, the Sapir-Whorf theory postulated that languages might influence, even control, thought patterns, and this was construed by some to suggest that meaningful translation was impossible. This is clearly an untenable position, but the different perspectives taken by different language users explains why a member of one speech community can declare that a text is correct from the grammatical point of view but that 'it is not English' or 'Italian' or 'German' or whatever. The Italian text below, based largely on the OV mentioned earlier, is an illustration of how important this mental picture of perspective is, even in a set of technical instructions. The frequent complaints on the part of customers about the incomprehensibility of translated instructions is arguably due as much to the text not matching the readers' set of conventional expectations as to semantic inaccuracy.

> Siamo lieti che abbiate acquistato un nuovo televisore a colori. E' un apparecchio modernissimo con numerose possibilità ed il modo migliore per conoscerlo è di leggere prima attentamente le presenti istruzioni d'uso. Se l'apparecchio è già stato predisposto per la ricezione delle trasmittenti dal vostro rivenditore, soltanto il capitolo 'Impiego del televisore' sarà di vostro interesse (ved. la pag. 4).

> **Impiego del televisore**
> Accensione del televisore
> Premete l'interruttore di rete sul televisore. Nella scala appare il programma numero 1 e sullo schermo la trasmittente memorizzata su questo numero.

> **Selezione dei programmi**
> Per la selezione dei programmi da 0 a 9 compreso premete il corrispondente tasto numerico.
> Per la selezione di un numero di programma composto da due cifre premete il tasto -/--. Nella scala (sul televisore) appaiono due linee.
> Per tornare ai numeri dei programmi da 0 a 9 compreso ripremete il tasto -/--

Immagine e suono

Mediante i tasti + e − potete aumentare o diminuire il livello della saturazione, della luminosità e del volume.

Questa modifica *non* è di carattere permanente. Premendo il tasto *verde* o riaccendendo il televisore otterrete l'immagine ed il suono nuovamente al livello preregolato.

Interruzione del suono

Mediante il tasto ⊠ potete disinserire il suono. Per inserirlo nuovamente ripremete il tasto ⊠ o premete il tasto verde.

Apertura del televisore

Solo un tecnico del Servizio assistenza può aprire il pannello posteriore del televisore.

Other sections of the text are now offered for practice:

Positioning the TV

To obtain a picture with good contrast, position your TV in such a way that no direct sunlight or lamplight strikes the screen. When viewing in the evening it is preferable to switch on subdued lighting for otherwise the picture will be too bright.

Tuning to the TV stations
this can be done in two ways:

Automatically: your TV searches for the channel numbers of the stations itself.

Press button ▷▷ on the TV or remote control. A channel number (recognisable by the red dot after the figures) appears in the window. The channel numbers will run up until the next station is reached. The sound is suppressed while the set is searching for a station.

Press button ▷▷ again if the channel number remains stationary in the window and there is no picture or the picture is poor. As soon as the station appears on the screen, fine tuning takes place automatically.

Directly: i.e. you can choose the channel numbers yourself.

Press button C/P (Channel or Programme selection) on the TV or remote control. A channel number (recognisable by the red dot after the figures) appears in the window.

Select the desired channel number with the digit buttons on the remote control. For numbers 1 to 9, first press button 0 i.e. you select 01, 02 etc. to 09. If you select a channel number that does not exist two horizontal bars appear in the window.

Speech/music
Press button 'Ð on the TV for clear reproduction of speech.
Release button 'Ð (press again for music reproduction).

Points to remember
If the picture disappears from the screen and only a bright white line can be seen you should switch the set off immediately, remove the plug from the socket and inform the dealer.

2.2.2 Memotel

Telecom Italia recently introduced their own answering service and provided the following instruction leaflet.

MEMOTEL: GUIDA BREVE ALL'USO PER ASCOLTARE I MESSAGGI
(UNA VOLTA CHE IL SERVIZIO È ATTIVO)

Per usare Memotel dal proprio telefono	**Da fuori casa – da un altro telefono**
Premere i tasti ✱ # 6 4 #	Comporre il proprio numero
Comporre il codice standard 1 2 3 4 #	Digitare il tasto # durante il messaggio di risposta della propria segreteria
Lasciarsi guidare dai messaggi vocali	Comporre il codice standard 1 2 3 4 #
0 è il tasto di aiuto che potete usare durante qualsiasi funzione	Lasciarsi guidare dai messaggi vocali

Da ricordare

- dal proprio telefono consultare la segreteria è sempre gratuito. Da fuori, da un altro telefono, costa quanto una telefonata.
- lasciandoti guidare dai messaggi vocali, puoi sostituire il codice standard con un tuo codice personale.

Tutte le informazioni dettagliate per l'utilizzo di **MEMOTEL** sono contenute nella guida all'uso che ti verrà recapitata a stretto giro di posta dopo la richiesta di prova gratuita al Numero Verde.

Literal translation

MEMOTEL: BRIEF GUIDE TO THE USE FOR LISTENING TO THE MESSAGES (one time that the service is active)

To use Memotel from own phone	From out of home – from another phone
Press the keys ******.	Compose own number.
Compose the standard code *****.	Digit the key # during the message of response of own secretary.
Let oneself guide by the vocal messages.	Compose the standard code *****.
	Let oneself guide by the vocal messages.

0 is the key of help which you can use during any function.

To remember	
- from own phone consult the secretary is always free. From out, from another phone, costs as much as a phone call.	All the detailed informations for the utilisation of MEMOTEL are contained in the guide to the use which you will come sent at tight turn of post after the request of free trial at Green Number.
- leaving you guide by the vocal messages can substitute the standard code with your personal code.	

To steer clear of any of the banal traps indicated in the literal translation, the translator of this kind of text would do well to check the latest equivalent literature produced by British or American companies in the same field. Changes take place rapidly nowadays, and the old translation couplet *comporre il numero/dial the number*, for example, runs the risk of being rendered obsolete by improvements in telephone design. However, although the push-button phones of today would seem to require a different action (e.g. *key the number*, which is now to be seen on some instructions), the latest British Telecom literature still uses the verb *dial* in some instances (e.g. *Dial 157*). Certain lexical items have entered the vocabulary of both languages recently: *segreteria (telefonica)/answering service, Numero Verde/ Freephone, il tuo codice personale/your personal identification number (PIN)*.

Other set expressions are still in current use: *una telefonata/a local call, informazioni dettagliate/detailed information, a stretto giro di posta/by return of post, prova gratuita/free trial.*

Apart from these considerations, care need only be taken in trying to find equivalent expressions where an automatic equivalent does not readily present itself. These must not sound forced to a native speaker's ear: *guida breve all'uso/a brief user's guide, attivo/in operation, lasciarsi guidare/follow, messaggi vocali/spoken instructions.*

This kind of text is generally straightforward from a grammatical point of view, consisting of uncomplicated syntax with much use of imperatives and infinitives. However, certain stylistic markers need to be adopted: *Da ricordare/Please remember.* This text contains no concealed pragmatic meanings which would detract from its purpose of providing clear instructions to potential customers.

MEMOTEL: A BRIEF USER'S GUIDE FOR RECEIVING MESSAGES
(once the service is in operation)

To use Memotel from own phone	**From outside – from another phone**
Press the keys ******.	Dial or key your own number.
Key the standard number *****.	Press key # during your own answering service's reply.
Follow the spoken instructions.	Key the standard code *****.
	Follow the spoken instructions.

0 is the help key you can use at any stage.

Please remember

- consulting the answering service from your own phone is always free. The cost of phoning from outside or from another phone is that of a local call.

- following the spoken instructions, you can replace the standard number with your own personal identification number.

More detailed information on how to use MEMOTEL is contained in the user's guide, which will be sent to you by return of post following your Freephone request for a free trial.

The practice text that follows is taken from Telecom's 'Guida ai Numeri Verdi':

Benvenuti alla seconda edizione della Guida ai Numeri Verdi
Consultatela. Vi aiuterà a risparmiare tempo e denaro.
Chiamare un Numero Verde infatti non costa nulla e vi può aiutare a risolvere qualsiasi problema, a chiedere informazioni, ad effettuare un ordinativo, a conoscere il punto vendita più vicino o semplicemente a ricevere assistenza.
Da dove chiamare? Da qualunque apparecchio abbiate a portata di mano. Anche da un telefonino.
Chiamare un Numero Verde è facile: basta digitare 167 seguito dal numero dell'Azienda o dell'Ente abbonato:

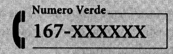

in qualunque città di Italia vi troviate. Non è necessario infatti comporre alcun prefisso teleselettivo, poiché il Numero Verde è unico a livello nazionale.
Utilizzate quindi la Guida ai numeri Verdi ogni volta che lo ritenete opportuno. Il Numero Verde è il fiore all'occhiello delle Aziende e degli Enti che hanno a cuore i propri Clienti. Essi saranno contenti di mettersi in contatto con voi, ascoltarvi e darvi il suggerimento più giusto. Vi stanno aspettando.

2.2.3 Combination lock

The final text in this subsection on instructions is taken from the small leaflet included in the packaging of a briefcase, and concerns the case's locking mechanism.

COMBINATION LOCK

The combination is set to 000 (zero-zero-zero).
To change it, proceed as follows.
1) Open the case. The release mechanism is located at the back of the combination.
2) Move the release mechanism to the lower position.
3) Set the combination to the required number, remembering to keep a note of it somewhere in case you forget it.
   We advise you to use 3 numbers you are familiar with such as part of your telephone number, date of birth or street number.

4) Reposition the release mechanism without moving the combination wheels.

Ensure that you have done this before closing the case

Your SPHERA case can now be opened only with its secret combination. If you wish to change the combination again, repeat points 2, 3 and 4. For total protection of your case also ensure that both locks are locked.

Write your secret number here

The text is of a semi-technical nature – the instructions for setting the combination lock on a briefcase. The participants in this discourse act are the writer of the instructions and the customer wishing to set the lock. The time is basically irrelevant and we will assume no particular accompanying circumstances. The present tense reinforces the timelessness of this communicative act. The text is organised in a conventional series of steps with predictable anaphoric cohesive devices (*The combination ... To change it ... the combination*), and the thematisation of verbs in the imperative mood is consonant with this text type. Being a written semi-technical text it is lexically dense, particularly with regard to the quasi-technical terms themselves. As the text is translated into numerous languages on a leaflet measuring approx. 10 x 25 cms., the accent is on succinctness.

From the lexical point of view, many of the terms used fall into the noun string pattern, though none exceed two items: *combination lock, release mechanism, street number, combination wheels*. The translator should seek the one-to-one relationship typical of terminology in Italian prepositional phrases and noun+adjective combinations, e.g. *combination lock/serratura a combinazione*.

In spite of the general economy of the text, item 3) breaks out of the mould and becomes more discursive, adopting a more informal, chatty style (*remembering to keep a note of it somewhere in case you forget it*) and spoken language norms such as post-placed prepositions (*use 3 numbers you are familiar with*). As the concept of user-friendliness takes hold, such register changes can be expected to become frequent across a whole range of texts.

The term *street number* is an accurate reflection of English housing patterns, while in Italian *numero civico* is the equation translation, again reflecting the less clear-cut concept of street address.

The final *ensure that both locks are locked* is clumsy, even given the English tolerance of repetition, but at least unequivocal.

The Italian translation found alongside the English on the leaflet is as follows, and will serve as a vehicle for further comment:

SERRATURA A COMBINAZIONE

Alla consegna la combinazione è regolata su 000 (zero-zero-zero).
Per variare la combinazione è necessario operare nel modo seguente:

1) Aprire la valigia. Nella parte posteriore della combinazione troverete la levetta di cambio.
2) Muovere la levetta di cambio nella posizione inferiore.
3) Ora impostare la combinazione sul numero desiderato tenendo presente di annotare il numero da qualche parte nel caso lo dimenticaste. Vi consigliamo di utilizzare 3 numeri a voi familiari come parte del numero telefonico, della data di nascita o numero civico.
4) Senza muovere le rotelline della combinazione, far ritornare la levetta nella posizione normale.

Assicuratevi di aver fatto questa operazione prima di chiudere la valigia

Ora la vostra valigia SPHERA si aprirà soltanto con la propria combinazione segreta. Se desiderate cambiare nuovamente la combinazione ripetere le fasi 2, 3 e 4. Per una protezione totale della vostra valigia assicuratevi anche che entrambe le serrature siano chiuse a chiave.

Segnate qui il vostro numero segreto

The Italian version is typically slightly longer, mainly due to the extra information provided on occasion (cf: *The combination is set/Alla consegna la combinazione è regolata*) and the amplification in *this/questa operazione*. Similarly, the second line *To change it, proceed as follows* diffuses into *Per variare la combinazione è necessario operare nel modo seguente*.

A final comment: although the briefcase was Made in Italy, it is assumed that the original set of instructions was written in English (this is common practice) and the other language versions are translations. The spontaneous informal stretch of language embedded in the English text would tend to corroborate this view, though the above-mentioned repetition of the word *lock* might raise the odd eyebrow. However, the fact that the original was not Italian is well documented by that same penultimate clause (*assicuratevi anche che entrambe le serrature siano chiuse a chiave*) – there are no keys (or keyholes) provided with the briefcase!

The following practice text is taken from the instruction leaflet accompanying the 'Thumper®' alarm clock:

1. Remove slide off cover at back of clock.

2. Insert the 'N' size battery into battery compartment, making sure + and – ends of battery are in proper positions (as shown in compartment) and the battery is well seated. We recommend you replace demonstration battery with an alkaline battery for long life.

3. Set time by sliding the set switch to time set. Press minute (M) button to correct time then press hour (H) button to correct time. Slide the set switch back to lock position.

4. Set alarm by sliding set switch to alarm position. Press minute button to desired time, then press hour button to correct time. Slide the set switch back to lock position.

5. To turn on alarm slide switch on right to 'on' position.

6. Hitting the Thumper® pad turns on light to illuminate dial and turns off alarm for the snooze feature which resets itself every four minutes till switched off.

2.3 Medical texts

Medical texts figure among the most frequently translated (and mistranslated) text types. Demand for medical translation stems largely from the needs of doctors to publish material in English language journals of varying degrees of prestige and deliver talks in English at international conferences. However, it is still uncommon to find specialist translators, even in fields as potentially rewarding as medicine, and this accounts for the often substandard nature of the work undertaken. While it is not so rare to find doctors with a good command of the English language, they rarely have any training in translation, and thus the uneasy symbiosis of doctor and non-specialist translator continues. The latter, however, can benefit from experience and a few relevant notions passed down from those who have already broken the ground. Many considerations relating to technical-scientific translation in general are pertinent to medicine, but the genre also has its own specificity.

It is also thought by some that technical translation in general, and medical translation through inclusion, is relatively problem-free, in that the only difficulty posed is at a lexical level. This theory assumes that technical texts consist of simple, unadorned syntax, peppered with technical terms which merely require the consultation of a good technical dictionary. The translator soon learns, however, that this is a gross oversimplification. A medical text may be grammatically tortuous for a number of reasons, not least of which the doctor's inability to express complicated ideas simply and in short manageable sentences, and medical lexis can often take on a syntax of its own, e.g. *glicogenosintesi tessutale*. Medical texts do, however, vary greatly in complexity, depending on the level of specificity. Tracts dealing in general medicine tend to use familiar terminology, while more specialised material contains terms that are often unfamiliar to medical specialists in other fields, e.g. *idiopathic hypocitraturia* in the field of nephrology. Other terms are being coined daily to keep pace with scientific achievement. There are, however, many paramedical areas such as quality control, hospital management and health policy which use an accessible language code, and publications for the general reader (witness the rising interest in medical problems shown by daily newspapers) use relatively straightforward language. There are, however, impenetrable concentrations of technical detail such as abstracts for conference papers on highly specialised areas of medicine which test translation techniques to the limits.

Another widely-believed myth is that doctors can understand even badly-translated texts, simply by piecing together the terminology. This notion is constantly refuted by journal referees who send back papers because of lack of clarity due to poor language use. A cause for sober reflection here is that many of these rejected translations are the work of mother-tongue, non-expert translators.

Two texts taken from the same journal now follow. The first is the beginning of the editorial which, while attempting to address the general problems encountered in the field, is less technically dense than the second extract, which is taken from one of the specialised articles found within this issue.

2.3.1 Giornale italiano di medicina riabilitativa (supplement): Editorial by N. Basaglia

1 Le disabilità più frequenti, anche se fortunatamente meno gravi ed abitualmente transitorie, riportate con costante omogeneità in tutte le indagini epidemiologiche realizzate nei paesi industrializzati sono quelle causate dalla patologia articolare.

2 Conseguentemente l'attività ambulatoriale dei medici di medicina
generale, dei fisiatri, degli ortopedici e dei reumatologi è in gran parte
dedicata a questa tipologia di patologie ed alle conseguenti menomazioni
e disabilità.

3 Questo settore della medicina è caratterizzato da frequenti approcci
parcellari, da visioni limitate ed a volte superficiali che hanno determinato
e giustificato interventi scarsamente scientifici, spesso fantasiosi e dato
spazio a tutta quella serie di interventi che passano sotto il termine di
'medicina alternativa', 'medicina esoterica' ed altro ancora.

4 Chi, come me, crede nella scientificità dell'approccio medico che, come
tale, non può mai essere alternativo di interventi valutativi e terapeutici seri
ma solo di un qualcosa di non scientifico (né orientale od occidentale, ma
universale), ritiene etico superare quelle ampie sacche di ignoranza ancora
esistenti nel settore e diffondere un vero approccio 'medico-scientifico'
sulla patologia articolare più frequente e le tecniche valutative e
terapeutiche validate e di rapida e dimostrata efficacia.

The literal translation of this text may actually pass the test of comprehensibility, but would still be unpublishable:

1 The most frequent disabilities, even if fortunately less grave and
habitually transitory, reported with constant homogeneity in all the
epidemiological investigations realised in the industrialised countries are
those caused by the articulatory pathology.

2 Consequently the surgery activity of the doctors of general medicine, of
the physiatrists, of the orthopedic surgeons and rheumatologists is in
great part dedicated to this typology of pathologies and to the consequent
disablements and disabilities.

3 This sector of medicine is characterised by frequent divided
approaches, by limited visions and at times superficial which have
determined and justified scarcely scientific interventions, often fanciful
and given space to all that series of interventions which pass under the
term of 'alternative medicine', 'esoteric medicine' and other still.

4 Who, like me, believes in the scientificness of the medical approach
which, as such, can never be alternative of serious evaluative and
therapeutic interventions but only of a something of non scientific (neither
oriental nor occidental, but universal), retains ethical to overcome those
ample sacks of ignorance still existing in the sector and to diffuse a true
'medical-scientific' approach on the most frequent articulatory pathology
and the evaluative and therapeutic techniques validated and of rapid and
demonstrated efficacy.

Lexicogrammatical analysis

The context of situation consists of a one-to-many participant structure featuring a specialised journal writer largely dislocated from his readers within the strictly medical world of joint pathology, though the interpersonal relationship is probably that of peer-to-peer. This context usually entails doctors writing for doctors, sometimes in a hierarchical 'teacher-student' way, but generally as an information-exchanging exercise. In any case, the text must be streamlined for the English medical reader, who expects more concision, even in an editorial. Syntactic as well as stylistic patterns at both clause and phrase level come into play in making Italian texts of this type more elaborate, and this should be constantly borne in mind. Firstly, the elegant phrase *con costante omogeneità* in paragraph 1 can be reduced to *regularly* in the hope that the homogeneous element is clear from the co-text *the result of* . . . . A wholesale shifting of the concessive phrase beginning *anche se* . . . can slim down the entire clause. The disjunct *fortunately*, which is a comment on the part of the author, can also be considered not strictly necessary. The adjective *grave/i* is usually translated as *serious* in medical contexts; the English *grave* has other well-prescribed collocations, e.g. *grave responsibility*. The Italian adjective *articolare* has to be transformed into the adjectival noun *joint*, which is the keyword of the whole journal. *Pathology* is a difficult item and will be dealt with later.

In paragraph 2, *Attività* is one of those many Italian words that are dealt with in this book that have a far higher frequency and different range to their transparent English equivalents (cf: *intervento* in this text). *Surgery time* could be opted for here, though it would appear that the potentially ambiguous *surgery* (*ambulatorio/chirurgia*) is also specifically British English, reflecting historico-administrative as well as medical norms. *Clinic* is an alternative, certainly in American English. Note that not all 'branches of medicine/specialist doctor' pairings follow the same pattern (cf: *rheumatology/rheumatologist, pediatrics/pediatrician, orthopedics/orthopedic surgeon*), though the rule is not rigid. For example, *orthopedist* can be found in the literature.

The participle *dedicata* is an example of a false friend which should be replaced by *devoted*, and *largely* is the adverbial collocation required for *in gran parte*.

It would seem that *menomazioni e disabilità* is rather tautologous, offering more scope for cuts: *(disablement and) disabilities*.

In paragraph 3, the search for a suitable translation of the rather unusual adjective *parcellari* could yield *fragmentary*, which would seem to strike the right register. The noun *visioni* must become singular in English while carrying the identical meaning. *Determinato (determinare)* is another verb form used more commonly than the English *determine. Led to* (from *to lead to*) is a useful alternative, as it is for the ubiquitous *portare a.* Following the reasoning that *scientifici* is not meant in the strict English sense of 'scientific' but in its often broader meaning of 'serious', 'academic' and 'acceptable', *interventi scarsamente scientifici* might reasonably be translated as *barely acceptable ... treatment. Treatment* replaces *interventi*, the latter being as common a term in Italian medical literature as *intervention* is rare in English texts. Two non-technical set expressions have clear one-to-one equivalents: *passare sotto il nome di/go by the name of* and *ed altro ancora/and so on.*

In paragraph 4 it is necessary to think a moment about *Chi, come me, ...* to realise that it needs diffusing and re-ordering to *All those like me, who ... .* The *scientificità dell'approccio medico* can probably be dealt with in many ways: *the scientific basis of approaches to medicine* is one. It should be noted that *alternative* requires a preceding indefinite article: *be an alternative.*

The adjective *valutativi/e*, which appears twice in this short stretch of text, does not appear in bilingual dictionaries, not even in medical bilingual dictionaries. Intuitively, *evaluative* feels right, though it is equally elusive in the same dictionaries. Its appropriacy is proved by consulting monolingual Italian and English dictionaries, a further indication that the latter are a greater help to the translator than the former.

Some syntactic fine-tuning is required in this last paragraph. The subject *Chi, come me, ... /All those like me, who ...* eventually links up with the verb phrase *ritiene etico superare/believe it ethical to want to overcome.* The dummy *it* is necessary to English syntax, while the addition of *to want* is dictated by questions of usage and even semantics – there is a desire involved. *Large pockets (of ignorance)* can be used to match the register of *ampie sacche.* A final phrase (*proven to be valid evaluative and therapeutic techniques*) is an attempt to streamline *le tecniche valutative e terapeutiche validate e di rapida e dimostrata efficacia.*

The translation thus rolls to:

1 The most frequent disabilities regularly reported in epidemiological investigations in industrialised countries, even if less serious and usually transitory, are the result of joint pathology.
2 Consequently the surgery time of doctors working in general medicine,

physiatrists, orthopedic surgeons and rheumatologists is largely devoted
to this pathology and the consequent (disablements and) disabilities.
3 This area of medicine is frequently characterised by fragmentary
approaches and limited, and at times superficial, vision which have led to
and justified barely acceptable and often fanciful treatment and provided
space for a whole series of therapies which go by the name of 'alternative
medicine', 'esoteric medicine' and so on.
4 All those like me, who believe in the scientific basis of approaches to
medicine which, as such, can never be an alternative to serious evaluative
and therapeutic treatment but only to something non-scientific (neither
eastern nor western, but universal), believe it ethical to want to overcome
those large pockets of ignorance that still exist in the sector and to
promulgate a real 'medico-scientific' approach to the most frequent joint
pathologies and proven to be valid evaluative and therapeutic techniques.

Further linguistic and pragmatic considerations

The above translation is largely the work of a non-specialist with experience
of medical translation, but it is salutary to observe the work of an expert in
the field, in this case a non-translator medic, who provided a sort of parallel
'interpretation' of the text in the journal in question. This version is much
too distant from the original to be considered a translation in the accepted
sense, though elements of it will also be found in this final brief analysis.

Firstly, the key concept in paragraph 1 emerges clearly as being that of
joint disorders, and it is fronted to theme position. *Disorders* replaces the
doubtful *pathology* – the latter term really belongs to a higher register in the
English consciousness, used mainly to refer to the study of medicine, and
not to refer to individual *disorders*. By getting down to the core message (. . .
are among the most common causes . . .), translators can condense the first
two paragraphs into one. They can reduce *less serious* to *mild* by adopting
the opposite perspective, and replace *transitory* with the near-synonym
transient, thereby achieving the right medical register in both cases. The
medici di medicina generale are correctly identified as *general practitioners*.

On further analysis, the very Italian use of <u>caratterizzato</u> *da frequenti*
approcci parcellari is avoided (*characterised* does not have the same range)
and replaced with *we can observe great variability in clinical approach*. Again
working from the opposite direction, <u>unsound</u> *diagnosis and treatment* is
preferred to the unmedical *fanciful*.

The *scientific basis of approaches to medicine* has been fine-tuned to *a*
correct scientific clinical approach. Similarly, the final rather clumsy phrase

and proven to be valid evaluative and therapeutic techniques has been revolutionised to *and thereby improve the diagnostic and therapeutic quality of our practice.* This latter solution admittedly takes translation licence further than is usually acceptable, but it is neat and simple and conveys the message perfectly. The result of this final roll is:

> Joint disorders are among the most common causes of disability in industrialised countries. Although they are often mild and usually transient, the surgery time of general practitioners, physiatrists, orthopedic surgeons and rheumatologists is largely devoted to these disorders and the consequent disabilities.
>
> In this area of medicine we can observe great variability in clinical approach and limited, and at times superficial, vision which have led to and justified barely acceptable and often unsound diagnosis and treatment, leaving room for a whole series of therapies which go by the name of 'alternative medicine', 'esoteric medicine' and so on.
>
> All those like me, who believe in a correct scientific clinical approach which, as such, can never be an alternative to serious evaluative and therapeutic treatment but only to something non-scientific (neither eastern nor western, but universal), believe it ethical to want to overcome those large pockets of ignorance that still exist in the sector and to promulgate a real 'medico-scientific' approach to the most frequent joint disorders and thereby improve the diagnostic and therapeutic quality of our practice.

The text continues as follows and is offered for practice:

> Per questi motivi ho accettato con entusiasmo la proposta di dar vita ad una rivista scientifica multimediale come supplemento al *Giornale italiano di medicina riabilitativa.*
>
> Non una rivista finalizzata a stimolare la ricerca, ma dedicata ad una serie didattica fondata su solide basi scientifiche, che con un carattere pluridisciplinare è aperta al contributo di fisiatri, reumatologi, ortopedici, neurologi, psicoterapeuti ed ad ogni altro specialista medico che opera nel settore.
>
> Uno strumento utile per omogeneizzare gli approcci valutativi e terapeutici di tutti coloro che operano quotidianamente negli ambulatori dedicati a questa tipologia di utenti nel tentativo di avvicinare la 'domanda' di interventi sanitari al 'bisogno reale'

evitando approcci inutili, dispendiosi e come tale dannosi all'individuo ed alla comunità.

Sono attualmente previsti tre numeri all'anno ed ogni fascicolo conterrà articoli esaurienti ed aggiornati su specifici argomenti in modo da fornire al lettore una visione aggiornata e completa della problematica trattata, comprese eventuali critiche e possibili dubbi sui singoli approcci.

2.3.2 Giornale italiano di medicina riabilitativa (supplement): La legamentite ileo-lumbare

As mentioned above, the next text is a more specialised piece on a specific impairment.

La legamentite ileo-lumbare

Definizione
La legamentite ileo-lumbare è una sindrome dolorosa lombare, spesso irradiata nella fossa iliaca o lungo l'arto inferiore omolaterale (Fig. 1) e caratterizzata dalla presenza di un tipico punto doloroso alla pressione nella zona postero-mediale della cresta iliaca.

Eziologia
La localizzazione del punto doloroso alla pressione nella zona postero-mediale della cresta iliaca ha indotto i vari autori a pensare che sia coinvolto il legamento ileo-lombare.
Ciò nonostante, non bisogna dimenticare che nella stessa area si inserisce un gran numero di tendini: del muscolo gran dorsale, del muscolo multifido, del muscolo quadrato dei lombi, del muscolo lunghissimo del torace (parte lombare), del muscolo ileo-costale, del muscolo trasverso-spinale e dell'ultimo muscolo inter-trasversario.

Anatomia
Il legamento ileo-lombare prende origine dal processo trasverso di L5 mediante due fasci: un fascio anteriore ed un fascio posteriore (Fig. 2).
Il *fascio anteriore* del legamento ileo-lombare è corto, largo e piatto. Esso trae la sua origine dalla zona anteriore ed inferiore dell'apice del processo trasverso di L5 ed espandendosi come un ventaglio va ad inserirsi sulla tuberosità iliaca.
Il *fascio posteriore* del legamento ileo-lombare, invece, trae la sua origine dall'apice del processo trasverso di L5, ha un diametro rotondeggiante di

circa 1-3 mm e, prima di inserirsi sulla cresta iliaca, si espande come un piccolo cono. Alla fine si inserisce sulla cresta iliaca, dal margine anteriore fino all'apice.

L'esistenza di una componente del legamento ileo-lombare ad origine dal processo trasverso di L4 è molto controversa.

Literal translation

Ileolumbar ligamentitis

Definition
The ileolumbar ligamentitis is a painful lumbar syndrome, often radiated in the iliac trench or along the inferior homolateral limb (Fig. 1) and characterised by the presence of a typical painful point to the pressure in the postero-medial zone of the iliac crest.

Etiology
The localisation of the painful point to the pressure in the postero-medial zone of the iliac crest has induced the various authors to think that is involved the ileolumbar ligament.

That notwithstanding, there is no need to forget that in the same area is inserted a great number of tendons: of the great dorsal muscle, of the multifidus muscle, of the square muscle of the loins, of the very long muscle of the thorax (lumbar part), of the ileocostal muscle, of the transverse-spinal muscle and of the last inter-transversal muscle.

Anatomy
The ileolumbar ligament takes origin from the transverse process of L5 through two bundles: an anterior bundle and a posterior bundle (Fig. 2).
The *anterior bundle* of the ileolumbar ligament is short, wide and flat.
It takes its origin from the anterior and inferior zone of the apex of the transverse process of L5 and expanding like a fan it goes to insert itself on the iliac tuberosity.
The *posterior bundle* of the ileolumbar ligament, instead, takes its origin from the apex of the transverse process of L5, has a diameter rounding of about 1-3 mm and, before inserting itself on the iliac crest, it expands like a little cone. At the end, it inserts itself on the iliac crest, from the anterior margin up to the apex.
The existence of a component of the ileolumbar ligament at origin from the transverse process of L4 is very controversial.

Lexicogrammatical analysis

La legamentite ileo-lumbare is referred to in English as *iliolumbar syndrome*, as a brief glimpse at any of the relevant literature will show. Indeed, articles on or around the subject in question are probably more useful in medical translations than in any other type. The fields have become so specific that the terminology used, and even the syntax, show a great deal of repetition and act as recurring models. Translators should thus constantly peruse similar material, if available, while working on a medical text, in order to guide them through an unfamiliar world.

The Italian text then actually refers to *sindrome*, but English style restraints are not so inflexible as to rule out its repetition in the target version.

Use of both mono- and bi-lingual dictionaries is of course necessary with this type of text, and theoretically not risky, in that one-to-one correspondences should be the norm. The temptation, however, to revert to common core language and translate *irradiata* with *spread* (the latter has a pseudo-medical feel to it, cf: *pain spreads*), should give precedence to a dictionary check, which will reveal that the correct terminology is *radiated* or even *irradiated*. The dictionary search for *fossa iliaca* is not so straightforward. The first item provided in a commercial publication designed for doctors, the Italfarmaco Dizionario Medico (1986), is an unchanged *fossa*, followed by four other options (*fovea, lacuna, lacune, pit*), while *iliaca* is given two different English spellings – *iliac* and *ileac* and an alternative *ileal*. This confusion is avoided totally in the OV of this text (published in parallel in the journal) by adopting a less technical description: *in the abdominal low region*. The Fig. 1 mentioned in the text (but not shown here) is an invaluable aid in identifying and understanding the verbal element, allowing for some simplification in places. For example, it would be possible to dispense with the adjective *omolaterale* – the figure shows the exact position of the syndrome. Nowhere are these considerations more important than in the task of simultaneous interpreting, but the translator of written technical texts can take refuge as well.

In general, the terms *inferiore* and *superiore* are translated by *lower* and *upper* respectively, even in technical texts, but *inferior* is correct in this context, as the medical dictionary will confirm. The literal translation of the Italian verbal expression *caratterizzata da* is *characterised by*, which sounds right on first (mental) hearing, but would almost always, on reflection, be reduced – for example, to *with*.

The question of semi-false friends in the form of simple adjectives is exemplified by the Italian noun phrase *un tipico (punto) doloroso alla pressione*. The perfect adjective to describe the latter in English is *tender (point)*, with the meaning of 'sensitive to the touch', providing an extra component to the usual Italian equivalent *tenero* in other contexts. In fact, *tenero* is an adjective that needs to be handled with the same circumspection as other seemingly 'easy' terms such as the previously-mentioned *gentle*, *kind*, *nice*, and so on. The end of the sentence can be allowed to form itself as a literal translation.

As regards the section on *Etiology*, the opening phrase picks up on the end of the previous paragraph in a typical pattern of repetition which the translator should be looking out for.

A grammatical question that frequently emerges in this kind of text is whether or not to keep the Italian present perfect tense in, for example, *ha indotto i vari autori*. There is an argument to say that the present perfect in English should be employed because the doctors involved are still dealing with the case and the results are important in the here and now, but an article in print tends to forfeit its temporal rights, and the past simple *led the authors to believe* covers the writers now and into the future.

The list of *muscoli* whose Latin-based names should create no real translation headaches, dictionary permitting, could actually be translated in Latin, as occurred in the OV of this text.

In the *Anatomy* section, the same principles generally applied to *inferiore* and *superiore* also pertain to *anteriore* and *posteriore*, namely *front* and *back*, though in these medical contexts *anterior* and *posterior (bands)* are pre-ferred. The translator, while initially tempted into looking for a verb phrase to replace *prende origine* and *trae la sua origine*, will opt sensibly for a simple *originates*.

The rather elaborate image of the *fascio anteriore* which *espandendosi come un ventaglio va ad inserirsi sulla tuberosità iliaca*, should put translators on their guard when they consider the weakness of the verb *va/goes* in an English clause of this type, and the impossibility of attaching *goes* to the verb *to insert*. The verb phrase can, in fact, be condensed into a preposition: *expands into the iliac tuberosity*.

In the next sentence, the problem of translating *invece* (*on the other hand*, *alternatively*, *on the contrary*, and hardly ever *instead*) can be solved by leaving it out – the distinction is implicit in the text. In the following sentence the translator may well wish to change the order of prepositional phrases to create a spatio-grammatical progression more typical of English:

si inserisce sulla cresta iliaca, dal margine fino all'apice/it inserts itself from the anterior margin to the apex of the iliac crest. Finally, the use of the Italian noun *esistenza* should send the same signals as the participle form *caratterizzata* earlier, namely is it being used for its own sake or as a component in a longer expression that can usefully be curtailed in a more succinct English clause? The translator may well decide that the latter is the case and translate *L'esistenza di una componente del legamento ileolumbare ad origine ...* with something like *The origin of the iliolumbar ligament ....*

The translation has rolled on:

Iliolumbar syndrome

Definition
The iliolumbar syndrome is a painful lumbar syndrome, often radiated in the abdominal low region or along the inferior limb (Fig. 1) with a tender point in the posterior-medial area of the iliac crest.

Etiology
The location of the tender point in the posterior-medial area of the iliac crest led the authors to believe that the iliolumbar ligament was involved. However, in the same area a large number of tendons are inserted: the latissimus dorsi, the multifidus, the quadratus lumborum, the longissimus thoracis pars lumbarum, the ileocostalis, the transversospinalis and the last lumbar intertransversarii.

Anatomy
The iliolumbar ligament originates from the L5 transverse process by two bands: an anterior band and a posterior band (Fig. 2).
The *anterior band* of the iliolumbar ligament is short, broad and flat. It originates from the anterior-inferior zone of the apex of the L5 transverse process and expands like a fan into the iliac tuberosity.
The *posterior bundle* of the iliolumbar ligament originates from the apex of the L5 transverse process, has a round diameter of about 1-3 mm and, before inserting itself on the iliac crest, it expands like a little cone. In the end, it inserts itself from the anterior margin to the apex of the iliac crest. The origin of the iliolumbar ligament from the L4 transverse process is very controversial.

As the text is purely technical, further analysis of a semantico-pragmatic nature is unnecessary. The text continues as follows and is offered for practice:

Innervazione

E' probabile che il legamento ileo-lombare abbia una doppia innervazione: sia dal ramo posteriore del 12° nervo toracico, sia dal ramo posteriore del 1° nervo sacrale.

In effetti, gli anatomisti descrivono a livello della regione lombare l'esistenza di molte fibre anastomiche sia tra le radici di altri tratti vertebrali che tra le branche laterali dei rami posteriori.

Queste anastomosi sono così frequenti che si può parlare di *plesso lombare posteriore*.

Anatomia Patologica

Il legamento ileo-lombare può essere coinvolto da quelle situazioni patologiche delle entesi definite col termine *entesopatie degenerative*.

Esse possono svilupparsi per fattori meccanici locali, quali macro-traumi unici o micro-traumi multipli da attività sportive, lavorative, ecc (*entesopatie localizzate o entesopatie meccano-degenerative*), oppure possono svilupparsi per fattori metabolici, quali il diabete, l'iperparatiroidismo, ipervitaminosi A, ecc (*poli-entesopatie degenerative*).

Sintomatologia

Il paziente lamenta un dolore lombare caratterizzato da un andamento infradiano tipico e caratteristico: il dolore è più intenso al mattino e durante le tipiche attività della vita quotidiana (ad esempio aumenta quando il paziente si piega sul lavandino per lavarsi il viso, o quando si veste, ecc). Tuttavia, la ripetizione del movimento allevia il dolore avvertito dal paziente.

A volte il dolore può irradiarsi all'inguine o all'arto inferiore omolaterale (pseudo-sciatica).

The following text offered for practice is an extract from an article on the metabolic side-effects of diuretic drugs:

I DISORDINI METABOLICI CONSEGUENTI ALLA TERAPIA DIURETICA

I diuretici non fanno eccezione alla regola generale dei farmaci, che è quella di essere potenzialmente dannosi.

La grande diffusione della terapia diuretica e l'introduzione di farmaci sempre più potenti sono certamente alla base dei numerosi effetti indesiderati che conseguono all'impiego dei diuretici.

Ricorderemo, tra questi, le alterazioni del metabolismo dei carboidrati, dell'acido urico, dell'ammoniaca e degli elettroliti e i disordini dell'equilibrio acido-base.

1. Le alterazioni del metabolismo dei carboidrati

In alcuni ipertesi curati con diuretici, Finnerty e Wilkins osservarono per primi che la somministrazione protratta di tiazidici era seguita talora dal deprimersi della tolleranza ai carboidrati. L'interesse suscitato da questo nuovo aspetto di patologia 'iatrogena', definito 'diabete tiazidico', ha stimolato numerose ricerche sperimentali e cliniche nell'intento di chiarirne la frequenza, gli aspetti clinici e la patogenesi.

Sul piano sperimentale, hanno dimostrato intenso effetto diabetogeno, a dosi normali, sopratutto i diuretici tiazidici e, a dosi molto elevate, anche l'acido etacrinico ed il furosemide.

Anche nell'uomo, sono apparsi potenzialmente diabetogeni soprattutto i tiazidici; meno sicuro appare l'effetto iperglicemizzante dell'acido etacrinico e del furosemide. Infine per altri diuretici, come il triamterene o lo spironolattone, non si è mai osservato un sicuro effetto iperglicemizzante alle dosi comunemente impiegate.

Chapter Three

Legal, Commercial and Promotional Texts

3.1   Legal and commercial texts

Legal documentation in general is a fertile field for translation and could easily find a place among the technical texts of the previous chapter. It is a notoriously difficult broad genre from a translation point of view, though a number of conventions help keep the translator on the right track (see Part One **3.4.3**). Such conventions are obligatory elements of the genre, whatever the subject matter might be, and in today's complicated world, this could be more or less anything. In an era of expanding communication across nations, the legal terminology of each individual country, already dense and opaque to their own peoples, often needs to be unequivocably translated into the legal language of another country. Momentous decisions and events may hinge on such translations, either at a personal or even national level.

At a personal level, compared to the relatively recent past, apart from being subjected to the terms of legal/commercial agreements practically every time they purchase an article, citizens of western societies are now more than ever likely to have to consult a lawyer and enter into contract agreements at certain moments in their lives. Accordingly, this chapter looks initially at a particular field of legalese, that associated with legal agreements in the form of licences and contracts, thereby linking up with the world of commerce, the other focus of this section. The first text examines translation from English to Italian and the second from Italian to English. The language of the commercial letter, based on a piece of English correspondence, will be analysed in the third text in this section, followed by an analysis of the translation of a European Union document originally prepared in English.

3.1.1 Licence agreement

The following document is a licence agreement for a US company's Interactive CD-ROM application:

PLEASE READ THIS LICENCE CAREFULLY BEFORE breaking the seal on the packaging. By breaking the seal on the packaging, you are agreeing to be bound by all terms of this Licence. If you do not agree to the terms of this Licence, promptly return the unopened software and its complete packaging for a full refund.

LICENCE
In consideration of payment of the licence fee, which is a portion of the price you paid, the software, including without limitation any images incorporated in or generated by the software, and data accompanying this Licence (the 'Software') and related documentation are licensed (not sold) to you by the Company. The Company does not transfer title to the Software to you; this Licence shall not be considered a 'sale' of the Software. You own the diskettes on which the Software is recorded, but the Company retains full and complete title to the Software on the diskettes, the accompanying documentation, and all intellectual and industrial property rights therein.

The following translation into Italian is to be found in the same booklet as the original, together with translations into fifteen other languages:

SI PREGA DI LEGGERE ATTENTAMENTE QUESTA LICENZA PRIMA DI USARE IL SOFTWARE. L'utilizzazione del presente software comporta l'accettazione di tutti i termini e le condizioni della presente Licenza. Chi non intendesse accettare i termini e le condizioni della presente Licenza è tenuto a restituire prontamente i supporti del software intatti con la confezione completa e verrà integralmente rimborsato.

LICENZA
Il software, incluse tutte le immagini incorporate nel software o generate da esso e i dati che accompagnano questa Licenza (di seguito il 'Software') e la relativa documentazione sono a Voi concessi in licenza (non venduti) dalla Società, a fronte del pagamento del corrispettivo della Licenza, che costituisce una parte del prezzo che avete pagato. La Società non Vi trasferisce la proprietà del Software: questa Licenza non può essere interpretata come una 'vendita' del 'Software'. Voi sarete proprietari dei CD-ROM sui quali il Software è registrato, ma la Società manterrà la piena ed esclusiva proprietà del Software contenuto nei CD-ROM, della documentazione di accompagnamento e di tutti i diritti di proprietà intellettuale ed industriale ad essi inerenti.

The text is marked by a number of typical features of this type of legal document. Firstly, standard vocabulary and expressions abound, matched by Italian equivalents: *PLEASE READ THIS LICENCE CAREFULLY/SI PREGA DI LEGGERE ATTENTAMENTE*, to be bound by all terms of/ *l'accettazione di tutti i termini e le condizioni*, In consideration of payment of/ *a fronte del pagamento*, related documentation/*la relativa documentazione*, transfer title/*trasferisce la proprietà*, retains full and complete title/*manterrà la piena ed esclusiva proprietà* , therein/*ad essi inerenti*.

There is much repetition of *(this) Licence* and *the Software*, which are the key words in the text, but also of other expressions, for example, *breaking the seal on the packaging* at the beginning. The Italian version responds with *(questa) Licenza* and *il Software* where the second example is a straight loan word, like so much computer-related lexis (it also exists as a loan in six of the other languages). In the case of *breaking the seal on the packaging*, the repetition is not identical, as the initial verbal form is nominalised on its second appearance in Italian: *PRIMA DI USARE IL SOFTWARE ... L'utilizzazione del presente software*. Furthermore, the semi-metaphorical *breaking the seal* is discarded in favour of a congruent *usare*. The key terms *Licence/Licenza* and *Software/Software* have an initial capital in line with the previously-mentioned legal document convention.

The more direct (user-friendly?) English language approach with the use of the second person pronoun (*If you do not agree ...*) is made more formal in Italian with a typical third person subjunctive usage: *Chi non intendesse ...* . The message continues in peremptory fashion in both languages though in slightly different ways. The English *promptly return the unopened software* puts an unequivocal adverb before a second person imperative, whereas Italian prefers *è tenuto a restituire prontamente i supporti del software*, maintaining the same force in the adverb, though placing it after the verb, but also keeping to the more distant third person instruction (*è tenuto*). This line is continued through to the information that the person *verrà integralmente rimborsato*. English is more concise with a simple prepositional phrase: *for a full refund*.

The long first sentence in the second paragraph is subjected to considerable re-ordering in translation, but remains an equally unwieldy example of 'legalese'. The repetition of *software* is maintained, and Italian prefers to add an anaphoric prononimal reference that English avoids: *any images incorporated in or generated by the software/incluse tutte le immagini incorporate nel software o generate da esso*.

In this paragraph, the Italian pronoun *Voi/Vi* takes over from the impersonal third person. The English refers continually to *you*, which is ambiguous as to register. There is an example of the deontic *shall* in *this*

Licence shall not be considered a 'sale', rendered by *questa Licenza non può essere interpretata come una 'vendita'*, which captures the obligation intended. The verb in the English *You <u>own</u> the diskettes* is nominalised to *Voi sarete proprietari*, with the verb *to be* in the future tense, which possibly makes the situation clearer for the purchaser.

Finally, it is interesting to note that the *diskettes* mentioned in the English text are translated as *CD-ROM* in Italian, as in all the other fifteen languages featured in the booklet.

The text continues as follows and is offered for practice:

RESTRICTIONS

The Software contains copyrighted material, trade secrets, and other proprietary material. You may not re-sell, decompile, reverse engineer, disassemble or otherwise reduce the Software to a human-perceivable form except as permitted by law. Except as provided for in this Licence, you may not copy, modify, network, rent, lease, or otherwise distribute the Software; nor can you make the Software available by 'bulletin boards', on-line services, remote dial-in, or network or telecommunications links of any kind; nor can you create derivative works or any other works that are based upon or derived from the Software in whole or in part. You shall not part with possession of, lend, or transfer any part of the Software or related documentation to any other person.

FURTHER RESTRICTIONS ON USE

The Software provides you with the ability to print images containing the Company's copyrighted characters. This Licence only allows you to print the images on paper only for your PERSONAL, NON-COMMERCIAL, AND NON-GOVERNMENTAL use provided that you preserve all copyright notices that are included with the images as generated by the Software. This means that you may, for example, use the Software to print invitations to your own family party. You may not, for example, use this Software to print invitations for functions or events sponsored by a business, charity, church or educational institution. Without limiting the foregoing, you may not use images generated by the Software in connection with any advertising or promotional materials, whether for profit or not for profit. Use of images generated by the Software for any purpose not specifically allowed by this Licence is a violation of the Company's copyrights, trade marks, registered and unregistered design rights and other proprietary rights and will result in the immediate termination of this Licence.

3.1.2 Contract

The text chosen for demonstration purposes in this case is an Italian leasing contract, drawn up not long after the leasing phenomenon took hold in Italy, and therefore an important example of contemporary business practice covered by conventional legal terminology. The 'official' translation act was the writing of a university thesis (Merlo 1986), part of which was subsequently published in the 'Rivista italiana del leasing 3/87'. The fact that the receiver of the original text was a graduation panel rather than a commercial customer perhaps encouraged the writer to mentally approach the text with extra analytical rigour.

CONTRATTO DI LOCAZIONE FINANZIARIA
(LEASING) MOBILIARE

La Società di Leasing, nel contesto del presente atto denominata anche 'il Locatore', e la Ditta nel contesto del presente atto denominata anche 'il Conduttore' qui rappresentata da ... (munito di necessari poteri):

PREMESSA

a) che il Conduttore ha chiesto in *leasing* al Locatore il macchinario e/o l'attrezzatura (comunque in prosieguo sempre denominato 'il macchinario') descritto alla successiva clausola 1) del presente contratto;

b) che tale macchinario, scelto e trattato direttamente dal Conduttore presso Fornitore di sua fiducia, dovrà essere appositamente acquistato dal Locatore con proprio ordinativo di acquisto che il Conduttore ha preventivamente esaminato ed approvato;

c) che a tal fine il Conduttore si è dichiarato disposto, sia nei confronti delle parti che di terzi, a manlevare e tenere indenne il Locatore di ogni rischio e responsabilità connessi con l'acquisto, custodia, conservazione ed impiego del macchinario per tutta la durata del presente rapporto, ivi compresi i rischi derivanti dalla scelta del Fornitore e quelli per i danni da caso fortuito o forza maggiore ed a corrispondere il canone pattuito per tutta la durata del contratto, anche in caso di mancata utilizzazione del macchinario, nonché ad assumere a proprio carico ogni onere relativo all'uso ed alla manutenzione ordinaria e straordinaria dello stesso;

Literal translation

FINANCIAL MOBILE LOCATION CONTRACT

The Leasing Society, in the context of the present act denominated also 'the Locator', and the Firm in the context of the present act denominated 'the Conductor' here represented by ... (armed with necessary powers):

PREMISED

a) that the Conductor has asked in *leasing* the Locator the machine and/or the equipment (in any case in following always denominated 'the machine') described at the successive clause 1) of the present contract;

b) that such machine, chosen and treated directly by the Conductor at Furnisher of trust, will have to be deliberately purchased by the Locator with proper order of purchase that the Conductor has previously examined and approved;

c) that to that end the Conductor has declared himself disposed, . both in the confrontation of the parts than of thirds, to indemnify and hold unhurt the Locator of every risk and responsibility connected with the purchase, custody, conservation and employment of the machine for all the duration of the present rapport, here comprised the risks derivating from the choice of the Furnisher and those for the damages from fortuitous case or major risk and to correspond the rent agreed for all the duration of the contract, even in case of lacking utilisation of the machine, not that to assume at proper load every burden relative to the use and to the ordinary and extraordinary maintenance of the same;

A literal translation of legal language inevitably produces a considerable amount of gobbledygook such as that above, though we shall see now that producing a correct translation requires a rather different mental approach than in many other genres. In their search for the right (or initially right-sounding) term, syntagm or expression, translators must remember that their choices are limited by collocational restrictions that are sacrosanct in legal discourse. It is possible that such language is unknown or only partially familiar to the translator, and recourse to authentic documentation, legal glossaries or indeed the kind of thesis material cited here (which is produced with this very purpose in mind) may be absolutely necessary.

Further analysis

Having stressed the importance of not betraying the conventional and obligatory elements that bind together a legal document such as a contract, that tight lexical cohesion that gives the discourse its juridical texture, it must also be pointed out that the fundamental difference in the Italian and English legal systems (Constitutional versus Common law) at times makes the matching of such conventions hazardous. At such times the all-important criterion must be that of obeying the dictates of the legal system within which the text is going to be used. This may on occasion require a certain limited flexibility in the choice of terms in order to make the concept fit the language.

As the Italian title gives us both *locazione* and *leasing* (Italian commercial bilingual dictionaries were already using the terms together in the seventies), the term *leasing* or *lease* will of course appear in the English. But when the Italian term *mobiliare* (*movable goods* cf: *immobiliare* = *buildings, property*) is seen in the light of the rest of the document, as is envisaged by the pre-translation analysis, it can be seen that it refers to the same thing as *l'attrezzatura* and *il macchinario*, and can thus already be termed *equipment*.

Società should be translated by *Company*.

The subject is followed by one of the many fossilised expressions so common in legal parlance (*hereinafter referred to as* . . .), which is repeated in the next clause forming a typical chain of both lexical and grammatical cohesion. The use of capital letters for the main protagonists of the contract echoes the Italian usage, but English extends this later to non-human entities. The translator should be familiar with the *-or(er)/-ee* distinction (*Lessor/Lessee*, as in *employer/employee*). *Munito di necessari poteri* would need to be translated at the level of the whole expression: *endowed with the authority required*.

PREMESSO = *WHEREAS*, and nothing else will do.

In the case of *ha chiesto in leasing*, again the translator would be advised to look for a translation at the level of the whole 'chunk' of information, as opposed to a word-for-word approach: *is desirous of leasing*. The meaning is the same, the wording is suitably archaic without being impenetratable, and thus identifiable from similar documentation. The question of the *equipment* has already been broached, the term *successiva* can be left out as redundant, so the only doubt remaining in paragraph a) is *del presente contratto*. The adjective can be replaced with the more concise deictic *this*, and logic might suggest that the translator follow it with the term *contract* – that is, after all, what it is! But the translator may think for a moment that yes, in the field of insurance, for example, it would surely be a contract, but in contexts such as these (rentals, hire, etc.), isn't the term *Agreement* more common? Looking it up in the dictionary, this suspicion would be confirmed. *Contratto* is a partial false friend.

Paragraph b) provides a clear example of the need for that flexibility of expression mentioned above. It is the syntax that is fossilised here rather than the terminology, and thus the 'Englishising' process may have to be drastic. The paragraph begins with *And*, as do all succeeding paragraphs in this section, fufilling one obligation of the genre (the Italian paragraphs all begin with *che* as they approach the subject from a different syntactic perspective). The verb form *scelto* can be nominalised and thematised, and the tricky *trattato direttamente* reduced to *free* before the new noun, covering also for *Fornitore di sua fiducia/And the free choice of the Equipment and the Supplier ...* . However, this exercise in pruning would have to be compensated in some way, especially in a legal text where missing elements would be treated with suspicion. One attempt to fill the gap and sound suitably juridical might be *... lies with the Lessee and is the Lessee's responsibility*. Having already mentioned the *equipment*, but having completed a first sentence in the English version, the translator would have an automatic opportunity to use a characteristic feature of legal language and begin a second sentence with *Said equipment ...* . The Italian use of the modal verb of obligation *dovrà* is a compulsory element in the genre, and is mirrored in English by the obligatory use of the deontic modal *shall*. The problem of avoiding gender bias by using a pronominal device such as *his/her* can be avoided if the translator thinks of the Lessor as a company or entity and translates *proprio* with *its own*. The final clause would probably sound more appropriate to the translator as a passive form: *previously examined and accepted by the Lessee*.

The use of archaic formulae emerges again at the beginning of paragraph c) where *si è dichiarato disposto* should provoke, through the translator's 'world knowledge' of legal terminology, the wording *hereby agrees to*. The paragraph then continues as one long, elaborate, though largely paratactic sentence (cohesion through conjunction) where a reordering of the syntax is inevitable. The translator into English would probably not split the verb chain *disposto ... a manlevare e tenere indenne* with the interposing phrase *sia nei confronti delle parti che di terzi*, but would unite them (*agrees to indemnify and hold (the Lessor) safe and harmless*), the last rather quirky type of expression being not uncommon in legal jargon (cf: *goods and chattels*, *aiding and abetting*).

Parti must be translated by *parties* (NOT *parts*), and *terzi* by *Third parties*.

The repetition of synonyms or near-synonyms noted above even extends to prepositions and pronouns, and *da ogni rischio e responsabilità* can become *from and against any and all risks and liabilities*. The latter term has a more legal feel than *responsibility*, just as *pertaining to* might be preferred to *connected with* when translating *connessi con*.

Falsish friends like *custodia* and *conservazione* should put translators on their guard and save them from neglecting such contextually-appropriate options as *storage* and *maintenance*. The sentence then runs fairly effortlessly, requiring merely a little fine tuning as regards word order, and the addition of a *thereby* before the verb *agrees* for stylistic rather than semantic reasons. The Italian term *durata* appears twice in this sentence (*... del presente rapporto* and *... del contratto*), and there can be no good reason for translating it differently on these two occasions – the item *term* would figure in many such documents. The 'official' version considered here actually alternates *term* with *currency* for no obvious reason other than a possible desire to exploit what scope for flexibility the text offers. As the sentence is already elaborate, the translator would be justified in toning down rhetorical elements such as *nonché* with a simple conjunction *and*, and perhaps in eliminating completely redundant elements such as *a proprio carico*. The English version would have rolled into the following:

FINANCIAL EQUIPMENT LEASE

The Leasing Company hereinafter referred to as 'the Lessor' and the Firm hereinafter referred to as 'the Lessee' herein represented by its agent ... (endowed with the authority required)

WHEREAS

a) the Lessee is desirous of leasing from the Lessor the machinery and/or the equipment (hereinafter referred to as 'the equipment') described in clause 1) of this Agreement;

b) And the free choice of the Equipment and of the Supplier lies with the Lessee and is the Lessee's responsibility. Said equipment shall be acquired by the Lessor through its own purchase order previously examined and accepted by the Lessee;

c) And to this end the Lessee hereby agrees to indemnify and hold the Lessor safe and harmless both against the parties and Third parties from and against any and all risks and liabilities pertaining to the purchase, storage, maintenance and use of the Equipment, including those risks arising from the choice of the Supplier and from damage caused by fortuitous event or force majeure during the whole currency of this Agreement and thereby agrees to pay the fixed rental for the entire term of this Lease even in the case of non-use of the Equipment and to assume any charge relating to the use and the normal and satisfactory maintenance of the same;

The text continues as follows, and is offered for practice:

d) che in vista del presente contratto il Conduttore ha presentato al Locatore la propria situazione giuridica, amministrativa, economica, patrimoniale e tecnica ed ha offerto inoltre di garantire il buon esito dell'operazione con la prestazione delle garanzie richiestegli ed al cui rilascio è condizionata l'assunzione da parte dell'*Italease* degli obblighi derivanti dal presente contratto;

e) che sul presupposto di quanto sopra e subordinatamente alle manleve e garanzie di cui ai punti c) e d) che precedono, il Locatore è venuto nella determinazione di acquistare il macchinario oggetto del presente contratto in conformità alla scelta ed alle indicazioni del Conduttore, al fine di concederlo in *leasing* al medesimo alle condizioni tutte convenute nel presente atto e sue eventuali aggiunte ed integrazioni;

f) che le parti hanno convenuto di rapportare l'ammontare del canone di *leasing*, tra l'altro, alla durata fissata alla successiva clausola 2) per l'utilizzazione del macchinario da parte del Conduttore ed ai costi complessivi che il Locatore incontrerà per l'acquisto del macchinario stesso (compresi gli oneri accessori quali spese trasporto, oneri doganali, spese per l'acquisto valuta, ecc. ed al netto degli sconti), qui indicativamente preventivati in Lit . . . .

3.1.3 Business letter

9th November 19___

Dear Sirs,

With reference to your letter of 27th October, in which you ask us to consider some revision in our existing arrangements in regard to commission, we inform you that we find it difficult to allow an increased commission on our goods.

We quite appreciate that it is a hard fight for you to win business against German and American competitors who are firmly established in your market, but our prices are very low and if we allow you an increased commission, the very small margin of profit on which the running of this business is based would be entirely absorbed.

However, as we agree that your volume of business does give some claim to special concessions, we are prepared to give you financial help to cover advertising costs.

Probably our action does not provide a complete solution to the problem but we trust the above offer will be of interest to you.

However, for further talks about the matter, we would like to advise you that Mr J.M. of this company will be visiting Italy about the first week in December. We should be pleased to know whether you will be interested in discussing with him all the aspects of the problem and whether you would be available for a meeting at the beginning of December.

We look forward to your reply.

Yours faithfully,

(from Codeluppi 1997:183)

The translation of this letter takes shape around a number of conventional expressions typical of the genre: *With reference to your letter/in riferimento alla Sua lettera, ... established in your market/ ... affermate sul mercato, we trust the above offer will be of interest to you/riteniamo che possa comunque interessarLe, we would like to advise you/siamo lieti di comunicarLe, We should be pleased to know/Voglia gentilmente farci sapere, We look forward to your reply/Restiamo in attesa di una Sua sollecita risposta.*

In spite of the 'businesslike' nature of commercial correspondence, in both languages we find occasional circumlocutions: *to consider some revision in our existing arrangements in regard to commission/di apportare alcune modifiche concernenti la provvigione precedentemente concordata.* Almost inevitably with circumlocutions exact equivalence is lost. However, compensatory mechanisms come into play (*existing arrangements/precedente-*

mente concordata) where the meaning in the noun group is transferred to an adverb + participle construction.

At times, one language may be more verbose than the other: *we are prepared to give you financial help to cover advertising costs/Siamo quindi disposti a venirLe incontro con un contributo finanziario per le spese relative alla pubblicità.* The Italian version is a third longer than the original, due mostly to the use in Italian of the longer verbal expression *a venirLe incontro con/to give you*, and the use in English of the economic noun string device *advertising costs/le spese relative alla pubblicità.* Conversely, the final English sentence (*We should be pleased to know whether you will be interested in discussing with him all the aspects of the problem and whether you would be available for a meeting at the beginning of December*) could be translated more succinctly (*Voglia gentilmente farci sapere se desidera avere un colloquio con lui per discutere la questione nei dettagli*) by not repeating the already-mentioned date of the proposed meeting, and by the use of shorter verb phrases: *se desidera avere un colloquio* (cf: *whether you would be available for a meeting*), *per discutere la questione nei dettagli* (cf: *in discussing with him all the aspects of the problem*).

The Italian reluctance to repeat lexical items (*commission ... commission*) would lead the translator to search for an alternative solution, for example, *we find it difficult to allow an increased commission/non ci sembra il caso di modificare quanto già fissato.*

The English letter seems to break out of the usual mould briefly in the wording *it is a hard fight for you* and the search for an Italian equivalent might produce *la difficoltà di controbattere.*

In the sentence *We quite appreciate ... our prices are very low* in the second paragraph, the English text handles the providing of a justification with the simple adversative *but*. The Italian translator would probably need a more elaborate strategy: *Pur rendendoci conto ... dobbiamo farLe notare che i nostri prezzi sono contenuti.*

The expression *the running of this business* may need to be made more specific: *la nostra politica delle vendite.*

The above comments refer to the following proposed translation:

> Egregio Sig.
> in riferimento alla Sua lettera del 27 ottobre, con la quale ci richiede di apportare alcune modifiche concernenti la provvigione precedentemente concordata, La informiamo che non ci sembra il caso di modificare quanto già fissato.
> Pur rendendoci conto della difficoltà di controbattere la forte competitività

delle ditte tedesche ed americane che da tempo si sono affermate sul mercato, dobbiamo farLe notare che i nostri prezzi sono contenuti e se dovessimo concederLe un aumento di provvigione, l'esiguo margine di profitto sul quale basiamo la nostra politica delle vendite risulterebbe completamente annullato.

Tuttavia in considerazione del volume di affari che Lei ci procura, riteniamo che abbiate diritto ad avere un certo riconoscimento. Siamo quindi disposti a venirLe incontro con un contributo finanziario per le spese relative alla pubblicità.

Anche se la nostra offerta non risolverà completamente le Sue difficoltà, riteniamo che possa comunque interessarLe.

Siamo lieti di comunicarLe che il nostro J.M. si troverà in Italia all'inizio di dicembre e sarà disposto ad approfondire ulteriormente i termini della nostra proposta. Voglia gentilmente farci sapere se desidera avere un colloquio con lui per discutere la questione nei dettagli.

Restiamo in attesa di una Sua sollecita risposta

Cordiali saluti

The following letter is offered for practice:

25th January 19_____

Dear Sirs,

Further to the conversation between you and Mr _____ in your office in Milan, we are pleased to offer you the agency for our Swatch watches in Italy.

Before the contract is drawn up for signature, we have prepared a preliminary draft of a suitable form of agreement for consideration by you and your partner Mr _____ . The conditions are as follows:

(1) We undertake to transact all business with Italy through you alone and in return you look after our interests to the best of your ability and you handle no other imported products of a competitive type.

(2) You will receive a commission of 10% on the net proceeds of watches sold.

(3) You are to render us quarterly account sales at the end of March, June, September and December respectively and you are to accept our drafts on you for the net amount of these sales. You are also to send us periodical reports on the market situation in Italy. As we are particularly keen on developing our trade in the south of Italy, we expect you to make every effort to further our interests in

that part of the country where our watches are not yet sufficiently known.

We are prepared to let you have samples to the total value of £ ... free of charge.

The contract comes into force on March 1st 19____ for a period of two years after which it is to be considered as renewed for one more year unless notice is given by registered letter at least two months before expiry.

Yours faithfully,

(from Codeluppi 1997:185)

3.1.4 European Union documents

A very important subsection of legal language can be subsumed under the rather clumsy heading 'bureaucratese', the language of national and international administration. The policy documents of international organisations such as the European Union, the United Nations, the International Monetary Fund, and so on, are ultimately aimed at framing legislation. Particularly in the case of the great supranational bodies, this kind of documentation must be constantly translated. The largest 'translation factory' in the world is probably to be found within the administrative division of the European Union, where a huge portion of the budget is devoted to making EU business linguistically available to an ever-growing number of nations. The text reproduced below, by Anton E. Kunst and Johan P. Mackenbach, was first presented in Copenhagen in 1994 at the European Health Policy Conference: Opportunities for the Future. The text was written by non-English university researchers, which may account for one or two slightly questionable linguistic choices, and is addressed to politicians and administrators, with the objective of sensitising the latter to the problem of socioeconomic inequalities in health. It is the kind of text that Sabatini (1990:632-40) refers to as being 'con discorso mediamente vincolante', that is it provides information to an uninformed reader who is required to interpret that information reasonably accurately, though not necessarily to the letter, as might be the case with a highly technical text.

The language used in the text is highly standardised, in keeping with its status as English as an international language. There is no pretence at creative writing, and hence there is much repetition of key terms within a predictable grammatical structure associated with the relaying of information. The style is impersonal and sterile, alternating rhetoric-free discursive passages with lists, categorisations, etc. The Italian version should be equally informative and equally unappetising.

MEASURING SOCIOECONOMIC INEQUALITIES IN HEALTH
Why should socioeconomic inequalities in health be measured?

There is consistent evidence throughout Europe that people at a socioeconomic disadvantage suffer a heavier burden of illness and have higher mortality rates than their better-off counterparts.

These socioeconomic inequalities in health are a major challenge for health policy, not only because most of these inequalities can be considered unfair but also because reducing the burden of health problems in disadvantaged groups offers great potential for improving the average health status of the population as a whole.

Recognising this, the member states of WHO in the European Region have adopted a strategy for health for all that has as its first target:

By the year 2000, the differences in health status between countries and between groups within countries should be reduced by at least 25%, by improving the level of health of disadvantaged nations and groups.

This is clearly a very ambitious target and may not be realised everywhere. Nevertheless, it gives a clear focus to health policy and promotes the monitoring of quantitative changes over time in socioeconomic inequalites in health, which is essential to assess the effects of health policy interventions.

Lexicogrammatical analysis

On seeing the title *MEASUR<u>ING</u>* ... the translator would get straight into nominal mode with *MISURAZIONE*; such transformations will be required throughout the text. The phenomenon of *socioeconomic inequalities in health* is the key concept in the text and must be decided on at the beginning and maintained: *le disuguaglianze socioeconomiche nella salute*.

The temptation to translate *Why should ...?* with *Perché si dovrebbe ...?* can be avoided by thinking the text structure through in Italian. Isn't *Perché misurare ...* more spontaneous?

Similarly, *There is constant evidence throughout Europe* is better translated by a very Italian verb-fronted construction like *E' stato riscontrato più volte in tutta Europa*. The lack of technical rigour in *più volte in tutta Europa* is justified by the fact that the text can be defined as being 'con discorso mediamente vincolante'. The neat English prepositional phrase *at a socio-economic disadvantage* would give the translator the chance to mould the Italian language into a circumlocution (*svantaggiate dal punto di vista socioeconomico*), which is better than a hazardous prepositional equivalent. The following expression (*suffer a heavier burden of illness*) is particularly English in its choice of verb and noun, and may need looking at from a slightly different perspective by the translator: *hanno una tendenza maggiore ad ammalarsi*. The neutral English verb *have* in *have higher mortality rates* would not satisfy the translator, who would look for one of the wide range of Italian function verbs to express this concept: *presentano un tasso di mortalità* (cf: *costituiscono* for *are* in the next sentence). The use of *better-off* seems to betray the semi-technical register of the text, but the translator can do no better than translate with *benestanti*.

The second paragraph can be more or less transparently translated at first, right down to the passive form *most of these inequalities can be considered unfair/per la maggior parte possono essere considerate ingiuste*. The verb *reducing* can be nominalised to *la riduzione* in the process alluded to at the beginning of the analysis. The English text repeats the noun *burden*, displaying the English lack of concern about repetition and providing evident lexical cohesion, but also reinforcing the sterility of the discourse. As the semantic components of the term *burden* were bypassed on the first occasion, the translator would feel no obligation to adhere to this particular cohesive device, nor to be creative on his/her own part. Exact meaning components not being compulsory, this text could continue with *la riduzione dell'entità dei problemi sanitari* . . . .

In the third paragraph, the verb *Recognising* . . . might be adjectivised (*Consapevoli di* . . .). The acronym *WHO* (World Health Organisation) belongs to that group whose initials are drastically different in Italian, as opposed to those which remain unchanged (*NATO/NATO*) or are simply reversed (*UNO/ONU*). In this case, the Italian is *OMS* (Organizzazione mondiale della sanità). It must simply be known, though good dictionaries usually contain a comprehensive list of the most frequently-used acronyms. As the English text continues, it may be misread, at least on a first reading, at the point *a strategy for health for all that has* . . . . Making it clearer in Italian by using, for example, inverted commas (*una strategia 'Salute per tutti' che ha* . . .) might well be considered.

It may be the sense of rhythm in an Italian sentence that occasionally urges the translator to add words to the original, for example: *between countries and between groups/fra i vari paesi e fra i diversi gruppi*. The *should* in *should be reduced* is vaguely deontic and has a slightly legal ring to it, possibly suggesting the translation *dovranno essere* (see legal text in this chapter).

By 25% should be translated as *del 25%*.

The final paragraph begins with *This is ...*, prompting a very Italian *Si tratta ... di* (cf: French *Il s'agit de ...*). The sentence continues in a transparently translatable way until *which is essential to ...*, which might lead the translator to another of those useful function verbs: *le quali rivestono un'importanza fondamentale per ...* . Finally, the verb *to assess* would find nominalisation in *la valutazione*. The translation would now look like the version printed below, in fact to be found in thesis form in Buttazzoni (1996):

Misurazione delle disuguaglianze socioeconomiche nella salute
Perché misurare le disuguaglianze socioeconomiche nella salute?

E' stato riscontrato più volte in tutta Europa che le persone svantaggiate dal punto di vista socioeconomico hanno una tendenza maggiore ad ammalarsi e presentano un tasso di mortalità più elevato rispetto alle persone più benestanti.

Tali disuguaglianze socioeconomiche nella salute costituiscono un grosso problema per la politica sanitaria, non solo perché per la maggior parte possono essere considerate ingiuste, ma anche perché la riduzione dell'entità dei problemi sanitari nei gruppi più svantaggiati fornisce una grossa opportunità per migliorare lo stato di salute medio della popolazione complessiva.

Consapevoli di ciò, gli stati membri dell'OMS nella Regione Europa hanno adottato una strategia della 'Salute per tutti' che ha come suo primo obiettivo:

Entro il 2000 le differenze nello stato di salute fra i vari paesi e fra i diversi gruppi all'interno di essi dovranno essere ridotte almeno del 25%, migliorando lo stato di salute delle nazioni e dei gruppi più svantaggiati.

Si tratta chiaramente di un obiettivo molto ambizioso, che può non essere raggiunto dappertutto. Ciononostante, esso pone l'accento sulle questioni di politica sanitaria e sull'analisi delle variazioni quantitative nel tempo delle disuguaglianze socioeconomiche nella salute, le quali rivestono un'importanza fondamentale per la valutazione dei risultati degli interventi di politica sanitaria.

Later in the publication, the following passage appears and is offered here for translation practice:

Measuring the association between socioeconomic status and morbidity and mortality

When data on socioeconomic inequalites in health are available, either from existing data sources or as the result of a new data collection effort, the magnitude of these inequalities can be measured. This chapter presents guidelines on the quantitative techniques that can be used for this purpose. This is done in two parts: the first part concentrates on the inequalities as they are observed at one point in time, and the second part focusses on changes over time in the inequalities. In both cases, the recommended approach starts by describing in detail the patterns of association between socioeconomic status and morbidity and mortality and, if appropriate, by calculating one or more summary indices.

Describing health inequalities at one point in time

A detailed description of the association between socioeconomic status and health starts by calculating the morbidity and mortality levels for each socioeconomic group. The classification of socio-economic groups should contain a hierarchical component: that is, it should be possible to distinguish people with a low position in the social hierarchy from those with a high position. In addition, the classification should be detailed enough to allow specific groups with excessive morbidity and mortality levels to be identified.

(*Measuring Socioeconomic Inequalities in Health*,
A. Kunst & J. Mackenbach,
World Health Organisation Regional Office for Europe)

3.2   Promotional material

The term 'promotional' is used to cover more than just the field of advertising, though an advertisement forms the first text to be analysed in this section. This is followed by a promotional piece taken from a company's presentation brochure. The third analysis is of a tourist leaflet, one of the most translated, and most abused, genres within the translating world. Finally in this section, the notes accompanying a compact disc are examined. English/Italian and Italian/English translation analyses are equally represented and alternated.

In terms of pure publicity, many of the distinguishing features of advertising copy are discussed in Part One, Chapter Three, but some broader aspects of the translation of such material also need to be considered. Firstly, it is perhaps true that most advertising is designed for national markets appealing to relatively homogeneous cultural groups. Secondly, advertising can be an extremely creative art form and, in many cases, if a product needs to be aimed at a foreign public, the 'translation' may take the form of a drastic, almost unrecognisable, re-elaboration of the original. However, the global market and the internationalisation of commerce have resulted in many products having or achieving international appeal and, where feasible, successful advertising copy is presented for translation. The example below of an advertisement for an Italian product is subdued by the standards of the genre, the message is universal and the text is almost translatable as it stands for the English-speaking market.

3.2.1 Advertising text

CONCORSO AMICA DIAMANTE DI VENERE DAMIANI

Un diamante è per sempre
De Beers

Questo Diamante
di Venere non è
irraggiungibile.
Basta chiederlo
Il concorso si è concluso e
le Veneri che si sono aggiudicate
i nove diamanti di Damiani
sono state premiate.
Ma anche voi potrete facilmente
provare la gioia di indossare
questi bellissimi Diamanti di Venere,
basta chiederlo.
Chiederlo a Babbo Natale, per
esempio.

Spiegategli che sarà un regalo splendido
e utilissimo, che potrete portare in tutte le
occasioni e che vi farà pensare a lui in ogni
momento della giornata. Non potrà resistere,
siccome vi ama, ve lo farà trovare sotto l'albero. E
se Babbo Natale volesse chiedere qualche
informazione in più, suggeritegli
di telefonare al numero verde di Casa
Damiani.
Vedrete: presto uno di questi diamanti
di Venere Damiani sarà vostro.

Damiani
Servizio clienti Tel. 167–565656

The text is accompanied by a close-up photograph of a beautiful woman
with a low-cut dress wearing a Damiani diamond on a chain round her
neck.

Literal translation

FRIEND COMPETITION DIAMOND OF VENUS DAMIANI

A diamond is for ever
De Beers

This Diamond
of Venus is not
unreachable.
Enough to ask it.
The competition has concluded itself and
the Venuses who adjudged themselves
the nine diamonds of Damiani
have been rewarded.
But also you can easily
try the joy of wearing these
very beautiful Diamonds of Venus,
enough to ask it.
Ask it to Father Christmas, for
example.
Explain to him that it will be a splendid and very
useful present, that you can wear in all the

occasions and that it will make you think to him in every
moment of the day. He will not be able to resist, as
he loves you, he will make you find it under the tree. And
if Father Christmas wanted to ask some more
information, suggest to him
to telephone to the green number of Casa
Damiani.
You will see: soon one of these diamonds
of Venus Damiani will be yours.

Damiani
Clients Service Tel. 167-565656

Lexicogrammatical analysis

The usual transformation of the Italian prepositional genitive to a saxon genitive or noun cluster can be foregone in the case of *Diamante di Venere*: such a serious (and seriously expensive) object can be left as *Diamond of Venus*. The translator would be aware of the rather colloquial, as well as the neatly efficient, properties of *Basta chiederlo – Just ask for it* would correspond on both counts. Note *chiedere = to ask <u>for</u>*.

The reflexive Italian verb form *si è concluso* should be considered in terms of what it is that is ending; a competition is likely to be *over*. The rest of this sentence is very Italian in style and would require a certain amount of re-ordering from a slightly shifted perspective. The first past participle in the verb group *si sono <u>aggiudicate</u>* can be substituted by an adjective *winning* before the noun *Venuses*, and the second, in the concluding passive phrase *sono state premiate*, can be reduced to *received* (cf: the frequent translation of the verb *premiare*, seen from the other perspective, as a simple *to give*). The expression *provare la gioia* is so common in Italian (cf: 'la gioia' constantly attributed to football fans) that it is tempting to translate it with something like *experience the joy*, but mentally transposing the idea into an English context might produce something more close to the English genre as *feel the thrill*. The adjective *bellissimi* contains a certain force that the English qualifier *fabulous* might match.

A little further on, the copular verb *sarà* in *Spiegategli che sarà un regalo* invites the English use of *make* in *Explain to him that it will make a really beautiful ...* . Interestingly, while *beautiful* is rarely a wholly suitable translation for *bello/issimo*, it is perfectly acceptable here as a translation of *splendido*. A subtle grammatical point emerges in the wider section

Spiegategli che sarà un regalo splendido e utilissimo, che potrete portare in tutte le occasioni ..., where the *che* refers to the *regalo*. The English version (see next section) would be better served by *Explain to him that it will make a really beautiful and useful present, that you can wear it all the time* ..., where *that* is connected to the verb *explain* and *it* refers back anaphorically to the *present*. In the last sentence of the paragraph, the verb phrase *suggeritegli* is persuasive in tone, and therefore *get him to* might be appropriate.

Servizio clienti should be translated as *Customer Service*.

Semantico-pragmatico-cultural analysis

The text is clearly vocative and persuasive and the writer's task is to capture the attention of potential customers. There is, therefore, a direct appeal to *voi* which clearly treats the sophisticated women who are targeted with a touch of respect and, at the same time, addresses all such women. The English *you* achieves this interpersonal aim effortlessly.

The main heading alludes to a *competition* (*concorso Amica*) which the English readership could not be expected to be aware of. On the other hand, there is no guarantee that all, or even most, Italian readers are familiar with it, so there is no compelling reason to remove all mention of it. It can remain vague, as in the first sentence of the main text: *Our competition*. The De Beers quotation is *A diamond is forever*, not to be confused with the James Bond-associated plural version *Diamonds are forever*. The adjective *irraggiungibile* would sound better as the phrase *out of reach*, and better still if anchored personally with a *your: out of your reach*.

Babbo Natale must be either *Father Christmas* or *Santa Claus*. The translator may opt for the latter and insert a mention of *Christmas* later (see below).

At the beginning of the next paragraph, in the case of *Spiegategli*, it is possible that a simple *Tell him* would suffice, but *Explain* might be preferred on account of the adjective *utilissimo/really useful*. The idea is that the diamond is not only a beautiful (and therefore frivolous) gift, and this requires explanation. Moreover, as mentioned earlier, the verb *Explain* then governs the following clauses: <u>*that*</u> *it will make a really beautiful and useful present*, <u>*that*</u> *you can wear it all the time* and <u>*that*</u> *it will make you think of him every minute of the day*. A substitution of a cultural nature for *ve lo farà trovare sotto l'albero/he'll put it in your Christmas stocking* might better reflect English customs, and at the same time provide a mention of

Christmas. The *him* and *he* which refer simultaneously to Santa Claus and a supposed boyfriend, husband, or lover are reinforced with a friendly *Santa* in *If Santa needs any further information.*

Numero verde is *Freephone.*

Lastly, the expression *Just wait and see* hits the right register for *Vedrete.* Summing the two analyses, the translation has rolled to:

DAMIANI DIAMOND OF VENUS COMPETITION

A diamond is forever
De Beers

This diamond
of Venus is not
out of your reach.
Just ask for it.

Our competition is now over and
the winning Venuses have
received their nine Damiani
diamonds.
But you too can easily
feel the thrill of wearing these
fabulous Diamonds of Venus;
just ask.
Ask Santa Claus, for
example.
Explain to him that it will make a really beautiful
and useful present, that you can wear it all the
time and that it will make you think of him every
minute of the day. He won't be able to resist, and
because he loves you, he'll put it in your Christmas stocking.
And if Santa needs any further
information, get him to
phone the Casa Damiani
Freephone number.
Just wait and see: a Damiani
Diamond of Venus will soon be yours.

Damiani
Customer Service Tel. 167-565656

Another Italian advertisement that appeared in the Corriere della Sera (8/12/96) is now offered for practice:

Da oggi la cultura va in vacanza con l'abbronzatura

E prima di Natale, prezzi niente male.

Messico, Cuba e Jamaica, in crociera sono tutta un'altra cosa! Da L.2.090.000 volo compreso.

Questa crociera è tutto un programma, state un po' a sentire. A bordo della Costa Playa si va nel mar dei Caraibi in grandissimo relax, navigando in acque azzurrissime e arrivando su spiagge favolose. Ma attenzione: un'intensa abbronzatura non è l'unica attrattiva di questa crociera. Infatti, tra un tuffo nel mare trasparente di Montego Bay, in Jamaica, e un'immersione nel paradiso sottomarino dell'Isola della Juventud e di Grand Cayman, vi aspettano anche appassionanti scoperte culturali. Prima a Cuba, dove avrete tutto il tempo di conoscere i mille volti dell'Avana, la capitale. Dal sontuoso barocco coloniale, passerete all'animatissimo lungomare, e dallo show Tropicana alle 'bodeguite', i caratteristici locali del centro storico dove si beve rhum gelato alla menta. Poi la nave vi porterà in Messico, ad ammirare le emozionanti rovine Maya di Tulum, a picco sul mare, e quelle di Cobà, circondate dalla foresta tropicale. E poi, ci sarebbe da parlare dell'ospitalità a mille stelle che vi aspetta sulla Costa Playa, il grande servizio a bordo che vi farà sentire molto, molto coccolati ... ma forse siete già impazienti di correre alla vostra agenzia di viaggi. Nessuna meraviglia, a questa crociera resistere è difficile.

3.2.2 Promotional text

The following text is taken from the Eurologos Multilingual Editing Network brochure, the original of which was written in French. It explains what multilingual document production is all about.

EUROLOGOS total quality
The three key words in multilingual document production

Multinational   (subsidiaries and European network)
Control   (mother tongue and revision)
High-tech   (C.A.H.T. and multimedia graphics)

We have long known that each word has its importance, but have had to wait for almost twenty years for these three words to take on their full meaning, and become the key to denote know-how of the very highest level.

Since 1977, the year in which the first EUROLOGOS company was founded in Brussels, our international organisation has enjoyed continuous expansion, leading to the establishment of the first of our European subsidiaries.

We have responded to the increasingly multinational nature of markets and companies by developing a **multinational** network of subsidiaries. The second key word **control**, has thus assumed even greater significance: the geo-style and socio-style of a text can only ever really be guaranteed when produced 'in situ', in the so-called mother tongue market. Furthermore, you cannot get more economical than revising (checking) a language in the country where it is spoken.

And finally, **high-tech**. The post-industrial revolution ushered in by computer science in the 1980s and 1990s is something that EUROLOGOS has been actively involved in from the word go, day in, day out.

Given that the purpose of the organisation is to provide high-standard multilingual translation, we should expect a high degree of fidelity and accuracy in the various versions that appear together in this same document. The material is factual, not creative, and the different language texts should thus be 'mirror images' of one another. With this in mind, it will be interesting to compare the Italian text below to the English version as if it were a translation of it.

Qualità Totale EUROLOGOS
Le tre parole chiave dell'editing multilingue

Multinazionale	(filiali e network europeo)
Controllo	(madrelingua e revisione)
High-tech	(C.A.H.T. e grafica multimediale)

Noi che conosciamo il peso delle parole abbiamo dovuto attendere quasi vent'anni perché questi tre termini si caricassero della totalità del loro significato per divenire le chiavi esplicative di un know-how d'eccellenza.

Dal 1977, anno di fondazione della prima società EUROLOGOS a Bruxelles, la nostra organizzazione internazionale è cresciuta fino alla creazione delle prime filiali europee. Alla multinazionalizzazione dei mercati e delle imprese, abbiamo risposto con la 'filializzazione' **multinazionale** delle nostre società.

Il termine **controllo**, la seconda parola chiave, è divenuto così ancor più significativo; il geostile e il sociostile di un testo sono realmente garantiti solo quando prodotti 'sul posto', all'interno del mercato detto *di lingua* *madre.* Nulla risulta allora più economico che revisionare (controllare) una lingua là dove essa viene parlata.

Infine l'**high-tech**. La rivoluzione (post-)industriale prodotta dall'informatica degli anni Ottanta-Novanta è stata vissuta da EUROLOGOS in diretta, giorno per giorno.

The main title starts with an automatic reordering mechanism, the key word remaining prominent through capitalisation. Interestingly, in the subtitle, Italian uses the loan word *editing* for the more elaborate English *document production*. This is one of many examples of loan words acquiring either a wider or narrower range of meaning in the borrower language. The loans continue with *network* and *C.A.H.T.* (computer-aided human translation). This phenomenon is common in technical writing and particularly common in the more recently-developed technical fields. The noun phrase *multimedia graphics* is an example of the short noun string that requires adjectivising in Italian: *grafica multimediale*.

As regards the main text, the first sentence is subjected to a degree of modification, as it is transformed from a partially paratactic structure with the coordinating conjunctions *but* and *and* to a totally hypotactic Italian construction containing a series of subordinate clauses: *che conosciamo ...*, *perché questi tre termini si caricassero ... , per divenire ... .* The result is that the two sentences sound perfectly natural in their respective languages. Within this same sentence, in the verb phrase *take on their full meaning*, the adjective *full* is nominalised in Italian to *totalità*. In another interesting case of noun/adjective use, the English collocation *key terms*, where *key* is the modifier, becomes *chiavi esplicative*, where the *chiavi* becomes the head word. There is a further loan in *know-how*, and the use of the convenient *d'eccellenza* for *of the very highest level*. English, in fact, has the French *par excellence* at its disposal as a loan expression, but neither the context nor the register would point to its use.

In the second sentence, the grammatical metaphor in *our international organisation has enjoyed continuous expansion* is reduced to a more standard metaphorisation with *la nostra organizzazione è cresciuta*, thereby avoiding the temptation to force an inappropriate expression onto the target language. The third sentence undergoes an interesting transformation marked by reordering, nominalisation and term creation. The typically English adverb-adjective-noun construction *increasingly multinational nature* is reduced to a lengthy nominalisation (*multinazionalizzazione*) and shifted to the left, setting up the model for the creation of a new term (*filializzazione*), which neatly takes care of *network of subsidiaries*. At the same time, it provides an escape from an overuse of loan words, in this case from *network*.

The second main section, on *control*, sees the noun *significance* adjectivised to *significativo*, in line with similar use in other kinds of technical text, for example in medical articles. The neologisms *geo-style* and *socio-style* translate effortlessly into *geostile* and *sociostile*. The prepositional phrase *all'interno del* replaces the simple English *in* in *all'interno del mercato detto di lingua madre/in the so-called mother tongue market* in a case of stylistic adaptation – the simple preposition would seem abrupt in Italian. In the following sentence, the Italian verb *risulta*, which so often has little more than a copulative role, is used to translate the copular *get*.

It is interesting to note that *informatica* is still seen as the equivalent of *computer science*, resisting the introduction of *informatics*. Finally, shifting the perspective but maintaining the dynamism and sense of energy, the rather colloquial English *EUROLOGOS has been actively involved in from the word go* is substituted by *è stata vissuta da EUROLOGOS in diretta*.

The text continues as follows and is offered for practice:

(The post-industrial revolution ushered in by computer science in the 1980s and 1990s is something that EUROLOGOS has been actively involved in from the word go, day in, day out)

... from the first rotary fax machine and the first computers (as dedicated as they were incompatible), which we were one of the first to purchase in 1981, through to our recent Interleaf network.

In turn, C.A.H.T. (Computer-Aided Human Translation) continues to combine superbly with new terminology software and extremely high-performance computer graphics systems such as our Silicon Graphics, with its 2-giga multimedia brain.

It is also on these key words that we have based this magazine. And as we speak no fewer than nine official languages in our European subsidiaries, it goes without saying that the pages you are reading had to be of a multilingual character.

What's more, as we know, document production has to be multilingual and of total quality.

For exports, that's a sine qua non.

3.2.3 Tourist information

The vast range of hastily-prepared multilingual brochures, information
leaflets, booklets, promotion material and the like on display in any location
where visitors are likely to stop or pass by (which these days means virtually
everywhere) continue to be the source of much merriment by virtue of the
translation 'howlers' that are so often found within their pages. Those with
knowledge of both the source and target languages involved, especially if
both are presented together in the same publication, point knowingly to the
'obvious' errors that have been perpetrated. Whole articles, even books,
have been devoted to showing up such amusing, at times vulgarly sugges-
tive, even potentially calamitous examples of this 'translationese'. Dodds
(1995:143), for example, explores the hilarious renderings into English of
various Italian restaurant menus. No attempt will be made here, however,
to provide a list of amusing specimens. Rather, an attempt will be made to
show the processes involved in providing as correct a translation as possible,
though authentic translations displaying some of the above-mentioned
peccadilloes will be provided for comparison.

Viaggio al centro del Friuli

The Comunità Collinare del Friuli produced a pull-out leaflet to advertise
the area in and around the hill-town of San Daniele, and published it in
three versions – Italian, German and English. Excerpts from the Italian
original went as follows:

> VIAGGIO AL CENTRO DEL FRIULI
> Tanti paesi, tutti da scoprire

> Molti sono gli interessi e i percorsi che possono portare il visitatore
> fra i nostri sedici Comuni: l'osservazione naturalistica, i castelli
> medioevali e le chiesette affrescate, l'architettura contemporanea, ma
> anche un artigianato di grande pregio, senza dimenticare le attrattive
> della gastronomia e sempre restando immersi in un ambiente
> verdissimo.

> *Buia*

> 6.657 abitanti. Comune sparso su numerosi colli con sede a S.
> Stefano e frazioni di Avilla, Madonna, S. Floreano, Tomba e
> Urbignacco. Sul colle più alto, detto 'Monte', il bel borgo chiuso di S.
> Lorenzo con l'omonima antica chiesa affrescata (in restauro) e un

panoramico parco con resti di fortificazioni medioevali e del castelliere preistorico; interessante shopping per i gioielli e le ceramiche. A fine aprile la festa della primavera, che vede un intero toro arrostito 'alla castellana', e il 12 luglio la festa delle campanelle.

Fagagna

5.947 abitanti con le frazioni di Battaglia, Ciconicco, Madrisio e Villalta. Grosso centro con un'economia completa. Da visitare i ruderi del castello e la cinquecentesca casa della Comunità, la medievale Porta di Borgo e, nella vicina Villalta, l'imponente maniero ben conservato e ancor oggi abitato. Interessanti la gastronomia e lo shopping per varie produzioni specializzate. La prima domenica di settembre si svolge la secolare e divertentissima corsa degli asini. Sui colli vicini, un campo da golf a nove buche e, appena fuori dell'abitato, la zona di tutela ambientale dei 'Quadri'.

Per chi ama il verde, la storia, la gastronomia

La Comunità Collinare si trova a due passi da Udine, nel cuore antico del Friuli, a un'ora di auto dalle spiagge dell'Adriatico, dai centri sciistici e dai confini austriaco e jugoslavo (*sic*). Due caselli dell'autostrada A23 'Alpe Adria' sono i suoi margini; scorrevoli strade statali la collegano con tutti i centri della regione Friuli-Venezia-Giulia e del vicino Veneto.

Gli aeroporti di Venezia, Ronchi dei Legionari e Klagenfurt la collegano con tutto il mondo. Di origine morenica, tre semicerchi di colline digradanti che guardano verso le montagne e alle spalle la pianura; è un ambiente dolce e verdissimo, punteggiato di piccoli centri e attraversato da innumerevoli strade e viottoli. E' il regno della bicicletta e delle passeggiate. Da sempre luogo di villeggiature tranquille, grazie al clima mite, con grandi mutevoli cieli …

The 'official' English version will be inserted at this point, as reference will be made to it during the analysis:

A TRIP TO THE HEART OF FRIULI
Lots of villages, all to be discovered

The interests and paths which may bring the visitor to our sixteen Communes are myriad: nature-watching, medieval castles and frescoed churches, contemporary architecture but also handicrafts of great value, without forgetting the attractions of good cooking, all while remaining immersed in the green country-side.

Buia

6,657 inhabitants. The Commune is scattered over numerous hills with its head office at S. Stefano and the villages of Avilla, Madonna, S. Floreano, Tomba and Urbignacco. The pretty, closed-in village of S. Lorenzo with its ancient, frescoed church (under restoration) is to be found on the highest hill, called 'Monte', and also possesses a panoramic park with remains of medieval fortifications and a prehistoric stronghold; interesting shopping for jewellery and ceramic ware. The Fete of Spring at end-April foresees a bullock roasted on the spit 'castle-style' and the Fete of the Handbells falls on 12th July.

Fagagna

5,947 inhabitants together with the villages of Battaglia, Ciconicco, Madrisio and Villalta. It is a big centre with a complete economy. Visit the ruins of the castle and the 5th century Community House, the medieval Village gateway and, in the nearby Villalta, the well-preserved, imposing manor which is still inhabited. Gastronomy and shopping prove interesting due to various specialised productions. The centuries-old and amusing Mule Race is held on the 1st Sunday of September. There is a 9-hole golf course on the nearby hills, and the area of the 'Quadri' protected ambient, is just outside the build-up zone.

For those who love nature, history and gastronomy

The Hill Community is in the vicinity of Udine, in the ancient heart of Friuli, an hour's drive from the the Adriatic beaches, the ski resorts and the Austrian and Yugoslavian borders. It is flanked by two motorway exits; traffic-free state roads connect it with all the town centres of the Friuli-Venezia-Giulia region and that of the nearby Veneto. The airports of Venice, Ronchi dei Legionari and Klagenfurt provide worldwide connections. The area is of morainic origin with three semicircles of sloping hills looking towards the mountains with the plain behind it; the beautiful, green countryside is dotted with small villages and crossed by winding roads and lanes. It is ideal for walking and cycling. It has always been a spot for peaceful holidays, due to its mild climate and great mutable skies ...

There is an inevitable temptation, when faced with a translation of this kind, to criticise with relish what seems to be a woefully inadequate performance. This is not the purpose of this exercise, though some reflection on what went wrong in a general sense is in order. It is also tempting to assume that this translation (and thousands of others like it and worse) must have been the work of a non-native speaker with no chance of revision. This is quite possible but by no means certain. But what leads a native-speaker translator into the kinds of stylistic, lexical and textual traps illustrated above, apart from general incompetence and lack of specific knowledge, neither of which can be remedied through this discussion? Basically, it would seem that no pre-analysis has taken place, and that the text has been transposed sentence by sentence with only marginal deference to the dictates of the target language. But perhaps more importantly, no consideration has been given to emulating the features of the particular genre in question. Similar English tourist publicity material is written in a particular way and obeys certain unwritten rules of style. Like its counterparts elsewhere in the world it can be gushing, self-adulatory and lexically dense, but so much of it has now been produced that certain stylistic and lexical elements have created what is a recognisable style or set of style features. Certain language functions become fossilised in such well-defined text types. These are, indeed, the factors that make a genre. And so to our 'rolling' approach with a first 'literal' draft:

Literal translation

A VOYAGE TO THE CENTRE OF THE FRIULI
Many towns, all to discover

Many are the interests and the routes that can lead the visitor between our sixteen Communes: the naturalistic observation, the medieval castles and the frescoed little churches, the contemporary architecture, but also an artisanship of great worth, without forgetting the attractions of the gastronomy and always remaining immersed in a very green environment.

Buia

6,657 inhabitants. Commune scattered on numerous hills with head office at S. Stefano and villages of Avilla, Madonna, S. Floreano, Tomba and Urbignacco. On the highest hill, said 'Monte', the pretty, closed borough of S. Lorenzo with the homonymous ancient frescoed church (in restoration) and a panoramic park with remains of medieval fortifications and of the prehistoric stronghold; interesting shopping for jewels and ceramics. At end-April the fete of Spring which sees a whole bull roasted 'castle-style' and the 12th July the fete of the handbells.

Fagagna

5,947 inhabitants with the villages of Battaglia, Ciconicco, Madrisio and Villalta. Big centre with a complete economy. To visit the ruins of the castle and the 5th century Community house, the medieval Borough Gate and, in the nearby Villalta, the imposing manor well-preserved and still today inhabited. Interesting the gastronomy and the shopping for various specialised productions. The first Sunday of September is held the centuries-old and very amusing race of donkeys. On the nearby hills a golf course at nine holes, and just outside the inhabited area the zone of environmental protection of the 'Quadri'.

For who loves the green, the history, the gastronomy

The Hill Community is found at two steps from Udine, in the ancient heart of the Friuli, at an hour of car from the beaches of the Adriatic, from the ski centres and the Austrian and Yugoslavian borders. Two tollbooths of the A23 Alpe Adria motorway are its margins; easy-flowing state roads connect it with all the centres of the Friuli-Venezia-Giulia region and of the nearby Veneto.

The airports of Venice, Ronchi dei Legionari and Klagenfurt connect it with all the world. Of morainic origin, three semicircles of sloping hills which look towards the mountains and at the shoulders the plain, it is a sweet and very green environment, dotted with small centres and crossed by innumerable roads and lanes. It is the kingdom of the bicycle and of the walks. Since always a place of quiet holidays, thanks to the mild climate with great mutable skies ...

Analysis

(As the OV has also been included in the examination of this long text, the translation will now 'roll' directly to a conclusion by incorporating all the lexicogrammatical, semantic, stylistic and cultural elements in a single analysis, making occasional reference to the OV).

The context of situation consists of a written and illustrated text designed to serve an indefinite number of potential visitors over an indefinite amount of time. An informer/persuader presents a pleasant-to-read description of a region for a willing readership. It is vital that the translator attempts to maintain this interpersonal rapport. A large number of colour photographs provide cohesion.

Title *Viaggio al centro del Friuli*: as it is not unreasonable to assume that the famous Jules Verne novel may have provided the inspiration for the title of the booklet there is no reason to eschew the literal *Journey to the centre of (the Earth) Friuli*. The more transparent term *voyage* generally refers only to *viaggi* by sea or in space. The OV *A trip to the heart* is, in fact, in keeping with the genre; it merely misses the literary reference. *Friuli*, as the name of a region, requires no article.

The subheading *Tanti paesi, tutti da scoprire* is disjointed, lacking the cohesive elements of a standard sentence, though effective in its message. The OV is weak: *lots of villages* sounds almost infantile; in line with the pseudo-poetic style of the genre, the translator could come up with an expression like *A (whole) host of* to begin the phrase. The Italian noun *paese* does not give precise indications as to size – *towns and villages* is a suitable amplification, especially if actual knowledge of the area tells the translator that these are what it consists of. The Italian *da* + verb construction often requires the passive infinitive in English (*to be* + past participle – see OV), though in this case the simple infinitive gives more dynamism to the potential action. Hence ... *to discover*, which also maintains the theme and information structure.

In the first long sentence, the OV shows all the signs of 'translationese', at times resembling the literal version above. *Molti sono ...* is an attractive stylistic variation on the more mundane *Ci sono molti ...* . The English *Many are ...* is also possible, but more marked than its Italian counterpart. Thus a decision could be made to play safe with *There are so many interesting places and itineraries ...*, the adverb *so* compensating the fronted *Molti*. The nouns *interessi* and *percorsi* can be adjectivised, and the modal verb group ... *possono portare* converted to the infinitive expression ... *to attract the visitor*, which is so much more English, and merits inclusion for this reason. If translators were to attempt to visualise a corresponding English publication, then constructions of this sort should appear before their eyes, leading them away from grammatically correct but unlikely structures.

Comuni is a question of readership awareness. It can be left intact for an educated, Euro-travelling public (highlighted by italics in the conventional manner for foreign words), though not converted into *communes* which has French connotations. *Towns* is possible, though not all the *comuni* in question fit that description.

The list of attractions begins with *l'osservazione naturalistica*, whose literal translation is too formal for English tastes. It can be diffused to something like *the sights and sounds of nature*, whereas *i castelli medioevali, le chiesette affrescate* and *l'architettura contemporanea* provide examples of translational equation. The *artigianato di grande pregio* transforms typically into a short multivariate string: *splendid craftwork. Le attrattive della gastronomia* can be reduced to *good food*; the translator may be guided here by knowledge of publications such as 'The Good Food Guide'. The expression *senza dimenticare* seems to invite the equation *not forgetting*, yet perhaps the real equation in terms of equivalent set expression is *not to mention*.

The non-finite clause at the end of the paragraph is difficult to link up to the preceding part of the sentence, requiring a reiterative *all this ... .* A device of this kind may often be necessary when translating long Italian sentences where the subject needs to be reintroduced. The *verdissimo* superlative could be treated literally and translated with *greenest. Ambiente* is another tricky noun, though the photographs portraying the various phenomena which accompany the text (the physical context of situation) suggest *setting*. The translator may, however, have second thoughts, and discard *greenest* in favour of a more natural *in such a green setting*.

The section on Buia begins with *6.657 abitanti* – the conventional equation is *population 6,657*. The Italian text continues in vaguely note form omitting articles, auxiliaries, etc., a style not readily transferrable to the English version. As the administrative details of the *comune* system do not pertain to the English-speaking world, the term *sede* has little meaning; a neutral term like *centre* should convey the basic idea. *Head office* (OV) turns the *comune* into a business. The problem of translating *comune* and *sede* is less irksome, however, than the finding of an equivalent for *frazione*. There is no place for explanatory footnotes in this type of publication, so something must be offered. *Suburbs* is too urban, and they do not lie out enough to be *outlying areas*, though this latter term may be suitable on occasion. An alternative solution is to forego the use of an equivalent term and verbalise the idea with *surrounded by Avilla*, etc. A *frazione* is, in fact, simply a place.

In the next sentence, beginning with *On the highest hill* maintains the marked theme structure.

Detto should be translated as *known as*.

The Italian continues to omit elements, though in English a verbal metaphor like *lies* is required to cement the sentence structure.

The term *borgo* further highlights the inadequacy of dictionary definitions in finding equivalent terminology in the field of urban geography. English is often reduced to superordinate terms such as *area, district* – *the S. Lorenzo district?* Local knowledge would confirm whether *walled* is an accurate rendering of *chiuso. Closed-in* (OV) is difficult to decipher.

Omonimo is one of those very useful Latin-based Italian words that need expanding in English into set locutions, in this case *of the same name.*

The dictionary gives *under repair* for *in restauro,* though *closed for restoration* would seem more familiar to most translators.

A *panoramic park* (OV) seems a tempting solution to *parco panoramico,* though it is not the park that is panoramic. At the risk of being over-pedantic, the translator might decide that *a park with panoramic views* is more logical.

Castelliere, as a much less familiar term than *comune* but, retaining a distinct meaning within the Italian historical context, can be amplified by providing an English quasi-equivalent in apposition: *'castelliere' stronghold.*

Shopping is an example of a loan word that has come into Italian with a rather different specific meaning to the original (cf: other gerundives – *parking/carpark, camping/camp-site, footing/jogging*). Transformation is therefore justified. Similarly, the Italian use of *interessante* often veers slightly from the meaning of the English *interesting,* as in this case where *fascinating* is more appropriate.

In the final sentence in this section, the grammatical metaphor *vede* can be replaced with a conventional *includes.* The context of situation, backed by world knowledge, suggests that *alla castellana* is *on the spit.* The *festa delle campanelle* can be bracketed and kept for local flavour though backed by its English translation.

The section on Fagagna begins in a similar way to the previous section, and the same considerations, particularly as regards omissions, apply. This time the translator may opt for *outlying areas* to translate *frazioni.* The second sentence lacks even a dummy subject (*It* in English), and the OV follows suit, but English style really begs the repetition of *Fagagna.* However, *grosso centro* is potentially misleading; it is not a 'large town' (world knowledge), the OV *big centre* is too vague and not very English, and *large village* destroys the effect of giving it importance. So perhaps *small town* is the best solution; it is an accurate description and the term *town* confers a certain prestige. But what does *economia completa* mean? Logic would suggest *(highly-)developed economy.*

Rather than the imperative opted for in the OV (though imperative use is often found in the genre), the sentence can undergo a thorough re-ordering, with *da visitare* becoming *are well worth visiting* following the list of attractions.

Again, by mentally juggling the long Italian sentence after baulking at trying to start it with the verb, the more English syntax and easier style should coalesce in the translator's mind. Note also the power of the Italian preposition *da* in this sentence.

Cinquecentesca is, of course, *sixteenth century*.

The *Casa della Comunità* is transparent enough to be left in Italian, even if the precise nature of this building is not clear; it is a tourist attraction, thus not requiring historical exactitude, which can be gained on visiting it. The translator should beware of easy solutions like the OV *Community House*, in that to the modern ear it may sound like a refuge for the poor or homeless in a large city.

The *Porta del Borgo*, as it can be left in Italian in support, can be translated simply by a capital-lettered *Gate*, which is sufficient to conjure up the image in the reader's mind.

Because of the syntactic upheaval mentioned above, the manor in Villalta needs to be introduced by *as is*.

Conservato = conserved, preserved, well-kept? This is one of those areas where native-speakers may disagree, but the conventional dictionary wisdom is that buildings are preserved, food is conserved and gardens are well-kept. But ... ?

More re-ordering is required in the next sentence where Italian fronts the adjective *interessanti*. The latter, together with *gastronomia*, can easily be reduced to sense and become *a pleasure* and *eating*.

On the model of the previous paragraph, the grammatical metaphor *see* can be used in the following sentence (*The first Sunday in September sees the holding ...*) with the consequent nominalisation of the verb phrase *si svolge*. *Secolare* requires the hyphenated compound *centuries-old*, an example of Italian providing a more economic version of the English compound.

As regards the *divertentissima corsa degli asini*, there is a tendency to associate the Italian *divertente* with *amusing* because of its occasional appropriacy, and perhaps because of misplaced scholastic conventions resulting from snap answers to the question '*Cosa vuol dire ...?*', '*How do you say ...?*'. Indeed, pairings of this nature are not uncommon, cf: *simpatico/kind, contento/happy, tranquillo/quiet*, which are only acceptable in some circumstances. Such cases can extend even to longer locutions: *Let it be/Lascia stare* (causing much consternation among Beatles fans – the song title 'Let it be' means 'Che sia ...'). The important thing again is for the translator to think in terms of the English genre, to imagine how an event of this type would be described. It would be described as *entertaining* and, as it is *-issima*, *highly entertaining*. And the event itself? Such 'races' are held in England and go by the name of *donkey derby* – a direct equivalent.

Filling in the grammatical gaps as usual, the last sentence would begin *There is a nine-hole golf course* (noun string) *in the nearby hills*. The grammatical metaphor *lies* can be used to provide cohesion in the following English clause, and for the *zona di tutela ambientale* the contracted *protected area* should suffice, the context of situation providing the implicit information that it is environmentally protected.

The title of the last section (*Per chi ama*, etc.) is rendered in the OV by *For those who love nature, history and gastronomy*. Perhaps a more careful consideration of what the visitors are expected to love would suggest the *countryside* rather than *nature* and certainly *good food* instead of *gastronomy*, but it is still clumsy in terms of the English genre. Here, the tension is between mentioning the 'love' of these things and simply giving a succinct informative heading (*Countryside, history and good food*), possibly accentuated by adjectival assistance (*Pleasant countryside, fascinating history and good food*).

The *Comunità Collinare*, as a semi-official denomination can be left in Italian but supported by an English gloss: *Hill Towns*. The colloquial expression *a due passi* invokes immediate substitution with the equivalent *a stone's throw*. The adverbial *a un'ora di auto* also has a direct substitute in the Saxon genitive form *an hour's drive*, highlighting the fact that the English verb/noun *drive* stretches much further than its dictionary equivalent *guidare/guida*.

Even elaborate Italian adjectives such as *centri sciistici* should not deter the translator from a constant endeavour to find the most natural equivalent. In these cases the 'lowest common denominator' is often the noun string, in this particular case *ski resort*.

There is much controversy over the extent to which the translator should intervene in cases of factual inaccuracy, ranging from the firmly non-interventionist lobby to those, like Newmark, who believe it is at times the translator's duty to set the record straight. In the case of *dai confini austriaco e jugoslavo*, it would seem that history has passed the writer by, and the translator would be justified in correcting *jugoslavo* to *Slovenian*.

In the second sentence, the *caselli dell'autostrada/motorway exits* in Italian simply *sono i suoi margini*, whereas English may prefer the grammatical metaphor _mark its borders_. The subject/theme of the next clause is _scorrevoli strade statali_ which, apart from a presumably fortuitous alliterative phonological effect, contains the almost onomatopoeic and evocative adjective _scorrevoli_. The word gives the idea of fast-moving traffic, but unfortunately is difficult to match in this context, in that equivalent items would refer to the traffic and not to the roads. Taking a different perspective on the same semantic idea, the _(main) roads_ are described as _uncongested_. The OV then refers to the airport of Ronchi dei Legionari, perhaps more clearly recognisable as _Trieste_.

The long hypotactic sentence beginning _Di origine morenica_, being in the typical note form, requires the odd cohesive tie, for example, _with three semicircles . . . ._ The _colline digradanti_ seem to shift effortlessly into _sloping hills_, but a moment's thought might suggest to the translator that the latter sounds tautologous in English. It would also seem advisable to avoid prepositional or phrasal verbs involving _look (look up to, look out over, look towards)_ to translate _guardano verso_ and opt for _facing_.

The description of the _ambiente (landscape?)_ as _dolce_ poses the problem of how to translate such a common adjective (_sweet, soft_) in a particular context. The pseudo-poetic nature of the genre would certainly not rule out _mellow_ in these circumstances. _Punteggiato di_ has its equivalent contextual collocation in _dotted with_. The metaphorical _E' il regno della bicicletta e delle passeggiate_ is not original and therefore begs a substitute expression that would trip off the tongue of an English-speaking reader: _It is cycling and walking country_.

In the case of the _villeggiature/holidays_, a more appropriate adjective for the translation of _tranquille_ than _quiet_ (see above) is _relaxing_. The final noun phrase _grandi mutevoli cieli_ should create some kind of image in the translator's mind, perhaps that of _wide rolling skies_. Certainly, the OV _great mutable skies_ is neither linguistically nor meteorologically acceptable.

Like the skies, the translation too has now rolled to a more definitive version:

> Journey to the Centre of Friuli
> A (whole) host of towns and villages to discover
>
> There are so many interesting places and itineraries to attract the visitor to our sixteen _comuni_: the sights and sounds of nature, the medieval castles and the small frescoed churches, or the contemporary architecture. But there is also splendid craftwork, not to mention good food, and all this in such a green setting.

Buia

Population 6,657. The *comune* is spread out over a number of hills:
the centre is S. Stefano, surrounded by Avilla, Madonna, S. Floreano,
Tomba and Urbignacco. On the highest hill, known as 'Monte', lies the
attractive (walled) S. Lorenzo district with its ancient frescoed church
of the same name (closed for restoration) and a park with panoramic
views containing the ruins of medieval fortifications and the
prehistoric *castelliere* stronghold. There are fascinating jewellery and
pottery shops. At the end of April the Spring Festival includes a whole
bull being roasted on the spit, and on 12th July the Festival of Bells
(*festa delle campanelle*) is held.

Fagagna

Population 5,947, including the outlying areas of Battaglia, Ciconicco,
Madrisio and Villalta. Fagagna is a small town with a highly developed
economy. The castle ruins, the sixteenth century *Casa della Comunità*,
and the medieval Gate (*Porta di Borgo*) are well worth visiting, as is
the imposing and well-preserved manor house in nearby Villalta, still
intact today. A series of specialist products make eating and shopping
a pleasure. The first Sunday in September sees the holding of the
centuries-old and highly entertaining donkey derby. There is a nine-
hole golf course in the nearby hills and just outside the town lies the
'Quadri' protected area.

Countryside, history and good food

The *Comunità Collinare* (the Hill Town area) is a stone's throw from
Udine in the ancient heart of Friuli, an hour's drive from the beaches
of the Adriatic, from the ski resorts and from the Austrian and
Slovenian borders. Two of the Alpe Adria motorway exits mark its
borders; uncongested roads connect it to all the towns in the
Friuli-Venezia-Giulia region and in the nearby Veneto.

  The Venice, Trieste and Klagenfurt airports provide connections to
the whole world. Of morainic origin, with three semicircles of hills
facing the mountains, with the plain behind them, it is a mellow green
landscape, dotted with small towns and crossed by countless roads
and lanes. It is ideal cycling and walking country. It has always been a
place for relaxing holidays, thanks to the mild climate and the wide
rolling skies ...

The text continues as follows, and is offered for practice:

La Comunità Collinare è un ambiente in cui storia dell'uomo e storia naturale si sono fuse nei millenni, lasciando ovunque i segni del passato. Degli oltre trenta castelli e fortezze di cui restano tracce più o meno consistenti, almeno sei si ergono ancora integri e possenti, spesso ben restaurati e abitati. In qualche caso il castellano può aprire le porte ai gruppi con guida, ed è un'esperienza indimenticabile. Dalla sommità dei colli, lasciati il panorama e le torri, si scende, per boschetti e prati, nelle conche, zone umide di torbiere, stagni e laghetti di grande interesse naturalistico.

Per gli amanti della gastronomia gli appuntamenti e gli indirizzi sicuri non mancano, come pure l'occasione di acquistare qualche cosa prodotto da artigiani di arte raffinata. Il prosciutto e le bigiotterie di San Daniele, le ceramiche di Buia, le pelletterie di Colloredo possono essere l'occasione per portare a casa più di un semplice souvenir.

E per lo sport, un campo da golf a nove buche a Fagagna, equitazione e volo a vela a Osoppo possono valere da soli una gita, senza dimenticare campi sportivi e da tennis e viottoli adatti alla mountain-bike, presenti quasi ovunque.

MORUZZO

2.136 abitanti con le frazioni di Alnicco, Brazzacco e S. Margherita del Gruagno. Un castello e un tiglio millenario sulla piazza, un borgo murato a S. Margherita (cripta del IX sec.), una splendida villa, che racchiude i resti del castello di Brazzacco, valgono la sosta su queste colline che sono un balcone naturale sulla pianura.

OSOPPO

2.703 abitanti con la frazione di Rivoli. Il centro è un interessante esempio di ricostruzione urbanistica e architettonica delle rovine del terremoto del '76. Lo storico colle fortificato conserva resti di architetture medievali, rinascimentali, napoleoniche, asburgiche e italiane. D'estate ospita manifestazioni pubbliche. Nei suoi pressi la grande zona di tutela ambientale delle risorgive di Bars ove si può praticare l'equitazione e il volo a vela.

3.2.4 Compact disc notes

The sleeve notes to records, tapes and compact discs are often translated into several languages for obvious commercial reasons. This kind of text represents a genre subdividable into a number of subgenres, such as potted biographies of the artists featured on the disc, historical notes on composers of classical music or, in the case of opera, synopses of the 'libretto'. The text chosen here is the first part of just such a synopsis of Donizetti's 'L'elisir d'amore'. The record was produced by Decca in London, and thus the original text is in English, subsequently translated into several languages including Italian. The latter will be used as the main point of reference for the analysis.

Synopsis
Act One

Scene 1. Nemorino, a shy and simple young farmer from a Basque village is in love with Adina, a wealthy country girl. But Adina is wilful and his offers of love are constantly rejected. As the curtain rises on Adina's farm, she is seated apart from a group of harvesters, reading, and Nemorino wonders how he could possibly win her love, since she is so wonderful and much better than himself. She has just come across the legend of the potion which bound Tristan and Isolde with undying love, and reads it aloud to amuse the others.

   At this point a drum is heard and a platoon of soldiers enters, headed by the dashing and bombastic Sergeant Belcore. Belcore at once begins to woo Adina, and in spite of his self-assurance and arrogance, she is flattered: however, to his hasty proposal of marriage she answers that she would like a little time to think it over. Nemorino, naturally, is very jealous and when everybody else leaves, he begs Adina to return his love, but in vain: she prefers to remain fancy free.

Analysis

The context of situation must be seen from two perspectives. First, the text forms part of a well-established text type with a writer doing a job for a record company, and thus obliged to work within the fairly rigid limits prescribed by this genre. The action is recounted in the present and present perfect tenses in order to create the effect of an event happening at the time of reading, thus recreating the effect of seeing the opera. However, at one remove, the 'field' of events is detached from the immediate experience of the writer and reader: it is a work of fiction set in the past and this has certain linguistic consequences, which the translator should bear in mind.

While *Nemorino* will remain untranslated, the rest of the first sentence throws up some interesting contrasts in article use and noun compounding. The translator into Italian may find that *a shy and simple young farmer* may sound better without an article: *Nemorino, timido e semplice giovane contadino, . . .* . The workaday translation of *village* is often *paese*, but given the time and space setting of this particular context, the register might point the translator in the direction of *villaggio*. As the translator then considers the simple solution of the literal translation of *country girl/ragazza di campagna*, he or she should always test whether a reducing device might be available, and it is: *paesana*.

In the second sentence, the importance of componential analysis can be seen. The adjective *wilful* is used in a rather unusual way, both syntactically and semantically. All the examples given in the Collins Cobuild Dictionary show this lexical item being used attributively, that is before the noun (*wilful neglect, wilful misconduct, he is a wilful . . . young man*), in recognisable collocations. In the text above it is used predicatively, as complement of the verb *to be*. Furthermore, the same dictionary gives the two main components of meaning as 'with the intention of causing someone harm' and 'stubborn'. This is confirmed by the meanings listed in the Sansoni bilingual dictionary: *premeditato, intenzionale* and *testardo, cocciuto, ostinato, caparbio*. These are indeed major components of the meaning of the word, but in this context there would seem to be something else. Going back to the original meaning of the word (full of wiles) and integrating a world knowledge element of spoilt young ladies in stories, the translator can mentally conjure up an image of an obstinate person who appears to be not too concerned about hurting others, but who acts this way through a certain frivolous thoughtlessness rather than real malice. When this element is added, *Adina* would seem to qualify for the adjective *capricciosa*, and her behaviour in the opera indeed bears this out.

It is very tempting to translate what follows (*. . . and his offers of love are constantly rejected*) with a more or less literal interpretation, which may well be formally acceptable, but if the translator lets him/herself be swayed by Adina's feelings on the matter, a more forceful (though less superficially faithful) Italian version might be *e non ne vuole sapere del suo amore*.

Again it is a question of asking oneself what an Italian would be most likely to say in these circumstances if writing an original version.

The next sentence begins conventionally for the genre (*As the curtain rises*). The equivalent is readily available: *La scena si apre*. The syntax of the several following clauses is then likely to develop in a different way, becoming gradually more and more differentiated as the translator lets his or her Italian grammatical instincts outweigh the word patterns on the page. Uncharacteristically, it is the Italian translator in this case who could well profitably opt to transform one long hypotactic sentence into two, separating Adina's actions and Nemorino's thoughts. The English version describes Adina as *wonderful* and *much better than himself*, both of which deserve some attention. The first epithet is rather vague, but all we have to go on at this early stage is the physical appearance of the girl, 'as the curtain rises', so the Italian translation could simply concentrate on her *bellezza*. Similarly, the use of *much better* begs the question 'migliore in che senso?' The native speaker and the translator attuned to native speaker awareness knows that *better* in this kind of context refers to social position – the Cinderella syndrome – and will translate accordingly *appartenenti ... a un ceto sociale superiore al suo*.

The final sentence of the first English paragraph begins with the use of the rather low-register phrasal verb *come across*. There is a tension here between attempting to match the rather odd, slight change in register (cf: *è appena saltata fuori la storia ...*) and maintaining the normal register of the genre, at least in Italian. The *potion* must be translated by the original Italian *elisir d'amore*, if for no other reason, in honour of Donizetti. The English then jumps from the modern phrasal verb to an old romantic register describing how the potion *bound Tristan and Isolde with undying love*. The mythical characters become *Tristano e Isotta* and a similar cliché might be found in *legò per sempre insieme*, or some other legendary wording.

The first sentence of the second paragraph with its examples of typically English passive, intransitive and participle verb use, should not deter the translator from syntactically transforming it into exquisitely Italian form through nominalisation (*al rullo di un tamburo*), re-ordering (*sopraggiunge un drappello di soldati*) and more nominalisation (*con in testa ...*). The adjective *dashing* (and *bombastic* to a certain extent) belongs very much to a particular set of time and space coordinates, namely the context of military prowess and elegance of a bygone age. Equivalents should be sought as much as possible within those parameters. The pairing of *baldo e spavaldo*, as well as providing the right kind of atmosphere, echoes the 2:3 syllable gradation of the original, and adds a further element of alliteration. Moreover, by shifting the adjective pair to the end of the clause, the translator can put the information focus on the sergeant's attributes, a justifiable change in view of the fact that such attributes are important to the plot and the consideration that the English writer might have done the same if not shackled by the restrictions of English syntax.

The language register that produced *bound Tristan and Isolde with undying love* and *dashing* re-emerges in the use of the old-fashioned, poetic verb *woo*, providing a consistency of register and a particular kind of lexical cohesion. Italian can correspond with, for example, *far la corte a*. The English projected clause with indirect speech (*she answers that she would like a little time ...*) can typically be rendered with a prepositional projection in Italian: *risponde di non aver premura ....* It is a sensitivity to these kinds of syntactic transformations that make for elegant translation without traces of translationese.

On the other hand, the last sentence can be translated more literally without the risk of a fall in tone. Care is required, however, when the register changes again with the expression *fancy free*. The modern British reader, consciously or otherwise, is likely to associate this phrase with the longer expression *footloose and fancy free*, which has come to lose some of its meaning of 'free from romantic attachment' and simply to indicate freedom to do as one chooses (consider '*The meeting's been called off, so tonight I'll be footloose and fancy free*'). However, the context of Adina and Nemorino suggests the accepted meaning (Sansoni bilingual: *non innamorato*); something like *avere il cuore libero*.

There follows the official Decca translation into Italian:

LA TRAMA
Atto primo

Scena 1. Nemorino, timido e semplice giovane contadino di un villaggio basco, ama Adina, una ricca paesana. Ma Adina è capricciosa e non ne vuole sapere del suo amore.

La scena si apre sulla fattoria di Adina, che è seduta in disparte da un gruppo di mietitori e legge. Nemorino si chiede come potrà mai conquistare gli affetti di una ragazza dotata di tale bellezza, e appartenente, per di più, a un ceto sociale superiore al suo. Adina sta leggendo la storia dell'elisir d'amore che legò per sempre insieme Tristano e Isotta, e legge ad alta voce per divertire gli altri.

In quel momento, al rullo di un tamburo, sopraggiunge un drappello di soldati, con in testa Belcore, il sergente, baldo e spavaldo. Belcore non tarda a far la corte ad Adina, che ad onta della sicurezza e arroganza di Belcore, ne rimane lusingata. Ma alla piuttosto affrettata proposta di matrimonio, Adina risponde di non aver premura e che ci vuole pensare.

Nemorino, naturalmente, è geloso e, quando gli altri si sono allontanati, prega Adina di ricambiare il suo amore, ma invano: la giovane preferisce avere il cuore libero.

The synopsis continues as follows and is offered for practice:

Scene 2. Dr Dulcamara, a picturesque and loquacious quack, arrives on the village square and, before the assembled villagers, he sings the praises of his wonderful remedy, guaranteed to cure all ills. The naive Nemorino is impressed and asks whether he also sells the love potion of Queen Isolde. Naturally Dulcamara obliges him, but warns him that the potion will take effect only after twenty-four hours – which will give him enough time to leave the village – and that no one must know about it. Nemorino is now so pleased and sure of himself that Adina is surprised to find him in a cheerful and confident mood: he assures her that his heart will be cured within one day. In a fit of pique she then tells Belcore that she will marry him in six days' time. Nemorino is not worried: he knows that tomorrow she will fall at his feet. But a message reaches Belcore with an order to leave the village in the morning, so Adina agrees to marry him that very day. Nemorino is now desperate, but his entreaties to Adina to postpone the wedding for just one day are all in vain: she invites everyone to the marriage feast and they all mock the distraught Nemorino.

A similar text, the synopsis of Bellini's 'Norma', accompanies the Decca compact disc recording of that opera, and is also offered as practice:

Act One
Scene 1. It is the night of a new moon. The druid members of a community in Roman-occupied Gaul (around 50 B.C.) are preparing for the ceremony of cutting mistletoe, which will be performed by the priestess Norma. They hope for a sign from the god Irminsul to break their peace treaty with the Romans and to go to war.

The proconsul for the territory is Pollione, who has secretly become Norma's lover and has fathered two children. Recently, however, he has met Adalgisa, a novice priestess, and fallen in love with her. He discusses his situation with the centurion Flavio while the druids are dispersed, waiting for the moon to rise. The two Romans hide as the druids return to where their altar stands. Norma appears and addresses the assembly. Despite the arguments of her father Oroveso, Norma insists that the time is not yet right for an attack against the Romans: she prophesies that the Roman Empire will one day collapse through its own vices. She performs the ceremony of the mistletoe and promises that when Irminsul demands the Romans' blood she will call them. However, while the people still talk of vengeance she is secretly preoccupied by the conflict which a rebellion would provoke between her duty and her heart.

Part Two of 'Language to Language' ends here with the hope that the range of analyses and examples has been sufficient to stimulate discussion and practice amongst teachers, students or translators of any capacity on the many facets of that varied and complex world that is English/Italian translation. No text can explain precisely how to translate more than a handful of specific examples, but if the reader can find some interest in the material in this book, and in turn think about or discuss the topics raised in a constructive manner, then this will equip that reader to approach texts for translation in a more confident and informed manner. This positive approach, allied to experience gained through constant practice in the field, will make that person a well-rounded translator, someone who can gain endless pleasure and satisfaction from accomplishing a challenging and at times arduous task.

Glossary of terms

adjacency pairs: connected pairs of utterances as found in such patterns as question/answer, complaint/apology, e.g. *Are you ready?/Yes I am, You are late!/I'm sorry.*

alliteration: the repetition of initial consonant sounds to create a particular effect and focus the reader/listener's attention on some element of meaning. (adj. **alliterative**)

anaphoric reference: in terms of cohesion, anaphoric reference describes the way elements in a text can refer back to other elements. The typical vehicles for this kind of reference are pro-forms, e.g. *Whales are not fish, they are mammals.* The pronoun *they* refers back anaphorically to *Whales.*

antonymy: the relationship of oppositeness (*The Good, the Bad and the Ugly*).

attitudinal disjuncts: adverbs showing speakers' attitudes to what they are saying, e.g. *obviously, fortunately.*

bottom-up processing: with reference to translation, the mental construction of a text situation starting from the words and clauses and working up to the broader features of the overall context. (cf: **top-down processing**)

bracketing: see **minimal bracketing**.

calque (loan translation): a literal translation of a lexical item, e.g. *basketball/ pallacanestro.* (v. **to calque**)

cataphoric reference: in terms of cohesion, cataphoric reference describes the way elements in a text can refer forwards to other elements. The typical vehicles for this kind of reference are pro-forms, e.g. *What I'm going to do is tell you a story*, where the pro-from *What* refers forward to *tell you a story.*

chunk: a unit of text corresponding to a unit of meaning for translation purposes.

classifier: a word or word group indicating a subclass of a noun, e.g. *film star, pop star, soap opera star.*

cleft sentence: a sentence where a single clause is split into two, usually through the use of the anticipatory *it*, which pushes the main subject to a position after the verb *to be*, e.g. *It is oxygen that keeps us alive.* A similar device is the **pseudo cleft sentence** where *what* is used to pre-empt a verb or an entire clause, e.g. *What she felt was real fear, What they did was break the door down.*

coefficient of intensity: a measure of the semantic force of a word. For example, the verb *annihilate* has greater force than the verb *destroy*, and thus a higher coefficient of intensity; the coefficiency could be matched by the addition of an adverbial, e.g. *totally destroy.*

cohesion: the way linguistic elements connect the various parts of a text, basically **conjunction, reference** and **lexical cohesion.**

collocation: the non-casual occurrence of words in recognisable combinations (**collocates**), e.g. *a heavy smoker, un fumatore accanito*; the restrictions on how words combine, e.g. *he's good at tennis, *he's clever at tennis.*

collocation-bound: connected to a linguistic item in a set combination, e.g. *slam the door.*

common core: the basic vocabulary and grammar of a language as opposed to the language required for advanced or special purposes.

communicative dynamism: the concept of **CD** is based on the premise that clauses consist of both **given information** and **new information**. Generally the given information (that already mentioned in the text or already known by receivers of the text) comes at the beginning of the clause and the new information at the end of the clause (see **theme** and **rheme**). The given information helps to 'anchor' the discussion, providing a guideline for the text receiver, while the new information provides the dynamic element, the part that keeps the receiver interested. Communicative dynamism is thus a function of the relative weighting of given and new information: given information has a low CD and new information has a high CD.

componential analysis: semantic analysis of words, consisting of the identification of their component parts, e.g. *tigress* (feline, female, fierce, etc.).

computational linguistics: the study of linguistics through the use of computers.

concision: the property of being brief and clear. (adj. **concise**)

concordancing: the technique whereby lists of sentences can be extracted from a corpus of language, and information on individual words and expressions can be analysed in relation to their context and co-text.

conjunction: the joining of words, phrases or clauses in relations of time, space, cause, etc.

connotation: ideas or qualities associated with a word or expression in addition to its literal sense. For example, the word *peasant* has negative connotations that the word *farmer* does not have. (adj. **connotative**, adv. **connotatively**. Cf: **denotation**)

contrastive lexicogrammar: the comparison of grammatical structures and lexis across languages.

context of situation: the situational 'context' in which a communicative act (text of some kind) occurs. All texts are produced and received within a set of circumstances of time, place, purpose, etc., they involve various persons in various roles, and are conveyed in a particular way (spoken, written, faxed, etc.). These elements combined form the context of situation. (see also **field, tenor** and **mode**)

copular: a term used to describe verbs that link a subject to a complement, principally the verb *to be* (*He is a teacher*), but also other verbs, e.g. *look* in *you look tired*, *turn* in *he's turning grey*.

corpus (pl. **corpora**): a large collection of written or spoken text, often stored in a computer memory or data-base, typically used for linguistic research.

co-select: one word co-selects another to form a combination. This may be a typical grammatical or lexical collocation (*go swimming, terribly sorry*) or simply a question of one word attracting another for reasons of semantic association or reinforcement (*scientific experiment, musical score*).

co-text: all the linguistic items in a text considered in relation to a specific word or expression, whether in the immediate vicinity or more distant within the same text.

culture: '… that complex whole which includes knowledge, belief, art, morals, law, customs and any other capabilities and habits acquired by man as a member of society' Encyclopedia Britannica, 1983, vol. 4.

culture-bound: referring only to the source language culture, e.g. *Guy Fawkes Night, polenta*.

declarative: a declarative sentence has the form of a statement, as opposed to a question or an order.

deep (structure) grammar: an abstract level of syntax that is basic to all languages. What is actually spoken by individuals in their various mother tongues is based on a **surface grammar** of concrete realisations in words.

deictic: a deictic word changes its meaning depending on the situation it is used in. For example, the pronoun *he* can refer to many different male persons according to the situation of use. (n. **deixis**)

delicacy: level of detail or specificity.

denotation: the property of a word to refer to or represent a concrete or abstract entity in the world, that is any object, event or concept (adj. **denotative**, adv. **denotatively**. Cf: **connotation**)

deontic: expressing control through obligation or permission, typically through modal verbs.

discourse: stretches of spoken or written language in context.

discourse community: those involved in a series of common actions recognisable as a distinct activity and the language they use, for example in a trade union executive or a scout troop.

ellipsis: the omission of words, phrases or clauses from text because they can be understood without explicit mention.

embedded clause: a clause contained in another clause, typically a relative clause, e.g. *The simple fact that he lived in the area was an advantage*.

epistemic modality: the grammatical realisation of attitudes and opinions as to the truth of a proposition, i.e. whether something is possible or necessary, typically through modal verbs (*can, must*) or adverbials (*possibly, definitely*).

epithet: an item, typically an adjective, indicating some quality, e.g. *beautiful, crazy*.

equivalence: in the field of translation, the semantic matching of terms, e.g. *dog/cane, piove a catinelle/it's pouring down.*

exophoric reference: the term used to describe the act of referring to some implicit entity that has not yet been referred to in a text, e.g. a sudden command like *'Come over here, you lot!'* where the place and the people concerned can only be identified through the context, not the co-text.

expressive function of language: the function providing an expressive outlet for speakers/writers, allowing them to exploit their creative skills, for example in a poem. (cf: **informative function, vocative function**)

extension: in semantic terms, any past, present or future example of an entity. For example, the extension of *zebra* refers to all the zebras that have ever existed, that exist now and that will exist in the future.

false cognates: items in one language that, through their morphological structure, would seem to correspond in meaning to words in another language, but which in fact have partially or totally different meanings, e.g. *actually/attualmente, barracks/baracche.*

felicity conditions: the conditions that must exist for a communicative act to be successful. For example, the exhortation *'Study Chapter Two for homework'* can only work if the speaker has the necessary authority, the reading of the chapter is relevant to the receivers of the order, the receivers have access to the book in question, and so on.

field: one of the components of the **context of situation**, cf: **tenor, mode**. It is the component that refers to what is happening in the situation: people use language differently depending on what they are doing.

finite verb: all forms of the verb except the infinitive and participles. In a verb phrase, only the first verb is finite, e.g. *He must have gone.*

fossilised: refers to terms that once had real meaning in the language but that are now accepted with a secondary significance, e.g. the name *Thomson* originally meant 'son of Tom'.

fricative: a consonant sound created by expelling air through almost closed lips, producing a hissing effect, e.g. *foot, this.*

fronting: the grammatical process of placing a word, often unusually, at the front of a clause. For example, in relation to the clause *John is a good player*, the noun group is fronted in the version *A good player, John is.*

function word: a word which has merely a grammatical function and no autonomous 'meaning', e.g. prepositions, conjunctions (*of, in, and*).

functional grammar: a functional grammar attempts to describe and explain how language is used; all language elements are seen as fulfilling some function.

functional sentence perspective: a grammatical analysis of how information is presented within clauses. The distribution of information is seen in terms of **theme** and **rheme**, which respectively provide **given** and **new** information. (see **communicative dynamism**)

genderlect: the variety of language considered to be specific to men or women.

generic: referring to a class of entities, e.g. animals.

genre: in this book, the term 'genre' is used in a similar way to 'text-type', but also to refer to more than just the broad subject-based and sociolinguistic distinctions. Thus a recipe, a protest song, or a church sermon can be considered genres, and at a greater level of delicacy, a more specific 'oral examination in Spanish' might be considered a genre consisting of a series of recognisable features. Some of these features will always be present (question/ answer routine, some form of greeting and dismissal, etc.) and be similar to related genres (an oral exam in geography, a driving test), and some will be specific to that genre (use of Spanish language, questions on Spanish grammar). The term has no rigid definition so the concept of genre runs into that of sub-genre. A narrative can be considered a broad genre, a fairy story a sub-genre, and 'the telling of a fairy story by a teacher to a class of infants' a further sub-genre.

given information: information in a clause that has already been mentioned in the co-text or is somehow known to the receiver of the text. For example, in the sequence *Paris was lively in those days. The city never slept*, the noun phrase *The city* in the second clause is given information, as it refers to the already mentioned *Paris*. (cf: **new information**)

grammatical metaphor: an alternative realisation of the most common way of expressing a semantic function. For example, most actions are most sponta- neously expressed by verbs, most descriptions by adjectives, etc., but these may sometimes appear in a different grammatical form, especially in the written language, e.g. *We drove through Tuscany and saw some beautiful countryside/ Our drive through Tuscany showed us the beauty of the countryside.*

holistic: describing the whole of something, as distinct from its component parts.

homonyms: words with the same form but different meaning, e.g. *a row of houses, to row a boat*. (cf: **homographs** = words which also have a different pronuncia- tion, e.g. *he had a row with his wife* and **homophones** = words with different form but the same pronunciation and different meaning, e.g. *salmon roe*)

hypertheme: the main theme of a text, appearing at or near the beginning, and to which subsequent themes refer back.

hyponymy: the relationship of a subordinate term (e.g. *Rolls Royce*) to a superordinate term (*car*).

hypotaxis: the organisation of clauses into main and subordinate structural and semantic units. The subordinate, or secondary, elements are dependent on the main clause, e.g. *(While waiting at the bus stop), he saw a person (he thought he recognised)*. (adj. **hypotactic**. Cf: **parataxis**)

idiomatic: describing the use of expressions which mean something different from the literal meanings of the words that make up those expressions, often peculiar to a particular language culture.

illocutionary intent: what speakers/writers actually mean by what they say/write. (cf: **illocutionary act** - see **locutionary act**)

imperative: the mood of the verb that is used to make people do things, or to give orders (*Bring me my coffee!*) but also to make offers, suggestions, etc. (*Have a nice day*).

implicature: the means by which a listener infers exactly what a speaker intends, if the speaker's utterance contains an indirect illocutionary element. For example, if a dinner party host says '*It's getting rather late*' then by implicature the guests understand that he means it is time to go home.

information focus: in spoken language, where the phonological stress lies, typically at the end of the clause in English.

informative function of language: the function providing information about the facts and events of the real world, for example in a newspaper article. (cf: **expressive function, vocative function**)

interlanguage: the language spoken by learners, i.e. a level of language lying at some point on a range that goes from beginner stage to almost total fluency.

interlingual: between languages. (cf: **intralingual** = within the same language)

interpersonal: the element in language involving the social relationships that exist between people.

intertextuality: how the producing or receiving of one text is influenced by previously-produced texts, typically within the same basic field.

iteration: repetition.

lexical cohesion: textual cohesion created by the repetition of words or their reiteration in some other way within the same text. (see **synonymy, hyponymy, antonymy, semantic field**)

lexical density: a measure of the number of **lexical words** (content words) in a text in relation to the number of **function words**. It is measured by dividing the number of lexical words by the number of clauses.

lexical item (lexeme): a word or combination of words and morphemes that form a single unit, e.g. *dog, guard dog, doggy*. A word with various inflected forms (e.g. *go, goes, went, gone, going*) is considered to be a single lexical item.

lexical word: a word referring to some thing, state or action, e.g. *hippopotamus, enjoyment, shoot, beautiful, severely.*

lexicogrammar: the words and grammar of a language. The use of the term 'lexicogrammar' shows the recent recognition of the fact that grammar/syntax and lexis/vocabulary are closely linked.

lexicography: the compiling of dictionaries.

lexis: the words and lexical items in a language.

linguistic options: the various members of a linguistic set, e.g. subject pronouns (*I, you, she/he/it, we, you, they*) which a speaker can choose from. (see **paradigm**)

loan (word): a lexical item, which may even be an expression, in one language that is used in its original form in other languages, e.g. *leader* in Italian, *dolce vita* in English.

locutionary act: a communicative act of speaking or writing. (cf: **illocutionary act**, which refers to what the speaker/writer is doing with the locutionary act, i.e. ordering, apologising, criticising, etc., even if this is not explicit, and **perlocutionary effect** which is the (often unpredictable) effect the locutionary act produces on the listener/reader)

marked: in contrast with the normal pattern. (cf: **unmarked** = normal, typical)

marker: an indicator of some linguistic feature, e.g. *-s* is a plural marker, *-ess* is a gender marker.

material process: a process, represented grammatically by a verb form, describing the actual occurrence of something, e.g. *Bill killed the rat. Jennifer coughed. The committee resigned.*

mental process: a process of sensing, thinking, etc., represented grammatically by a verb form, e.g. *to feel, to see, to think, to like.*

metaphor: a word or expression used in a different context to the usual and not with its literal meaning, e.g. *the world's a stage.*

metonym: a figure of speech where one item is replaced by another, related item, e.g. *Downing Street* to mean the Prime Minister.

minimal bracketing: in a translation context, the dividing of text into the fewest semantically autonomous units possible. For example, the expression *and the same to you* can be considered a single semantic unit for translation purposes and translated *altrettanto* without, misleadingly, analysing each individual item.

mnemonic: something that assists memory, e.g. the English spelling aid '*i before e except after c*'.

mode: one of the components of the **context of situation**, cf: **field**, **tenor**. It is the component that refers to what the language is being used to do, e.g. deliver a speech, sing a song, direct traffic. It also refers to the medium employed, e.g. spoken or written. Language use varies accordingly.

monosemic: with only one meaning.

morpheme: the smallest analysable unit of the lexicogrammar, which may be a complete word, e.g. *elephant*, or a meaningful part of a word, e.g. *un/distinguish/ed.*

morphology: the form and structure of words.

new information: information in a clause that has not already been mentioned in the co-text and is not known to the receiver of the text. For example, in the sequence *Paris was lively in those days. The city never slept*, the information *never slept* in the second clause is new information, as it tells us something new about *Paris/The city*. (cf: **given information**)

nominalisation: the process of forming nouns or noun phrases from other parts of speech, e.g. from verbs and adjectives. For example: *He believed that . . ./It was his belief that . . .*

non-finite: a non-finite verb form has no person or tense. For example, *he goes* is a finite form in the third person singular, present tense. The forms *to go, going* and *gone* are non-finite forms.

noun string: a noun phrase consisting solely of nouns, e.g. *Environment department air pollution report.*

onomatopoeia: the use of words that, through their phonological features, resemble the sound of the entity or process they represent, e.g. *splash, click.* (adj. **onomatopoeic**)

paradigm: a list or pattern showing, for example, the various forms of a word, or a set of **linguistic options** to choose between. The adverb **paradigmatically** refers to the way one linguistic item is chosen in place of another possible substitute from such a list:

HE	LOVES	YOU
SHE	HATES	HIM
....	....	....

etc.

In first position the choices available are *I, you, he, she, it, we, they*; in second position the choices available are *loves, hates, despises, adores, kills, kicks, kisses,* etc. (cf: **syntagmatically**)

parataxis: the organisation of clauses or phrases into related units of equal stature. For example, the famous line from Caesar *'I came, I saw, I conquered'* contains three autonomous yet semantically-connected clauses of equal status, i.e. no one is subordinate to the others. (adj. **paratactic**. Cf: **hypotaxis**)

parsing: the splitting up of stretches of text into constituent parts.

partitive: in the field of terminology, 'partitive' refers to the various types of entity that exist within a general class, e.g. *(cuisine) Italian, French, Chinese,* etc.

performative: with reference to verbs, a verb which actually carries out an action, e.g. *I declare you man and wife.*

perlocutionary effect: see **locutionary act**.

phatic: intended only to establish social contact, not to provide information, e.g. *Good morning, Nice day,* etc.

phonological equivalence: the repetition or overlap of sound features (alliteration, rhyme, etc.) in recognisable patterns.

phonology: (the study of) the sound system and intonation patterns of a language and how they are used to express meaning. (adj. **phonological**)

plosive: a consonant sound created by a sudden release of air from the lips, producing an explosive effect, e.g. *ball, pike.*

political correctness: a term describing a use of language whose purpose is to avoid offending particular groups in society or particular ideological positions, e.g. *native Americans* instead of *Indians,* or the pejorative *Redskins.* (adj. **politically correct**)

polysemy: the property of having two or more related meanings, e.g. *mouth* (organ of the body or river outlet). (adj. **polysemous**)

pragmatics: the study of meaning in particular situations, or of what speakers actually mean by what they say. For example, a speaker may say *'What a lovely day!'* on a grey and rainy November morning with the purpose of being ironic. (adj. **pragmatic**)

presentative: a presentative clause presents the subject by means of an adverbial such as *here*, e.g. *'Here comes the bride'*.

pro-forms: any kind of pronoun.

pronominalisation: the use of pronouns, which are often omitted in Italian.

prototype: the image of a typical example of an entity, presenting only the typical characteristics of that entity. For example, the drawings that children make of cats, houses, cars, etc. usually conform to the idea of the prototype.

pseudo cleft sentence: see **cleft sentence**.

pun: a play on words, typically exploiting the polysemy or ambiguity of lexical items.

reference (1): in terms of cohesion, 'reference' describes the way elements in a text can:
- refer back to previous elements (*The Prime Minister is visiting Scotland. He will take this opportunity to speak about the proposed new parliament*), where the pronoun *He* refers back through a relationship of **anaphoric reference** to *The Prime Minister*.
- refer forwards (*What I'm going to do is tell you a story*) in a relationship of **cataphoric reference**.
The term used to describe the act of referring outside the text (*I hope everyone will understand*) is called **exophoric reference**.

reference (2): in semantic terms, the relationship between linguistic items (words and expressions) and things in the real world. Words and expressions that are used to refer to specific entities are known as **referring expressions** and the things to which they refer, whether they are concrete or abstract, are known as **referents**. For example, the lexical item *John's house* consists, at one level, of nothing more than spoken or written words, but it is a referring expression that refers to the actual place where John lives. Through this relationship of reference between words and things, people are able to indicate verbally what they wish to communicate to others.

register: the variety of language used in particular texts (e.g. medical text, legal text) or in particular circumstances (e.g. between friends, at work) distinguished by choice of vocabulary or style.

rheme: clauses can be seen as consisting of two parts, a **theme** and a rheme. In simple terms, the theme establishes what the clause is about and the rheme says something about it. In the clause *Beauty is in the eye of the beholder*, *Beauty* is the theme and *is in the eye of the beholder* is the rheme. (adj. **rhematic**)

rhetoric: an effective use of language such as that displayed by an accomplished orator. (adj. **rhetorical**)

scenario: a mental representation of a situation constructed from knowledge and memory.

semantic equivalence: the repetition or overlap of semantic features in a text through synonymy, figures of speech, word association within distinct semantic fields, etc.

semantic field: the grouping of words that are related in some systematic way, e.g. *Brothers* and *Sisters* gather round.

semantic prosody: the semantic content or force of a lexical item in a given context.

semantics: the study of meaning, for example through an examination of the relations existing between words and the things and events they stand for in the world. (adj. **semantic**)

service encounter: a situation involving a buyer and a seller, typically in a shop setting.

sign: a symbol (a sound or a written item) corresponding to an entity in the world.

simile: an explicit metaphor, in the sense that the term being metaphorised is joined to the metaphorical expression by a connector (*like, as, if,* etc.), e.g. *Life is like a box of chocolates.*

social semiotic: a term used by Michael Halliday to define language as a system of meaning (a way of making meaning) that is in turn an integral part of the social system or culture.

sociolinguistics: the study of language in its social and cultural contexts.

source text: in translation terminology, an original text that is to be, or has been, translated.

speech act: any meaningful utterance. (cf: **locutionary act**)

string: a succession of linguistic items, e.g. **noun string** = a succession of nouns.

Structuralism: a term used to describe the area of linguistics concerned with describing linguistic systems and patterns.

Structuralist: a term used to describe the linguists who worked in this field, particularly in America, in the middle of the twentieth century.

stylistics: concerning a writer's choice of particular forms and expressions. (adj. **stylistic**)

surface grammar: see **deep grammar**.

syllable gradation: the progressive increasing of the syllable length of words in sequence, e.g. *old, lonely and forgotten* (1, 2, 3).

synchronic linguistics: the study of language and linguistics as they exist at a particular point in time. (cf: **diachronic linguistics** = the study of linguistics over historical time)

synonymy or **near-synonymy:** the relationship between words or expressions of similar or almost identical meaning, e.g. *There were thirty* ladies *present at the* Women's Club *meeting.*

syntactic equivalence: the co-occurrence of identical or similar grammatical forms with a higher than usual frequency.

syntagm: a combination of two or more linguistic items to form a recognisable unit of grammatical structure (a word, a phrase, a clause).

syntagmatically: the way language is organised horizontally to create meaningful clauses and sentences: For example, SHE → LOVES → YOU forms a **syntagmatic sequence**. Any other arrangement of these words would not make the same (or any) sense. (cf: **paradigmatically**)

syntax: the way words are arranged to form grammatical units.

system: in the linguistic sense, a set of options to choose from, e.g. singular or plural; past, present or future tense. (adj. **systemic**)

target text: in translation terminology, the text into which the translator works.

tenor: one of the components of the **context of situation**, cf: **field, mode**. It is the component that refers to the relations subsisting between the people involved in the situation. Language use varies according to who is speaking to who, and what roles and status these people have vis-a-vis one another.

term: in the technical sense, a word or expression with an unambiguous meaning used in a specific field, e.g. a medical term, a football term.

terminology: specialised words and expressions used in specific fields such as medicine, ship-building, stamp-collecting. (adj. **terminological**)

theme: clauses can be seen as consisting of two parts, a theme and a **rheme**. In simple terms, the theme establishes what the clause is about and the rheme says something about it. In the clause *Beauty is in the eye of the beholder*, *Beauty* is the theme and *is in the eye of the beholder* is the rheme. (adj. **thematic**)

three-part list: a speech act containing three connected items in order to create some effect. For example, *The Good, the Bad and the Ugly* and, in the Churchill speech from Part One, 2.1.1 (Reference), '… has *so much* been owed by *so many* to *so few*'.

top-down processing: with reference to translation, the mental construction of a text situation from an understanding of the features of the context of that situation. (cf: **bottom-up processing**)

transparent translation: a translation based on clear equivalence between similar interlingual terms, e.g. *Prime Minister/Primo Ministro*.

trope: the non-literal use of words, e.g. **metaphor, simile**, etc.

universe of discourse: the (real or imaginary) world assumed by interlocutors when they communicate. For example, small children, unlike adults, assume a universe of discourse in which Father Christmas exists.

unmarked: in line with a normal, typical pattern, e.g. subject-verb-object.

vocative function of language: the function persuading or influencing others, for example in a political speech. (cf: **expressive function, informative function**)

Bibliography

Translation and language

Agard, F. B. & Di Pietro, R. J. 1965. *The Grammatical Structures of English and Italian*. Chicago: University of Chicago Press.

Arcaini, E. 1986. *Analisi linguistica e traduzione*. Bologna: Patron.

Arendt, H. (ed.) 1970. *Illuminations*. London: Jonathan Cape.

Asher, R. E. (ed.) 1994. *Encyclopedia of Linguistics Vol 5*. Oxford: Pergamon Press.

Atwell, E. 1986. 'Beyond the Micro'. In Leech & Candlin 1986: 168–183.

Austin, J. L. 1962. *How to Do Things with Words*. London: Oxford University Press.

Baccolini, R., Bollettieri Bosinelli, R. M. & Gavioli, L. (eds) 1994. *Il doppiaggio: trasposizioni linguistiche e culturali*. Bologna: CLUEB.

Baker, M. 1992. *In Other Words*. London and New York: Routledge.

Baker, M. 1993. 'Corpus Linguistics and Translation Studies: Implications and Applications'. In Baker, Francis & Tognini-Bonelli 1993: 233–250.

Baker, M., Francis, G. & Tognini-Bonelli, E. 1993. *Text and Technology. In Honour of John Sinclair*. Amsterdam and Philadelphia: John Benjamins.

Baker, M. 1995. 'Corpora in Translation Studies'. *Target* 7, 223–243.

Bassnett, S. 1980. *Translation Studies*. London: Routledge.

Bayley, R. & Preston, D. (eds) 1996. *Second Language Acquisition and Linguistic Variation*. Amsterdam: John Benjamins.

Benjamin, W. 1923. 'The Translator's Task'. In Arendt 1970.

Bloor, M. 1996. 'Academic Writing in Computer Science: A Comparison of Genres'. In Ventola & Mauranen 1996: 59–87.

Bolinger, D. 1971. *The Phrasal Verb in English*. Cambridge, Mass.: Harvard University Press.

Bonnes, R. & De Re, P. 1989. *Progetto Natura 3*. Florence: Editore Bulgarini.

Browne, V. & Natali, G. 1989. *Bugs and Bugbears*. Bologna: Zanichelli.

Brownless, N. & Denton, J. 1987. *Translation Revisited*. Florence: Edizioni Cremonese.

Bruti, S. 1996. 'Pragmatic and Discursive Functions of *in fact* and *infatti*'. Genoa: paper delivered at 'Associazione Italiana di Anglistica' annual congress.

Bühler, K. 1934. *Sprachtheorie*. Jena: Fischer.

Caldiron, O. & Hochkefler, M. 1992. 'I signori degli anelli'. In Castellano 1992: 25–48.

Castellano, A. 1992. *L'attore dimezzato? Quaderno di filmcronache*. Rome: ANCCI.

Chesterman, A. (ed.) 1989. *Readings in Translation Theory*. Losmaa: Oy Finn Lectura Ab.

Chomsky, N. 1957. *Syntactic Structures*. The Hague: Mouton.

Christie, F. 1995. 'From Reconstruction to Abstraction'. Beijing: paper presented at the International Systemic Functional Linguistics Association Congress, University of Beijing.

Coates, J. & Cameron, D. (eds) 1989. *Women in their Speech Communities*. Harlow: Longman.

Codeluppi, L. 1997. *A Practical Handbook of Business Theory and Commercial Correspondence*. Florence: Casa Editrice Le Lettere.

Cole, P. & Morgan J. (eds) 1975. *Speech Acts*. New York: Academic Press.

Cortelazzo, M. A. 1990. *Lingue speciali. La dimensione verticale*. Padua: Unipress.

Cortese, G. (ed.) 1992. *Her/his Speechways: Gender Perspectives in English*. Turin: Libreria Cortina.

Cortese, G. 1996. 'L'intervento del traduttore, tra la realtà e la virtualità del testo'. In Cortese 1996: 237–263.

Cortese, G. (ed.) 1996. *Tradurre i linguaggi settoriali*. Turin: Libreria Cortina.

Coseriu, E. 1967. 'Lexicalische Solidaritäten'. *Poetica* 1, 293–303.

Coulthard, M. (ed.) 1992. *Spoken Discourse Analysis*. London: Routledge.

Coulthard, M. (ed.) 1994. *Advances in Written Text Analysis*. London: Routledge.

Crystal, D. 1981. *Linguistics*. Harmondsworth: Pelican.

Crystal, D. 1987. *The Cambridge Encyclopedia of Language*. Cambridge: Cambridge University Press.

Crystal, D. & Davy, D. 1969. *Investigating English Style*. London: Longman.

Danes, F. 1974. *Papers on Functional Sentence Perspective*. The Hague: Mouton.

de Beaugrande, R. & Dressler, W. 1981. *Introduction to Text Linguistics*. London: Longman.

de Saussure, F. 1974. *A Course in General Linguistics*. London: Fontana.

de Vanna, M., Marinucci, M., Melato, M., Taylor, C. & Valenti, A. 1989. *Progressi della nosografia psichiatrica e risvolti linguistico-terminologici: glossario inglese-italiano*. Trieste: Università degli Studi di Trieste.

Delderfield, E. R. 1966. *Kings and Queens of England and Great Britain*. Newton Abbott: David & Charles.

Denton, J. 1995. 'Translation Teaching and Translation Assessment'. Misano Adriatico: paper delivered at Tempus Symposium 'Communicating Cultures', Istituto San Pellegrino.

Di Sabato, B. 1993. *Per tradurre*. Naples: Edizioni Scientifiche Italiane.

Dodds, J. 1994. *Aspects of Literary Text Analysis and Translation Criticism*. Udine: Campanotto Editore.

Dodds, J. 1995. 'All'Antica Commedia degli Errori: Or Crappy English in Italian Restaurants'. *Rivista internazionale di tecnica della traduzione* 1, 143–147.

Dodds, J., Brady, M., Taylor, C. & Moore, G. 1997. *Five Fits of Anger*. Udine: Campanotto Editore.

Dollerup, C. & Loddegaard, A. (eds) 1992. *Teaching Translation and Interpreting, Training, Talent and Experience*. Amsterdam and Philadelphia: John Benjamins.

Downing, A. 1997. 'Nominalisation and Topic Management in the Daily Press'. Halle-Wittenberg: paper delivered at Ninth Euro-International Systemic Functional Workshop.

Eco, E. 1995. 'Umberto Eco'. In Nergaard 1995: 121–146.

Ervin-Tripp, S. 1979. 'Children's Sociolinguistic Competence and Dialect Diversity'. In Pride 1979: 27–41.

Faerch, C. & Kasper, G. (eds) 1987. *Introspection in Second Language Research*. Clevedon: Multilingual Matters.

Falinski, J. 1990. *Translating into English*. Florence: Valmartina Editore.

Firth, J. R. 1957. *Papers in Linguistics 1934–57*. London: Oxford University Press.

Firth, J. R. 1959. *Papers in Linguistics 1934–1951*. London: Oxford University Press.

Firth, J. R. 1968. 'Linguistic Analysis and Translation'. In Palmer 1968.

Fisiak, J. 1993. *Further Insight into Contrastive Analysis*. Amsterdam: John Benjamins.

Flege, J. F., Munro, M. J. & Mackay, I. 1995. 'Factors Affecting Degree of Perceived Foreign Accent in a Second Language'. In Bayley & Preston 1996: 47–74.

Flood, J. (ed.) 1984. *Understanding Reading Comprehension*. Newark, Delaware: International Reading Association.

Fowler, R. 1977. *Linguistics and the Novel*. London and New York: Methuen.

Fraser, J. 1996. 'The Translator Investigated'. *The Translator* 2, No. 1: 65–80.

Fries, C. 1945. *Teaching and Learning English as a Foreign Language*. Ann Arbor, Michigan: University of Michigan Press.

Fries, P. 1995. 'Theme Development and Texts'. In Fries & Hasan 1995: 317–360.

Fries, P. & Hasan, R. (eds) 1995. *On Subject and Theme*. Amsterdam and Philadelphia: John Benjamins.

Galassi, G. 1994. 'La norma traviata'. In Baccolini, Bollettieri Bosinelli & Gavioli 1994: 61–70.

Garzone, G., Miglioli, F. & Salvi, R. 1995. *Legal English*. Milan: EGEA.

Ghadessy, M. (ed.) *Registers of Written English*. London: Pinter Publishers.

Giambagli, A. 1992. 'Un aspetto particolare della traduzione tecnica: la traduzione presso la Comunità Europea. Studio di un caso'. *Rivista internazionale di tecnica della traduzione* 0, 61–66.

Giglioli, P. P. (ed.) 1964. *Language and Social Context*. Harmondsworth: Penguin.

Giusti, F. 1989. *Statistica Applicata*. Bari: Cacucci Editore.

Goodwin, M. H. 1992. 'Directive-response Speech Sequences in Girls' and Boys' Task Activities'. In Cortese 1992: 151–169.

Gotti, M. 1996. *Robert Boyle and the Language of Science*. Milan: Guerini.

Gottlieb, H. 1992. 'Subtitling. A New University Discipline'. In Dollerup & Loddegaard 1992: 161–170.

Gran, L. & Taylor, C. (eds) 1990. *Aspects of Applied and Experimental Research on Conference Interpretation*. Udine: Campanotto Editore.

Grice, H. P. 1975. 'Logic and Conversation'. In Cole & Morgan 1975: 41–58.

Grundy, P. 1993. *Newspapers*. Oxford: Oxford University Press.

Gumperz, J. J. & Hymes, D. (eds) 1972. *Directions in Sociolinguistics: The Ethnography of Communication*. New York: Holt, Rhinehart & Winston.

Hajicova, E. 1994. 'Mathesius Vilem (1882–1945)'. In Asher 1994: 2395–2396.

Halliday, M. A. K. 1973. *Explorations in the Functions of Language*. London: Edward Arnold.

Halliday, M. A. K. 1976. 'Theme and Information in the English Clause'. In Kress 1976: 174–188.

Halliday, M. A. K. 1978. *Language as Social Semiotic*. London: Edward Arnold.

Halliday, M. A. K. 1985. *Spoken and Written Language*. Oxford: Oxford University Press.

Halliday, M. A. K. 1988. 'On the Language of Physical Science'. In Ghadessy 1988: 162–178.

Halliday, M. A. K. 1994. 'The Construction of Knowledge and Value in the Grammar of Social Discourse with Reference to Charles Darwin's 'The Origin of Species'. In Coulthard 1994: 136–156.

Halliday, M. A. K. & Hasan, R. 1975. *Cohesion in English*. London: Longman.

Halliday, M. A. K. & Hasan, R. 1989. *Language, Context, and Text: Aspects of Language in a Social-semiotic Perspective*. Oxford: Oxford University Press.

Hasan, R. 1984. 'Coherence and Cohesive Harmony'. In Flood 1984: 181–219.

Hatim, B. & Mason, I. 1990. *Discourse and the Translator*. London: Longman.

Heiss, C. & Bollettieri Bosinelli, R. M. (eds) 1996. *Traduzione multimediale per il cinema, la televisione e la scena*. Bologna: CLUEB.

Hjelmslev, L. 1953. *Prologema to a Theory of Language*. Bloomington: Indiana University Press.

House, J. (1981) (1997) *A Model for Translation Quality Assessment*. Tübingen: Gunter Narr Verlag.

Hurford, J. & Heasley, B. 1983. *Semantics: a Coursebook*. Cambridge: Cambridge University Press.

Hymes, D. 1964. 'Towards Ethnographies of Communicative Events'. In Giglioli 1964: 21–44.

Hymes, D. 1972. 'Models of the Interaction of Language and Social Life'. In Gumperz & Hymes 1972: 35–71.

Jakobson, R. 1960. 'Closing Statement: Linguistics and Poetics'. In Sebeok 1960: 350–377.

Jakobson, R. 1966. 'On Linguistic Aspects of Translation'. In Chesterman 1989: 37–52.

Johnson, C. M. & Johnson, D. 1988. *General Engineering*. London: Cassell.

Johnson-Laird, P.N. 1980. *Mental Models. Towards a Cognitive Science of Language, Inference and Consciousness.* Cambridge: Cambridge University Press.

Just, M. A. & Carpenter, P. A. (eds) 1977. *Cognitive Processes in Comprehension.* Hillsdale, New Jersey: Erlbaum.

Katan, D. 1996. *Translating across Cultures.* Trieste: SERT, Università di Trieste.

Katz, J. & Fodor, J. (eds) 1964. *The Structure of Language.* Eaglewood Cliff: Prentice Hall.

Kovacic, I. 1996. 'Subtitling Strategies. A Flexible Hierarchy of Priorities'. In Heiss & Bollettieri Bosinelli 1996: 297–305.

Kress, G. (ed.) 1976. *Halliday: System and Function in Language.* Oxford: Oxford University Press.

Krings, H. P. 1987. 'The Use of Introspective Data in Translation'. In Faerch & Kasper 1987: 159–176.

Labov, W. 1972. *Language in the Inner City.* Philadelphia: University of Pennsylvania Press.

Leech, G. 1966. *English in Advertising. A Linguistic Study of Advertising in Great Britain.* London: Longman.

Leech, G. N. 1981. *Semantics.* Harmondsworth: Penguin Books.

Leech, G. N. 1983. *Principles of Pragmatics.* London: Longman.

Leech, G. & Candlin C. (eds) 1986. *Computers in English Language Teaching and Research.* London: Longman.

Lemke, J. 1990. *Talking Science.* Northwood, New Jersey: Ablex Publishers.

Lindquist, H. 1984. 'The Use of Corpus-based Studies in the Preparation of Handbooks for Translators'. In Wilss & Thome 1984: 260–70.

Lionello, O. 1994. 'Il falso in doppiaggio'. In Baccolini, Bollettieri Bosinelli & Gavioli 1994: 41–50.

Lombardo, L. 1995. *Advertising and the English Language. A Linguistic Analysis.* Cassino: Università degli Studi di Cassino, Working Papers.

Lyons, J. 1977. *Semantics* (2 vols.). Cambridge: Cambridge University Press.

Malinowski, B. 1923. 'The Problem of Meaning in Primitive Languages'. In Ogden & Richards 1946: supplement.

Malone, J. L. 1988. *The Science of Linguistics in the Art of Translation.* Albany: State University of New York Press.

Mellor, R. G. & Davison, V. G. 1994. *How to Pass English for Business.* Mainz: Logophon Lehrmittel Verlag.

Minsky, M. 1975. 'A Framework for Representing Knowledge'. In Winston 1975.

Nergaard, S. (ed.) 1995. *Teorie contemporanie della traduzione.* Milan: Bompiani.

Neubert, A. 1995. 'Text and Translation'. *Rivista internazionale di tecnica della traduzione* 1, 63–76.

Newmark, P. 1981. *Approaches to Translation.* Oxford: Pergamon Press.

Newmark, P. 1982. 'The Translation of Authoritative Statements: A Discussion'. Meta **XXVII–4**.

Newmark, P. 1988. *A Textbook of Translation*. Hemel Hempstead: Prentice Hall.

Newmark, P. 1991. *About Translation*. Clevedon: Multilingual Matters.

Newmark, P. 1993. *Paragraphs on Translation*. Clevedon: Multilingual Matters Ltd.

Nida, E. A. 1964. *Towards a Science of Translation*. Leiden: Brill.

Nida, E. A. 1974. 'Translation' in Sebeok 1974: 1045–1068.

Nida, E. A. 1996. *The Sociolinguistics of Interlingual Communication*. Brussels: Editions du Hazard.

Nord, C. 1991. *Textanalyse und Übersetzen*. Heidelberg: Julius Groos Verlag.

Nord, C. 1992. 'Text Analysis in Translator Training'. In Dollerup & Loddegaard 1992: 39–48.

O'Connor, J. & Seymour, J. 1990. *An Introduction to Neurolinguistic Programming*. London: Mandela.

Ogden, C. K. & Richards, I. A. (eds) 1946. *The Meaning of Meaning*. London: Kegan Paul.

Palmer, F. R. (ed.) 1968. *Selected Papers 1952–9*. Bloomington: Indiana University Press.

Palmer, F. R. 1976. *Semantics*. Cambridge: Cambridge University Press.

Parks, T. 1994. 'Rethinking the Task of the Translator'. *Rivista internazionale di tecnica della traduzione* 1, 33–44.

Partington, A. 1995. 'Unusuality in Newspaper Headlines'. In Atti del XVII congresso 'Associazione Italiana di Anglistica – Il Centauro Anglo-Americano', Bologna. (in print)

Pinchuk, I. 1977. *Scientific and Technical Translation*. London: André Deutsch.

Pride, J. P. (ed.) *Sociolinguistic Aspects of Language Learning and Teaching*. Oxford: Oxford University Press.

Quirk, R., Leech, G., Svartvik, J. & Greenbaum, S. 1985. *A Comprehensive Grammar of the English Language*. London: Longman.

Rega, L. 1992. 'Didattica della traduzione specializzata: un primo approccio metodologico sulla scorta del sottotipo bilancio'. In *Rivista internazionale di tecnica della traduzione* 0, 67–78.

Reiss, K. & Vermeer, H. 1984. *Grundlegung einer allgemeinen Translationstheorie – Linguistische Arbeiten 147*. Tübingen, Niemeyer.

Sabatini, F. 1990. *La comunicazione e gli usi della lingua, 2° edizione*. Turin: Loescher.

Sager, J. 1990. *A Practical Course in Terminology Processing*. Amsterdam and Philadelphia: John Benjamins.

Salvi, G. & Vanelli, L. 1992. *Grammatica essenziale di riferimento della lingua italiana*. Florence: Le Monnier.

Salvi, R. 1996. 'Semantica, pragmatica e retorica nella dinamica del discorso economico'. Milan: paper delivered at II Seminario Didattica delle lingue di specialità: problemi e difficoltà traduttive, Università Bocconi. (in print)

Sanford, A. J. & Garrod, S. C. 1981. *Understanding Written Language*. New York: Wiley.

Savory, T. 1968. *The Art of Translation*. London: J. Cape.

Sapir, E. 1929. 'The Status of Linguistics as a Science'. *Language* 5: 207–214.

Schank, R. C. & Abelson, R. P. 1977. *Scripts, Plans, Goals and Understanding*. Hillsdale, New Jersey: Erlbaum.

Searle, J. R. 1969. *Speech Acts: An Essay in the Philosophy of Language*. New York: Cambridge University Press.

Sebeok, T. A. (ed.) 1960. *Style in Language*. Cambridge, Mass.: M.I.T. Press.

Sebeok, T. A. (ed.) 1974. *Current Trends in Linguistics vol. 12*. The Hague: Mouton.

Simpson, P. 1992. 'Teaching Stylistics: Analysing Cohesion and Narrative Structure in a Short Story by Ernest Hemingway'. *Language and Literature* 1: 47–67.

Sinclair, J. 1991. *Corpus, Concordance, Collocation*. Oxford: Oxford University Press.

Sinclair, J. 1992. 'Priorities in Discourse Analysis'. In Coulthard 1992: 79–88.

Snell-Hornby, M. 1988. *Translation Studies. An Integrated Approach*. Amsterdam and Philadelphia: John Benjamins.

Snelling, D. 1992. *Strategies for Simultaneous Interpreting*. Udine: Campanotto Editore.

Steiner, E. 1997. 'An Extended Register Analysis as a Form of Text Analysis for Translation'. In Wotjak & Schmidt 1995: 235–256.

Steiner, E. 1996. *Übersetzungswissenschaft im Umbruch, in Festchrift für Wolfram Wilss zum 70. Geburtstag*. Tübingen: Gunter Narr Verlag.

Strutt, P. 1992. *Longman Business English Usage*. Harlow: Longman.

Swales, J. M. 1990. *Genre Analysis*. New York: Cambridge University Press.

Swales, J. M. 1996. 'Occluded Genres in the Academy: The Case of the Submission Letter'. In Ventola & Mauranen 1996: 45–58.

Tannen, D. 1992. *You Just Don't Understand*. London: Virago.

Taylor, C. 1984. 'Realism and the Language of Realism in the Works of Alan Sillitoe'. In Dodds, Brady, Taylor & Moore 1997: 55–80.

Taylor, C. 1990. *Aspects of Language and Translation*. Udine: Campanotto Editore.

Taylor, C. 1990. 'Coherence and World Knowledge'. In Gran & Taylor 1990: 21–27.

Taylor, C. 1994. 'Il doppiaggio delle canzoni: un commento alla traduzione di Cats and Rabbits da Alice in Wonderland'. In Baccolini, Bollettieri Bosinelli & Gavioli 1994: 142–149.

Taylor, C. 1996. 'Linguaggi settoriali: linguistica testuale e 'nuovi tipi' di testo'. In Cortese 1996: 281–291.

Taylor, C. (ed.) 1996. *Aspects of English 2*. Udine: Campanotto Editore.

Taylor Torsello, C. 1984. *English in Discourse I & II*. Padua: Cleup Editore.

Trimble, L. 1985. *English for Science and Technology*. New York: Cambridge University Press.

Trompenaars, F. & Turner, C. H. 1993. *Riding the Waves of Culture*. London: The Economist Books.

Ulrych, M. 1992. *Translating Texts*. Rapallo: Cideb Editrice.

Ventola, E. & Mauranen, A. (eds) 1996. *Academic Writing*. Amsterdam and Philadelphia: John Benjamins.

Viaggio, S. 1992. 'Contesting Peter Newmark'. *Rivista internazionale di tecnica della traduzione* 0, 27–58.

Viëtor, W. 1884. *Elemente der Phonetik des Deutschen, Englischen und Französischen*. Heilbronn: Gebr. Henninger.

Viezzi, M. 1996. 'Patricia D. Cornwell's Novels and the Translation of Cultural Items' in Taylor 1996: 89–120.

Weinreich, U. 1953. *Languages in Contact*. New York: Linguistic Circle of New York.

White, P. R. R. 1997. 'Racism, Hegemonic Discourse and the News Story: Modelling Genre in a Cross-cultural, Cross-discoursal Training Context'. Halle-Wittenberg: paper delivered at Ninth Euro-International Systemic Functional Workshop.

Whorf, B. 1956. *Language, Thought and Reality: Selected Writings of Benjamin Lee Whorf*. Carroll, J. B. (ed.) Cambridge, Mass.: M.I.T. Press.

Widdowson, H. 1978. *Teaching Language as Communication*. Oxford: Oxford University Press.

Widdowson, H. 1979. *Explorations in Applied Linguistics*. Oxford: Oxford University Press.

Wilss, W. & Thome, G. (eds) 1984. *Translation Theory and its Implementation in the Teaching of Translating and Interpreting*. Tübingen: Gunter Narr.

Winograd, T. 1977. 'A Framework for Understanding Discourse'. In Just & Carpenter 1977: 63–88.

Winston, P. (ed.) 1975. *The Psychology of Computer Vision*. New York: McGraw-Hill.

Wotjak, G. & Schmidt, H. (eds) 1997. *Models of Translation? Festschrift für Albrecht Neubert*. Leipzig: Leipziger Scriften zur Kultur-, Literatur-, Sprach- und Übersetzungswissenschaft.

Yates, C. St. J. 1988. *Earth Sciences*. London: Cassell.

Theses

Buttazzoni, R. 1996. 'Measuring Socioeconomic Inequalities in Health, Traduzione e Commento'. Trieste: (unpublished thesis) University of Trieste.

Chighine, A. 1994. 'Inquinamento atmosferico dell'ambiente urbano. Aspetti tecnici e linguistici'. Trieste: (unpublished thesis) University of Trieste.

Corbolante, L. 1987. 'La traduzione di un successo umoristico 'culture-bound' –

The Growing Pains of Adrian Mole di Sue Townsend'. Trieste: (unpublished thesis) University of Trieste.

Crescenzi, A. 1993. 'Analisi critica del film *Do the Right Thing* di Spike Lee'. Trieste: (unpublished thesis) University of Trieste.

de Poli, A. M. 1988. 'Indagine terminologica nel settore della meccanizzazione agricola: glossario italiano-inglese-tedesco delle principali macchine per la raccolta dei cereali'. Trieste: (unpublished thesis) University of Trieste.

Guerra, M. G. 1987. 'Il factoring: un nuovo strumento di gestione aziendale. Lessico ragionato in italiano, inglese, francese'. Trieste: (unpublished thesis) University of Trieste.

Merlo, M. 1986. 'Tre contratti di leasing: traduzione e analisi del linguaggio giuridico. Glossario italiano-inglese-spagnolo'. Trieste: (unpublished thesis) University of Trieste.

Ondelli, S. 1995. 'La drammatizzazione dei titoli nei quotidiani in Italia e in Gran Bretagna'. Trieste: (unpublished thesis) University of Trieste.

Romele, A. 1992. 'Lo stampaggio a caldo: contributo ad una standardizzazione terminologica. Glossario inglese-italiano'. Trieste: (unpublished thesis) University of Trieste.

Sandrelli, A. 1996. '*Caro Diario* di Nanni Moretti. Studio comparato delle versioni sottotitolate in inglese e spagnolo'. Trieste: (unpublished thesis) University of Trieste.

Zamponi, C. 1995. '*The Wind in the Willows*. Analisi e traduzione dell'adattamento teatrale dell'omonimo romanzo'. Trieste: (unpublished thesis) University of Trieste.

Dictionaries

Collins Cobuild English Dictionary. 1995. London: Harper Collins.

Grand Larousse de la Langue Francaise. 1975. Paris.

Le Nouveau Petit Robert. 1993. Montreal: Dictionnaires Le Robert.

Longman's Dictionary of Language Teaching and Applied Linguistics 1. 1992. Richards, J. C., Platt, J. & Platt, H. (eds) Harlow: Longman.

I Dizionari Sansoni KEY. 1995. Schmid Bona (ed.) Florence: Sansoni Editore.

The New Roget's Thesaurus. 1984. Norman Lewis (ed.) New York: Berkley.

Vocabolario della lingua italiana. Roma: Istituto della Enciclopedia Italiana.

Literary works

Anderson, E. 1966. *Letters of Mozart and his Family*. London: Macmillan.

Atwood, M. 1977. *Dancing Girls and other stories*. Toronto: Seal Books.

Atwood, M. 1991. *Wilderness Tips*. Toronto: Mclelland & Stewart.

Bennett, A. 1991. *The Wind in the Willows*. London: Faber & Faber.

Dickens, C. 1986. *Martin Chuzzlewit*. London: Penguin.

Doyle, R. 1993. *Paddy Clarke ha ha ha*. London: Minerva.

Fielding, H. 1983. *Tom Jones*. Harmondsworth: Penguin.

Goldoni, L. 1987. *Se torno a nascere*. Milan: Arnoldo Mondadori Editore.

Lawrence, D. 1982. *Sons and Lovers*. Harmondsworth: Penguin.

Lennon, J. & McCartney, P. 1968. *The Beatles Songbook*. Milan: S.B.K. Ed. Manioli.

Magris, C. 1986. *Danubio*. Milan: Garzanti.

Mandela, N. 1994. *Long Walk to Freedom*. London: Little Brown & Co.

Marpillero, G. 1980. *Essere di paese*. Milan: Arnoldo Mondadori Editore.

Moravia, A. 1965. *L'Angoscia*. In Trevelyan 1965: 133–147.

Oates, J. C. 1994. *Haunted*. New York: Dutton.

Orwell, G. 1984. *Animal Farm*. Harmondsworth: Penguin.

Parks, T. 1985. *Tongues of Flame*. New York: Grove Press Inc.

Parks, T. 1993. *Italian Neighbours*. London: Mandarin.

Severgnini, B. 1992. *L'Inglese: lezioni semiserie*. Milan. Rizzoli.

Shaw, G. B. 1929. *Androcles and the Lion & Pygmalion*. Leipzig: Bernhard Tauchnitz.

Sillitoe, A. 1975. *Saturday Night and Sunday Morning*. London: W.H. Allen.

Townsend, S. 1982. *The Secret Diary of Adrian Mole aged $13\frac{3}{4}$*. London: Methuen.

Townsend, S. 1983. *The Growing Pains of Adrian Mole*. London: Methuen.

Trevelyan, R. (ed.) 1965. *Italian Short Stories 1*. Harmondsworth: Penguin.

Wilde, O. 1982. *A Woman of no Importance*. In *Oscar Wilde/Plays*. Harmondsworth: Penguin.

Wilde, O. 1982. *The Importance of Being Earnest*. In *Oscar Wilde/Plays*. Harmondsworth: Penguin.

Translations (of literary works)

Aldridge, A. (ed.) 1972. *Il libro delle canzoni dei Beatles*. Milan: Arnoldo Mondadori.

Anderson, E. 1966. *Letters of Mozart and his Family: Mozart alla moglie a Baden* (trans. G. Cervone). Wittingen: Neef.

Carroll, L. 1993. *Alice nel paese delle meraviglie* (trans. A. Busi). Milan: Feltrinelli.

Dickens, C. 1927. *Le avventure di Martin Chuzzlewit: II La Palude* (trans. S.S. Filippi). Milan: Treves.

Lawrence, D. 1971. *Figli e amanti* (trans. F. Cancogni). Milan: Arnoldo Mondadori.

Magris, C. 1986. *Danube* (trans. P. Creagh). New York: Farrar, Straus & Giroux.

Moravia, A. 1965. *L'Angoscia* (trans. A. Davidson). In Trevelyan 1965: 133–147.

Parks, T. 1995. *Lingue di fuoco* (trans. R. Baldassare). Milan: Adelphi Edizioni.

Rizzo, S. (ed.) 1972. *Bob Dylan, blues, ballate e canzoni*. Rome: Newton Compton Italiana.

Shakespeare, W. 1949. *Amleto principe di Danimarca* (trans. W. Montale). Milan: Cederna.

Shakespeare, W. 1963. *Amleto*. In *Opere complete di Shakespeare* (trans. G. Baldini). Milan: Rizzoli.

Townsend, S. 1991. *Il diario segreto di Adrian Mole* (trans. C. Brera). Milan: Sperling & Kupfer.

Wilde, O. 1994. *Una donna senza importanza*. In *Oscar Wilde: Tutte le opere* (ed. M. d'Amico). Rome: Newton.

Wilde, O. 1979. *L'importanza di essere probo* (trans. M. d'Amico). Milan: Arnoldo Mondadori.

Acknowledgements

The authors and publishers are grateful to the following copyright holders for permission to reproduce copyright material. While every endeavour has been made, it has not been possible to identify the sources of all materials used and, in such cases, the publishers would welcome information from copyright sources. Apologies are expressed for any omissions.

pp. 6, 32: from *The Wind in the Willows* by Alan Bennett, reprinted by permission of The Peters Fraser and Dunlop Group Limited on behalf of Alan Bennett ©: as printed in the original volume; pp. 6, 24, 175, 179: from *Secret Diary of Adrian Mole* by Sue Townsend, published by Methuen 1982; pp. 6, 178: from *Il diario segreto di Adrian Mole* by Sue Townsend, translated by C. Brera, published in Italy by Sperling & Kupfer Editori; p. 8: from *Tongues of Flame* by Tim Parks published by Grove/Atlantic, Inc.; p. 8: from *Lingue di fuoco* by Tim Parks published by Adelphi Edizioni; p. 15: from *Pygmalion* by Bernard Shaw, permission was given by The Society of Authors on behalf of the Bernard Shaw Estate; p. 17: from *Animal Farm* by George Orwell, published by Penguin Books Ltd, by permission of A. M. Heath & Company Ltd; pp. 20–21: from 'Dancing Girls' in *Dancing Girls and other stories* by Margaret Atwood by permission of Curtis Brown on behalf of Margaret Atwood. Copyright 1977 O. W. Toad Limited; pp. 21, 118–20: from *Wilderness Tips* by Margaret Atwood. Copyright © 1991 by O. W. Toad Limited. Used by permission of Doubleday, a division of Bantam Doubleday Dell Publishing Group, Inc. in the USA; and by permission, McClelland & Stewart, Inc. *The Canadian Publishers*; p. 25: from the Italian translation of "Chimes of Freedom" in *Bob Dylan, blues, ballate e canzoni*, used by permission of Newton & Compton Editori, Italy; p. 39: from "Clearing the Air" by Lewis in *Complete Car* (December 1994); p. 41: from *Dizionario Sansoni Italiano/Inglese* 3rd edition by Vladimiro Macchi; p. 43: from Cobuild *English Dictionary* (1995); p. 49: 29 words (p. 135) from *Italian Short Stories: Racconti Italiani* edited by Raleigh Trevelyan (Penguin Books, 1965) © Penguin Books Ltd, 1965. Reproduced by permission of Penguin Books Ltd; p. 52: from the lyrics of Walt Disney Pictures *Alice in Wonderland*, "In a World of My Own". Music by Sammy Fain, words by Bob Hilliard. Italian lyrics by PERTITAS. © 1949 Walt Disney Music Company. Copyright renewed. All rights reserved. Used by permission; p. 55: from *Saturday Night and Sunday Morning* by Alan Sillitoe © Alan Sillitoe 1958 and 1986; pp. 59–60: 'Good Day Sunshine', lyrics by John Lennon and Paul McCartney © 1966 – Sony/ATV Music Publishing Ltd; pp. 111, 196, 202: from *La Repubblica* 16 November 1995, 13 November 1996, 20 April 1996; p. 115: from *Paddy Clarke, ha ha ha* by Roddy Doyle published by Minerva in the UK, Italy & Australia; and Copyright © 1993 by Roddy Doyle. Used by permission of Viking Penguin, a division of Penguin Putnam Inc. in the USA; p. 124: from *Haunted: Tales of the Grotesque* by Joyce Carol Oates. Copyright © 1994 by The Ontario Review, Inc. Used by permission of Dutton, a division of Penguin Putnam Inc. in USA and Canada, and Copyright © 1994 by The Ontario Review, Inc. Reprinted by permission of John Hawkins & Associates, Inc.; p. 143: from radio advertisement for Mistsubishi Motors, copyright The Colt Car Company Limited; p. 165: from *Le Avventure di Martin Chuzzlewit*, translated into Italian by S. Filippi, published by Treves, used by permission of Garzanti Editori; p. 174: from *L'Inglese: lezioni semiserie* by Beppe Severgnini, © 1992, Rizzoli Libri Spa, Milano; pp. 179–80: from *Italian Neighbours* by Tim Parks, published by William Heinemann in the UK, and by Grove/Atlantic in the USA; p. 185: from *The Letters of Mozart and his Family* edited by E. Anderson and published by Macmillan Press Ltd; p. 187: from *The Letters of Mozart and his family* edited by E. Anderson and translated into Italian by Cervone, published by Macmillan Press Ltd; pp. 189, 195: from *Danubio* by Claudio Magris, published by Garzanti Editore; p. 194: from *Danube* by Claudio Magris, translated from the Italian by Patrick Creagh. First published in 1986 by Garzanti editore, Milan, in Great Britain in 1990 by the Harvill Press. © Garzanti editore s.p.a. 1986. Translation © William Collins Sons & Co. Ltd, & Farrar, Straus & Giroux. Reproduced by permission of The Harvill Press and Farrar, Straus & Ginoux, Inc.; pp. 202–3: from *Observer Review* 12 November 1995, (p1); p. 203: from *Internazionale*, 12 January 1996, translated from the English by Francesca Terrenato; pp. 205–6: from "Town that grew too fat on salt is falling into hole no one will fill" from *The Observer* 18 January 1998 (p1); pp. 206–7, 207–8: from *Arrivederci* in-flight magazine of Alitalia; p. 212: from 'YOUNG FRANKENSTEIN' ©1974 Twentieth Century Fox Film Corporation. All rights reserved; pp. 227, 232: from *Progetto Natura 3* by

Bonnes & De Re, published by Editore Bulgarini; pp. 232–3: from *Statistica Applicata* by F. Giusti published by Cacucci Editore; pp. 233–4, 236: from *National Geographic* April 1987, vol. 171, no. 4; pp. 236–7, 243–4: from *Un modello etologico* by Massimo Bardi in "Sapere", n.2(983), aprile 1996 published by Edizioni Dedalo; pp. 245–6, 249–51:, from Philips Instruction Manual for 26CS 3270 Television by permission of Philips Consumer Electronics; p. 257: from advertisement for "Thumper® Alarm Clock" used by permission of Outlook Zelco Europe in Europe, and by Zelco Industries, Inc. in the USA; pp. 258–9, 263–4, 269: from editorial by Basaglia, and "La Legamentite Ileo-lumbare", by Gasparini, Basadonna and Rucco in *Giornale italiano di medicina riabilitativa* (supplement), by permission of Dottore Vincenzo Rucco, Ospedale di Medicina Fisica e Riabilitazione; pp. 272–5: used by permission of a US company; pp. 281, 283–4: from *A Practical Handbook of Business Theory and Commercial Correspondence* by Codeluppi, published by Casa Editrice Le Lettere; pp. 285, 288: from "Measuring socioeconomic inequalities in health" by Kunst, A. E. & Mackenbach, J. P.; Copenhagen, WHO Regional Office for Europe, 1994 (unpublished document EUR/ICP/RPD 416); pp. 294–7: from Multilingual Editing Brochure published by Eurologos; pp. 298–302: from *Viaggio al Centro del Friuli* by permission of Comunità Collinare del Friuli Colloredo di Monte Albano (Udine).

Lightning Source UK Ltd.
Milton Keynes UK
UKOW010605260112

186040UK00003B/2/P